SMART WORLD

SMART WORLD

BREAKTHROUGH CREATIVITY
and the NEW SCIENCE *of* IDEAS

RICHARD OGLE

Harvard Business School Press
Boston, Massachusetts

The views expressed in this book are those of the author and not those of Mattel, Inc.

Library of Congress Cataloging-in-Publication Data
Ogle, Richard.
    Smart world : breakthrough creativity and the new science of ideas / Richard Ogle.
        p. cm.
    ISBN 978-1-59139-417-4 (hardcover : alk. paper)
    1. Creative thinking. 2. Creative ability. 3. Idea (Philosophy). 4. Philosophy of mind. I. Title.
    BF408.035 2007
153.3—dc22   2006035420

The paper used in this publication meets the minimum requirements of the American National Standard for Information Sciences—Permanence of Paper for Printed Library Materials, ANSI Z39.48-1992.

For Laura and Elizabeth

CONTENTS

ACKNOWLEDGMENTS

In writing this book I was strongly influenced by the ideas of two seminal thinkers. Andy Clark's concept of the extended mind lies at the very foundation of what I have to say. Similarly, Albert-László Barabási's discoveries in the emerging science of networks provided the basis for the principles and laws that form the book's organizing framework. I would also like to acknowledge a number of other people who influenced me more deeply than the references scattered through the work may indicate. Steven Strogatz and Duncan Watts initiated the scientific study of networks in the late 1990s, developing several crucial insights drawn on here. Mark Buchanan provided a lucid and highly readable introduction to network science. George Lakoff and Mark Johnson's pioneering treatment of metaphorical thinking, and Gilles Fauconnier and Mark Turner's groundbreaking work on conceptual networks, had a significant impact on my thinking. Much the same is true of Clifford Geertz's approach to cultural anthropology, to which I owe the concept, if not the phrase, "spaces to think with." Similarly, Stuart Kauffman's exploration of the idea of self-organization and "order for free" provoked many interesting trains of thought. Steven Pinker's always lucid and insightful exposition of what might be termed the "standard theory of mind" proved invaluable, even as I found myself arguing for a different approach. Richard Florida's exploration of the emerging creative economy provided an essential basis for the rationale of this book. The underlying idea that runs all through this book, that the mind is not exclusively inside the head, I first encountered working with Fernando Flores. Most if not all of these thinkers would probably be surprised to find their ideas developed and applied in the way I have in this book, and may well disagree with much of what I have to say. I alone bear responsibility for their exposition and use here.

Many people have supported and encouraged me in writing this book, including notably my sister Rosemary Ogle, Dorothy Edwards, Gail Clinton,

Karen Aberle, Bob Dunham, Norman Bookstein, Pete Kalajian, Matthew Bonazzoli, Brian Bonazzoli, Barry Stavro, and Victor Suchar.

Mike Graves, John Nirenberg, Lloyd Nirenberg, and Greg Chilenski all undertook the onerous task of reading through the manuscript in its entirety. Their many comments and suggestions were valuable in a multitude of ways. I am also grateful for the comments of the four anonymous reviewers contacted by the publishers, which were similarly helpful.

Special mention must be made of the staff of the Camden Public Library, headed by Dottie Morales. My many requests for inter-library loans were always promptly and courteously met, as were my frequent inquiries to the reference staff. Without their kindness and professionalism, this book could never have been written. I am similarly appreciative of the help provided by the staff of the Rockport Public Library.

Jeff Kehoe, my editor at Harvard Business School Press, has overseen this project virtually from its inception. Throughout, he has been a source of enthusiastic encouragement and support, and much sage advice regarding the book's organization and content. Sarah Weaver proved to be a first-rate copyeditor, tactfully offering many suggestions for improvement. Jane Gebhart expertly shepherded the manuscript through production while allaying my various concerns about this process.

My agent David Miller endlessly talked through the ideas in this book with me, frequently making suggestions regarding its content, focus, and direction that had a major impact on its final form. Whenever I was in danger of straying too far from the book's central theme, he astutely guided me back. Supported by Lisa Adams, David also undertook a detailed edit of the entire manuscript, going through several revision cycles of some chapters. I could not have asked for a better agent or thinking partner.

My wife Laura Bonazzoli somehow found the time and energy in the midst of her own busy professional life to edit every line of the book, improving it immeasurably. I also benefited greatly from our many discussions, which covered practically all of the book's major ideas, as well as its detailed arguments and illustrations. Above all, she has been an unwavering source of loving support. My eight-year-old daughter Elizabeth, who was in preschool when I began this project, has continually surprised me with the strength and liveliness of her imagination. I learned more from observing her than from most of the books I read on this still poorly understood human faculty. I owe Laura and Elizabeth a great debt of gratitude, not only for their help and inspiration, but also for their patience and understanding in cheerfully putting up with the many, many hours expended on writing this book that would otherwise have been spent with them.

THE MYSTERY OF
BREAKTHROUGH CREATIVITY

Intelligence is not the measure of how much we know how to do,
but of how we behave when we don't know what to do.

—John Holt[1]

How does the mind work? For the past seventy years philosophers, cognitive and evolutionary psychologists, linguists, neuroscientists, and researchers in artificial intelligence have intensively studied this question. Their efforts have made the logical and biological structure and functioning of the mind visible as never before. We now possess a good understanding of how we acquire language; how the visual system works; how we learn, extending knowledge through rational thought processes; and how our emotions affect our beliefs and actions. Nevertheless, our knowledge of the mind remains frustratingly incomplete.

One of the biggest gaps in our understanding is breakthrough creativity, which stands among the human mind's greatest yet most enigmatic forms of achievement. Relativity theory, DNA, cubism, printing with movable type, the personal computer, the Internet, and the iPod may be comprehensible enough in themselves, but the mental processes that led to them have remained largely beyond our grasp. Where do truly innovative ideas come from, and how does the mind make the leap to embrace them? What role do existing cultural and social factors play? Above all, what are the primary mental faculties involved in creativity, and how do they work? These are genuinely important questions, but until recently, the answers have been distinctly unsatisfactory. Creative leaps? Ah, we say, that's genius. Which is just another way of saying we don't have the foggiest idea how to talk about them.

1

Too bad, because creative breakthroughs shape how the future unfolds. As the creative economy begins to replace the knowledge economy, business leaders are increasingly relying on innovation rather than productivity as the key to expansion.[2] Penetrating the mystery of breakthrough creativity would significantly improve our ability to envision the future and the opportunities for growth it presents. To do so, we need to enlarge our standard ways of thinking about the mind. The goal of this book is to introduce you to an extended view of the mind and its role in intelligently structuring the world around us that will finally begin to solve the mystery of how we make creative leaps.

Over the past two decades a series of profoundly important advances have occurred in both the philosophy of mind and the empirical mind/brain sciences that, taken together, are finally opening the way to a new understanding of breakthrough creativity. Three developments are of particular significance: recognition that the mind extends beyond the brain, a renewed interest in the mind's imaginative faculties and the analogical reasoning that underlies them, and the emergence of a new science of networks.

First, cognitive scientists, researchers in artificial intelligence, psychologists, and philosophers have begun to talk about how the mind *extends out into the world*. This revolutionary expansion of the traditional concept of mind directly challenges our belief in the individual mind's internal self-sufficiency. We are coming to understand that in making sense of the world, acting intelligently, and solving problems creatively, we do not rely solely on our mind's internal resources. Instead, we constantly have recourse to a vast array of culturally and socially embodied *idea-spaces* that populate the extended mind. These spaces—manifested in forms as various as myths, business models, scientific paradigms, social conventions, practices, institutions, and even computer chips—are rich with embedded intelligence that we have progressively offloaded into our physical, social, and cultural environment for the sake of simplifying the burden on our own minds of rendering the world intelligible. *Sometimes the space of ideas thinks for us.* We live in a smart world.

Second, philosophers and cognitive psychologists are expanding our understanding of how we think. The conventional view, drawing on a tradition that extends from Plato through Descartes to modern-day rationalism, holds that the foundation of intelligent, intelligible, creative thought is *reason*. Rational thought essentially enables us by virtue of knowing one thing (e.g., the earth is round) to know that something else is also true (you won't fall off the edge, no matter how far you go). This mode of thinking is the foundation not only of everyday common sense and intelligence, but also of advances in physical science, technology, economics and other social sciences, business, and many other spheres of activity. Reason, then, is rightly taken as one of the mind's principal creative faculties. Operating in both our personal and professional lives, it reliably enables us to expand our knowledge beyond our immediate experience and thus to think freshly and intelligently about the nature of our world.

But reason clearly isn't the whole story. Our deep understanding of analytical reasoning tells us nothing about the extraordinary mental processes of *imagination, intuition,* and *insight* that underlie many forms of creative thinking: the sudden flash of inspiration; the surprising emergence of a meaningful pattern in the midst of complexity; the insightful reframing of a problem; the leap to a whole new space of ideas. Such mental reconfigurations are familiar to anyone who has engaged in serious creative activity, and yet until recently we had virtually no way of describing them or theorizing about them in a useful way.

Fortunately, we are finally beginning to understand the role of imagination, insight, and intuition in creative thinking. An important part of this advance stems from renewed recognition among philosophers and mind/brain scientists that, alongside analytical reasoning, the mind possesses a second, very different mode of thinking based on what we may loosely term *analogical* reasoning. This typically involves not analysis, but rather the imaginative and insightful transfer of whole patterns of knowledge from a familiar domain to one whose structure and character are less well defined, for the sake of making sense and thus creating new understanding.

Consider metaphor, a central form of analogical thought. We're all familiar with the power of metaphor to clarify one thing by referring to another. When Shakespeare has Macbeth, contemplating the murder of Duncan, say,

> . . . *I have no spur*
> *To prick the sides of my intent, but only*
> *Vaulting ambition, which o'erleaps itself*
> *And falls on the other [side].* [3]

we vividly apprehend by means of a concrete image drawn from the world of horsemanship something of the heedless exercise of will and the danger of ensuing calamity that certain acts of ambition involve. Similarly, when a business leader describes a colleague as a "loose cannon," the metaphor succeeds with just two words in evoking certain crucial aspects of the sphere of naval warfare—the need to run a tight ship, the risk of seriously damaging others by being out of control, the dangers in battle of uncoordinated action—and efficiently transfers them to a specific situation in the competitive world of business. Conventional metaphors such as "silo organization," "shepherding someone along," and so forth are equally effective in bringing to life concepts that might otherwise remain hard to articulate.

This brings us to the third and perhaps most radical development of all: the emergence within the last five years of *network science*, a branch of complexity theory that seeks to establish universal laws and principles of networks, ranging from links between brain cells to the structure of the Internet.

For over three decades now, the trend in the mind/brain sciences has been toward what might be termed the progressive *networking of the mind*. This has ranged from the demonstration that the crucial structure of long-term memory resides in the links between neurons, to the treatment of visual perception in terms of neural networks, to recent research suggesting that even concepts are formed dynamically from the interaction of semantic webs.[4] As I'll show, the interaction of the idea-spaces of the extended mind can be described equally well in network terms. Such spaces form themselves into surprisingly dynamic webs that constantly shift under cultural, social, scientific, and technological pressures, creating new patterns as old ones collapse, fragment, connect, merge, and integrate.

The emerging science of networks tells us that such pattern formation is not random, but obeys certain laws governing the dynamics of all networks. It thus provides us with a powerful new set of tools for modeling the dynamics of both the individual and the extended mind. Its newly discovered laws have led to two highly significant insights regarding creativity. First, the networks of the extended mind, like all dynamic networks, are self-organizing: *they drive their own transformation*, thereby enabling the intelligence embedded in the idea-spaces of our smart world to provide a vast and potent external source of creative energy and ideas. Second, the human mind's imaginative faculties not only actively piggyback on these dynamics, deriving much of their creative power from them, but turn out to be themselves driven by universal network laws.

The developments I have been describing, although loosely connected, have until now been proceeding independently of one another. The central claim of this book is that by bringing them together we can gain radically new insight into how creative breakthroughs happen. Simply put, creative leaps arise from the imaginative and insightful transfer of powerful, externally embedded intelligence from one idea-space to another. Furthermore, when scientists, artists, architects, inventors, and entrepreneurs make such dramatic advances, their achievements can be described in terms of network laws.

Consider, for example, one of the turning points in the history of postwar jazz, the Dave Brubeck album *Time Out*. Brubeck had been advised by his mentor, the French classical composer Darius Milhaud: "Travel the world and keep your ears open, and use everything you hear from other cultures. Bring it into the jazz idiom."[5] While visiting Turkey, Brubeck heard some folk musicians playing a very catchy tune to the beat 1-2, 1-2, 1-2, 1-2-3. Initially he was puzzled. Then it came to him: they were playing in 9/8 time, improvising around it just like jazz players. At that period jazz, in spite of having gone through a series of revolutionary harmonic and chromatic changes wrought by such giants as Louis Armstrong, Duke Ellington, Charlie Parker, and Thelonius Monk, was still solidly based on the 4/4 time inherited from marching bands. Rhythmically, it had barely progressed at all.

Back in America, Brubeck decided to do an album based on time signatures not previously used in jazz. *Time Out* opens with "Blue Rondo à la Turk" in 9/8, preserving the original 1-2, 1-2, 1-2, 1-2-3 beat. We can even hear the strains of a Turkish folk song coming through. The album continues with Paul Desmond's celebrated composition, *Take Five*, in 5/4, "one of the most defiant time signatures in all music," as Steve Race put it in his liner notes. The album sold over a million copies, the first jazz recording ever to do so, earning Brubeck a *Time* magazine cover story in November 1954. What Brubeck's musical breakthrough reveals is that we have the capacity to *transfer whole patterns of significant form* (gestalts) from one world to another, with powerful creative effect.

A more recent example of this kind of creative thinking is the runaway success of the Apple iPod. A number of factors, including excellent design and styling, permissible downloading, and intense publicity, clearly played a major role. Underlying this, however, was a deeper move on Apple's part. The fact is that in pre-iPod days, portable digital music players were a niche market of no great interest to major electronics or computer companies (by Steve Jobs's own admission, Apple nearly missed the market altogether). Apple's real achievement was to have brought into the somewhat disarrayed, inchoate world of portable media (which now extends beyond music to embrace text, podcasts, television programs, and even movies) the immensely sophisticated power to *manage digital content* that has been developed within the mainstream computing world over the past twenty-five years (not least by Apple itself), embodied in everything from exponential increases in storage capacity to interface design to ease of downloading. It was above all Jobs's recognition of this wide-open opportunity to transform one domain by importing into it hard-won knowledge and design from another long-established one that launched the iPod on its extraordinary trajectory.

Both these cases illustrate not only how the creative mind shifts culturally or technologically embedded intelligence from one idea-space to another, but also how it does so by interacting with the law-governed dynamics of the extended mind. As will become evident, the successes of *Time Out* and the iPod both exemplify the workings of network laws, demonstrating how the law of hotspots and the law of the fit get fitter lead to tipping points.

By integrating the developments discussed here—the idea of the extended mind, our new understanding of the mind's imaginative faculties and analogical powers of thinking, and the advent of an emerging science of networks—we can for the first time give a theoretical and practical account of achievements that before were generally regarded as the unfathomable products of genius: How Jobs and Wozniak took the lead in inventing the personal computer, and why it was they and not the brilliant but ill-fated Alto team at Xerox who succeeded in the marketplace. Why Crick and Watson, two rank outsiders, succeeded in solving the enigma of DNA when Linus Pauling couldn't. How Gutenberg managed to design a truly effective printing press when so many before him had failed. Where Ruth Handler got the idea for Barbie, and why it turned the doll business upside down. How Maya Lin's precedent-shattering design for the Veteran's War Memorial in Washington unfolded in her mind. How Frank Gehry transformed the world of architecture, setting it on a new path. How supersizing portions came about, and why it became the most potent idea in the fast-food industry since sliced bread.

Businesspeople—and though they may be more loath to admit it, scientists, technologists, artists, and other professionally creative people—constantly scan the horizon for the Holy Grail of creative leaps, the Next Big Thing. Where will the next big breakthrough come from, when will it appear, and how will it evolve? If the past is any guide, the NBT has a remarkable capacity to show up unannounced, to the surprise and irritation of all concerned—witness the PC revolution and the Internet, to name just two of a long list of exemplars.

In truth, of course, we still can't predict its next appearance. What we can do is gain a better understanding of how the mind's imaginative intelligence, interfacing with the embedded intelligence of the networked idea-spaces of the extended mind, brings about creative leaps. This new understanding, firmly grounded in the laws of network science, will help us respond to radical innovations more quickly and intelligently than before. It may even help us create some of our own.

Chapter One

OUTING THE MIND

He who does not expect will not find out the unexpected,
for it is trackless and unexplored.

—Heraclitus[1]

The Musée d'Ethnographie du Trocadéro was an unlikely site for the start of a revolution. Established in 1868 as a result of the decision by the Louvre to clear out the museum's haphazard collection of curios, it was a grimy storehouse for loincloths, weapons, musical instruments, masks, fetishes, sculpted figurines, and other odd-looking bric-a-brac brought back by sailors from France's newly acquired colonies in Africa and the South Seas. Such objects, constituting "completely second-rate collections," were, the authorities declared, "far removed from the fine arts," and thus quite inappropriate for a museum dedicated to exhibiting "art works of the highest order."[2] Drastically underfunded and not even properly catalogued, at the turn of the century the Musée d'Ethnographie had the air of a seedy indoor bazaar.

Into its dusty halls wandered a twenty-five-year old artist. At first he was revulsed: "When I went to the Trocadéro it was disgusting. The flea market. The smell. I was all alone. I wanted to get away. But I didn't leave. I stayed. I stayed . . ." Something he could not articulate held him transfixed.

And then it came to him:

I understood something very important . . . The masks weren't like other kinds of sculpture. Not at all. They were magical things . . . The Negroes' sculptures were intercessors . . . Against everything; against unknown, threatening spirits. I kept looking at the fetishes. I understood: I too am against everything. I too think that everything is unknown, is the enemy! Everything. Not just the details—women, children, animals, tobacco, playing—but everything! I understood what the purpose of the sculpture was for the Negroes . . . [The fetishes] were weapons. To help people stop being dominated by spirits, to become independent. Tools. If we give form to the spirits, we become independent of them . . . I understood why I was a painter. All alone in that awful museum, the masks, the Red Indian dolls, the dusty mannequins. Les Demoiselles d'Avignon *must have come to me that day, but not at all because of the forms: but because it was my first canvas of exorcism.*[3]

The *Demoiselles* marked a profound turning point, not just for Picasso but for modern art itself. It is one of the most sublimely beautiful and at the same time deeply disturbing works of art ever produced, by some standards the most important painting of the twentieth century. Prior to completing it, Picasso had seemed to race through one style after another, drawing inspiration from artists as far apart as El Greco and Toulouse-Lautrec, and periods ranging from ancient Greek to postimpressionist. Now he finally knew who he was as a painter.

The painting was unquestionably a breakthrough in purely formal terms. With its drastically flattened perspective and fractured planes, it leaped far beyond anything Cézanne had achieved, clearing the way for cubism's dazzling recomposition of forms, and smashing forever the idea that the main purpose of art was to produce beautiful, realistic-looking illusions (see figure 1-1). Western art had finally sprung free of its compulsion to render the human face and figure realistically in terms of its skeletal structure and musculature. Instead, shape, volume, and plane were now in the grip of a tradition that had never bowed to the ethic of representation.

FIGURE 1-1

Pablo Picasso: *Les Demoiselles d'Avignon* **(1907)**

Source: Museum of Modern Art, New York. © 2007 Estate of Pablo Picasso/Artists Rights Society (ARS), New York. Digital Image © The Museum of Modern Art/Licensed by SCALA/Art Resource, N.Y. Used with permission.

Above all, however, the *Demoiselles* was a revolution in function. Perhaps no painting of human flesh so shocks us in its depiction of the artist's agonized relationship to his subject matter. As Picasso himself makes clear, what he overwhelmingly felt enthused by was the essentially magical purpose of African sculpture. By reframing art as exorcism, as an act of protecting oneself from domination by "unknown, threatening spirits," Picasso irrevocably changed the twin roles of artist and spectator. Painting transcended the status of object, effectively becoming a way of propitiating our spiritual and psychological demons. Cubism has come and gone, but the radical transformation Picasso prompted in how we look at art and the act of painting, as well as our own involvement in it as viewers, remains deeply embodied in the culture to this day.

Experiences like Picasso's in the Trocadéro, with their sudden flashes of inspiration and insight, lie at the very heart of creative breakthroughs. So let's press a little further into exactly what happened that strange day in 1906, and in the crucial following months. The *Demoiselles* evolved over a period of time through hundreds of sketches that suggest the partial influence of Iberian and Catalan sculpture. When we look at the finished painting, however, there is no question that the leap it constitutes over what had preceded it is due primarily to the powerful effect of African sculpture.[4] In an interview just three or four years later, Picasso confirmed this: "My greatest artistic revelation came about when I was suddenly struck by the sublime beauty of the sculpture done by the anonymous artists of Africa. In their passionate and rigorous logic, these works of sacred art are the most powerful and beautiful products of the human imagination."[5]

We want to say it was Picasso's genius that, inspired by African art, enabled him to make that leap. To characterize Picasso's experience in this way, however, is simply to admit we don't have any clear way to think about it. It would be more accurate to say he surrendered his genius to a strangely exotic *world* that, with the shock of the new, radically reorganized and reshaped his art. Picasso invented neither the nonrepresentational, fractured planes nor the exorcist function that would leave such a searing mark on twentieth-century art. African art possessed its own aesthetic and logic, and this became *a space to think with*. Almost immediately, its energy, forms, and purposes began to drive his own. Encountering a powerful new idea-space, he entered it fully and began to let its strange but compelling logic think for him.

Humankind's Promethean ability to make creative leaps like Picasso's both fascinates and frustrates us. The printing press, the Copernican revolution, Darwinian evolution, abstract art, the Xerox machine, the World Wide Web: these are just a few examples of the paradigm shifts that have shaped the pace and direction of Western development since the ancient Greeks.

Indeed, the drive for creative breakthrough is one of the central dynamic forces of the Western world, the means whereby it has transformed itself into the most complex, powerful, wealthy, culturally enriched, and scientifically and technologically advanced society in history. Breakthrough creativity has been, in the historian Joel Mokyr's trenchant phrase, the West's "lever of riches."[6]

The aim of this book is to establish a new paradigm for exploring the creative mind, one in which external idea-spaces such as the one Picasso so dramatically encountered play a central role. A good place to start constructing this paradigm is by asking a seemingly innocuous question: Where does thinking happen?

THINKING OUTSIDE THE BRAIN: EMBEDDED INTELLIGENCE AND THE EXTENDED MIND

If there's one truth most of us would confidently assent to, it's that we think—form beliefs and opinions, make decisions and judgments, intelligently solve problems, *create*—with our brains. Indeed, how could it be otherwise? It's hard to even imagine an alternative, and there has been little effort on the part of philosophers, psychologists, and other scientists investigating the physical basis of mind to do so. Until recently, that is.

About a decade ago, an influential group of leading philosophers, neuroscientists, AI (artificial intelligence) researchers, and others involved in the mind/brain sciences began to probe more deeply into the issue of exactly where human thinking takes place. Their conclusions, stated for the most part in academic journals and books, amount to a profound challenge to the basic *mind-inside-the-head* or *MITH* model.[7]

"[T]he human mind was never contained in the head," asserts Andy Clark, boldly disposing of several centuries of post-Cartesian mental modeling in a single sentence.[8] In a series of influential books and papers, Clark, professor of philosophy at Edinburgh University, brilliantly and incisively synthesizes a decade of research in the mind sciences that collectively supports the project he wittily terms "outing the mind."

Clark's central point is both simple and radical: the human mind could barely function at all without *external* help of some kind, given the level of information overload and sheer complexity of the tasks that we face daily: "We use intelligence to structure our environment so we can succeed with *less* intelligence. *Our brains make the world smart so that we can be dumb in peace.*"[9]

There is a dramatic illustration of this in the movie *Apollo 13*. Anyone who has seen the film, starring Tom Hanks as Captain James Lovell, probably remembers one particular scene. With *Odyssey*, the fatefully named command module, rapidly dying following the explosion of one of its oxygen tanks, the astronauts are faced with a rapid decamp to *Aquarius*, the Lunar Excursion Module (LEM) that will serve as their lifeboat. With just fifteen minutes to complete a lengthy power-down of the command module and power-up of the LEM, one of the most vital tasks to be completed is to recompute the coordinates of the Odyssey's guidance system to allow for the LEM's slightly different orientation. The movie shows Hanks scribbling down numbers on a piece of paper, and then frowning at his own calculations. A single digit wrong would send the spacecraft's crew hurtling off forever into outer space. "OK, Houston, check me. I've completed these gimbal conversions, but I need a double-check of the arithmetic. The roll CAL angle is minus 2 degrees. The command module angles are 355.57, 167.78, and 351.87." Back in Mission Control, white-shirted engineers at their consoles frantically recalculate Lovell's numbers. They are using slide rules!

The tools we use in our everyday lives tend to remain largely invisible, in the sense that we hardly notice their presence. Whether we are engaged in some mundane task like using a word processor or the altogether more exhilarating one of putting a man on the moon, we simply get on with the immediate task at hand, typically taking our equipment for granted. It's only when some breakdown occurs and we are suddenly forced to pay attention to it that we begin to recognize how much intelligence is already embedded in its design, and how this is already organizing our thinking without our previously having noticed.

In the case of *Apollo 13*, a safe return to earth depended crucially on the guidance system data being recalculated not only accurately but very fast— the power systems in the *Odyssey* were on the point of complete failure. NASA had at its disposal whole banks of sophisticated computers, of course, but these were not programmed to do the basic calculations Lovell needed. So the engineers reverted to that most mundane pre–pocket calculator workhorse, the slide rule, an instrument that, Clark notes, "transforms complex mathematical problems (ones that would baffle or tax the unaided subject) into simple tasks of perceptual recognition."[10] Had the engineers at Mission Control been forced to do the necessary calculations on paper, *Apollo 13* might well have missed the trajectory needed to bring it back to earth altogether. Instead the slide rule, designed specifically to exploit human beings' highly developed visual acuity, allowed them to perform a set of complicated calculations in seconds.

If thinking denotes the capacity to intelligently solve novel problems, then we can say that the slide rule *thinks for us*. In the *Apollo 13* case, it solved the problem of both performing and certifying the correctness of a tricky set of calculations. Attributing intelligence to a slide rule may seem counterintuitive, given our MITH-influenced tendency to identify thinking strictly with conscious human agents, but consider some further cases. Drivers of the first cars were forced to manually adjust the ignition timing and choke, change gears, and apply just the right amount of brake pressure to avoid skidding.[11] In other words, they had to continually think about what to do as they encountered each new set of driving conditions. Now this thinking is done automatically by computer-controlled mechanisms. Jumbo jets can be flown on automatic pilot, and spaceships landed on the moon by software programs.

If these technological artifacts can continually figure out how to control the craft in all manner of conditions and flight modes, then they are essentially engaging in the same problem-solving process as a human pilot—in other words, they are *thinking*. As Clark observes, what such cases imply is that "our [mental] boundaries extend further into the world than we might have initially supposed."[12] Or as the philosopher Daniel Dennett puts it, "The primary source [of our greater intelligence] . . . is our habit of offloading as much as possible of our cognitive tasks into the environment itself—extending our minds (that is, our mental projects and activities) into the surrounding world."[13]

This capacity of technological artifacts and systems to think for us represents a form of *embedded intelligence*, that is, a specific capacity to solve novel problems that is embedded in the world around us, in the extended mind (the term is Clark's). Interestingly, this external capacity for thinking is by no means limited to technological artifacts such as computer chips or slide rules. As we'll see, it exists in many forms, in myths, cultural and social practices, scientific paradigms, business models, and yes, art forms. What Picasso encountered at the Trocadéro was a physically embodied form of a whole space of social intelligence, a specific set of social practices for exorcising the fears evoked by spirits perceived as hostile.[14]

A more familiar instance of a cultural form of embedded intelligence is the Arabic number system, which gradually replaced the old Roman numeral system in western Europe during the thirteenth century.[15] The advantages of this system are readily apparent when we perform even a relatively simple arithmetical calculation. Try subtracting 333 from 666. The problem is so easy my seven-year-old daughter Elizabeth could do it in her head. Now try doing the same thing using Roman numerals: DCLXVI–CCCXXXIII. As Elizabeth would say, yikes! Our unfamiliarity with the Roman system (ever tried to read the year at the end of an old movie before it disappears from the screen?) is only a minor part of the problem. The fact is, the Roman form of notation is nothing more than a system of abbreviation: DCLXVI is just shorthand for six hundred and sixty-six. It's no more help in doing the calculation than the words are.

The genius of the Arabic system is that it embeds actionable intelligence about cardinal numbers right into the notation itself. When we use the decimal system, modularizing numbers to base 10, we only have nine numerals (plus zero) to deal with. Larger numbers are created using a simple notational convention: every time a numeral moves one position to the left, its value increases ten times, with zero used as a placeholder to help indicate leftward positioning. To perform basic arithmetical calculations, all we have to do is memorize the results for the first ten digits (0–9), and then move from column to column, "carrying over" or "borrowing from" in the familiar way.

Like the slide rule, this system exploits our natural visual acuity and aptitude for spatial pattern recognition, making what would otherwise be an extremely challenging task into a simple one. As something we learn in childhood and use the rest of our lives, the Arabic system constitutes a standardized, easily manipulable, shared cultural artifact of enormous power, yielding potentially infinite output from a small finite input. By offloading much of the intelligence about numbers into the system of notation, we've made a part of our world smart "so we can be dumb in peace." The system thinks for us, significantly augmenting our cognitive powers.

IDEA-SPACES

We have jumped from the sublime to the everyday, from high art to arithmetic. The fundamental point remains the same, however. The mind—seat and organ of human intelligence—is broader and deeper than we thought. It extends far out into the world, more outside than inside. Even without our being aware of it, this extended mind engages closely with our individual mind, shaping and organizing our thinking. Sometimes an encounter with the intelligence of another world dramatically transforms our thinking, leading to a breakthrough like Picasso's at the Trocadéro. More mundanely, the intelligence we routinely offload into the environment enables us to easily and quickly perform tasks that would otherwise prove difficult or time-consuming. But whether we are simply adding numbers or triggering a revolution in art, we don't have to do it all ourselves.

An *idea-space* is a domain or world viewed from the perspective of the intelligence embedded in it, intelligence that we can use—consciously or not—both to solve our everyday problems and to make the creative leaps that lead to breakthrough.[16] The Arabic number system and African art are both idea-spaces in this sense. Creative leaps arise not from exclusively internal operations of the individual mind (genius or otherwise), but from navigating the idea-spaces of the smart world we have built for ourselves; locating the powerful, structured forms of intelligence embedded in them; and analogically transferring these to new spaces. This is what Brubeck, Picasso, and Apple Computer did, with radically transformative effect.

In some instances, the space used to think with, rather than preexisting in the culture, is purposely constructed to facilitate thinking. Consider the corporate practice of developing an innovative business model.[17] A typical model will likely include a variety of shared assumptions, basic principles, policies, and declared intentions relating to the current global competitive environment; the range of products and/or services required to profitably exploit it; and the best strategy and organizational structure to effectively execute it. Like an architect's model of a building, it doesn't attempt to show every relevant detail, but rather represents the main components and their relationships to one another reduced to their essentials. As a relatively tightly organized idea-space, a business model encodes actionable intelligence about competitive markets, products, and organizational structure designed to allow a company to survive, profit, grow, and even transform itself. This intelligence—sometimes embedded in a formal document, but also learned and shared by employees and executives via meetings, e-mail, and even water-cooler conversations—is sufficient to form the basis of the thousands of decisions that make up the company's strategic and tactical operations.

Consider IBM. When Lou Gerstner came to the company in 1993, IBM had begun to embrace the then-fashionable view that the future of IT lay in decentralization, a trend that boded ill for a corporate monolith committed to mainframe computers. Gerstner, who knew from firsthand experience at American Express and RJR Nabisco what a nightmare it could be to get myriad different programs, applications, and systems to work together, concluded that "there was a very important role for some company to be able to integrate all of the pieces and deliver a working solution to the customer."[18] He accordingly put together a business model, drawing heavily on his prior corporate experience, designed to enable IBM to take on precisely that service role, thereby creating a shared space for others to think with.

Just over a decade later, IBM has completely refashioned itself in accordance with that insight, in the process returning to stable growth and profitability. The model itself drove the company's innovative thinking, from the strategic level of R&D, product and service development, competitive pricing, and marketing to everyday tactics used by sales reps on customer calls. Instead of having to confront each problem and situation anew, managers and employees alike could use the model to shape, organize, and formulate their ideas. The business intelligence embedded in it was rich and powerful enough to guide their thinking most of the way, pointing to certain goals and solutions while manifestly ruling out others.

A very different form of business model was the sudden emergence of the so-called new economy in the late 1990s. Its precepts, formed in a thousand start-up plans, magazine articles, and above all, in the myriad conversations of Silicon Valley venture capitalists, entrepreneurs, and company executives, gradually coalesced into a surprisingly specific and cohesive idea-space embedded with intelligence about how to be successful in business—a kind of metamodel for business models. Unfortunately, key aspects of the intelligence embedded in the new economy turned out to be largely wrong. However, this shouldn't blind us to its power as an idea-space, for several years marking out the mental territory within which many a promising new start-up formulated its goals, tactics, and products as it rushed to embrace the future.

Idea-spaces can take many different forms. Established scientific disciplines and paradigms, for example, represent idea-spaces that embed collective intelligence about the most effective way to carry out research, typically providing an overarching framework of established theory, principles, practices, heuristics, methodological assumptions, lab techniques, and so forth. Preexisting models and theories encapsulating prior empirical research strongly guide hypothesis formation. As in the case of a business model, this intelligence is embodied in a variety of quite distinct but publicly shared forms: class notes, conversations with mentors and colleagues, textbooks and journals. Often, its workings are just as invisible to the researcher as those of an automatic fuel injection system or word processor. Just as we "simply" drive or type, blissfully unaware of all the work being done to make things easy, so the researcher, immersed in work, simply proceeds, largely unaware of the vast apparatus of cognitive equipment that supports, shapes, and organizes his or her thinking and practice every step of the way.[19]

Other important idea-spaces range from art movements such as abstract expressionism or minimalism (embodied in a recognizable style, manifestos, critical articles, and shared values among artistic communities) to vast social institutions such as market-oriented capitalism. Cultural idea-spaces frequently influence behavior in ways we are barely aware of. For example, Robert Frank, an economist at Cornell University, recounts being subtly rebuffed by a French wine merchant who disapproved of his choosing a high-quality Champagne to use in a cocktail because it was on sale. Frank surmised that for many French, the American concern with saving money is trumped by an unwritten aesthetic principle about which Champagnes are right for specific uses.[20]

Professional anthropologists (as we'll see in detail in chapter 3) have long recognized such cultural norms as a form of "space to think with," acknowledging that the intelligence embedded in such spaces helps us solve both routine and novel problems. Correspondingly, they have also been among the first to recognize the many ways in which idea-spaces can also subtly disempower us by limiting the scope of our thinking. Spaces reveal, and they also conceal.

The impact of the Trocadéro's African sculptures on Picasso is a case in point. Other artists, including de Vlaminck, Derain, and Matisse, had begun to take an interest in African art, and yet in no instance was its effect on them revolutionary. Even Braque, Picasso's cubist collaborator, didn't get it:

> [Braque] loved the Negro pieces, but . . . because they were good sculptures. He wasn't ever afraid of them. Exorcism didn't interest him. Because he didn't feel what I called Everything, life, or I don't know what, the earth? Everything that surrounds us, everything that isn't us, he didn't find it at all hostile. Not even—imagine!—not even strange! He always felt at home. And still does. He doesn't understand these things at all; he isn't superstitious![21]

Picasso was able to "read" the idea-space of African sculpture in a very different way from his fellow artists because, paradoxically, however alien it at first appeared, it was also weirdly familiar to him. He suddenly realized that he shared what he took to be the anonymous African artists' superstitious attitude to an essentially hostile reality. Braque (and, we may suppose, Matisse and the others) evidently lived in an altogether more comfortable, bourgeois world that left them comparatively blind to the whole exorcist dimension of African art that so transformed Picasso.

Clayton Christensen, author of The Innovator's Dilemma, has identified similar examples of blindness in business. As he incisively points out, high technology is littered with companies that failed to survive, not because their managers weren't smart enough, but because they had trapped their thinking inside a mental space that blinded them to the realities of the emerging competitive game they were in.[22] Notoriously, for example, Digital Equipment Corporation collapsed in the 1980s because it failed to grasp the significance of the emerging PC industry. Every corporate document, from sets of strategic guidelines to marketing directives to daily executive briefings and team meeting agendas, propagated the fundamental belief that the future of IT lay in the continued growth of minicomputers. Given that collective idea-space, the incipient threat of the personal computer simply didn't compute. The prevailing corporate intelligence essentially derailed such thinking before it could even get going.

In a similar vein, scientists get stuck in outdated paradigms or models and fail to make the next breakthrough, as happened (as we'll shortly see) in the discovery of DNA. Architects and critics deride a new movement because it doesn't fit the criteria embedded in their own school of thinking. Tribes in thrall to ancient myths are initially unable to make any sense of the rude intrusions of modern civilization. Such examples can be multiplied indefinitely.

Einstein observed, "The significant problems we face cannot be solved at the same level of thinking we were at when we created them."[23] Clearly, Einstein grasped the paradoxical power of idea-spaces dense with accumulated intelligence to both empower and blind us.

The radical conclusion to be drawn from all this is that thinking—in the sense of novel problem solving—happens outside as well as inside the brain, in the intelligence embedded in the idea-spaces of the extended mind.[24] The individual mind/brain interacts with this extended mind, the two working together via a series of tightly interconnected loops.

All right, you may say, I get it: whether I'm driving my car, trying to get a crippled spacecraft back to earth, working on a scientific problem, refining my company's marketing plan, or even just adding up a bunch of numbers, the gray matter inside my skull can't do it alone. Constantly, it goes out into the world and loops through the intelligence embedded in a wide variety of physically and culturally embodied idea-spaces. Fine. But—Picasso notwithstanding—*can we really apply this new view of mind to breakthrough creativity?* Aren't we basically talking about pretty routine stuff here, like using a slide rule or following the rational dictates of a business model? How does the embedded intelligence in the idea-spaces of the extended mind explain major breakthroughs like the discovery of DNA, or the development of the personal computer? Are we going to deny that Crick and Watson, Gutenberg, or for that matter Picasso, were geniuses?

THE PROBLEM WITH GENIUS

As already noted, we long ago evolved a standard story about this exceptional level of creativity, one that is of course tightly interwoven into the MITH narrative. Great artists, scientists, writers, inventors, and discoverers are geniuses. Some undoubtedly got lucky, literally stumbling into the breakthrough they subsequently became famous for, but the majority are presumed to possess some quality that sets them apart. They're wired differently, their brain cells packed more tightly together than ours. Sounds logical, but like the MITH myth, this story too has started to implode under the pressure of some rather serious unaddressed problems.

First, psychologists have been unable to provide a theoretically coherent account of genius. Not only does the phenomenon remain a mystery; to date, despite decades of research, no satisfying explanation exists even for everyday creativity.[25] The central tool of psychological research for the last fifty years—diagnostics using rationally based intelligence tests—remains completely blind in the face of creative capacities and behavior. Beyond the level of 115, *there is no observable correlation between IQ and creativity.*[26]

The second and altogether more serious problem with the genius story is its inability to throw much light on three human capacities that are of fundamental importance to human creativity: imagination, insight, and intuition. These abilities are clearly involved in precisely those mental leaps that seem to characterize creative breakthroughs. Yet we know little about them, and perhaps because of this are inclined to relegate them to secondary status. The imagination in particular has invariably been treated as a poor cousin to analytical reasoning. Shakespeare's lovely lines from *A Midsummer Night's Dream* associate imagination with "the lunatic, the lover, and the poet":[27]

> *As imagination bodies forth*
> *The forms of things unknown, the*
>   *poet's pen*
> *Turns them to shapes, and gives to airy nothing*
> *A local habitation and a name.*

Such sentiments, vivid and enticing though they are, have hardly helped bolster the imagination's cognitive role. Disparaging the imagination in fact has a healthy history going right back to Plato, who scorned the *phantasmata* (images) conjured by the mind.

Intuition, often referred to (especially in business circles) as trusting your gut,[28] and more seriously as unconscious pattern recognition, has hardly fared better. As Malcolm Gladwell emphasizes in *Blink*, we simply aren't privy to what goes on behind the "locked door" of the unconscious.[29] Holistic reasoning, to which pattern recognition clearly belongs, has typically suffered the same fate, ending up as the poorly understood handmaid of analytical reasoning. As for insight, it has all too often been glossed as the sudden flash of inspiration, the latter word betraying in its etymology (Latin *inspirare*, to breathe into, with its ancient connotation of a divine source of "airy nothing") its strictly lightweight and somewhat suspect status.

In addition to these two problems, genius theory leaves a whole set of urgent questions unanswered: Why are creative leaps so difficult to achieve, even in cases where afterwards the outcome seems obvious? Are such leaps more or less unique, as genius theory implies, or are there universal patterns and principles underlying how they are conceived, evolve, and take off, possibly opening the way to a scientific approach? And where do radical new ideas come from, anyway? Underlying these questions is a deeper issue: Why do creative breakthroughs—and by implication, the phenomenon of genius itself—remain such a mystery? Put differently, why has a scientific approach to imagination, insight, and intuition, the acknowledged drivers of break-throughs, eluded us for so long?

The simplest answer to this last question is that until recently, we lacked any theoretically insightful, empirically based way of *modeling the notion of discontinuity*. The Cartesian model of thinking, inherited ultimately from Plato, is crucially based on continuity: logical and probabilistic reasoning cannot abide gaps. But creative breakthroughs involve leaps into the unknown. By their very nature they are not only disruptive but profoundly discontinuous.

THE ART AND SCIENCE OF DISCONTINUITY

It was the economist Joseph Schumpeter who in modern times famously drew attention to the violently disruptive nature of breakthrough creativity, noting the capacity of technological change to revolutionize economic structure through ongoing acts of creative destruction. Schumpeter was flying in the face of mainstream economics, which even today remains focused on smooth, linear deviations from and returns to a state of equilibrium. Modern economics still lacks a straightforward way of accounting for sudden leaps or violent disruptions—Adam Smith's famous invisible hand doesn't make jumps! Of course, that this should be so is hardly surprising: the core assumption of economic theory—that human beings are rational actors optimizing their benefits and opportunities by means of empirically driven analytical reasoning—leaves little room for modeling discontinuities.

During the past century, however, a number of disciplines began to come to grips with this enigmatic concept of discontinuity. In the arts, cubism broke up the smoothly continuous planes of representational painting, thereby with astonishing prescience embracing the theme of discontinuity at the very outset of the twentieth century. In the 1920s and 1930s, quantum mechanics explored the dynamics of the quantum leap and action at a distance. Kurt Gödel's incompleteness theorem, published in 1931, demonstrated that even mathematics, the sanctum sanctorum of rational continuity, had gaps: Gödel showed that there are truths that cannot be proved within a given system but must be apprehended by an intuitive leap. By the early 1960s, Thomas Kuhn was attacking the orthodox view of incremental progress in science, proposing in its place his now famous theory of paradigm shifts and scientific revolutions.

Around the same time, postmodernist thinkers such as Derrida, Foucault, and Baudrillard deepened anthropologists' challenge to the basic assumption of continuity underlying our traditional view of rationality.[30]

This holds that as human beings universally endowed with powers of analytical reasoning, we think, perceive, and act alike, essentially all living in the same world. Postmodernism recognized that we live in socially and culturally distinct worlds, and that moving between worlds may require a significant, disorienting, though potentially transformative jump that in extreme cases may prove difficult or even impossible. In the latter part of the 1970s, Stephen Jay Gould challenged orthodox Darwinian gradualism by proposing a new theory of evolution based on the concept of punctuated equilibrium—sudden periods of change followed by comparatively long periods of incremental development.

It wasn't until the mid-1980s, however, that discontinuity finally took center stage as a serious field of scientific inquiry in its own right. Researchers drawn from such diverse fields as physics, biology, chemistry, mathematics, computer science, and evolution began to collaborate in developing what became known as *complexity theory*, in which discontinuous change, from the sudden emergence of a tornado to the unexpected collapse of a sand pile, could be modeled using powerful new mathematical methods for describing chaos.[31] By the end of the 1990s, complexity theory had prompted the rise of the highly abstract field known as *network theory*, a radical set of ideas concerning the dynamics of connectivity recently developed by two mathematicians at Columbia University, Steven Strogatz and Duncan Watts, and by Albert-László Barabási, Emil T. Hofman Professor of Physics at the University of Notre Dame.

Barabási demonstrated that certain types of networks spontaneously self-organize themselves into a series of densely linked hubs.[32] The discovery of hubs, which create discontinuity by controlling links to surrounding nodes (in the same way an airline hub controls links to other cities), overthrew centuries of mathematical thinking that assumed dynamic networks formed new links in random fashion, spread smoothly and continuously through the available space. Barabási also discovered in network theory the basis for tipping points, those sudden, seemingly inexplicable discontinuous state changes underlying everything from avalanches to epidemics. During this same period, Strogatz and Watts uncovered the mathematical basis of the now-familiar network phenomenon of six degrees of separation, which demonstrates how even in very large networks, any node is easily reachable through a series of long-distance leaps.

As the century came to an end, the idea of discontinuity reemerged in theories of business innovation. Picking up where Schumpeter left off, Clayton Christensen, flying in the face of business's characteristic focus on continuous improvement and incremental change, argued convincingly for the essentially disruptive nature of much innovation. In similar vein, Larry

Downes and Chunka Mui, in their 1998 bestseller *Unleashing the Killer App*, boldly claimed that "discontinuity . . . is the primary characteristic of the new business environment."[33]

What remains to be done, and will be undertaken here, is to forge a deep connection between the discoveries concerning discontinuity made in the emerging science of networks, the imaginative processes underlying creative leaps, and the law-governed dynamics of a networked model of idea-spaces in the extended mind.

THE NETWORKED DYNAMICS OF IDEA-SPACES

When the new economy got going, it was explicitly promoted as a sharp break with the conventional wisdom that had preceded it. In other words, it was regarded (by its supporters, at least) as a leap into a radically new space of ideas that manifested little or no continuity with past economic precepts or practices. Similarly, Crick and Watson's research methods broke sharply with existing practices in biology. Since network theory models dynamic discontinuity, it should be able to shed light on the processes underlying such breaks. But how? To answer that question, let's first remind ourselves of the traditional account of change—that is, linear causality. A precedes B and causes B. I carelessly knock a china cup from the table onto the floor, where it smashes to pieces. My arm, gravity, the hardness of the floor, and the brittleness of the china all play a role. Until the advent of complexity theory in the 1980s, this was pretty much the only type of account, scientific or otherwise, that we had of change. It turns out, however, that in many dynamic systems, this linear notion of causality is incapable of elucidating what actually happens. It cannot explain, for example, how water freezes, or ant trails form, or diseases become epidemics. Rather, in each of these cases and thousands like them, the system itself is self-organizing: that is, there is no identifiable cause of change. Instead it's the dynamic properties of the system as a whole that guide and shape the system's parts into their resultant state. The output of dynamic, holistic, self-organizing systems such as these are referred to as "emergent."

For example, as architects well know, the best way to plan the paths between buildings on a campus is to let them emerge. At first, individuals will make their own way across the intervening grass or mud. After a time, however, the resulting multitude of paths will unexpectedly converge on just one or two optimal pathways between adjacent buildings. No one individual causes these paths to emerge, nor do they come about by conscious consent between individuals, or by design. Their structure is simply self-organizing. Ant trails emerge in precisely the same way.[34]

The mathematical biologist Stuart Kauffman, a former fellow of the Santa Fe Institute, where complexity theory was born, has come up with a lovely name for this type of phenomenon. He calls it "order for free."[35] Once identified, we find it everywhere: in biological networks, evolution, even social fads.

Obviously, there is enormous latent creative power in such self-organizing systems—systems that, in other words, drive their own transformation. The laws that can turn randomly organized water molecules into highly symmetrical ice crystals, the haphazard occurrences of a disease into a self-perpetuating killer epidemic, or a disordered set of nodes into a highly connected network hub are creative laws par excellence. Furthermore, the transformations they produce are typically discontinuous. There is, for example, no simple linear ratio of energy or effort between cause and effect, initial state and final state. Nor is the shift from one state to another either gradual or continuous. Rather, there is typically a sudden, unpredictable state shift, often of the entire system—the water abruptly turns to ice.

The conclusion to draw from all this is simple. When we find discontinuity in a dynamic system, we expect to find creative laws of self-organizing networks at work. Creative breakthroughs are by definition discontinuous, and typically occur in dynamic cultural, social, and intellectual systems. It's therefore reasonable to suppose that the laws of self-organizing networks are at work in creative breakthroughs, too. This hypothesis translates into the following two key claims, which we will investigate in detail in this book:

1. The extended mind, embodied in a world we ourselves have made smart, is a self-organizing network of idea-spaces, spaces of embedded intelligence that creatively form and reform themselves in accordance with laws based on principles of network science.

2. Imagination, insight, and intuition, the core individual mental capacities underlying creative analogical reasoning, engage dynamically with these spaces, giving rise to creative leaps.

When idea-spaces connect, merge, integrate, expand, dominate, take control, collapse, self-transform, or simplify, they do so in law-governed ways. Applying well-established principles of network science, I have formulated a series of nine laws applying to the dynamics of the extended mind that enable us to begin to crack the code of creativity:

The law of tipping points

The law of the fit get rich

The law of the fit get fitter

The law of spontaneous generation

The law of navigation

The law of hotspots

The law of small-world networks

The law of integration

The law of minimal effort

By the same token, these laws also transform how we think about imagination, insight, and intuition, revealing with surprising clarity their precise roles in the creative process.

If until now we have failed to formulate the laws governing creative breakthroughs, this is partly because we have been looking for them in the wrong place. Analytical reasoning, in spite of its central role in human thinking, is shockingly blind to the dynamics of the extended mind. Its unbreakable commitment to continuity (reason abhors gaps) forces it to proceed one step at a time, instead of making long-distance leaps typical of imaginative thinking. Its very analytical character makes it poor at recognizing patterns (which are inherently holistic), and thus of little help in guiding intuition. Furthermore, its basic dynamic is from simple to complex: wholes are built up from (and known in terms of) their simplest parts and the relationships between them. There is thus no mechanism in analytical reasoning that can account for emergent properties (in which the properties of the whole play a role in shaping the parts), or that allows for the sudden shift from complex to simple so typical of sudden insight.[36] No wonder psychometric tests based primarily on analytical reasoning could find no link between intelligence (so defined) and creativity!

Smart World claims that the *right* place to look for laws governing creative leaps is in network science, whose newly discovered principles drive the dynamics of the extended mind's component idea-spaces.

We are now in a position to propose a powerful new theory of breakthrough creativity, a genuine science of ideas. Imagination, intuition, and insight, together with the intricate ways in which, working through analogical reasoning, they expand and transform human mindspace, are no longer the enigmas they once seemed. We can begin to grasp how both individuals and groups meet the challenge of creativity by boldly venturing into new idea-spaces and directly engaging with the ceaselessly self-organizing intelligence of the extended mind—the mind out there. The dynamics of discontinuous breakthroughs—where radically new ideas come from, and how they form, evolve, get taken up, and are successfully integrated into the culture at large—can now be mapped.

INTO THE FUTURE

While we naturally tend to think of major creative achievements in terms of the past, what really matters about breakthrough creativity is its power to transform the future. Breakthrough creativity is one of the central mechanisms through which the future unfolds, the means by which dynamic societies use invention, discovery, and innovation to avoid stasis, stagnation, and decline. Printing, steam power, cubism, electric light, relativity theory, the Xerox copier, the personal computer, the World Wide Web—all were discontinuous leaps forward that opened up whole new worlds of exploration, development, and growth, setting the direction of change for decades or even centuries to come. Creative breakthroughs, in short, have fundamentally shaped our world.[37]

Ours is an era when the future seems to be coming at us faster than ever, even as it becomes more complex and harder to understand. Nowhere is this crisis of the future more apparent and more deeply felt than in business. As Larry Bossidy and Ram Charan write in *Confronting Reality*, businesspeople everywhere now find themselves dealing with a world in which conventional principles and practices of commerce have been upended. Citing factors such as global cost parity, hypercompetition, compressed margins, rapid commoditization, and reduced cycle times, they conclude that "more and more business leaders are getting blindsided, with a speed that was almost unthinkable in the past."[38] In particular, in an era when capital can move unrestrictedly across borders and the Internet radically speeds up the global flow of information, "Challenges to your business model, your strategies, and the very existence of your organization arise in improbable quarters. You are dealing today with something very close to the hypothetical butterfly of chaos theory, whose beating wings in China can ultimately generate a tornado in Iowa."[39] In such an environment, success requires "acute radar . . . you need to 'look around corners' and specifically discern the parts of the external environment that will affect the future of your business."[40]

As business leaders well know, and indeed as history teaches us, nothing is more dangerous to existing business than an unanticipated creative breakthrough. Gutenberg's printing press ended a thousand-year tradition of scribal text copying in just twenty years. *Encarta*, one of the first digital encyclopedias, caused the market for the printed version of *Encyclopedia Britannica* to collapse in under four years. The World Wide Web and the advent of a graphical user interface for the Internet famously caught Bill Gates off guard, compelling Microsoft to completely alter its corporate strategy. In the food industry, both the low-carbohydrate fad and the *trans* fat crisis seemed to emerge out of nowhere, in a matter of months, obliging it to radically transform its product lines and marketing, not to mention its profit forecasts.[41] Such examples can be multiplied indefinitely.

For successful business leaders, possessing a thorough understanding of breakthrough creativity and the three core mental capacities that drive it is more urgent than ever. Many of the examples used in the following pages—the invention and development of the personal computer, Barbie, supersizing, the Xerox copy machine, the new economy—are drawn from business; an equal number, however, are not. The laws governing the dynamics of breakthrough creativity are universal, not domain-specific. We can learn as much about creative breakthroughs from Crick and Watson, Frank Gehry, J. M. W. Turner, the invention of the alphabet, and the Cambrian explosion as we can from Steve Jobs, Ruth Handler, Chester Carlson, and the dot-com explosion.

Our study of breakthrough creativity must inevitably draw from a broad array of disciplines, ranging from economics, anthropology, and philosophy to the mind/brain sciences, complexity theory, and network science. To help navigate this complexity, I employ two readily accessible core elements: a series of in-depth accounts of men and women who succeeded in creating something radically new, and the nine laws that jointly determine the path that creative breakthroughs take.

We begin with a new look at one of the greatest scientific achievements of all time, the discovery of the structure of DNA, examining it in some detail as a classic instance of the power of idea-spaces to both block and enable radical new insight. We then step back for a moment to review the background of the study of creativity, the various approaches that have been taken, and the basis of the new theory of the extended mind. The main part of the book explores in detail each of the nine laws governing the dynamics of breakthrough creativity. In the final chapter, "Leadership, Imagination, and the Art of the Long Bet," we turn to more practical issues, such as how we can anticipate or quickly recognize critical breakthroughs in a given area, how to more accurately estimate their likely impact and direction of growth, and how we can ourselves achieve creative breakthroughs.

In his recent book, *Evolution's Captain*, Peter Nichols describes how, as late as the mid-1850s, sailors regularly put to sea equipped with neither instruments (barometers, for example) nor anything for forecasting weather save the most primitive and ancient doggerel: "A red sky in the morning is a sailor's warning"; "When rain comes before wind, halyards, sheets, and braces mind!"[42] Until recently, we have been in rather the same situation with regard to creative breakthroughs. We had little idea when or from what quarter the winds of change would blow, and whether they would herald fair prospects or possible disaster.

As we move more deeply into the creative economy, such a situation is increasingly intolerable. Though the existence of human genius is an undeniable fact, relying on it as the sole means to explain the dynamics of breakthroughs leaves us feeling helpless to either predict or shape our future. As you will have already noticed, the framework I'm elaborating here represents a radical break with the past, challenging some of our most deeply held beliefs regarding the mind's creative powers. Flying in the face of a 2,500-year-old tradition, it implies that some of our deepest and most creative ideas and patterns of thought are actively shaped by highly structured forms of intelligence that exist outside us: *the space of ideas thinks for you!*

The recent emergence of network science is enabling us to begin to measure and map the dynamics of the idea-spaces of the extended mind. No longer bound to wait like the seamen of yore for the next good wind or storm system to blow up over the horizon, we can now begin to advance into the future with greater confidence concerning the likely direction from which the next radical wave of progress will come, how it will unfold, its staying power, its probable impact on other areas of development, and how we should respond. On the basis of our new understanding, we may even be emboldened to undertake the challenge of achieving a breakthrough ourselves. In sum, we can begin to grasp how the future unfolds, and how we can help create it.

Chapter Two

SPACES TO THINK WITH

Reason, Imagination, and
the Discovery of DNA

There was in the early fifties a small, somewhat exclusive biophysics club at Cambridge, called the Hardy Club . . . Jim was asked to give an evening talk to this select gathering. The speaker was customarily given dinner first at Peterhouse. The food was always good but the speaker was also plied with sherry before dinner, wine with it, and, if he was so rash as to accept them, drinks after dinner as well. I have seen more than one speaker struggling to find his way into his topic through a haze of alcohol. Jim was no exception. In spite of it all he managed to give a fairly adequate description of the main points of the structure and the evidence supporting it, but when he came to sum up he was quite overcome and at a loss for words. He gazed at the model, slightly bleary-eyed. All he could manage to say was "It's so beautiful, you see, so beautiful!" But then, of course, it was. [1]

The discovery of the structure of DNA by Francis Crick (from whose memoirs this anecdote comes) and James Watson is an oft-told tale. It bears retelling, not only because the discovery represents an instance of profound, beautiful, and imaginative thinking, but also because it strikingly illustrates a key idea of this book—the power of idea-spaces to enlighten, and also to blind.[2]

If the race for DNA—and it was a race—had been handicapped from the start, Francis Crick and James Watson would have been very long odds indeed. Both were of course highly intelligent. But Crick—whose mother had insisted her infant first-born son be taken to the top of the house so as to ensure that in later life he would "rise to the top"—had received only an "indifferent" second-class honors degree from University College, London. Watson, though he had attained his PhD from Indiana University at the age of twenty-two, was generally regarded as "too bright to be really sound."[3]

In addition, neither man had trained well for this particular race. Crick had switched from physics to biology partly from sheer boredom—as a graduate student he had been put to work measuring the density of boiling water. Well grounded in physics, physical chemistry, and mathematics, he knew little organic or biochemistry. In addition, Crick was by temperament a rigorous theoretician, and had more than a little disdain for the messy business of laboratory experimentation. Watson was by his own account similarly ignorant of biochemistry and, equally inept in the lab, was something of a tinkerer. Moreover, the two were poorly equipped, working not in a biochemistry department but the Cavendish—one of the most distinguished physics labs in the world.

Nor would the theory that genius is mostly a matter of hard work explain Crick and Watson's success. At times, in fact, the two central protagonists behaved like people whose day job was working up skits for *Monty Python* instead of unlocking the secret of life. In addition to engaging in a veritable comedy of errors, they had distinctly lackadaisical work habits: Watson played several sets of tennis every afternoon and spent his evenings alternately chasing "popsies" at Cambridge parties and going to the movies. Crick, who rarely showed up at the lab before 10 a.m. and took a coffee break an hour later, repeatedly appeared to lose interest in the problem of DNA. On more than one occasion, vital pieces of information were obtained not through hard work but as a result of chance conversations in the tea line at the Cavendish laboratory. If, as Thomas Edison claimed, genius is 1 percent inspiration and 99 percent perspiration, Crick and Watson were evidently unaware of it.

And yet they triumphed. In spite of—or perhaps precisely because of—their limitations and distractions, these two minds spun and coiled around each other until together they cracked the genetic code. How did they do it? The story of how their thinking evolved, and where their competitors' stalled, reveals not just the twisting path to one of the greatest scientific discoveries of all time, but also a key characteristic of the extended mind: the ability of idea-spaces not just to promote fresh insight, but also to constrain thinking so that it cannot envision the way forward. The story also reveals how, in interacting with idea-spaces, the individual minds of creative people move back and forth between linear reasoning and leaps of the imagination.

THE BAFFLING PROBLEM

Before we can appreciate the brilliance of the solution, we have to understand the complexity of the problem. On the cover of Watson's recent book, imposingly entitled *DNA: The Secret of Life*, is a picture of the DNA molecule. When the book is turned to a slightly different angle, however, the famous double helix is replaced by a picture of a honeybee extracting nectar from a flower. It's a brilliant visual trope: the bee evokes the hive, ancient symbol of the creation of knowledge, as well as (more popularly) fertility and procreation; but it also reminds us of nature's fecund power to produce myriad species of complex yet functionally effective organisms. How biological organisms develop and reproduce themselves through metabolic mechanisms occurring within an individual cell, as well as through cross-generational replication, is what Crick called the "baffling problem" that both he and Watson had each determined to solve even before they met.[4]

In this age, when the structure of DNA is routinely taught in high school biology, when the human genome has been mapped, and every other day brings news of some new discovery about the role of genes in disease, it's easy to forget how complicated a problem DNA originally represented. The complexity falls into three distinct but related domains: molecular, genetic, and methodological.

Part of the difficulty lay in conceiving the physical structure of the DNA molecule itself. As elegant as a double reversed helix may seem to us now, no one had even imagined such a geometry inside a living cell before it gradually emerged into the light. Each aspect of this geometry—double helical backbones, with bases facing inward and conjoined in complementary fashion—had to be imaginatively conceived and then painstakingly proven empirically.

The "baffling problem" also forced researchers to confront three genetic puzzles in the form of conceptual tensions that verge on paradox. The first of these is *specificity versus invariance*. As a human being, your genetic inheritance is both complex and unique: even at the level of physical characteristics such as height, eye color, and so on, you have hundreds of specific traits that make you different from every other being on the planet. This specificity must be inherited through parental egg and sperm, as well as replicated invariably every time new cells are created. The second tension is *variation versus universality*. Just as humans vary, so do species. Nature has produced hundreds of thousands of different species, and yet the same universal process of heredity appears to be at work in humans and peas, mice and microbes. The third tension is the *one-dimensional versus the three-dimensional*. Physical organisms exist in the round, but genetic structure needs to be linear, purely a matter of sequencing units of information. Each of these conceptual tensions can be thought of as an instance of a deeper underlying paradox of *identity in difference*: highly specific structures must be endlessly copied; almost infinite biological differences are produced by some universal process; a common structural form integrates the one-dimensional into the three. Only slowly did these problematic issues resolve into the more general question of how the genetic code (an entirely novel concept in biology) could be physically embodied at the molecular level.

The third dimension of complexity (apart from DNA's physical structure and the three genetic puzzles) in solving the enigma of DNA's structure was primarily methodological. Keys to the solution of the multiple conundrums DNA presented lay scattered in several different disciplines: genetics, physics, physical chemistry, biochemistry, X-ray crystallography, and even linguistics and art. Furthermore, each represented a distinct idea-space differing not just in terms of facts, ideas, and theories, but of widely varying *ways of thinking*— of defining problems, developing hypotheses, interpreting data, and establishing the criteria for a satisfactory solution. At a deeper level, these approaches fell for the most part on one side or the other of the divide, running through all of science, between theoretical and experimental modes of investigation.

To be successful, then, any scientist working on the "baffling problem" needed to be able to cross from his or her own discipline's idea-space to other relevant idea-spaces in order to grasp the valuable intelligence embedded there. As we'll see, the scientists who failed to decipher DNA were unsuccessful precisely because they lacked this capacity to cross over into new idea-spaces and harness their intelligence. Physical chemists in thrall to their three-dimensional molecular models completely missed the importance of one-dimensional genetic data. X-ray crystallographers obsessively focused on finding telltale patterns in their results, scorned the boldly simplifying methods of physics that could penetrate to the essence of a problem. Biochemists, unschooled in genetic logic, failed to grasp the import of their own experiments. Remaining entrenched in their primary disciplines and the principal methodology they had been trained in, they were capable of proposing only a variety of partial solutions. In the end, the prize went to a pair of brash young shape-shifters whose confident imaginations and sharp intuitions enabled them to connect the dots by leaping from one idea-space to another without getting trapped in any single one.

THE STORY RETOLD

As far back as 1866, Gregor Mendel was able to show that inheritance in carefully chosen varieties of peas was controlled by discrete factors that could exist in two forms, called alleles. On the basis of this discovery, he developed an algebra of inheritance that allowed him to predict the characteristics of future generations.[5] It wasn't until 1903, however, that genes (as we now call them) were given a physical anatomy in the form of a sequence of points on chromosomes. This opened the way for T. H. Morgan's famous experiments with fruit flies, confirming that genes do indeed control the development of specific anatomical features of organisms. In spite of Morgan's success, however, the gene itself remained largely a mystery. What was it made of, and by what mechanism could it possibly control the production of the immense variety and highly organized complexity of living things?

Since a complete set of genes had to fit into each cell, it was deduced by the early 1940s that a gene (whatever its physical manifestation turned out to be) could be no larger than a molecule, and this in turn implied that from now on genetic research would have to focus on molecular chemistry. The physical chemistry of molecules has to do with the exact spatial configurations of atoms relative to one another. Henceforth genetic research would become essentially geometric.

In 1944, while Watson was still an undergraduate studying ornithology in Chicago, and Crick, living in wartime London, was designing acoustic and magnetic mines for the British Admiralty, Oswald Avery, a biochemist at the Rockefeller Institute, published a paper that subsequently came to be regarded as rigorous proof that DNA (the other main component of chromosomes besides proteins) was the genetic material. At the time, however, Avery's results were not widely accepted, since most biochemists were convinced that genes were proteins. DNA was thought to be too *stupid* a substance to possibly carry the complex genetic message. Nevertheless, the data linking DNA to genes was now out there in the extended mind. Thus, the stage was set for a serious attempt at resolving the conceptual paradoxes that made the gene such an enigmatic phenomenon.

The Grammar of Biology

Erwin Chargaff, a biochemist at Columbia University, had been impressed with Avery's data, and decided to focus his entire research efforts on analyzing DNA biochemically. It's worth quoting here the brief description Horace Judson, in his magisterial account of the discovery of DNA, provides of the method—known as paper chromatography—Chargaff used to get his results, since it offers a graphic glimpse into the world of experimental biochemistry:

> *Chromatography is simple, in principle: dissolve DNA in something that will chop it up into its separate components; float the solution down a sheet of wet filter paper; examine the paper under ultraviolet light to find the spot where*

each kind of base comes to rest; cut the spots apart with scissors; wash each fraction off its paper with another solvent and measure it.[6]

Thus described, it sounds straightforward. In reality it took Chargaff two years just to adapt the technique for use with nucleic acids.

What he found was astonishing: DNA, far from being the simple, monotonously repetitive molecule it was thought to be, turned out to be capable of tremendous variation, due to the widely differing proportions in different organisms of its four bases: adenine, thymine, cytosine, and guanine (A, T, C, and G). Chargaff thus concluded that if the long molecules of DNA were to "form an essential part of the hereditary process," the specificity that could be carried by different sequences of its bases was essentially infinite.

Chargaff's results, published in 1950, revealed for the first time a possible structural mechanism for carrying the genetic code. "I saw before me in dark contours the beginning of a grammar of biology," he later remarked.[7] There was more, however. Almost as an afterthought, Chargaff noted that the bases revealed an unexpected symmetry: in every sample he examined, the total amount of A invariably equaled T; and, correspondingly, C equaled G. Whether this was merely accidental he could not determine.

From a purely biochemical perspective, what we would have expected to find was wide variation in the proportions of A, T, C, and G in different organisms, reflecting the vast differences in their genetic makeup. Chargaff's experiments thus revealed what appeared to be an unanticipated identity in the midst of almost infinite difference. To a geneticist, the discovery of such an identity would have been extremely exciting, immediately suggesting a starting point for somehow resolving the identity/difference paradox in structural terms. But Chargaff, a biochemist, failed to recognize the significance of his discovery.

Chargaff was not alone in his failure to see what he had. His ratios quickly became known to many of the major figures involved in the search for the genetic code, yet their significance was not even the subject of serious speculation. Certainly Chargaff made no further progress in interpreting them. The reason for this blindness, of course, was that no one was looking at the data from the perspective of genetic geometry. The logic dictated by that idea-space would remain hidden until Crick finally found out about the ratios a couple of years later.

Enter the Genius: Linus Pauling and the α-Helix

Linus Pauling knew about Chargaff's ratios. Academic showman, bon viveur, and double Nobel laureate, Pauling was without question the leading physical chemist of his day. One of Pauling's most enduring contributions to the emerging discipline of molecular biology was the technique he and others developed at the California Institute of Technology for building models of biological molecules. The advantage of models was that, if constructed accurately, they could enormously simplify theoretical investigation, eliminating the need for endless analytical calculations.

Pauling's biggest success, one that contributed directly to Crick and Watson's ultimate triumph, was to have figured out the structure of keratin, a protein found in skin, hair, fingernails, and animal horn. The outcome of over fifteen years of research, Pauling's result convincingly demonstrated that the protein consisted of a triple helix—the so-called α-helix—with the backbones placed at the center. What inspired Crick and Watson more than the structure of the protein, however, was Pauling's demonstration "that exact and careful model building could embody constraints that the final answer had . . . to satisfy. Sometimes this could lead to the correct structure, using only a minimum of the direct experimental evidence."[8] This latter benefit was indeed fortunate, since neither Crick nor Watson was particularly adept at lab work. Crick was a theoretician, and Watson was clumsy ("One had only to see him peel an orange," Crick remarked to Judson).

Pauling's paper on the α-helix was published in 1951, eliciting many accolades from his professional peers. It was, unquestionably, something of a tour de force, and Pauling was showman enough to play it up for all it was worth. Just over a year later he would start applying his formidable intellect to figuring out the structure of DNA.

Rosalind Franklin and X-Ray Diffraction

Thousands of miles away from Cal Tech, in a cramped basement biophysics lab at King's College, London University, Rosalind Franklin and her fellow researcher, Maurice Wilkins, were already investigating the structure of DNA. Using X-ray diffraction, a painstaking method of determining the repeating structures of atoms arrayed together in crystals, Franklin was amassing hundreds of X-ray images, each revealing a discrete and minute detail about the structure of the DNA molecule. Franklin's technique yielded a vast quantity of data, including the position of the backbones and extremely precise measurements relating to the distances and angles at which the bases of DNA repeated themselves, as well as data indicating an essential symmetry to the DNA molecule. Nevertheless, Franklin was unable to produce a meaningful synthesis of her data. Working long hours, rarely socializing with other scientists, and disdaining a more theoretical, less datacentric approach (which she evidently regarded as "too flashy"),[9] Franklin failed, like Chargaff, to see what she had before her largely because she had closed herself off from other idea-spaces where the missing pieces of the DNA puzzle could be found.

Crick Meets Watson, and Idea-Spaces Multiply

What happened next in the saga of DNA is the stuff of legend. It is also comedy, farce, even tragedy, "a tale full of sound and fury," signifying in the end . . . a very great deal. The sound mostly came from Crick and Watson's endless talk. They met at Cambridge in the fall of 1951, and hit it off immediately. Both were already convinced that the big prize in biochemistry would be to figure out the precise physical chemistry of the gene, and they wasted no time in starting to speculate aloud about what it might be.

One of the principle advantages Crick and Watson had over their rivals lay in what at first might appear to be a weakness: their failure to specialize in any one discipline. The upside of this was the relative ease with which they moved from one discipline to another, multiplying the number of different idea-spaces they could think with. Watson had been trained in bacterial genetics by Salvador Luria, an Italian geneticist and future Nobel Prize winner. After being packed off to Copenhagen by Luria to learn some biochemistry(!), Watson had wandered his way, via Naples and London, to the Cavendish laboratory at Cambridge. He brought with him a firm conviction, rare at that point, that DNA, not a protein, was the genetic material. Crick, already working on the physical chemistry of the protein hemoglobin, was expert in X-ray diffraction. At the time, this technique, developed by Sir Laurence Bragg (head of the Cavendish) and his father in the 1920s, was the only serious rival to Pauling's model building for accurately ascertaining the atomic structure of large biological molecules.

Aware of Franklin's work at King's College, and knowing that Pauling was bound to turn his attention to DNA sooner or later, Crick and Watson nevertheless decided to press ahead with their own research, which progressed in dramatic fits and starts. In doing so, they made the most of their two key instruments of research—a huge appetite for speculative conversation, and an unbreakable commitment to the priority of theory over data.

Fed by some preliminary details leaking out of King's (whose high-quality equipment and excellent DNA sample they were unable to match), and aided by Crick's rigorous mathematical analysis of how a helix would show up in an X-ray diffraction photo, they built a preliminary model of the DNA molecule in the summer of 1952, a triple helix with the backbones in the middle. This model, which clearly owed more than a little to Pauling's model of the α-helix, was almost immediately shot down by Franklin, whose own research clearly showed that there were just two backbones, and that these had to be on the outside. Watson, it turned out, had gotten a key measurement of water content wrong by a factor of ten, although Crick admitted that he too should have figured out this elementary biochemical fact. Conventional biochemistry was never Crick's or Watson's strong point!

Immediately following this fiasco, Bragg forbade them to do further research on DNA, though given their almost complete lack of lab work, this ban was hardly a major deterrent. Following Franklin's critique, Crick began to consider two-stranded models in which the bases—now facing inwards, not outwards—were what bound the molecule together, most probably through hydrogen bonding. But bonded how? His first hypothesis was the obvious one: *like with like*, A bonding with A, C with C, and so forth. Not knowing enough about the nature of chemical bonds in DNA to make further progress on such a model, he enlisted the help of a young Cambridge mathematician, John Griffith, to figure out if such a pairing were possible. A couple of days later, meeting Griffith in the tea line at the Cavendish, Crick asked him if he had an answer. Yes, Griffith replied, but it wasn't like with like. The evidence, still quite tentative, pointed rather to A bonding with T and C with G. Ignorant of Chargaff's results (as evidently was Griffith), Crick's response was extraordinarily prescient: "Well, that's all *right*, that's perfectly O.K. A goes and makes B, B goes and makes A—you just have complementary replication."[10]

Crick's extraordinary grasp of the logical dictates of genetic geometry enabled him to see what the hypothesized base pairings appeared to imply. If the bases A and C on one strand of DNA always matched up respectively with T and G on the other, then the two strands were mirror images: for example, the base sequence ATTGCC on the first backbone would be matched by TAACGG on the second. Consequently, the infinite possible variability of the sequence of bases on one strand was balanced by the rigidity of producing its exact complement on the other. In his memoirs, Crick notes that he had originally gotten the idea of complementary replication from sculpture: a figure can be exactly reproduced by pressing it into a soft material, which can in turn be used as a mold for copying it. Of course, if what had to be copied were a three-dimensional structure such as a protein, then replicating the inside would prove extremely difficult, but in this case, the sequence of DNA bases was for practical purposes one-dimensional, so the problem disappeared.

If Crick failed for nearly nine months to recognize the significance of his insight, this was largely because of the sheer number of unsettled issues still facing him and Watson: How many backbones were there? Were they really on the outside, or inside, as Watson continued to believe up to a few days before they got the final structure right? And how did the bases bond, if indeed they did?

By an extraordinary coincidence, in late May, shortly after Crick's conversation with Griffith, Chargaff himself visited the Cavendish, precipitating one of the most farcical and, as it later turned out, most crucial events in the whole DNA saga. Watson's adviser, John Kendrew, arranged for Chargaff, Crick, and Watson to have dinner together. Evidently, it wasn't long before mutual contempt emerged on both sides. Chargaff was almost apoplectic in his scorn: "They impressed me by their extreme ignorance . . . I never met two men who knew so little—and aspired to so much . . . It struck me as a typically British intellectual atmosphere, little work and lots of talk."[11] Bitterly sardonic though the remark was (it was made more than two decades *after* the discovery of DNA), it was not totally unjustified, as Crick's own account of the meeting reveals.

Crick challenged Chargaff to say what all his work in nucleic acid had led to, tartly remarking, "It hasn't told us anything we want to know."

Chargaff answered, "Well, of course, there's the one-to-one ratios." So I said, "What's that?" So he said, "Well, it's all published." Of course, I'd never read the literature, so I wouldn't know. So he told me. Well, I mean—the effect was electric, this is why I remember it, you see. I suddenly realized: by God, if you have complementary replication, you can expect to get one-to-one ratios.[12]

Crick had instantly grasped what had eluded everyone else, including Watson: *the significance of the Chargaff ratios.* Given the almost infinite number of possible variants among strings of A, C, T, and G bases, the existence of one-to-one ratios between pairs of them confirmed in Crick's mind the insight that originally came after his meeting with Griffith: whatever the sequence along one backbone, it had to be matched by the complementary sequence along the other. (Had the matchup been like with like—A / A and so on—the Chargaff ratios would have been a coincidence of astronomically low probability.) Genetic replication was now straightforward: assuming the backbones eventually separated, each could be used as a template to produce further copies (strand 1 reproducing strand 2 and vice versa).

In January 1953, before Crick and Watson had figured out what to do with their realization, Linus Pauling completed a draft of a paper on the structure of DNA. He promptly sent a copy to his son, Peter, who was at the time doing research at the Cavendish and shared an office with Crick and Watson. When the paper arrived in the first week of February, Peter immediately went to show it to them. Watson, fearful that Pauling had got the structure, frantically grabbed the paper from Peter's outside coat pocket and began reading it. As it turned out, there were a number of things wrong with it, among them the fact that it posited a triple helix with the backbones at the center and the bases facing outward. This was unlikely, given Franklin's data. It also didn't make any sense in terms of the genetic logic, since the structure gave no clue as to how replication took place. Specifically, it made no mention of Chargaff's ratios, even though Pauling admitted later he knew about them. Crick and Watson's relief that Pauling hadn't beaten them turned to glee when it became apparent that he had made an absolutely elementary mistake in the atomic structure: the hydrogen bonds holding the triple backbones together had the effect of canceling the local electrical charges, so that, as Watson put it, "Pauling's nucleic acid in a sense was not an acid at all." Watson records his "pleasure that a giant had forgotten elementary college chemistry."[13]

Crick and Watson both knew that it could only be a matter of time, perhaps as little as six weeks, before Pauling caught his errors and began a second attack on the problem. But now Fortune would smile on them, as a series of events all running in their favor would carry them to victory.

The DNA Molecule Finally Emerges from the Shadows

The first in this series of events was a seemingly undramatic Medical Research Council (MRC) report released on December 15 summarizing Rosalind Franklin's research results to date. These included extremely precise measurements of the distances and angles at which the bases repeated themselves, as well as the fact that units of DNA possess a unique symmetry: when rotated a half turn they come back to congruence, with one half matching the other half in reverse. Neither Wilkins nor Franklin made anything of this last fact. When Crick read it, however, he was electrified.[14] Putting this symmetry together with Franklin's other results, Crick was immediately able to settle several of the outstanding issues regarding the structure of DNA: that there were indeed two strands of backbone, not three, arranged in a double helix; that they lay on the outside with the bases facing in, rather than the opposite; and most crucial of all (and this was where the symmetry he had instantly recognized played a vital role), that the two identical strands of the DNA molecule were reversed: *they ran in opposite directions*. In other words, for each gene, which might be a sequence of thirty or more "letters" (i.e., bases) attached to a backbone, there existed a *complementary* copy on the other strand.

Crick's insight was further confirmation of the conception of replication he had been developing since meeting with Griffith and Chargaff. As the two helical strands unwound, each carried an identical copy of the genetic code that could act as a template for the building of further double helixes.

The only question remaining was how the bases attached. This had been a stumbling block in the path of model-building efforts from the outset. The problem was that the obvious answer, via hydrogen bonding, appeared to be impossible on quantum-mechanical grounds: the available atoms for forming bonds were not stable. However, this supposition, notwithstanding that it was repeated in practically all the standard textbooks, turned out to be wrong. Here again, fate intervened. Jerry Donohoe, a former student of Pauling's who had studied hydrogen bonds intensively, happened to be a resident at the Cavendish at that time, and was able to put Crick and Watson right about the correct form of bond structure. The last barrier had finally been removed. As Crick noted, "There was no further jump to be made."[15]

A week later, on Saturday morning, Watson went to the lab early, and began tinkering with the cardboard cutouts he'd made of the atomic structure of the bases. Trying various combinations, he suddenly became aware that A could bond via the free hydrogen atoms with T, and correspondingly C with G. Furthermore, the bases laid over one another so perfectly that there was no need for the external backbone to be pinched or squeezed, a major problem with most prior models, including Pauling's. Crick came into the office an hour later and quickly confirmed that this arrangement of the bases looked right. As Horace Judson notes,

> That morning, Watson and Crick knew, although still in mind only, the entire structure: it had emerged from the shadow of billions of years, absolute and simple, and was seen and understood for the first time . . . A melody for the eye of the intellect with not a note wasted. In itself, physically, the structure carried the means of replication—positive to negative, complementary. As the strands unwound, a double template was there in the base pairing, so that only complementary nucleotides could form bonds and drop into place as the daughter strands grew . . . for the first time, at the ultimate biological level, structure had become one with function, the antinomy dialectically resolved. The structure of DNA is flawlessly beautiful.[16]

After a full model was built using metal jigs, Crick and Watson were finally willing to show their structure to the world. Franklin, Pauling, and Delbrück, among others, quickly concurred that it looked right. Only Chargaff remained sour, continuing years later to refer disparagingly to the kind of science Crick and Watson represented as "a direct symptom of the decline of the West . . . the barbarism of the twentieth century." It took years of extremely careful work to test the structure biochemically, validating their hypothesis of semiconservative replication. Their Nobel prizes came in 1962.

FAILURE AND SUCCESS: THE POWER OF IDEA-SPACES TO CONCEAL AND REVEAL

The story of DNA is unique in the annals of science. Virtually no other revolutionary scientific achievement has been chronicled in sufficient detail to enable us to follow each incremental step in reasoning and each imaginative leap involved. Here, we analyze more deeply the failures and successes of the key players in the story in order to highlight the power of idea-spaces—spaces to think with—to limit or expand the range of our thinking.

In seeking to understand scientific breakthroughs, we can learn much from failure. Thus, we begin by exploring the question of why several highly qualified people couldn't see what appeared to be right in front of them. This will help us understand the ways in which scientific paradigms (archetypal idea-spaces) *conceal* as well as reveal.

We can divide our key players into two groups according to their principal mode of doing science: the *experimentalists* and the *theoreticians*. No doubt the division is too neat—plenty of scientists both past and present can claim to do both competently—but one invariably predominates. In a very real sense, the experimental and theoretical approaches to scientific discovery represent quite separate high-level paradigms. They arise from distinct methodologies and laboratory practices grounded in different assumptions about how scientific advances are best made, lead their practitioners to focus on divergent sets of core questions and problems, and employ dissimilar professional standards for evaluating competing claims. In short, the experimental and theoretical approaches to scientific research represent two quite distinct *spaces to think with*.

On occasion, practitioners of the two modes within the same discipline or subject area appear to live in different worlds, even to the point of being completely blind to what a colleague claims to see. In the case of DNA, this division of labor (for both sets of skills are needed for science to advance) played a central role in determining who ultimately won and lost in the race to solve its structure.

The Experimentalists

Erwin Chargaff was an experimental biochemist in thrall to "the complexities that biologists destroy by describing them."[17] At the time, biochemistry was anything but a theoretical discipline. Men like Avery and Chargaff spent most of their time in the lab, growing nucleic acids in weird broths (in some cases made of beef hearts and rabbit organs), separating variant strains in centrifuges (one famous result used a Waring blender), coaxing the results to slide down wet filter paper, and similar highly practical activities. The challenges were primarily technical: avoiding contamination of samples, designing the experiment so as to demonstrate a desired result unambiguously, and refining techniques to eliminate undesired outcomes.

Of course, theory did play a role. Avery and Chargaff both understood at some level the potential *genetic* significance of DNA, and it framed their experimental work. Mostly, however, biochemists were glad enough of *any* insight they could glean experimentally as to biochemical structure, given how hard it was to do so in an era when the electron microscope was still undergoing initial development and a common kitchen appliance could do duty for a centrifuge. It was experimental data, not the logical dictates of genetic theory, that guided their work.

A man in want of his dinner is not much given to abstract thinking, Dr. Johnson remarked, and neither is a scientist who spends his days straining beef broth. Once the most fundamental characteristic of DNA's structure—the quantitative identity of the two sets of base pairs—had been discovered in the lab, the way lay open to matching that structure with the logic of genetic geometry. That was armchair science, the abstract thinker's preferred mode, a huge opportunity to perform an intricate but in the end relatively straightforward thought experiment. But Chargaff, with destiny staring up from his lab bench, didn't have a taste for it. It's not hard to imagine his scorn for such theorizing—more talk and no work. He never made the connection, which is of course just what scientific talk is designed to do. Nevertheless, Chargaff's results were vitally important, and for this alone he must be accorded part of the credit for solving the enigma of DNA.

In her own way Rosalind Franklin was no less scornful than Chargaff of Crick and Watson's peripatetic version of armchair science—endlessly trading ideas while strolling along the riverbanks at Cambridge—and the theory-determines-data approach that went along with it. There is a famous episode, made much of in *The Double Helix*, when Franklin appeared to advance menacingly on Watson, causing him to flee her lab. Evidently, Franklin's action was prompted by Watson's ill-judged remark that she couldn't interpret her own data because she didn't know enough theory. Franklin certainly had a head for abstract thinking that Chargaff may have lacked: X-ray diffraction required an abstruse, painstaking form of mathematical reasoning known as Patterson analysis. But being an experimentalist is as much a matter of orientation as actual knowledge. "We are going to let the data tell us the structure," Franklin told Crick when the latter made suggestions about letting theory be the guide. In short, methodologically Franklin was a radical inductive empiricist—that is, someone who believes that theory must be constructed step-by-step directly from the data.

Crick has observed that Franklin was just two steps away from the solution. Her recent biographer, Brenda Maddox, takes much the same view.[18] Without her MRC report results, obtained via meticulous lab work of the highest level, Crick and Watson unquestionably could never have arrived at their own model of DNA, and Franklin deserves full credit for them.[19]

Famously, she largely missed recognizing the helical structure of DNA (her notes indicate that she went back and forth about this, though for the most part she resisted the idea). She also missed the significance of the fact that the DNA molecule is uniquely symmetrical. To make sense of that in the way Crick immediately did, Franklin would have had to make several leaps, connecting things—such as paradoxes of genetic geometry and the mathematical analysis of helices—that lay in different disciplinary worlds.[20] Immersed in the Byzantine technicalities of X-ray crystallography, Franklin's inductive mind-set would not allow her imagination to leap into this crucial idea-space.

In short, both Chargaff and Franklin were operating deep within a methodological paradigm that blocked them from undertaking the kind of theoretical speculation that solving the enigma of DNA demanded. Their datacentric methods strictly limited both the kinds of reasoning they could engage in and, more important, their use of intuition and imagination to formulate insightful, testable hypotheses. It was, as much as anything, the idea-spaces they were thinking with that in the end frustrated their efforts.

What about Watson? He is so inextricably paired with Crick that it's sometimes hard to separate them. In reality, even while they acted as a team, their styles of thinking differed sharply. Watson's methodological paradigm was, as we'll see, closer to that of Chargaff and Franklin than to his celebrated partner's.

As *The Double Helix* reveals, Watson was among other things an outstanding nonfiction novelist. In spite of its many flaws (Crick, feeling a friendship betrayed, described it as at the level of "the lower class of women's magazines"[21]), the book remains unmatched in scientific literature for its sheer vividness and the force with which it destroyed a variety of myths about how science is done. Even as it promotes Watson's role, however, it also reveals the limitations of his thinking, which in spite of receiving periodic jolts of theory from Crick, remained in certain crucial respects experimentalist in nature. Nowhere are the key differences between the two men's approaches and styles of thinking more clearly revealed than in Watson's own description of the eureka moment itself.

Recall that in mid-December 1952, Crick, having finally seen Franklin's MRC report, had concluded that the DNA molecule was a double reversed helix, one chain running up, the other down. Crick's insight regarding the complementary symmetry of the DNA molecule's bases testifies to his extraordinary skill in abstract mathematical visualization of the kind physicists use. But according to Crick, Watson found it hard "to grasp that the chains were running in opposite directions, and what that meant."[22] Thus, Watson went ahead with building a model in which the two chains ran in the *same* direction, and featuring like-with-like (A/A, C/C, etc.) pairing of hydrogen-bonded bases.

There were several serious errors in Watson's model.[23] The most glaring of these was the flaw in genetic logic: if the bases were paired identically, then as Crick reminded Watson at the time, Chargaff's ratios remained entirely unaccounted for, turning them into a coincidence of staggering proportions. In effect, Watson was trying to solve the specificity/invariance paradox in too simple a way, using plain duplication in place of complementary replication. He recognized the need for identity in difference but located it in the wrong place—in the base bonding rather than in the overall complementary structure of the chains themselves.

On Saturday, February 27, a week after Donohoe had shot down his like-with-like model, feeling dejected but determined to press on, Watson began fiddling with some cardboard cutouts he'd made of the bases:

> *Though I initially went back to my like-with-like prejudices, I saw all too well that they led nowhere.*

Accordingly, Watson started shifting the bases in and out of various other pairing possibilities.

> *Suddenly I became aware that an adenine-thymine pair held together by two hydrogen bonds was identical in shape to a guanine-cytosine pair held together by at least two hydrogen bonds. All the hydrogen bonds seemed to form naturally; no fudging was required to make the two types of base pairs identical in shape.*

Watson immediately saw what this implied in terms of complementary replication:

> *Chargaff's rules then suddenly stood out as a consequence of a double-helical structure for DNA. Even more exciting, this type of double helix suggested a replication scheme much more satisfactory than my briefly considered like-with-like pairing. Always pairing adenine with thymine and guanine with cytosine meant that the base sequences of the two intertwined chains were complementary to each other. Given the base sequence of one chain, that of its partner was automatically determined. Conceptually, it was thus very easy to visualize how a single chain could be the template for the synthesis of a chain with the complementary sequence.*[24]

Watson's talent as a writer, presenting here with verve and clarity one of science's truly great breakthrough moments, only serves to bring out more vividly the somewhat accidental nature of his method. Notice first of all that, in spite of Crick's cogent theoretical criticisms, Watson initially went back to his like-with-like model, which essentially ignored the significance of the Chargaff ratios.[25] The question is, why? The only plausible explanation is that Watson could not see how combining unlike pairs of bases could possibly permit identical replication, and so chose to give Chargaff's result little theoretical weight. Watson's difficulty, like everyone else's, lay in *failing to imagine the genetic geometry correctly.*

Watson was led to abandon his like-with-like model only when he recognized, on the basis of direct visual evidence from his cutouts, that the hydrogen bonding simply wouldn't work. At this point, in matching up like with unlike, he was faced with just *six* possible pairings: AT, AC, AG, TC, TG, and CG.[26] So discovering the correct pairings—A/T, C/G—was a simple matter of trying each one out.

In his 1988 memoir, Crick remarks on the nontheoretical, trial-and error nature of Watson's breakthrough:

> The key discovery was Jim's determination of the exact nature of the two base pairs (A with T, G with C). He did this not by logic but by serendipity. The logical approach—which we would certainly have used had it proved necessary—would have been: first, to assume Chargaff's rules were correct and thus consider only the pairs suggested by these rules, and second, to look for the dyadic symmetry . . . shown by the fiber patterns. This would have led to the correct base pairs in a very short time.[27]

Crick, while not overtly disparaging Watson's approach here, is pointing to his own quite different, rigorously theoretical approach. Watson lacked the physics-trained scientist's ability to visualize, by the use of logic and imagination, the abstract geometry of the DNA molecule. Instead, he more or less blundered into it. In the end, we must conclude that Watson was at heart an experimentalist.

The Theoreticians

The early 1950s mark the definitive entry of physics into biochemistry, the integration of an inherently experimental discipline into an intensely theoretical one. Wet met dry, and dry prevailed. During the first decades of the twentieth century, physics had achieved an unparalleled series of breakthroughs, from Einstein's theory of relativity to the development of quantum mechanics. There are many reasons for this extraordinary success, but one of the most important was undoubtedly the powerful conjectural methodology developed by the leading physicists themselves.

This consisted of two core activities: bold speculation, often involving radical simplification, and model building.[28] Together these generated a potently dynamic thinking space for the intelligent interplay of reason with the mind's creative mental capacities: imagination, intuition, and insight. Physics methodology thus represented a *meta-idea-space for creating idea-spaces*; in other words, a space within which physicists could produce conjectural theories and models that constituted idea-spaces in their own right. Like business models, these guided thinking in the successful construction of solutions to specific scientific problems. When the physics methodology was first introduced into the biological sciences, it immediately produced two spectacular results, one at the hands of Pauling, the other at Crick's.

Twentieth-century physics was the special arena of those who delighted in first imagining how the world might be, and only then found the data to demonstrate it. Playing the game at a breakthrough level required a strong belief in the supremacy of theory over data, a capacity to clearly visualize highly abstract structures in terms of a concrete model (especially when imaginatively pursuing a whole chain of what-ifs), sharp intuition, excellent mathematical skills, and a willingness to criticize ideas, including one's own.

Pauling had these capacities in spades. Trained in quantum mechanics during the twenties, he was one of the first to bring the theory-oriented approach of physics to biochemistry. His profound understanding of chemical bonding enabled him to pioneer the all-important technique of modeling biological structures at the molecular level. As Crick himself noted: "What Pauling . . . show[ed] us was that exact and careful model building could embody constraints that the final answer had in any case to satisfy. Sometimes this could lead to the correct structure, using only a minimum of the direct experimental evidence. This was the lesson that we learned and that Rosalind Franklin and Maurice Wilkins failed to appreciate in attempting to solve the structure of DNA."[29]

Crick puts his finger here on the core difference between the experimentalists and the theorists, and why it was the latter who succeeded so dramatically. Experimental data, contrary to what Franklin believed, didn't reveal structure. Instead, what worked was theorizing about the constraints that a successful solution had to meet, and building these into the model, which in turn became a space of embodied ideas from which the correct structure could emerge. The role of empirical data was more to confirm the model than to reveal it.

Pauling's delineation of the molecular structure of the α-helix for the protein keratin—one of the first important results in the nascent field of molecular biology—was achieved, with characteristic audacity, confidence, and simplicity, using the theory- and model-building paradigm of physics. So why did he miss the structure of DNA? Certainly, with his mastery of this method, his access to a first-rate lab well equipped with both machinery and bright, ambitious postdoctoral students, and of course, his innate talent, he was well-positioned to take the prize. Yet his hasty model of the DNA molecule, with its triple helix and backbones facing outward, bore an uncanny resemblance to Crick and Watson's own first model of a year earlier, itself closely modeled on the α-helix. Pauling, still in thrall to his earlier success, was imitating himself.

Pauling knew about Chargaff's ratios, and could have used them to create a logical connection between physical structure and genetic function, but he didn't. His passion was physical chemistry, and he had risen to dominate it as no one else just as it was turning to focus on biological molecules. He appears to have seen DNA simply as one more molecule to be deciphered, rather than as what it turned out to be—the mother lode of genetics. Ironically, it was Pauling's very mastery that undid him. He knew too much about one dimension of the problem—chemical architecture—to spend a lot of time reflecting on the mystery posed by another. In the end, the idea-space of genetic geometry and its knotty but suggestive paradoxes remained largely a closed book to him.[30] Like Chargaff and Franklin, the mindspace he lived in professionally prevented him from imagining a conceptually richer way of making sense of the data.

Solving the structure of DNA would take an extraordinary leap of the imagination—in fact several extraordinary leaps—into an array of seemingly unrelated idea-spaces. It was precisely here, in insightfully combining the intelligence embedded in these spaces and bringing it to bear on the problem, that Crick's own mastery would shine through.

CRICK'S TRIUMPH

As an undergraduate Crick had read physics and mathematics at University College, London, acquiring by his own admission "the hubris of the physicist, the feeling that physics as a discipline was highly successful, so why should not other sciences do likewise?" His special interest as a graduate student became "the borderline between the living and the non-living"—in other words, essentially between the wet and the dry. While confessing he knew little about conventional biochemistry or organic chemistry, he read deeply in biophysics, finding in this emerging discipline "a healthy corrective to the rather plodding, somewhat cautious attitude I often encountered when I began to mix with biologists."[31]

Crick undoubtedly had the special talent for visualizing very abstract mathematical structures that has often enabled physicists to advance their insight and knowledge.[32] But the kind of bold, speculative simplification that made him a gifted theoretician he learned from Lawrence Bragg: "Bragg had a great gift for seeing problems in simple terms, realizing that many apparent complications might fall away if the basic underlying pattern could be discovered."[33] Crick notes that Bragg "made bold, simplifying assumptions; looked at as wide a range of data as possible; and was critical but not persnickety . . . about the fit between his model and experimental facts." Bragg's work, done in collaboration with Perutz, "was a revelation to me as to how to do scientific research and, more important, how *not* to do it."[34] It was a lesson Franklin in particular never learned.

Physical model building, which Crick learned from Pauling, was essentially an extension of this speculative, simplifying approach. Well-established facts, such as interatomic angles and distances, could be combined with more conjectural elements, such as, in the case of DNA, the number and position of the backbones. The resulting model could again be used as a space to think with, this time with the added benefit of concretely aiding visualization. Even fairly crude model building by Crick and Watson, for example, showed that some of their earlier models were wrong because the bases would cause excessive distortion of the backbones, a conclusion that could be established by visual inspection alone, without having to go through the complex calculations involved in establishing this theoretically. Like the slide rule, molecular models could do some of the thinking for you.

The conjectural, model-building approach to science Crick learned from Bragg and Pauling was an immensely powerful idea-space that had produced a string of spectacular successes in physics, but even so, didn't guarantee results. Bragg had been chasing the α-helix at the same time as Pauling, but came up with an erroneous structure. Pauling got DNA wrong. Similarly, Crick, in collaboration with Watson, took several tries before finally getting it right. Something more than just method was needed.

Uncoiling the Baffling Problem: The Genetic Code as a Space to Think With

Nothing in science so marks the gifted individual as the capacity to frame a key problem insightfully. In endeavoring to elucidate the structure of DNA, most of the protagonists, whether their field of expertise lay in physical chemistry, biochemistry, or X-ray crystallography, framed the problem from within the thinking space of their specific disciplines. This carried with it a double risk: first that they would fail to see the relevance of key elements—both ideas and ways of thinking—embedded in other idea-spaces; and second that in focusing on the purely physical, three-dimensional aspects of the problem, they would drop the all-important one-dimensional perspective of genetics.

Crick's genius, in addition to his mastery of the conjectural method, lay not only in grasping almost from the outset that solving the enigma of DNA would take a synthesis of ideas, facts, and ways of thinking embedded in multiple disciplines, but also in recognizing that crucial questions relating to constructing hypothetical molecular models had to be framed in terms of the logic of genetic replication. The gradual emergence of the double helix's celebrated twin, the concept of a genetic code, played a fundamental role, in Crick's mind at least, in figuring out the molecular model itself. It's easy to assume that the idea of a code simply followed from the physical structure, but this isn't the case. It has a quite distinct history of its own. In fact, in following Crick's thinking as it unfolded, we'll see that hypotheses about the two—code and structure—spiraled around one another, each from time to time illuminating the other, until they finally became integrated in a seamless whole.

When Crick and Watson published their famous two-page paper in *Nature* in April 1953, the idea of a genetic code was never mentioned explicitly, but was alluded to indirectly in the paper's famously coy conclusion: "It has not escaped our notice that the specific pairing we have postulated immediately suggests a possible copying mechanism for the genetic material."[35] Watson had resisted its inclusion, apparently fearing that the structure might still turn out to be wrong. Significantly, it was Crick who insisted. As written, it sounds almost like an afterthought; in reality it was the first allusion, however indirect, to the double helix's soon-to-be-famous inseparable complement.

The surprise that the idea of a genetic code caused can be gauged from a remark the geneticist Max Delbrück made to Horace Judson: "Even if [DNA] did carry specificity, then nobody, absolutely nobody, until the day of the Watson-Crick structure, had thought that the specificity might be carried in this exceedingly simple way, by a sequence, by a code . . . That there was so simple a trick behind it . . . this was the greatest surprise for everyone."[36]

If the idea of a genetic code didn't simply derive from the structure, but rather played an active role in its discovery, where did it originate, and how did it emerge over time into the full-blown concept embodied in Crick and Watson's model? Following this thread will take us to the core of Crick's thinking, clearly revealing how attuned he was from the outset to the importance of the intelligence embedded in the idea-space of genetics.

We saw earlier that genes, as the mechanism of genetic replication, had somehow to embody identity in difference along three core parameters. What were the elements of a genetic code that could do this, and how did they evolve? A code, in the sense Delbrück used the word, has four key characteristics: linear information, open-ended combinatorial power (i.e., in the sense that combining the letters of the alphabet creates endless new words and phrases), programming capability, and the ability to self-replicate. The first two of these were present in Mendel's algebraic formulae familiar from school textbooks. A whole array of differences within species could be captured in varied combinations of a few repeated elements representing heritable traits: AB, ABb, AaB, AaBb, and so forth. Genes' programming capacity, their ability—like computer code—to actually produce changes, was demonstrated in Morgan's work on chromosomes. Still, even at this point, the gene remained an indivisible unit, its internal structure concealed and its ability to code for almost limitless specificity as yet undeciphered. Both the code and what it coded were still inchoate, the relationship between them murky at best.

The logic of genetic geometry pointed to the need for a linear form of combinatorial generativity (which would enormously simplify the copying task), but for a long time none was in sight on either the protein side or, in terms of its physical manifestation, on the gene side.[37] Then, unexpectedly, a break came. In research for which he subsequently won the Nobel Prize, Frederick Sanger, an English biochemist at Cambridge, showed that what determined the precise structure of a protein was the sequence of its twenty amino acids. Although it wasn't then talked about in these terms, here, in the heart of the protein, were three of the four essential characteristics of a code: purely linear information, combinatorics (twenty amino acids could be combined into strings of several hundred), and programming capacity. Crick wasn't slow to grasp the genetic implications:

> *All a gene had to do was to get the* sequence *of the amino acids correct in that protein. Once the correct polypeptide chain [i.e., the string of amino acids] had been synthesized . . . then, following the laws of chemistry, the protein* would fold itself up correctly into a unique three-dimensional structure . . . *By this bold assumption the problem was changed from a three-dimensional one to a one-dimensional one, and the original dilemma [of how to copy a three-dimensional genetic structure] largely disappeared.*[38]

Finally, there was some kind of bridge from the protein side to the genetic side. Crick notes that the insight had come to him "before Jim Watson and I discovered the double helical structure of DNA"—in other words before anyone had any idea how genes themselves could carry out this linear programming function.

Chargaff's twin discoveries filled in the missing pieces. The fact that the bases in DNA were capable of carrying genetic specificity through variations in their sequencing meant that DNA could in principle carry out its role as a linear, generative, programmable code to direct the synthesis of proteins. As Crick put it (combining Sanger and Chargaff): "The genetic information is not conveyed and expressed by a large number of intricate symbols—it's not Chinese—but in two very simple and as it were alphabetic languages. Genetically, the information is carried by the nucleic acid, in the sequence of bases; but many such sequences can be translated into the other language—the amino-acid sequences of proteins—by special pieces of biochemical machinery."[39]

DNA's alphabet of just four letters could code the sequencing of the twenty or so naturally occurring amino acids, thereby enabling the infinite variation displayed in nature to be specified. Chargaff's second key result, the one-to-one ratios between pairs of bases, neatly solved the one remaining puzzle: how does the code self-replicate across generations of cells? Franklin's X-ray crystallography data suggested twin strands of DNA that were base-joined. If so, then when they separated, each would be a linear template for making a further copy. Crick, with this in mind, instantly recognized that Chargaff's one-to-one ratios brought back into play and in effect validated the discarded idea of complementary replication. The genetic code replicated itself, but in two steps, not one.

None of the other main protagonists came close to emulating Crick's skill in weaving back and forth between the genetic and the molecular, the informational and the physical, letting each play against the other until the twin end results, code and double helix, finally emerged in a harmonious unity. Even a maverick mind like Watson's couldn't match Crick's ability not only to move with ease between multiple idea-spaces—physical chemistry, biochemistry, X-ray crystallography, mathematics, and genetics—but also, on a higher level, to constantly allow the informational and physical dimensions of the problem to act as mutual frames for one another.

The odd thing is how little Crick did himself. This wasn't just a matter of others fashioning key parts of the puzzle for him (though in several cases they did). Rather, it was that once key ideas from idea-spaces that otherwise had little contact with one another were connected, they began, quasi-autonomously, to make new sense in terms of one another, leading to the emergence of a whole that was more than the sum of its parts. Thus the conditions genetic geometry logically had to satisfy automatically limited the choice of molecular models; correspondingly, these gave new meaning to the idea of a code. Complementary replication, which made no sense in three dimensions (because of the difficulty of copying the *inside* structure), almost magically became a key concept in the one-dimensional, informational context of sequential base bonding. Whole patterns of embedded intelligence engaged with one another, moving in a kind of back-and-forth dance of mutual influence, until eventually something wholly new emerged.

Without taking any credit away from Crick, we can truthfully say that much of the time, it was the dynamic interplay of spaces of ideas that was doing the thinking.

The Hidden Dynamics of Reason and the Scientific Imagination

Some idea-spaces, like X-ray crystallography or physical chemistry, cannot be separated from the empirical domains they are concerned with. Others, like the speculative method of theorizing that originated in physics, are sufficiently abstract to be transferable to other domains. Crick used this method, as we have seen, to great effect. Underlying this, however, was the interplay of the two most fundamental idea-spaces governing how the mind thinks creatively: reason and imagination.

We are so used to identifying scientific thinking with analytical reasoning that we can hardly begin to conceive how other mental capacities could be involved. The whole point of the scientific method appears to be to make and validate discoveries in a step-by-step, logical fashion. How else can new knowledge be proven correct? But as Kuhn pointed out a long time ago, the logic of justification is not the same as the logic of discovery. In the latter, as Crick himself emphasized, both reason and imagination play a role: "The most important requirements in theoretical work," he wrote, "are a combination of accurate thinking and imaginative ideas."[40]

Even a glance back at the path Crick and Watson's thinking took shows that there was rarely a linear path from one hypothesis, insight, or model to the next. The conjectural method Bragg taught Crick required that the imagination boldly leap out ahead of both reason and the available evidence, and therein lay both its power and risk. As Crick explained to Judson, the reason discoveries are difficult to make "is that you've got to take a series of steps, three or four steps, and if you don't take them you won't get there, and if you go wrong in any one of them you won't get there. It isn't a matter of one jump—that would be easy. You've got to make several successive jumps."[41]

In making such jumps, Crick was following his intuition, instinctively recognizing patterns whose underlying logic he could not yet fully articulate rationally. A good example of this is when, after being told by Griffith about the A/T, C/G base pairing, he immediately jumped to the idea of complementary replication without having any real idea of how this could work physically.

The danger of this mode of thinking is, of course, that you can blithely jump in the wrong direction, energetically creating a chain of erroneous conjectures. This need for imagination and intuition to be held in check by analytical reasoning, and correspondingly for reason to be prodded into action by them, explains one of the more puzzling features of how Crick and Watson's thinking unfolded. On several occasions, they seemed to have the pieces they needed in their hands, and yet held back. Why, for example, when Crick finally heard about Chargaff's ratios, which appeared to confirm his insight about complementary replication, didn't he go ahead and build a model there and then, instead of waiting another nine months? Again, why the delay after Franklin's data had confirmed the all-important symmetry of the DNA molecule?

The answer appears to be that right up until the end, there were just too many unsettled issues, ranging from details like the number of backbones and whether these were positioned inside or outside, to continuing questions about whether DNA really was the genetic material. As Crick notes, "There were always nagging doubts that one or more . . . assumptions might be dangerously misleading. In research the front line is almost always in a fog."[42] A case in point was hydrogen bonding between the bases. If this had turned out to be impossible, as for a long time appeared likely, then the whole double helix model would have collapsed, taking the idea of a genetic code with it. Crick needed the "accurate reasoning" provided by Donohoe concerning the correct form of the hydrogen bonds before he could be sure the model he and Watson had been constructing was the right one.[43]

The imagination reaches places where reason cannot go. Moving ahead of reason, it connects previously discontinuous webs of ideas, letting them play off one another until a new space to think with begins to emerge. Gradually things begin to cohere in a new pattern that first makes sense to intuition alone: "the pennies," Crick notes, "drop one after another until eventually it all *clicks*," and the insight comes. Only now can reason, confined to working over short distances in a well-defined space, start moving along the network, checking each link and along the way filling in some of the details.

Reason and imagination, continuity and discontinuity, rational inference and intuitive insight. The story of DNA is a beautiful illustration of this fundamental dialectic that drives creative breakthroughs. The step-by-step logic of scientific discovery in what Kuhn aptly called "normal science" has been well understood for centuries. But the nature and workings of the scientific imagination, surfing across the networked idea-spaces of the extended mind and, in a series of surprising leaps, constructing new ones, has until now remained obscure.

The imagination leaps out ahead of knowledge and the path of analytical reason. The arc it follows is neither random nor unfathomable, however. Through network theory, the science of emergent systems, it's possible to show how the unfolding, self-transforming path of the questing imagination follows a surprisingly law-governed trajectory, shaped by idea-spaces, tipping points, navigational strategies, hotspots, the integration imperative, small-world networks, and the discontinuities of the extended mind.

In the ensuing chapters I'll show how network science is beginning to shed light on how imagination, intuition, and insight, working together with analytical reasoning, generate breakthrough thinking. In all, I'll propose nine laws governing the self-organizing dynamics of networked idea-spaces, and the ways the human mind interacts with these. But first we'd better take a closer look at what we claim to know scientifically about the nature of mind itself and its various creative faculties.

Chapter Three

GENIUS, IMAGINATION, AND THE NATURE OF MIND

[T]he public is wonderfully tolerant.
It forgives everything except genius.

—Oscar Wilde

Reality leaves a lot to the imagination.

—John Lennon

On January 17, 1779, while making his way home on HMS *Resolution* from an unsuccessful attempt to discover the near-mythical Northwest Passage around Canada, the English explorer and navigator Captain James Cook landed in Kealakekua Bay, Hawaii. As he stumbled ashore with his officers and crew, Cook found himself surrounded on the beach by an awed but excited crowd of native inhabitants. Kuali'i priests swiftly conducted him with huge pomp and ceremony to the great temple of Lono, the chief deity of fertility and peace. Baffled but intrepid, the Englishman played along and was feasted and feted in an elaborate series of rituals lasting several days. Cook departed on February 4, but several days later he was forced back to the same bay to repair a broken foremast. This time the reception was distinctly hostile, and after a series of increasingly tense encounters over a period of days between the Hawaiians and Cook's crew, Cook himself, surrounded by hundreds of hostile, armed Hawaiians, was clubbed and stabbed to death.

How did this tragic reversal of fortune, bringing to an untimely end the career of one of England's greatest maritime explorers, come about? According to anthropologist Marshall Sahlins, Cook was apparently the victim of initially fortuitous but ultimately ill-fated timing. He had originally chanced to disembark in the middle of the annual Makahiki rites celebrating peace, abundance, and stability. His arrival coincided in various ways with myths relating to Lono, and he was immediately taken to be an incarnation of the god himself, the spirit dramatically and unexpectedly made flesh. The auspiciousness of this event was matched only by the singularly unpropitious fact of the deity's return after his season had officially ended and that of Kū, the god of war, had already begun. In the eyes of the Kuali'i priests, this presaged nothing less than a potential disordering of the narrowly circumscribed universe of Hawaiian life that could lead directly to social and religious upheaval. Cook therefore had to be sacrificed in the interests of sustaining continued cosmological order and stability.[1]

The deification and subsequent sacrificial death of Captain Cook is cited by anthropologists as a classic illustration of how allegedly primitive societies use their religious rituals and mythical beliefs as a kind of external mind to "think with." The priests who greeted Cook, imbued with centuries-old spiritual traditions, saw him not as the seafarer he actually was, but as the incarnation of one of their most important ruling deities, and acted accordingly. An intricately structured space of embedded intelligence, in the form of cultural patterns of religious beliefs and practices, thus determined what they thought and how they acted.

It is easy to smile disparagingly at this seemingly "primitive" reliance on external cultural forms to shape belief and action. Our Western tradition of mind, dating back to Plato, is rooted in an unshakable faith in the power and self-sufficiency of the individual's rational intelligence. We, at least, would have recognized Captain Cook for who he really was.

Perhaps so. And yet the fact is we all routinely rely on a whole web of social and cultural practices and knowledge to guide our behavior. Who among us doesn't unthinkingly depend on the supposedly accurate, trustworthy guidance provided by the high priests of our own times—professional experts such as stockbrokers, physicians, academics, or even the nightly weather forecaster? Nor is science itself, last bastion of Western rationalism, free from this tendency: in making their triumphant discovery of the structure of DNA, Crick and Watson at one point wrongly assumed that information regarding the configuration of hydrogen bonds in the DNA molecule was accurate simply because it was printed in a textbook. Chargaff, in thrall to the dictates of the reigning paradigm in biology, was blind to what others recognized instantly as crucial data. In business, executives trapped inside a deeply entrenched business model lead their companies to disaster. On a more mundane level, as we saw earlier, even simple mental operations like doing a straightforward arithmetical calculation or picking a wine are shaped by culturally embedded idea-spaces.

If Andy Clark and other proponents of the extended mind are right, then without resorting almost daily to this vast external web of cultural and social embedded intelligence, we could hardly function at all. For the most part, however, we pay little heed to how automatic this reliance is, or the extent to which it invisibly shapes how we think, act, and make sense of the world. In many regards our own thinking and behavior are just as bounded as that of the Hawaiians Cook encountered.[2]

Our overriding concern in this book is to gain insight into the role played in creative leaps by the networked idea-spaces of the extended mind. We want to understand how embedded intelligence can create a space to think with in the pursuit of radically new ideas, just as the culturally embedded myth of Lono shaped what the Hawaiians thought of Cook. But first we need to take a second look at an issue touched on briefly in chapter 1. Perhaps by default (because we can't think of a better explanation), most of us continue to attribute major creative leaps to genius. Is it possible that this idea, which has such a hold on our thinking, really can throw some light on creativity, or can we now replace it with a more insightful explanation?

TWO THEORIES OF GENIUS

. . . Newton with his prism and silent face,
The marble index of a mind for ever
Voyaging through strange seas of Thought, alone.

Wordsworth, encountering a moonlit statue of Newton at Trinity College, Cambridge, points to a widely accepted truth.[3] Of all the properties we attribute to genius, second only to extraordinary ability is that of being solitary. Millions have seen an apple fall, but only Newton, sitting alone deep in thought in his garden at Woolsthorpe, could see an analogy with how the moon falls toward the earth and the planets toward the sun.[4] In Western culture (and the very concept is quintessentially Western), genius and solitary individuality are indissolubly linked.

As Peter Kivy has shown in *The Possessor and the Possessed*, his illuminating study of musical genius, we owe this view of genius to Longinus's *On the Sublime*.[5] According to Longinus, genius is above all inborn, a gift of extraordinary ability that sets certain individuals apart from other less fortunate human beings. The possessor of genius imitates no one, but through the sheer force of his or her originality, is a maker rather than a follower of rules. The characteristically Romantic picture of the great artist pouring forth into the world the light within is matched by our modern conception of the scientist whose innate brilliance allows him or her to grasp truths to which others, mere appliers of scientific methodologies, are blind. As Kivy makes clear, for Longinus (and for Kant, who gave us the theory in its modern form), the source of power genius so clearly manifests comes from within.

In sharp contrast to the Longinian/Kantian theory of inner genius, Schopenhauer speaks of genius as "added from the outside . . . something foreign to the will, i.e., to the I or ego proper," and of genius taking possession of the individual.[6] Schopenhauer, though he owes something to his readings of Eastern mysticism here, is primarily repeating Plato's view. In the *Ion*, Socrates argues that poets such as Homer and Archilochus cannot be taken to be the primary source of what they say, which instead is to be found in divine inspiration. In a momentary fit the poet, possessed by divine frenzy, utters not his or her own words but those of some god. In a famous metaphor, Socrates mischievously suggests that power passes from the god through the poet to the spectator, like a series of linked magnetic rings.

"So antiquity gave us two notions of creative genius in the arts," Kivy notes, "the genius of the possessed and the genius of the possessor; the passive genius, possessed by the God, and the active genius, a God himself, possessor of the table of laws which he gives to his work; a genius to which creation happens and a genius who makes creation happen."[7]

We are all children of the Renaissance. The cult of the individual, not to mention secular modernity, is in our blood, a given in our settled view of things. A picture of creativity based on passivity and divine possession is barely comprehensible to us. We want our geniuses to be active, heroic even, not mere vehicles, unwitting subjects to whom creation simply "happens."

In modern times, the ideal of the equal opportunity society has given a new twist to this view of genius. Not "Everyone has won and all shall have prizes," as Lewis Carroll put it, but anyone *could* win and take the prize. Genius has come to look like an elitist concept, and so needs to be cut down to size. The only thing that distinguishes the genius from the rest of us is sheer hard work. "Geniuses are wonks . . . They work day and night," cognitive psychologist Steven Pinker confidently declares.[8] The idea is hardly new. What Kivy refers to as the "workaholic" theory of genius predates Edison's famous quip about perspiring geniuses by several centuries: Newton claimed he made his discoveries "by always thinking unto them . . . I keep the subject constantly before me and wait till the first dawnings open little by little into the full light."[9] J. M. W. Turner, the English painter who bequeathed to the world more than nineteen thousand works of art, remarked that "the only secret I have got is damned hard work."[10] Graham Greene echoed the sentiment: "I have no talent. It is a question of working hard, being willing to put in the time."[11] Of course, as Kivy notes, against this we must set the Mozart of Peter Shaffer's *Amadeus*—all inspiration and no work—but on the whole, the idea of the individual artist or scientist possessed of extraordinary powers of concentration and in little need of sleep is probably the closest we have come to a modern myth of genius. If it's "a boring myth . . . [lacking] the panache . . . of the Platonic genius possessed or the Longinian genius-god,"[12] it nevertheless satisfies our modern egalitarian instincts.

In the final analysis Kivy is not sanguine about our prospects of truly understanding genius: "Genius *is* a mystery. Not a supernatural mystery . . . but a *natural* mystery: a natural phenomenon that, as yet, we have no explanation for and, indeed, no idea of what form an explanation might take; what an 'explanation' would mean. It may, for all we know, be a natural mystery we will *never* understand."[13] Summarizing his view, he speaks of "the basic truth of the genius concept . . . that getting good ideas cannot be learned, cannot be taught, cannot be explained, cannot be methodized, and is an intensely personal matter . . . It is *as if* these ideas were the word of God or the gift of Nature."[14]

Mystery or not, the Longinian/Kantian view of genius remains popular. Today we scarcely know what to make of Plato's idea of divine frenzy, unless we opt for its Dionysian implications of an excess of alcohol or drugs. Even the workaholic genius is still presumed to draw his or her powers from within. Which brings us full circle back to the MITH (mind-in-the-head) theory of mind: genius or not, it's all *inside*.

THE COMPUTATIONAL THEORY OF MIND

How does the mind work? If we had a better understanding of this, then perhaps we could begin to lift the veil from the enigma of how creative breakthroughs occur. For centuries, the study of mind was strictly the province of philosophers. In the past hundred years or so, however, it has become the object of research in a dizzying array of disciplines: anthropology, cognitive psychology, social science, artificial intelligence, neuroscience, and linguistics, to name just the more prominent ones. In so vast and complex a field as the mind sciences, we can hardly expect to find the kind of uniformity of views encountered in more mature scientific fields such as physics and chemistry. Nevertheless, in regard to the mind's core cognitive functions that underlie intelligence, a fairly solid mainstream movement, grounded in nearly half a century of research, has emerged. While this movement certainly hasn't gone unchallenged, there is a surprisingly broad consensus that in its essentials at least, it is correct.

How do we know that an entity—a machine, a human being, or other living organism—is intelligent? Basically when, to cite Andy Clark again, it "looks like it knows what it is doing."[15] When you take your umbrella with you because you see storm clouds, you are acting intelligently. So too is the robot that avoids an obstacle in its path, the monkey that uses a short stick to pull over a longer one that can reach a banana, the mathematician who proves a new theorem, and the CEO who turns a company around.

Clearly, there's a lot of intelligent behavior around. Even if we restrict ourselves to humans, it's obvious that intelligent responses to novel situations must be based on some kind of *generative* or rule-based mental capacity. From some finite set of elements and rules for combining them, it must be possible to produce a potentially infinite output of intelligent behavior. Just as it's possible to create any written sentence in English from twenty-six letters plus the rules of English grammar, so our minds must have the capacity to use some limited set of elements and combinatorial rules to deal intelligently with the unlimited number of novel circumstances we may find ourselves in.[16] As Steven Pinker notes in *How the Mind Works*, "An intelligent system . . . cannot be stuffed with trillions of facts. It must be equipped with a smaller list of core truths and a set of rules to deduce their implications."[17] He refers to this idea as the *computational theory of mind*, citing as sources such luminaries of artificial intelligence and cognitive science as Alan Turing, Alan Newell, Herbert Simon, Marvin Minsky, Hilary Putnam, and Jerry Fodor.[18]

As humans with finite memories, Pinker observes, "we can't know everything about every object. But we can observe some of its properties, assign it to a category, and from the category predict properties that we have *not* observed."[19] The most fundamental of these categories or mental concepts aren't based on socially or culturally derived knowledge (the sort of things we learn in school, for example). Rather, they spring from our innate, evolution-derived capacity to structure streams of sense data into categories that reflect the fact that the world naturally clumps together in certain recognizable ways.[20] The categories don't represent objects themselves, but conceptual properties that characterize them. These will presumably include such basic dimensions of human experience as liquid/solid, edible/nonedible, friend/stranger, male/female, animate/inanimate, capable of locomotion, round, flat, and so forth.

At some point, such categories begin to mix with empirically derived knowledge. For example, on first encountering a puppy an infant may instinctively grasp that it is alive, friendly, and can move around. Later the child may learn from his or her parents that Mopsie is a dog, a female that can itself have puppies, and a species of miniature poodle. Further increments of knowledge will gradually yield a whole web of inferentially related conceptual knowledge, and from this a still greater store of inferences that will help in future encounters with the doggy universe. On being given a Sony Aibo for Christmas, for example, the child will quickly infer that even though it can move around, wag its doggy tail, and respond to commands, it is not, in fact, a dog.

Of course behaving intelligently—that is, looking like we know what we're doing—doesn't just depend on having a comprehensive set of categories for things, people, forces, and the like plus some basic rules of inferences for deriving new knowledge about instances within a category. We also have to have some way of reasoning about the way life happens and how we can and/or should interact with things. At the most basic level this capacity too, Pinker asserts, is inborn: "Many cognitive scientists believe that the mind is equipped with innate intuitive theories or modules for the major ways of making sense of the world. There are modules for objects and forces, for animate beings, for minds, and for natural kinds like animals, plants, and minerals."

Pinker supplements this list with one of his own, including "modes of thought and feeling for danger, contamination, status, dominance, fairness, love, friendship, sexuality, children, relatives, and the self."[21] Again, knowledge derived from experience gets mixed in with this list of innate components as the basis for acting sensibly and effectively.

Pinker refers to the operation of the multiplicity of innate modules that underlie and direct how we make sense of the world as "intuitive psychology."[22] At the core of this lies the idea that intelligent, rational thinking is "computation."[23] The mind, Pinker asserts, "owes its power to its syntactic, compositional, combinatorial abilities. *Our complicated ideas are built out of simpler ones*, and the meaning of the whole is determined by the meanings of the parts and the meanings of the relations that connect them."[24] The mind's innate machinery (concept formation, and intuitive theories of how objects, forces, and people behave), combined with empirically derived knowledge and some simple rules of inference, allows us to behave intelligently. It enables us to make sense of our environment and confront a potential infinity of novel situations rationally and effectively. Science, though using a stricter set of consciously derived concepts, theories, and inference rules, works in a similarly computational manner:

> We grasp matter as molecules, atoms, and quarks; life as DNA, genes, and a tree of organisms; change as position, momentum, and force; mathematics as symbols and operations. All are assemblies of elements composed according to laws, in which the properties of the whole are predictable from the properties of

the parts and the way they are combined. Even when scientists grapple with seamless continua and dynamical processes, they couch their theories in words, equations, and computer simulations, combinatorial media that mesh with the workings of the mind. We are lucky that parts of the world behave as lawful interactions among simpler elements.[25]

In Pinker's view, this fortunate meshing of the way the world works with the way the mind works makes the computational mind extremely powerful. "Because human thoughts are combinatorial (simple parts combine) and recursive (parts can be embedded within parts)," he notes, "breathtaking expanses of knowledge can be explored with a finite inventory of mental tools."[26]

It's hard to argue with Pinker's conclusion. Equipped with a limited set of innate mental modules and inference rules, plus inputs of domain-specific knowledge derived from experience, we can in theory extend human knowledge, and hence our ability to think and act intelligently in novel situations, more or less indefinitely. It's a compelling, expansive theory of mind, grounded in decades of research by leading figures in philosophy, psychology, and AI, and adopted (implicitly, at least) in fields as diverse as the physical sciences, technology, economics, education, mainstream cognitive psychology, and business management. Pinker is so confident of the theory that he boldly proposes that in principle if not in detail, this computational model of cognition, with its varied modules and chains of inference, has essentially solved the mystery of what makes intelligence possible: "With the advent of cognitive science, intelligence has become intelligible. It may not be too outrageous to say that at a very abstract level of analysis the problem has been solved."[27]

If advocates of the computational theory of intelligence are right, then no further theoretical innovations of any consequence will be required to account for our various ways of "looking like we know what we're doing," all the way from everyday common sense to important business decisions to the most profound scientific discoveries. Pinker doesn't have much to say about creativity, drily noting that "the genius creates good ideas because we all create good ideas; that is what our combinatorial, adapted minds are for."[28] In other words, no additional explanation is required for the creative leap: it's just all computation, all the way down.

But is this really the whole story? Can we construct a satisfying explanation of breakthrough creativity using just the kinds of computational operations Pinker discusses? Were Crick and Watson, for example, in fact that linear in their thinking? To address these questions, we turn to Thomas Kuhn, whose book *The Structure of Scientific Revolutions* remains the most insightful and popularly acclaimed account of creative leaps in science.[29] As we'll see, Kuhn in several ways anticipates the approach I am developing here.

CULTURAL BLINDNESS, PARADIGMS, AND THE FRAMING PROBLEM: VIEWING THE WORLD THROUGH THE LENS OF EMBEDDED INTELLIGENCE

Of all the assumptions underlying Thomas Kuhn's theory of scientific revolutions, none has been more controversial than the claim that scientists working in different paradigms within the same field are actually *living in different worlds*—not perhaps as wildly at odds as the worlds of the Hawaiians and Captain Cook, but quite distinct nevertheless. The claim was radical when Kuhn originally made it, and it remains so. Nevertheless, it merits serious examination, since it is central to his whole book.

Kuhn's fundamental point in *Structure* is of course that scientific development doesn't proceed smoothly in the form of a steady progression of improved theories, but rather as "a succession of tradition-bound periods punctuated by non-cumulative breaks."[30] The former Kuhn labeled "normal science." But real progress of the kind often associated with genius, the great revolutions in science, crucially involve a change of paradigm.[31] In claiming this, as the scientific historian Thomas Nickles has observed, Kuhn challenged the whole master narrative of modern science, derived directly from the Enlightenment program: *the idea of linear scientific progress toward ultimate truth.*[32] Discontinuity, Kuhn argued, not continuity, is the natural—in fact inevitable—order of things.

Why does Kuhn insist that paradigms are needed in the first place? The reason is simple, but as we'll see, it represents a challenge to certain core assumptions of the computational theory of mind that resonates closely with arguments for the role of idea-spaces in guiding intelligent thinking. Nature, Kuhn suggests, "is too complex and varied to be explored at random."[33] The scientist needs a map telling him or her what to look for, how to evaluate the various puzzles and anomalies that present themselves, and how to solve them. Providing this map is the role of paradigms. Just as the Hawaiians needed to resort to their myths to make sense of what was for them a novel and puzzling phenomenon, so a scientist, faced with a confusing series of factual anomalies, needs a new paradigm in order to understand what is going on. In other words, a paradigm frames the data in a way that allows meaningful patterns to emerge.

Paradigms as Lenses

If all Kuhn meant by paradigm were a set of theoretical principles and claims that impose a certain interpretation on empirical data, then there would be no controversy. The word *theoretical*, after all, comes from the Greek *theōrein*, to look at. A theory, in other words, is something that lets us see something in a different way. The wooden table I am sitting at as I type this gives every appearance of being solid. If I bang it, my hand stops, unable to pass through. A physicist observes the same table I do, but arrives at a very different interpretation of the sense data. Through the lens of theory, he or she can see an object made up mostly of empty space. Operating from a highly abstract set of axioms, laws, and principles, together with empirical observation, the physicist is led to this counterintuitive conclusion by a long but unbroken chain of deductive and inductive inferences.

As Kuhn recognizes, this idea of science as simply providing different interpretations of the same sense data is grounded in the post-Cartesian belief that we all, scientists and laypersons alike, live in the same observable world, even if our explanations of it may differ radically. *At the level of sense data, at least, things are basically the same.* This view, which fully accords with our commonsense intuition, continues to be widely held, not only by many working scientists, but also by educators, economists, psychologists, and businesspeople. Kuhn, however, adamantly rejects it, claiming that we are none of us neutral observers of the world, even at the level of everyday perception. Our various acts of making sense of the world (this white blur on the table in front of me is a cup of coffee, that tall blob over there is the Eiffel Tower) are unavoidably shaped by our prior beliefs and expectations.

To demonstrate his point, Kuhn cites an experiment in the psychology of perception conducted by Jerome Bruner and Leo Postman.[34] In the experiment, subjects were briefly shown a series of playing cards. Most were normal, but some were anomalous, such as a red six of spades or black four of hearts. Typically, subjects would identify the anomalous cards without any awareness of their being abnormal, as though they had actually seen the black six of spades, or the red four of hearts. In other words, they fitted what they saw (or thought they saw) to the conceptual categories they were already familiar with. The subjects' existing knowledge of cards constituted a paradigm that shaped direct perception.

Kuhn goes so far as to suggest that "something like a paradigm is prerequisite to perception itself. What a man sees depends both upon what he looks at and also upon what his previous visual-perceptual experience has taught him to see. In the absence of such training there can only be, in William James's phrase, 'a bloomin' buzzin' confusion.'"[35] For example, a neophyte physics student, looking at a bubble-chamber photograph, will see just a confused mass of broken lines. The trained physicist, on the other hand, viewing the same photo through the paradigm of advanced physics theory, will instantly recognize these as recording familiar subnuclear events.[36]

According to Kuhn, then, paradigms mediate *even our immediate sensory perception*. Whether in the form of a simple empirical belief (e.g., in cards, hearts are red) or a complex scientific theory, paradigms are disclosive spaces that allow us to see certain things while remaining blind to others. Data that don't fit into a particular paradigm "are often not seen at all."[37] Western astronomers, for example, only began to observe such variable phenomena as sunspots, comets, and new stars in the half-century immediately following the emergence of the Copernican paradigm. The Chinese, on the other hand, had systematically recorded these centuries before. Why? Certainly not because they had better equipment—they lacked even the crudest telescopes. Rather, Kuhn suggests, they were free of the pre-Copernican Western astronomical paradigm that insisted on an *immutable* cosmos, fixed in the same state for all eternity. In this case, the reigning paradigm constituted a restrictive lens that even rapidly developing telescopic technology couldn't overcome.[38]

A paradigm then, like a lens, reveals the world to us, but it also conceals.[39] If Sahlins is right, the Hawaiians who first deified and then clubbed Captain Cook to death never even saw him as a human being, let alone as an eighteenth-century English maritime explorer. For them he was a god incarnate. Similarly, according to James Watson, Rosalind Franklin, operating from a very different paradigm from the one used by himself and Crick, failed to recognize the telltale X in her photos that jumped out at Watson as a sure sign of a helix. Paradigms, in short, are idea-spaces.

Another way to think about paradigms is in terms of *framing*. Business-people, for example, often debate how to frame a problem or set of data, the better to understand it. We like to think that a frame is something we consciously construct. But if Kuhn is right, how we make sense of and think about the world is already shaped, from the level of perception on up, by a series of frames—paradigms that are often largely invisible to us, as water is proverbially invisible to the fish that swim in it.

Engineers, for example, frame a design problem for a consumer product differently than marketing people would. The two groups live in very different worlds shaped by different training, concerns, standards, practices, values, and goals. Similarly, entrepreneurs frequently encounter resistance to their inventions from mainstream companies or investor groups that, in spite of possessing excellent analytical skills, seem baffled by what is being offered them.

If you are over age sixty, you can probably still remember stencils, the mimeograph machine, and the smudgy purple ink copies that they made. Yet when Chester Carlson took his new xerographic process to A.B. Dick executives in the late 1950s, he was unable to spark any interest in it. From their point of view, stencils and carbon paper, the then dominant copying technologies, were much cheaper and did the required job. As John Seely Brown and Paul Duguid point out in *The Social Life of Information*, however, what they failed to imagine was how xeroxing would transform the way documents are created, distributed, and used to organize work.[40]

When A.B. Dick rejected Carlson's invention, no one was in the habit of walking into a harassed secretary's office and requesting twenty copies of a fifty-page report, with colored charts and diagrams, to be ready in half an hour. In short, in the paradigm/idea-space of 1950s business culture, where cheapness was a key market value and efficiency wasn't really an issue, A.B. Dick's (and subsequently IBM's) rejection of the xerographic process made a lot of sense. Given the highly novel and unproven technology, together with the relatively high switching costs, it represented a *rational* decision. It is only now, viewed from within a very different context of what has become standard business practice, that we can see how irrational the rejection was, and the enormous opportunity that was lost.

The lesson to be drawn from all this is that how we see and make sense of the world, from the level of sense perception to that of trying to make intelligent strategy decisions or scientific discoveries, is deeply shaped by the framing that, consciously or not, we unavoidably bring to bear. Kuhn emphasizes again and again that paradigms—his term for frames used in science—are not just purely mental sets of principles or theoretical knowledge. Rather, they also manifest in the form of practical training, established methodologies, lab techniques, available technology, and group preferences about what questions and problems are important and so worth investigating. As a form of idea-space, paradigms are ultimately rooted in society, or what Brown and Duguid call communities of practice.

Although Kuhn focuses his attention on the effects of paradigms in science, there can be little doubt from his references to Bruner and Postman's card experiments and other psychological research that he has no problem with extending the paradigm concept to all human cognition. To generalize, paradigms can be thought of as forms of embedded intelligence, the vital core of socially and culturally embodied idea-spaces that pervasively shape cognition, and in particular our human capacity for intelligent thinking and problem solving. In short, they represent a core part of the extended mind, and thus of our smart world.

In considering the ways in which paradigms or spaces of embedded intelligence limit thinking and sense making, it's important we not conclude that they are therefore in essence bad. Kuhn's whole point is that they are *unavoidable*. Without them, we can't make sense of the world at all. Being socially grounded, they represent relatively stable spaces within which the work of analytical reasoning—building up chains of inferences that enable us to vastly extend the range and depth of our knowledge—becomes possible. Kuhn takes pains to emphasize, in fact, that paradigms are precisely what make available the basic principles, assumptions, and methods from which the highly inferential, logical work of normal science—puzzle solving, as he termed it—can proceed. Thus, within their respective idea-spaces, the Hawaiians, and business leaders at companies like A.B. Dick and IBM, were acting rationally: they were making sound linear inferences from widely accepted beliefs and expectations about how the world works. We may now view their actions as misguided, but without being deeply embedded in the idea-spaces they lived in, they couldn't have thought or acted at all.

We're interested in Kuhn because of his insights into how creative breakthroughs, in the form of scientific revolutions, happen, and paradigms of course play a key role here. Paradigms conceal, in the sense of imposing limits on how far inferential thinking can go, but they also reveal. The formation of a new paradigm opens up new ways of seeing and thinking that can overcome the limitations of the old one, leading to major scientific advances and discoveries. Kuhn points to the history of electricity as an example.[41] The causes of electrical phenomena of attraction and repulsion had been speculated about since antiquity. None of the proposed theories, however, was able to explain a seemingly confusing range of observed phenomena. One of the competing theories was based on the idea that electricity was a fluid and could therefore manifest conduction. Several scientists who held this view began to think about how electricity could be bottled, and this led directly to the discovery of the Leyden jar in the early 1740s. Benjamin Franklin's attempts to explain this device in turn led to the formation of his own paradigmatic theory of electricity. The paradigm of electricity as a fluid thus made a scientific breakthrough possible, even though it ignored other aspects of the available data that were explained only later. Galileo's theory of pendulums, Newtonian mechanics, Dalton's discovery of atomic weights, and Einstein's relativity theories all represented the emergence of new paradigms that revolutionized the course of scientific research.

Why Paradigms Challenge the Computational Theory of Mind

When *The Structure of Scientific Revolutions* first appeared, the noted philosopher of science Israel Sheffler called Kuhn a radical irrationalist, subjectivist, relativist irrealist for denying, as Kuhn seems to, that science gives us objective truth. More recently, the physicist Alan Sokal charged Kuhn with being a principal source of postmodernist relativism and culture-based treatments of science.[42] Nor are such accusations just so much high-level academic mudslinging. Working scientists, mainstream economists, and business and management theorists, among others, remain deeply wedded to the idea that analytical reasoning can provide a linear path to objective truth. For them, being charged with embracing relativism, and hence discontinuity, is tantamount to courting intellectual dismissal.

The computational theory of mind, as we've seen, is committed to the view that we acquire, build up, and advance objective knowledge through a step-by-step process of logical inference. Beyond our initial endowment of innate knowledge, we make sense of our world and act intelligently primarily by using rational rules of inference. Admittedly, human reasoning is fallible, but science, with its more rigorous procedures, acts as a corrective in advancing human discovery and knowledge.

Kuhn would by no means disagree with all of this. To a large extent, it matches his account of how normal "puzzle-solving" science operates. Nevertheless, his theory of paradigms poses three significant challenges to the computational account of mind.

First, framing—the basic mental function performed by paradigms—is holistic, not computational. A paradigm consists of interacting, and hence interdependent, sets of principles, methods, goals, values, questions worth investigating, and so forth. Consequently, there is no straightforward way of building up a paradigm linearly, step-by-step, moving from the simple to the more complex. In other words, paradigms can't be constructed *inferentially*. However they develop, there is nothing in the computational theory of mind's approach to intelligence that throws much light on the process.

Second (and relatedly), paradigms are grounded in the shared ideas, ideals, practices, preferences, values, and training of a community. A paradigm that is grounded in a community of working scientists comes alive: it grows, changes, gains converts, preempts competing paradigms, and thus comes to constitute the stable context within which science's normal, inferential, puzzle-solving activities can proceed. In this sense, paradigms are typical forms of embedded intelligence, embodying not only knowledge but also preferred ways of doing things, standards, methods, and other normative components. The intelligence these embody, contrary to what Pinker and others imply concerning the elements of thinking processes, cannot easily be represented in terms of purely verbal knowledge, nor can it be built up inferentially from its component elements.

Third, scientific revolutions, constituting some of the clearest and best-documented examples of breakthrough creativity, do not happen smoothly, in an identifiable series of steps. A paradigm may take time to emerge and become fully formed and broadly accepted, but the switch in understanding, according to Kuhn, is akin to a gestalt flip: "What were ducks in the scientist's world before the revolution are rabbits afterwards."[43] So different are the paradigms that not only is it impossible to derive the new one from the old; they are in fact incommensurable. Time and space, for example, don't differ from one another in analytically identifiable ways in the Newtonian and Einsteinian paradigms. They partake of *quite distinct networks* of fundamental assumptions, theoretical concepts, underlying questions and issues, ways of evaluating and theorizing about data, and so forth, to the point where they represent different worlds of research, and even distinct ways of deciding what counts as data.

If Kuhn is right about paradigms and the fundamental role they play in breakthrough discoveries, then his ideas pose a serious challenge to the currently widely accepted computational theory of mind. Appeals to a mysterious "genius factor" aside, it's logical to conclude that creative leaps arise from some form of intelligent thinking process. For the reasons just cited, however, such a process cannot be characterized solely in terms of linear, simple-to-complex inferential operations. Kuhn's theory of paradigm change remains controversial. But it has two factors in its favor.

First, no credible account of paradigm-type framing has yet been given in strictly analytical terms. By extension, no account of how breakthroughs can be explained in inferential terms looks at all convincing. If smart inferences plus an adequate stock of empirical data were all it takes, Pauling should have gotten his second Nobel Prize for working out the structure of DNA. Second, Kuhn's concept of scientific revolutions as arising within community-based paradigms aligns with my claim that creative leaps have their origin in the analogical transfer of embedded intelligence from one idea-space to another.

Suppose genius (or whatever term we want to use for the mental capacities underlying creative leaps) turned out to be *a very high level of navigational skill in surfing the networked idea-spaces of the extended mind and locating powerful forms of embedded intelligence.* Such an idea would square with the notion, inherent in Kuhn and Clark, that the mind needs additional support beyond its own internal resources to act intelligently at all, let alone make bold creative leaps. This looks promising, since as we've seen, the concept of the extended mind is a compelling explanation even for everyday cognition. But we're still left frustratingly short of a theory of creative breakthroughs. How is the trick turned—whether by geniuses or mere mortals? If the intelligence embedded in the idea-spaces of the extended mind is deployed in some way in breakthrough thinking, how is it accessed and "downloaded"? Furthermore, we want to know where analytical reasoning—old-fashioned linear inferential rationality—fits into the picture. Surely it can't simply be dispensed with.

We seem to have a puzzle for which none of the pieces quite fit together. The problem is, of course, that there's a piece missing, a whole faculty of mind that's been left out. What we need is an account of the faculty that lies at the very heart of all creative endeavor: *the human imagination*.

THE FOUR I'S: IMAGINATION, INTUITION, INSIGHT, AND INTELLIGENCE

When Kenneth Grahame, a clerk at the Bank of England and writer of children's stories, first approached publishers with his latest manuscript, he was repeatedly rejected. The book was about a group of talking animals, something that was regarded as just too fantastic. Victorian educators believed in discouraging children from pretending and daydreaming, and a lot of fairy tale nonsense about a friendship between a rat and a mole could only be detrimental to a child's mental and social development. Grahame's book was finally saved by the intervention of Teddy Roosevelt, an avid fan of his earlier stories. The book's subsequent success enabled Grahame to retire for the rest of his life.

The Wind in the Willows still sells about eighty thousand copies a year.[44]

The imagination has long had a bad rap. As the psychologist E. L. Murray summarized it, in the history of Western thought, "meaning, respectable meaning, was identified with the logical thinking of humankind, while human imaginative thought was identified with the animistic, the irrational, the illogical, the instinctual, the repressible, and ultimately the dangerous."[45]

Freud, true Victorian that he was, distinguished between what he termed primary and secondary process thinking; the first was associated with impulses and fantasies arising from the unconscious, the second with planning and rational control. Taking their cue from this, psychologists distinguish between so-called *autistic* and *realistic* thinking, with the former characterized by when a person, relatively free of external constraints, "imagines, fantasizes, dreams, hallucinates, or has delusions," as opposed to "judging, conceptualizing, and problem solving."[46] We're back with the *Midsummer Night's Dream* version of imagination.

In both the hard sciences and the social sciences, the term *imaginative* is hardly a valued quality, the preferred epithets for research being rational, objective, predictive, explanatory, and the like. Management theory had a brief infatuation in the 1990s with the visionary leader, but it quickly faded with the dot-com crash, and was anyway largely interpreted as a savvy ability to catch onto emerging trends ahead of the competition. Realism and rationality rule.

And yet: Einstein asserted that in examining his methods of thought, "the gift of imagination has meant more to me than my talent for absorbing absolute knowledge."[47] Crick believed that part of what held Rosalind

Franklin back was that while she was an adequate theoretician, "she wasn't what I would call very imaginative."[48] For Crick, "The most important requirements in theoretical work are a combination of accurate thinking and imaginative ideas."[49] John Dewey was of the opinion that "every great advance in science has issued from a new audacity of imagination."[50] Breakthroughs ranging from Einstein's famous thought experiments to the invention of the personal computer to creating the Barbie doll were all vivid exercises of the imagination. Correspondingly, commerce is littered with missed opportunities that can be traced directly to imaginative blindness, an inability to think creatively about how the future might unfold. A.B. Dick's rejection of Carlson's copying machine, Bill Gates's tardiness in recognizing the significance of the Internet, and the failure of the media industry to anticipate the inevitable arrival of file-sharing technologies such as Napster and Grokster are merely the more notorious cases among a long list.

Imagination is the creative faculty par excellence. For both late Enlightenment thinkers and the Romantics, it was the most valuable part of mind, far more powerful than reasoning.[51] The problem lies not in doubting imagination's power, but rather in taking its measure and in figuring out how to adapt it to one's more rational purposes. Perhaps this is the main reason why philosophers, psychologists, and cognitive scientists have been so wary of the imagination: it's as incorrigibly mysterious as the creative process itself.

The Intelligent Imagination

As we've seen, psychologists have tended in the past to worry about the imagination's role in creating fantasies, delusions, and dreams. Perhaps in reaction to this, other researchers narrow imagination to the capacity for visualization.[52] Images are an important component of imagination, but studying imaging doesn't explain how the faculty of imagination empowers intelligent thinking. We're more interested here in what might be termed the *intelligent* imagination: in other words, the imagination that enables us to make sense of our experience, and to solve problems creatively and effectively, presenting us with a way of seeing the world that offers a better fit with our goals, needs, and hopes for the future.

The most fundamental characteristic of the imagination is its ability to let us *free ourselves from the grip of present reality*. This is most obvious when we bring to mind something not in our visual field, as when I imagine my late Aunt Edith, or the Statue of Liberty. More important, however, this characteristic enables us to construct and play with alternative ways of seeing, understanding, and acting in the world that allow something new, interesting, and useful to emerge.

In their groundbreaking book, *The Way We Think*, Fauconnier and Turner give the imagination a fundamental role in basic cognition, characterizing it as "the central engine of meaning behind the most ordinary mental events."[53] Since meaning and sense making lie at the very heart of intelligent behavior—looking like we know what we're doing—their concern is clearly with the intelligent imagination. To see why they make this assertion, essentially allowing imagination to partly usurp reason's traditional role in mental life, let's briefly look at some of the examples they adduce as evidence. Human language is central to thinking, constituting the consciously expressed basis of conceptual meaning as well as communication. In a sentence such as "The cow is brown," we tend to think of the adjective as assigning the fixed property *brown* to *cow*. The example is misleadingly simple, however. Consider, for instance, *safe*, as in "The child is safe," "The beach is safe," "The shovel is safe." As Fauconnier and Turner note, "'Safe' does not assign a property but, rather, prompts us to evoke scenarios of danger appropriate for the noun and the context . . . Technically, the word 'safe' evokes an abstract frame of *danger* with roles like victim, location, and instrument."[54]

In the scenario of a child at play in the sand, in the first case the child is a (potential) victim, and in the second and third the beach and shovel the (potential) instruments of harm. If the context changes, however, so does the meaning. In an ecological context, the beach assumes the role of potential victim of harm from an unspecified instrument such as wave erosion. If the shovel were a valuable antique locked in a museum case to protect it from theft, then it is neither potential instrument nor victim, but a possession, with the potential victim the museum itself. In each case, the meaning implied by "safe" *must be constructed from a network*, consisting of concepts connected by various roles (e.g., instrument, victim) that are combined to match either a hypothetical or a real situation. Thus meaning is dynamically created, with irrelevant combinations being tried and discarded in a (largely unconscious) imaginative process (e.g., as in the case of the shovel hurting the museum or the case it's in). Since the imagination is a space where the brain can run such simulations even in the absence of an external stimulus, it's logical to view it as the primary locus and faculty of meaning creation.[55]

In many cases, the relevant meaning-building structures are already embedded in the culture itself.[56] Consider, for example, the phrase "dolphin-safe tuna." Here, making full sense of the phrase involves invoking a world in which fishermen use methods that prevent harm coming to dolphins (contrast "shark-safe beach"). This in turn invokes worlds in which on the one hand consumers have concerns about the safety of dolphins, are aware of different types of fishing methods, and wish to be responsible in their eating habits, and on the other, marketing departments of food producers seek to induce shoppers to purchase their brand. The full meaning emerges from a mental process in which the imagination dynamically integrates these net-worked idea-spaces with the networked elements of the conceptual frame for "safe."

What these examples demonstrate is how the creative powers of the imagination are involved even in the most basic of cognitive processes. We stressed earlier the role of analogical reasoning in creative thinking, ranging from metaphor to the very highest level of scientific breakthrough (e.g., electricity is a fluid).[57] Here too, analogy can be treated in terms of networked frames processed in the imagination. The expression "to dig one's own grave," for example, vividly renders meaningful any situation in which someone is unwittingly causing significant harm to themselves through their own actions. The meaning depends on integrating the salient elements of the concrete situation (e.g., an employee risks being fired for spreading malicious gossip about her boss) with the networked cultural idea-space of death, grave digging, corpses, and burial, and the social idea-space of failure based on mistakes arising from voluntary action. Making sense of the expression as applied to a given situation crucially involves recognizing differences between these networks and appropriately integrating them. Thus digging a grave is normally the consequence of death, not the cause of it.[58]

Fauconnier and Turner clearly demonstrate several points: that the imagination, not reason, is the primary site of meaning construction and sense making; that even the most basic meaningful concepts emerge from a dynamic creative process of conceptual network integration, or what they call *blending*; that analogical reasoning, in which significant structure is mapped from one domain or world to another for the sake of creating better understanding in the less well-defined sphere, can be modeled in network terms; and that the mental operations involved in creative meaning building and sense making move seamlessly back and forth between structures inside the mind and the idea-spaces of the extended mind. The intelligent imagination invokes the smart world we live in at least as much as the mind inside the head.

Fauconnier and Turner claim that "we are now entering an age in which the key intellectual goal is not to celebrate the imagination but *to make a science of it*. Imagination is at work, sometimes invisibly, in even the most mundane construction of meaning, and its fundamental cognitive operations are the same across radically different phenomena, from the apparently most creative to the most commonplace."[59] The foundation they have laid, which includes principles of analogical reasoning, opens the way for a rigorous approach to the kinds of imaginative leaps of human intelligence that underlie scientific, artistic, technological, business, and other creative breakthroughs of the highest order.[60]

Imagination is not the poor cousin of reason, trafficking in desire-driven fantasy, dreaming, and delusion, but rather, as Fauconnier and Turner show, the very basis on which intelligent, sense-making thought builds. Independently, the philosopher Colin McGinn has reached a similar conclusion in his recent book *Mindsight*, arguing that without the faculty of imagination, there could be no thought, rational or otherwise.[61] To think intelligently is to create webs of meaning about how the world might be, and this is the work of imagination. Reason follows, creating the rational links and chains of inference that validate and extend our knowledge of reality. Fundamentally we are, as McGinn asserts, *Homo imaginans*.[62]

Intuition and Insight

As the history of breakthrough creativity shows, and as the examples in succeeding chapters will confirm, the intelligent, creative imagination is closely allied with two no less mysterious-seeming human capacities: intuition and insight. Psychologists have recently returned to studying these topics, which were often neglected on the grounds that they were too enigmatic for academic research.[63]

Intuition is often taken, correctly, as the unconscious pattern perception.[64] And therein lies the problem. How can we analyze what isn't present to the conscious mind? Clearly, intuition guides the imagination, pointing out some new place to look or an as yet unarticulated set of elements that somehow link together in a novel and interesting pattern. Intuition is our navigation system for exploring novel idea-spaces. It's what gives scientists hunches and leads businesspeople to trust their gut. Without it, the imagination would find itself searching blindly.

Working together, intuition and imagination give rise to insight, the quintessential phenomenon of breakthrough creativity, the eureka moment, the sudden flash that brings new light to what previously lay in darkness. Archimedes went to the baths for a soak, and suddenly saw how to figure out whether or not the king's crown was solid gold. Richard James, a naval engineer, watched a tension spring fall to the ground and keep bouncing, and the idea for the Slinky toy was born. The list goes on and on.[65] But how such insight happens continues to mystify us. One leading group of psychological researchers investigating creative cognition complains that "if creative insights occur in sudden, unpredictable ways and if [as Arthur Koestler claimed] conscious thought might inhibit insights, how could they ever be studied under controlled laboratory conditions?" Their conclusion is that insightful leaps are among "the most mysterious-seeming of creativity topics."[66]

The imagination, aided by intuition, gives rise to those sudden flashes of insight that underlie many instances of breakthrough creativity. Putting aside for a moment its seemingly enigmatic character, let's add this new piece to our jigsaw of the mind, and try to put the pieces of the puzzle back together in a way that makes sense. Suppose creative thinking works something like this. To act intelligently and look like we know what we're doing, we constantly offload our hard-won intelligence into the world. The resulting idea-spaces form themselves into vast, highly dynamic webs, giving intelligible structure and meaning to the smart world we have created for ourselves. Our inference-driven faculty of analytical reasoning, forced to move step-by-step, is far too slow and limited to be able to exploit the power of this embedded intelligence for creative purposes. Worse still, these webs aren't even connected by strictly logical links.

Instead the imagination, guided by the pattern-recognizing powers of intuition, boldly jumps across intervening space to connect to whole new networks of meaning. Bringing entire groups of elements into contact with one another for the first time, it sets up the space in which insight, the mind's capacity to form new coherent patterns or gestalts, can operate. And so, suddenly the breakthrough occurs. A new space is born, a new framework within which the puzzle-solving powers of analytical reasoning can go to work. Eureka!

But does this really help? Or are we just exchanging one set of mysteries for another? Of course the imagination leaps, intuition looks for emerging patterns, and insight happens in a flash. Who has ever doubted it? But are we really any closer to understanding the central enigma, the process of creativity?

THE SCIENCE OF IDEAS

Both Fauconnier and Turner and Colin McGinn insist that all acts of meaning creation and sense making, whether in everyday communication or genuine creative leaps, are at bottom acts of the imagination. Without imagination we could not think, or mean, at all. This view is beautifully summed up by scientific philosopher Michael Polanyi's well-known saying: "We must imagine and believe before we can know." The imagination frees us from the mesmerizing grip of reality, allowing us to invent, play with, and even try out alternative worlds. Only when such an imagined world has come into being can reason go about its work of organizing, structuring, validating, and extending. Knowledge (i.e., justified true belief), the very thing we seem to build our sense of reality on, comes late in the game. But how are we going to gain any genuinely new understanding of this *intelligent* imagination? As McGinn himself asks in regard to the imagination, "Where is the science?"[67]

Part of the answer has already been given. The currency of intelligent thinking is meaning—what else could it be?—and meaning, as Fauconnier and Turner have shown, arises from the dynamic integration of networks of concepts. The mistake is to think these networks are necessarily organized in the familiar hierarchies of linear, analytical reasoning.

The individual mind, operating analogically, continually makes use of non-linear networks of intelligible ideas, often by surfing the dynamic networks of intelligence embedded in the idea-spaces of the extended mind. So to understand creative leaps, we sorely need a delineation of the law-governed dynamics of such networked spaces, particularly in regard to their capacity for self-organization, and the discontinuities this gives rise to. And that is just what this book provides. In the chapters ahead, I will describe in detail nine laws that provide real insight into how imagination, intuition, and insight work, and how they drive the intelligent thinking that underlies creative break-throughs. These laws, which are grounded in universal principles drawn from the emerging science of networks, give us a means to describe the familiar but seemingly inscrutable processes that underlie creative thought: the leaps of the imagination, linking previously unconnected idea-spaces; the way contexts are created out of arrays of related elements; the pattern-recognition characteristic of intuition; and the sudden transitions from complex to simple that are typical of insight. For the first time, we will have the possibility of a real *science of ideas*.

Chapter Four

THE FOOLS ON THE HILL

Tipping Points and
the Microcomputer Revolution

*How do you convey the magic of a new dawn? It was a time when
cranks and dreamers saw the power they dreamed of drop into their
hands and used it to change the world. It was a turning point when
multinational corporations lost their way and kitchen-table entrepreneurs seized the banner and pioneered the future for everyone . . . It
was a bona fide revolution.*

—Paul Freiberger and Michael Swaine, *Fire in the Valley*[1]

On the evening of April 16, 1975, an assorted group of over a hundred professional engineers and computer hobbyists began assembling in a second-
floor classroom of the Peninsula School, located in a wooded area of Menlo
Park, California. They were joined by a number of somewhat less neatly
attired counterculture devotees whose mantra was *Computer power to the people!*[2] The group had come from all over Silicon Valley, some from as far away
as Berkeley, and their rather nondescript appearance couldn't dampen the
sense of expectation and energy that crackled in the room that night. They
were there to attend the fourth meeting of the Bay Area Amateur Computer
Users Group, better known as the Homebrew Computer Club.[3]

In one corner of the room, a slender young man with hair down to the
middle of his back began setting up an Altair 8800 computer, at the time one
of the very few in private hands. Manufactured by a small company called

MITS based in Phoenix, the Altair had debuted three months earlier when the cover of the January *Popular Electronics* had announced its existence. Running on an Intel 8080 chip originally developed for calculators, it consisted of a tiny 256-kilobyte memory, a primitive bus, and a series of switches and eight flashing lights located on the front panel of its metal case.

To program the Altair, the operator had to flip each of the switches in a precise order, entering one binary digit of machine language at a time. Assuming the operator made no mistakes inputting the instructions, the machine would eventually compute a simple math problem such as, How much is 6 + 3? Impressively, the answer, indicated by the winking lights, would soon come back: 1001. If you were sharp enough, you could quickly translate the binary code back into normal English: 9! That night, however, Steve Dompier, who had flown to Albuquerque to pick up his Altair personally, was planning to demonstrate something a little more impressive. He hadn't made a round trip of over four thousand miles just to prove that a metal box with a rat's nest of wires inside could do first-grade arithmetic.

Bent over his machine, and fending off all inquiries about what he was up to, Dompier laboriously flicked switches for seven or eight minutes. Just when he was almost done programming, a couple of kids tripped over the long extension cord stretched to the only working electrical outlet down on the first floor, instantly wiping out the Altair's memory. Undaunted, Dompier began entering the program all over again. Finally he quietly said that he was ready.

The chattering gradually subsided and a hush fell over the room. Out of the small radio wired to the Altair came a scratchy but distinct rendering of the Beatles' hit, "Fool on the Hill." As it ended, Dompier shouted, "Wait, there's more," and the astonished crowd began to make out a second tune. This time it was "Daisy, Daisy (A Bicycle Built for Two)," the first song ever sung by a computer—a major feat achieved by Bell Labs in 1957. Now a kid with a crude tin box, a tiny microprocessor, and a thimbleful of memory had just recreated that moment. History was being made that night, and everyone knew it. As the song ended, the room exploded, giving Steve Dompier a standing ovation.

As Paul Freiberger and Michael Swaine have noted in their engrossing history of the rise of the personal computer, *Fire in the Valley*, "the Homebrewers understood the revolutionary implications of Dompier's act . . . by claiming this machine for such a trivial, thoroughly unprofessional use, he was planting a flag on newly conquered ground. This thing belongs to *us*, he was saying, and it was this act of rebellion against the spirit of the computer priesthood, more than his technical prowess, that the Homebrewers applauded that night."[4]

Less than a mile away from the Peninsula School, in a building shaped like an Aztec temple complex, another small computer was also under development. Like the Altair, it too had been designed and built well away from the mainstream. In 1970 the Xerox Corporation, not wanting to be left out of the growing computer business, had set up a research facility in Palo Alto, far from the company's headquarters in Connecticut. Given a free rein, little pressure to produce a commercially viable product, and plenty of corporate funding, the Xerox PARC team had not wasted their time. The product they had come up with, the Xerox Alto, began as the brainchild of Douglas Engelbart, a legendary computer pioneer who had led a development team at the Stanford Research Institute. That team, minus Engelbart, had eventually migrated to Xerox PARC, and what they had produced was a wonder to behold: a computer the size of a briefcase with a video monitor; a bit-mapped graphical user interface that included windows, scrolling, files, and pull-down menus; an advanced programming language called Smalltalk; a mouse; and Ethernet communication capabilities. It even boasted a word-processing program, and an official promotional slogan: "Office of the future."

Had a venture capitalist (a rare breed in those days) happened to see a demo of the Xerox Alto and then dropped by the Homebrew meeting that night, there can be little doubt where he would have put his money. In comparison with the Alto's impressive hardware and software capabilities, the Altair was a joke, a toy for kids like Dompier to amuse themselves with on weekends.

The venture capitalist would, of course, have been wildly wrong. . . .

Over the next four or five years, the Homebrew Computer Club, using the Altair as its jumping-off point, would be the principal source of practically every major development that led to the birth of the personal computer industry. Within three years of the Altair's debut, some thirty or so computer-related companies sprang up, the majority located in the Bay Area and with close links to the Homebrew Club. In time these would in turn seed literally hundreds of other companies manufacturing computers and peripherals and designing software for the new breed of machine. Among Homebrew's regular attendees were such future luminaries as Bill Gates, Paul Allen, Steve Wozniak, and Steve Jobs.

Within two years of its debut, the Altair was doing $13 million a year in sales. Its successor as market leader, the Apple II, would go on to become the best-selling personal computer model ever, making Apple Computer the fastest-growing company in Wall Street history. Meanwhile, the ill-fated Alto was destined to become one of the most famous and expensive flops in the history of computing. As its parent company vacillated, "fumbling the future,"[5] the increasingly frustrated core members of the PARC team would progressively migrate to Apple, where under Jef Raskin's leadership they would in time produce the Mac. The Alto eventually made its commercial debut in 1977, three years after it had been developed. Priced like a minicomputer, however, it completely missed the exploding personal computer market, and sold only 2,000 units.[6]

How do you see the future before it arrives? The personal computer was the original Next Big Thing in high tech. Veteran venture capitalist L. John Doerr famously declared it the "single largest legal accumulation of wealth in the century."[7] Why, then, did every one of the major corporate players in the computer industry, including IBM, HP, Control Data, DEC, and in a sense even Xerox, *fail to see the PC revolution coming*? Even more important, how do you go about inventing the future when no one has the foggiest idea what it looks like? The span of time from the Altair's crude beginnings to the Apple II's triumph was a scant four and a half years. By any measure, the sheer amount of invention and group learning needed to pull this off was breathtaking.

As we will see, idea-spaces played a central role, both negatively and positively. The failure of the mainstream computer industry to anticipate the arrival of the personal computer—an enormous failure of insight and imagination—exemplifies once again the fact that being in thrall to the wrong idea-space can blind you to what seems obvious to others. Correspondingly, the achievements of extraordinarily gifted individuals like Steve Jobs, Steve Wozniak, and other microcomputer pioneers make sense only when seen in the context of their deep engagement with a network of idea-spaces whose dynamic interactions largely drove the trajectory the industry would follow.

In exploring the emergence of the home computer, we will find ourselves confronting a fundamental question that underlies the mystery of all truly creative leaps: *How does order emerge out of disorder?* How does something that is organized precisely and powerfully enough to make a big impact come out of what looks like confusion and disarray? When Crick and Watson solved the structure of DNA, the idea of a genetic code embodied in a reversed double helix conjoined by complementary bases wasn't even on anyone else's radar. The rise of the microcomputer was characterized by disorder that at times verged on chaos.

At the outset, there was little more than a ragged band of hobbyists, engineers, hippies, garage entrepreneurs, journalists, and small-time retailers united by their passionate desire for change, but possessing little concrete idea of what they wanted, let alone of how things would turn out. Then there was the clashing encounter of three communities: the hobbyist electronics groups, the Bay Area counterculture, and the (mostly East Coast) mainstream computer industry. Out of this mishmash there gradually emerged an industry, complete with competing brands and models, component suppliers, hardware and software developers, retail chains, conferences, marketing campaigns, user clubs, and magazines.

Naturally, we want to understand the role the mind's imaginative faculties played in the emergence of this powerful new order of things, the birth of a wholly new idea-space in the high-tech world. How did the early microcomputer pioneers imaginatively and insightfully engage with the new space that was emerging? Were they the prime movers, or did their genius lie more in skillfully exploiting a series of dynamics that were already under way in the networked idea-spaces of the extended mind? The answers to all these questions lead to a single law of networks whose fundamental property is to effect the shift from disorder to order, or in other words, from complexity to simplicity.

THE LAW OF TIPPING POINTS

In his best-selling book *The Tipping Point,* Malcolm Gladwell popularized the idea that small things can have great effects.[8] However, he did not invent the concept. Physicists had long theorized about so-called *phase transitions*, the critical point at which water turns to ice or metal becomes magnetized.[9] In a metal such as iron or nickel, for example, each atom has a specific magnetic spin. At high temperatures, such as in molten lava, these spins randomly point in all directions. As the temperature of the metal cools, clusters of atoms with spins pointing in the same direction begin to form, getting larger and larger. Suddenly a single large cluster with all spins aligned emerges, at which point a magnet is created. Informally we can refer to this phase transition, in which the structure of the metal shifts from random to coherent, as the tipping point of the metal. Scientists have discovered similar processes underlying such sudden transformations in many other areas, including the way lead becomes a superconductor, sand piles collapse, and slime mold suddenly coalesces into a single organism.

Tipping points violate what scientists used to think of as a fundamental principle of physical systems: that there is a direct, quantifiable relationship between cause and effect. Suppose you are using a crowbar to pry a rock loose in your garden, and the rock isn't budging. Probably, you'll either push down harder or get a longer lever. Either way, the effect (moving the rock) is caused by the precise amount of force used. It's just this familiar relationship of quantifiable causality that is missing when a system is said to tip.

If you've ever been in a traffic jam, you may well have experienced the phenomenon firsthand. Let's imagine you're driving at sixty miles per hour on a large freeway system. Traffic starts to slow down, and you find yourself doing thirty, then fifteen, although there isn't an accident or some other cause for the slowdown in sight. Before you know it, you've come to a complete stop. The system has tipped into a new state. What caused the jam? Certainly not you; not one of the cars ahead of you, nor one of those trying to enter the freeway from the various on-ramps. The truth is, no one element causes a tipping point to happen. Rather, the system as a whole undergoes a sudden, qualitative change: the traffic stops.

The fact of tipping points presents us with two puzzles: How does progressive *quantitative* change suddenly produce a *qualitative* shift? And why is our normal concept of linear causality violated? These puzzles turn out to be closely related.

Unlike physical change caused by an agent of some kind, the dynamic process underlying a tipping point is typically *emergent*: in other words, a higher-level of structure emerges as the result of the *self-organizing interaction* of otherwise uncoordinated lower-level elements. No fundamental factor directs the activity.[10] To put it more simply, stuff just happens: more cars drive onto the freeway. But in the process, a higher-level pattern gradually builds that is more than the sum of its parts. This pattern directs a major change in the system as a whole. Disorder becomes order: a new idea-space emerges seemingly from chaos.

An emergent system violates the normal relationship of cause and effect because it is *indirect*. It's the emergent higher-level pattern, not the lower-level elements, that causes the system to tip and from then on governs the activity of the system. The jam directs traffic flow, not the other way round. A purely quantitative process morphs into a qualitative shift.[11]

There is a huge technical literature on phase transitions, especially in physics and sociology, much of it dealing with rather arcane technical matters such as power laws, exponents, and renormalization. For present purposes, however, we can settle for the following rather simple statement of the law of tipping points, formulated (for reasons that will shortly become apparent) in network terms:

THE LAW OF TIPPING POINTS

In an open, dynamic network, under certain critical conditions, *more becomes different*. More change in lower-level elements prompts a self-organizing process that gives rise to a new, qualitatively different pattern.[12]

The "more" here can range from an ongoing process of like changes (as in the cooling of certain metals) to chance events and interactions (Picasso's visit to the Trocadéro). Unlike in the case of prying a rock loose, there's no direct connection between more (i.e., greater force) and the outcome. Rather, what matters in tipping points is the relationship between more and the *context* in which it occurs. As we'll see, this is exactly where idea-spaces and the dynamically linked networks they form play a key role in triggering tipping points.

A creative breakthrough by definition represents a sharp break with the past, typified by the emergence and rapid growth of something qualitatively new and different. In this sense, inventions, discoveries, and radical innovations are all paradigmatic outcomes of tipping points. The development of the personal computer resulted from no fewer than *three* of them.

Since context does most of the "heavy lifting," the individual's creative effort (i.e., force) need not be commensurate with the change that is created. The missing causal energy is provided by the system itself—the network of idea-spaces with which individuals engage. *Les Demoiselles d'Avignon* didn't leap fully formed from Picasso's head, but emerged from the deep immersion of his imagination in the idea-space of African art. Similarly, the idea-space of the personal computer, as artifact, industry, and idea, can't be traced directly to the brain waves of a few gifted individuals, but rather arose as a result of their imaginative engagement with powerful existing idea-spaces. What were those idea-spaces, and how did the pioneers of the microcomputer revolution draw creative energy from them? Let's go back to the beginning of the story.

OUT OF THIN AIR?

By the early 1970s computing was big business, with companies like IBM, Honeywell, and Control Data Corporation all making mainframes, while DEC, Wang, Data General, and HP were pioneering the hugely profitable minicomputer market. Two things characterized the industry during this period. First, the available computers were so expensive that only businesses and government or academic institutions could afford them. Second, access to the machines themselves was controlled by a computer "priesthood" that not only strictly determined time-sharing schedules, but also ensured programming was sufficiently opaque to force most users to rely on a small coterie of highly specialized software engineers to develop usable programs. The net result was that owning a computer to which they had exclusive access and for which they could develop usable programs was a nearly impossible dream for most people.[13]

But dream they did. Engineers who had spent the day designing chips or programming big iron for the defense industry at Lockheed Missiles and Space Corp. in Sunnyvale, students with access to mini- or mainframe computers at Stanford and other college campuses, teenagers and their dads with an aptitude for electronics, all came home at night and started fiddling around in their bedrooms, garages, and workshops. Out would come the soldering irons, the reams of wire, and the surplus electronics parts by the dozen. The hobbyist electronics market, spurred by magazines like *Popular Electronics* and *Radio Electronics*, caused the burning of a lot of midnight oil, especially in Silicon Valley. The overall spirit was both anarchic and enterprising. One energetic thirteen-year-old, needing some additional parts for the electrical circuit frequency counter he was building, found Bill Hewlett's name in the phone book and called him up to request that he arrange to send him what he needed. Perhaps the founder of HP was persuaded by his youthful enthusiasm, or maybe he sensed the kid had a future. Either way, Steve Jobs got the parts, and was on his way.

At the time, most hobbyist activity was focused on building minor electronic gadgets such as radios, oscillators, and primitive calculators. But what everyone dreamed of building was a machine, no matter how crude, they could play around with at night and that would begin to mimic the computers they worked on by day:

> What these enthusiasts wanted most often was more control over the machines they used. They resented having to wait in line to use the very tool of their trade or to engage in their favorite hobby. They wanted immediate access to the files they created on a computer, even if they were off somewhere on a business trip. They wanted to play computer games at their leisure without someone telling them to get back to work. In short, what these enthusiasts wanted was a personal computer. [14]

The Altair was the brainchild of Ed Roberts, a physically imposing engineer, entrepreneur, and chronic tinkerer who had learned about electronics in the air force. Roberts's company, MITS, had nearly gone bankrupt trying to compete with Texas Instruments by selling kits for programmable calculators. But when Intel launched the 8080 microprocessor in April 1974, Roberts saw his chance. Finally, here was a chip that could serve as the brain for a small computer.

Roberts wasn't the first to market with a home computer kit. In July 1974, *Popular Radio* had announced the Mark-8, a kit computer designed by Jonathan Titus based on an earlier chip and selling for around $1,000. And there were others. The Mark-8 generated few orders, but galvanized Roberts, with the encouragement of Les Solomon, the technical editor of *Popular Electronics*, to come up with a better computer at a significantly lower price.

More is different. The Altair wasn't first on the block, but its arrival led the embryonic microcomputer industry to tip, creating overnight the market for a buildable hobbyist computer. Engineers young and old, amateur and professional (you didn't need an advanced degree, but soldering the kit together and debugging it were not for the technically challenged), went hog wild over the Altair.

Hobbyists rushed to mail in their checks for $397. Since the combined MITS headquarters, assembly plant, and salesroom were all jammed together in a storefront squeezed between a laundry and a bowling alley in Phoenix, a long waiting list immediately developed. Within weeks a back order for over four thousand built up. As a result, MITS was able to turn itself virtually overnight from a failing calculator-kit firm with debts totaling $400,000 to a company with a massive and enthusiastic customer base, a $250,000 bank balance, and a huge order book.

Crossing Harvard Square in mid-January, 1975, Paul Allen caught sight of the Altair boldly displayed on the cover of *Popular Electronics*. With considerable prescience, he recognized that this presaged a huge new opportunity. Allen promptly raced off to tell his friend Bill Gates he'd better forget his freshman studies at Harvard right now and focus on writing some software for the new machine or they'd miss out on the revolution. Six weeks later, they had completed a demo of BASIC (a simple programming language) for the machine.

Not surprisingly, the Altair rapidly spawned a host of competitors. By the end of 1975, other hobbyist kits developed by start-ups with such fanciful names as Kentucky Fried Computers, Golemics, Inc., Itty Bitty Machine Company, and Sphere had sprung up. More serious competition came in the form of Processor Technology's Sol and the IMSAI 8080. Additionally, numerous start-ups quickly formed themselves into profitable businesses supplying peripherals, add-ons, and circuit boards that provided enhanced and/or more reliable performance in place of the Altair's notoriously buggy hardware. Whether it was competing or collaborating, however, the Altair was the catalyst for and de facto leader of an exploding industry no one pretended to understand. By August 1977, three months after MITS was acquired by Pertec for $6 million, and a mere two and a half years since the Altair had debuted, it was estimated that over fifty thousand privately owned microcomputers were in use.

In other words, the microcomputer world had tipped. But how? The predictable answer—that individual genius overturned conventional business models and economic laws—takes us only so far. What it fails to take into account is the organizing energy supplied by an underlying network of idea-spaces. Over time, the dynamic patterns they formed drove the emergent microcomputer industry through a series of qualitative transformations. Since the microcomputer revolution was as much social as technological in nature, a good place to start in analyzing this transformative role of idea-spaces is with some interesting characteristics of social networks.[15]

COMMUNITIES OF PRACTICE, STRONG VERSUS WEAK TIES, AND HUBS

In their groundbreaking book *The Social Life of Information*, John Seely Brown (former head of Xerox PARC) and Paul Duguid resist the temptation to explain invention and innovation solely in terms of technological genius, entrepreneurial drive, and luck. While these elements are invariably present, they rightly emphasize the necessary complementary role played by social and organizational innovation: "The challenge in moving systematically from an initial invention . . . to innovation is the challenge of coordinating diverse, disparate, and often diverging, but ultimately complementary, *communities of practice*."[16] Such communities are made up of a tightly knit group where most people know one another, often through face-to-face contact, and share similar professional backgrounds, ideas, values, and goals. In other words, they are idea-spaces rich in shared embedded intelligence. The great strength of such communities lies in their members' capacity to mutually influence and learn from one another, allowing ideas and changes to propagate quickly and easily through the group. As a consequence, communities of practice tend to be especially good at the kind of collaborative, tightly coordinated creativity that often underlies knowledge development and invention. Their corresponding weakness, however, resides in their tendency to become insular, unable to communicate effectively with outside groups. As Brown and Duguid put it, communities of practice tend to have high *reciprocity* but low *reach*.[17] Successful innovation typically requires both.

In the early 1970s, Mark Granovetter, a UC–Berkeley sociologist, developed an important distinction between *strong* and *weak ties* in social groups that makes it possible to distinguish reciprocity and reach in network terms.[18] Strong ties represent the bonds of mutual acquaintance, shared values, and collaborative activities that bind together families, close-knit groups of friends, club members, and work groups. Figure 4-1 shows part of a typical "skunk works"—a close-knit, project-oriented community of practice that excels at collaborating and sharing ideas.

FIGURE 4-1

A typical "skunk works" group manifesting strong ties

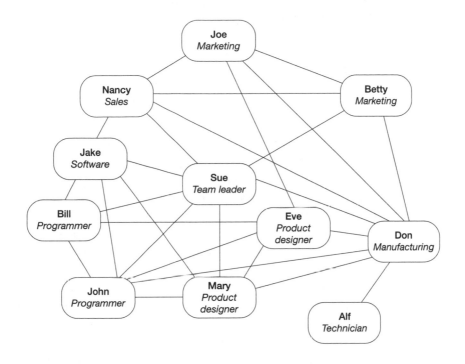

Source: Adapted from *Nexus: Small Worlds and the Groundbreaking Science of Networks* by Mark Buchanan. Copyright © 2002 by Mark Buchanan. Used by permission of W. W. Norton & Company, Inc.

The ties are strong in the sense that many of the various sets of relationships, reflecting informal ties or in some cases membership of cross-functional teams, overlap. Thus Jake, John, and Sue all share ties with one another and with Mary; Don and Betty share ties with Sue, Joe, and Nancy, and so forth. Such overlapping makes the group very close-knit: even someone who doesn't share a direct relationship with another group member can usually reach that person in a single step via a third party. For example, Jake doesn't have a direct link with Eve, but can still reach her through Bill. Only the poorly connected Alf usually needs more than one step to reach most other people. Overlapping relationships also mean that even if one person leaves, the basic structure of group relations and interactions remains intact. Thus if Bill left, Jake could still interact with Eve via John.

Such a network could equally well represent various groups of family relatives or friends, again defining overlapping relationships. When Picasso was in Paris in the early part of the twentieth century, for example, he was part of a loosely knit group of artists and patrons who knew each other with varying degrees of intimacy. Picasso was particularly close friends with Matisse and Gertrude Stein (who also included Matisse in her circle). Matisse was close to Derain and Vlaminck, who met Picasso mostly in the company of the former. Braque mainly related to this group via Picasso. It was Vlaminck who first got interested in African art, but the idea quickly spread through the group, although only Picasso was strongly affected by it.

Strong ties, then, characterize social networks with a high link-to-node (tie-to-member) ratio. Such closely interlinked social clustering is the defining characteristic of communities of practice. This helps to explain why information, values, and new ideas can diffuse so rapidly in the idea-space around a community of practice, and how its members can continue to collaborate flexibly and effectively even if one or more members aren't present. But the very degree of internal cohesion in communities of practice, while invaluable for close cooperation, also makes such groups vulnerable to becoming insular, thereby cutting them off from potential sources of new information and ideas.[19]

Weak ties lack this cohesion and multidimensionality, typically representing connections with acquaintances rather than family, friends, or coworkers. Sometimes, as in the case of the debutante who rushed home from the ball to tell her parents that she danced-with-a-boy-who-danced-with-a-girl-who-danced-with-the-Prince-of-Wales, the connection is quite ephemeral. On the other hand, in effective social networking, weak ties can be usefully exploited—in job hunting for example—to put you in touch with someone you would otherwise never meet. This led Granovetter to speak paradoxically of "the strength of weak ties," which lies in their reach rather than their reciprocity.

Weak ties often act as a bridge between two groups that normally wouldn't have contact with each other (see figure 4-2).

As Gladwell notes, connectors like A and B are "masters of the weak tie." As such, they play a powerful role in promoting diffusion throughout the networks they participate in.[20] This is especially the case when multiple connectors link up, connecting otherwise separate groups or individuals in one huge network (see figure 4-3).

Epidemics—including social fads—spread precisely because well-linked connectors are so effective in spreading the contagion. A single individual from Hong Kong infected with avian flu, for example, can spread the disease from his or her own community to one in New York simply by boarding a plane. One of the infected New Yorkers then travels to Los Angeles, spreading the flu there. In this case, the "connector" is someone who literally links communities via travel. More typically, connectors serve to spread ideas, act-

FIGURE 4-2

Weak ties bridge two groups with strong internal ties

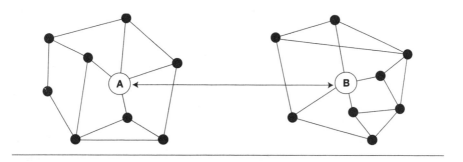

FIGURE 4-3

A network of connectors linked by weak ties

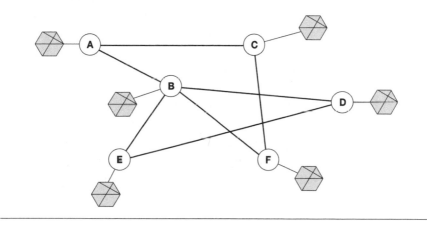

ing as persuasive intermediaries between groups that otherwise have little contact with one another. This is how fads can spread so fast, jumping from one geographic or social group to another. It's also how enthusiasm for a radically innovative product can spread through a company from one department to another. Connectors are often good salespeople, adept at spreading the word.

In part it was the lack of such connectors that doomed the Alto. As a classic skunk works, the developmental team at Xerox PARC was high on reciprocity (collaborating and sharing ideas), but low on reach. It lacked weak ties to the rest of the company—and to the hobbyist community—that could break its insularity. No one proved effective in gaining support for a commercially viable microcomputer from largely uncomprehending senior management strategists or even other engineering departments that would implement production. As a result, the necessary financial and human resources to turn brilliant invention into effective innovation never occurred.

Albert-László Barabási, one of the pioneers of network science, has shown that a network containing a series of connectors linked by weak ties is a type of *small-world network*. In such networks, hubs (highly connected nodes—in roughly the same sense as hubs in an airline network) ensure that any two nodes are separated by only a few steps.[21] A powerful advantage of Barabási's approach is that it is abstract enough to apply to virtually any network of elements—including humans, communities, idea-spaces, products, and so forth. Thus even patterns of electric grid lines turn out to be examples of small-world networks. It is consequently ideal for modeling the dynamics of idea-spaces (which, recall, can themselves represent a broad and quite disparate range of things). Furthermore, using Barabási's research on hubs, two European researchers, Alessandro Vespignani and Romualdo Pastor-Satorras, have conclusively shown that *a dynamic network dominated by one or more hubs will inevitably tip*, thus providing a powerful connection between qualitative transformation and network topography. In other words, linked hubs (essentially abstract connectors) form the crucial context in which even a small input (more is different) will lead to a tipping point.

As we'll see, Barabási's theories about hubs and small-world networks will provide us with a way to model how new ideas, inventions, and practices propagate with powerful transformative effect on the idea-spaces they enter. Specifically, we'll discover how order emerged from disorder in the rise of the microcomputer industry through the network dynamics that give rise to tipping points.

THE DYNAMICS OF DISRUPTIVE INNOVATION

According to Clayton Christensen, decisions concerning whether to invest resources and effort into an emerging technology are typically made on the basis of a *value network*:

> A value network is the context within which a firm establishes a cost structure and operating processes and works with suppliers and channel partners in order to respond profitably to the common needs of a class of customers. Within a value network, each firm's competitive strategy, and particularly its cost structure and its choices of markets and customers to serve, determines its perceptions of the economic value of an innovation.[22]

A value network, then, is a useful tool for understanding how an innovative industry developed out of the strategic and tactical decisions of the competing firms involved. Essentially, it represents the core intelligence embedded in the idea-space of an emerging industry.

The rise of the microcomputer is a classic case of what Christensen terms a *disruptive innovation*, that is, a new type of product whose significance the mainstream industry was largely blind to.[23] So from the standpoint of the central theme of this chapter—how order arises out of disorder—the issue becomes, How did the highly ordered idea-space of the microcomputer's value network evolve seemingly out of nothing? What role did tipping points play, and what were the underlying network dynamics that gave rise to them? The answers yield some surprising insights.

THE FIRST TIPPING POINT

The hobbyist community to which the Altair was marketed with such explosive success had a profoundly antiestablishment streak that set it sharply at odds with the mainstream computer industry. Hackers gloried in causing havoc by breaking into mainframe computers (Bill Gates achieved early notoriety by managing to crash Control Data Corporation's nationwide proprietary Cybernet system). The general attitude of amused contempt, mixed with vague aspirations to some sort of rivalry, is well captured in a sardonic remark by Don Lancaster, an aerospace technician who frequently wrote articles for hobbyist magazines: "I was working on . . . a military project with $1.5 million to build a [terminal] display. It occurred to me maybe I could make a few concessions and do it for $99 instead."[24]

Others seriously protested the refusal of mainframe and minicomputer companies to consider making the vast potential of computers available to ordinary individuals or even schools. Robert Albrecht left Control Data Corporation for this reason, going on to start a nonprofit alternative education organization in Silicon Valley called the Portola Institute, as well as the tabloid newspaper *People's Computer Company*. David Ahl was part of a team at DEC designing a TV-sized computer for school use, only to have the project contemptuously squashed by the company president, Kenneth Olsen. Ahl promptly resigned, and later became editor of *Creative Computing*. Lee Felsenstein, master of ceremonies at the Homebrew Club, left Ampex in 1969 out of general disgust with working for corporate America. Sympathizing deeply with a growing Bay Area movement that wanted to bring computing power to ordinary people, he set to work helping to organize Community Memory, a project to give the public access to local bulletin boards via terminals placed in storefronts and supermarkets.

The Community Memory project symbolized an excruciating paradox faced by those hobbyist pioneers who desperately wanted to make computing more widely accessible. Even as they distanced themselves from the mainstream computer industry, they found themselves forced to rely on it, not just for many of the parts they scrounged, but also for any real computing power: Community Memory's terminals were hooked up to an old Xerox mainframe inherited from SRI in Stanford. The project, which was hopelessly buggy and confused people not used to working with computers, failed.

It was part of Ed Roberts's genius that he found a way to overcome this impasse by reconnecting the hobbyist community to the mainstream industry while appealing directly to its anticorporate ethics. MITS was itself a victim of big business, having almost gone bankrupt when Texas Instruments' aggressive price cutting ruined its kit calculator business. The Altair's design neatly flipped three key elements of the mainstream computer industry so that they fully addressed hobbyist desires for an affordable machine (the Altair's retail price was two hundred times less than the cost of a small minicomputer) in kit form that with some tinkering could still do real computing. The Intel 8080 was the first microprocessor with sufficient power and ease of programming to act as the brain of a microcomputer. And yet the mainstream industry had no use for such chips. Robert Noyce, head of Intel, voiced a widely held view that the future of the microprocessor lay in watches. Other candidates included kitchen blenders, carburetors, and elevators. What the mainstream marginalized, the hobbyists could use.

The Altair's price was also kept low by adopting a characteristic design element of minicomputers: slots for additional boards. These were originally intended to allow minicomputers to be configured to the customer's precise needs. In the Altair, they allowed the initial purchase price to be kept rock bottom by providing absolutely minimal functionality the user could add to later. Moreover, the hobbyists were by the same token given a much bigger sense of ownership of the new type of machine that would be designed and built in a thousand garages. Nor was this new machine just a toy. Equipped with the right add-ons and peripherals plugged into various of its eighteen expansion slots, in combination with the more powerful 8080 chip, the Altair, *Fire in the Valley* notes, "had the potential, at least in miniature, of doing everything a large mainframe computer could do."[25]

Once the Altair had established the link with the mainstream industries, a series of positive feedback loops began to operate. As hobbyists finally got their hands on an affordable machine with no limits in principle to its future development, sales soared, ensuring costs stayed low. By building and configuring the computer themselves, Altair users were able to satisfy their hobbyist instincts while increasingly taking ownership of the very concept of the microcomputer. As the once amorphous hobbyist community increasingly focused its attention on the Altair and the possibilities it seemed to hold out, ties between its members strengthened through user clubs, newsletters, conferences, and bulletin boards cannily organized by MITS. Excitement mounted as news of the latest improvements, new user-inspired designs, and even software circulated. Meanwhile, MITS created a future business supplying add-on components that would further the development of the microcomputer outside of the mainstream industry.

The Altair was more than the latest of a string of machines aimed at jump-starting the microcomputer market. It succeeded in tipping the disordered space of hobbyist dreams into the reality of a usable, openly modifiable design with real computing potential. In network terms, the hobbyist community and the Altair became twin hubs joined by a series of strong feedback loops, a configuration that inevitably provokes a tipping point. The Altair crucially acted as a connector to the mainstream industries (mainframe, minicomputer, and semiconductor). The strength of this weak tie was that it enabled hobbyists to tap into essential technological elements of those industries (processor power, programmability, the ability of Moore's law to continually improve price / performance ratios, modular architecture), without which their dreams didn't have a future.

THE SECOND TIPPING POINT: THE EMERGENCE OF A SOCIAL-INDUSTRIAL COMPLEX

When the Altair arrived in the Bay Area, it came into contact with a mixed group of microcomputer enthusiasts whose skills, values, and ambitions constituted a far richer idea-space than that of the average hobbyist community. Users were typically engineers or hackers with strong hardware and software design skills. Furthermore, in varying degrees they were imbued with two sets of beliefs with deep roots in the region: faith in the Silicon Valley myth of garage-based entrepreneurship and in the goal of starting a revolution that would finally give ordinary people access to computer power, thereby ending for good the mainstream industries' gatekeeper role.

Dompier's demo acted as a perfect catalyst for this volatile mix. Like a magnet aligning iron filings, it served to focus the Bay Area enthusiasts' previously scattered and unorganized ideas and ideals into a coherent vision. Many of the people who came to the first few Homebrew Club meetings not only didn't know one another, they barely knew others of a like mind even existed. Most must have felt a significant sense of isolation, working in large corporate data centers or at major hardware firms where talking openly of a personal computer would have invited disbelief verging on ridicule. What a relief to discover there were others who shared their dreams and who had begun to hold regular meetings. They might still have their heads in the clouds, but they knew what they wanted to do, and they were now well on their way. "The Fool on the Hill" could be the anthem for the entrepreneur in all of us.

But it was "Daisy, Daisy (A Bicycle Built for Two)" that clinched things. The sheer whimsical nature of the song belied its profound symbolic signifi-cance. If Dompier's feat was technologically crude (his program simply manipulated static on the attached radio), it nevertheless proclaimed that Bell Labs had henceforth better look to its laurels. More than that, anyone in the room who had seen Stanley Kubrick's *2001: A Space Odyssey* remembered how the spacecraft's evil, all-powerful supercomputer HAL (widely though erroneously believed to be a sly reference to IBM) had sung the song as the surviving astronaut *disabled* it through removing its memory banks. So too the Altair, named after a distant world in a *Star Trek* episode, might one day strike at the heart of the computer industry's evil empire.

As the crowd rose in unison to cheer the song, a new vision of the future was born. In the next few months, Homebrew attendance rose, quickly top-ping seven hundred, and conversation shifted from technical shop talk to set-ting up new businesses. The Homebrew Club had transformed itself into something new: not just a meeting ground for hobbyist enthusiasts, but the very epicenter of an emerging *social-industrial complex* consisting of dozens of entrepreneurial start-ups offering everything from software to hardware components to brand models of microcomputers, retail chains, user clubs, and so on. The underlying pattern driving development had changed again. Low cost, together with an expandable architecture, combined to create a huge opportunity with low barriers to entry for entrepreneurial firms bent on complementing the Altair's base model or even competing directly with it. Garage-based hobbyists became garage-based entrepreneurs. Inevitably, the sheer availability of talent led to a flood of improvements at every level that MITS simply couldn't match.

As the market grew, accompanied by sharply increased user demands for improved performance and functionality, the motivation to innovate intensi-fied. More firms (by 1976 there were over fifty hardware companies in the microcomputer market) meant more competition, keeping costs low even as performance improved. Moore's law—the claim (first made in 1965 by Intel cofounder Gordon Moore) that the number of transistors per unit cost on an integrated circuit doubled every two years)—had now passed over into the new microcomputer industry. Competitors to Intel's 8080 swiftly appeared, including the Motorola MC6800 processor and the Zilog Z80. The weak tie to the mainstream industries proved useful in other ways too. In the spirit of Don Lancaster, cheap knock-offs or substitutes were designed for such key components as input-output devices, high-level languages, and an operating system. As hard drives became smaller and affordable, this crucial feature of mainframe and minicomputers was adopted too (first by the Northstar).

The emerging social-industrial complex of the microcomputer was self-organizing into a networked idea-space possessing an almost ideal combination of strong and weak ties, reciprocity and reach, collaboration and competition. At its heart, the Homebrew Computer Club became a community of practice whose members knew one another, set up businesses together, and freely shared information. Chains of connectors—both human and institutional—spread from there through the entrepreneurial enclave of Silicon Valley to user clubs, fairs, magazines, newsletters, retail chains, and bulletin boards, as well as to the mainstream industries themselves.

Crucial to the growth of this network was an ethos of cooperation and information sharing that was sharply at odds with conventional business practice among high-technology firms. This was partly inherited from the idealism of the Bay Area counterculture community, whose members often played leadership roles in the Homebrew Computer Club and its entrepreneurial offshoots. But it also had roots in the antiestablishment, revolutionary ethos of the hobbyists themselves. Intensely conscious that they were ushering in a revolution that was social as well as technological, microcomputer enthusiasts and entrepreneurs "were more interested in exploring the potential of the microcomputer than in making a fortune."[26] Openness won out over proprietariness (supported by a minority that included Ed Roberts and Bill Gates), in the belief that it was "more important to create the next invention than to protect the last one."[27]

The clear source of the revolution was *network dynamics*. The emerging networked idea-space of the microcomputer was dominated by a series of major hubs linked by positive feedback loops. These drove the space through two important tipping points, each resulting in the emergence of a qualitatively different, radically higher level of order. The information that traveled along these loops kept individual and group participants—including users, entrepreneurs, designers, hardware manufacturers, magazine editors—in the loop, facilitating rapid enhancement of collective intelligence. Participants in the microcomputer revolution understood the benefit of listening to the network and acting accordingly. When the space of ideas is thinking for you, it's the smart thing to do!

By now it should be obvious why the mainframe and minicomputer manufacturers not only didn't see the microcomputer revolution coming, but continued to ignore it when it arrived. Trapped inside the idea-spaces of their own highly profitable value network, they had nothing pushing them to reach outside. As a result, unlike the semiconductor and hard-drive manufacturers, they failed to develop even a weak tie into the emerging network of the microcomputer, and thus had no means of evaluating what was happening.

What about Xerox? It's bad enough to miss the Next Big Thing, but when you've apparently already developed it, it's distinctly careless not to run with it. Here we come to the nub of the matter: the PARC scientists hadn't, in any meaningful sense of the word, *developed* the personal computer (which the hobbyist microcomputer would shortly become). What they did do was invent some of the personal computer's key technologies that would subsequently be incorporated into the Macintosh and Windows computers.

As noted earlier, part of the PARC team's problem stemmed from its being a fairly insular community of practice lacking weak ties into other corporate departments such as manufacturing and marketing that are essential to launching a successful product. But there's more to it than that. The fact is, developing the microcomputer wasn't just a matter of coming up with a whole array of new technologies, or even of pulling them together in an expensive prototype, however innovative the machine might be. It also entailed developing a supply chain that could provide cheap components and complementary technologies; an initial niche market of highly informed, enthusiastic customers who could both help develop the product and form a base from which to cross the chasm to mainstream users; an information-sharing ethos that drove the pace of innovation while keeping it tightly focused on the market; and software that users understood and wanted. Xerox didn't develop any of these essential elements for inventing the microcomputer, and indeed *could not have done so*. The fact is, these elements all emerged as a direct result of the multiple links between the industrial, social, commercial, and technological hubs and networks of the microcomputer's social-industrial complex. Xerox, isolated as it was, lacked significant links to this complex. It was, quite literally, out of the loop![28]

In focusing on the role of dynamic network topography in shaping the early stages of the microcomputer and its social-industrial complex, we seem to have largely deflated the conventional story of heroic pioneers succeeding through sheer brilliance, drive, and a measure of luck. Surely individual imagination, intuition, and insight played a part in all this?

The question of the role of the mind's imaginative faculties in creativity will be explored in more depth in succeeding chapters. For the moment, let's keep in mind that their dynamics can themselves be thought of in network terms. Take the two most salient cases in this chapter, Ed Roberts and Steve Dompier. As an entrepreneur, Roberts seems to have started out with some intuitive notion of the kind of machine hobbyists wanted. It's unlikely, however, that the Altair's specifications simply leapt fully formed into his head one day. Rather, he must have tried out one combination after another, until gradually a pattern began to emerge. Weak links became strong ones, with a high degree of coherence (i.e., reciprocity): "Stripped down functionality plus modular architecture means ultra-low cost without limiting future development; hobbyists like to tinker, and MITS can make a business out of supplying add-ons . . . Aha!" Dompier must have gone through a similar process in figuring out what kind of demo would have the maximum impact on those attending the Homebrew Club that fateful night. In the eye of the imagination, the dots connect, intuition becomes insight, and something new is born. *The imagination too has its tipping points.*

By the end of 1977, the microcomputer industry was thriving and rapidly expanding. It was now poised to go through its final transition into a mass-market personal computer. The third tipping point was about to happen.

Chapter Five

DARWINIAN NETWORKS, OR WHY THE FIT GET FITTER

You didn't do shit!

—Jerry Wozniak to Steve Jobs, who was
demanding a 50–50 split with his son of
stock in Apple Computer[1]

During the infamous late 1990s dot-com boom, one start-up after another was funded by venture capitalists who had been persuaded that the product or service in question, since it would be first to market, would gain the enormous advantage of being *first mover*. Driven by a kind of pioneer land-grab mentality based on the belief that this assured long-term success and even dominance, start-ups spent millions of dollars in an effort to speed up product and service development and market penetration. Although most of these entrepreneurial ventures eventually failed, the first-mover principle has some basis in fact. Market-dominating companies like Yahoo!, Amazon.com, eBay, and (outside of high tech) Southwest Airlines and FedEx all provide solid evidence for it. Indeed, as a determinant of strategic success, the principle seems quite plausible. Invariably, the first firm in a market establishes a whole array of links with suppliers, distributors, promotional media, and customers. New entrants will naturally try to compete for this network of connections, but as the industry, and pool of customers, grows, the market leader's share of this network of connections—essentially its value network—expands proportionately.

Nevertheless, the principle isn't universally valid. Even before the great high-tech bust of 2000, there were counterexamples that placed limits on its scope. Quicken, for example, was the forty-third personal finance software package to market, yet swiftly rose to a dominant position.[2] Far simpler to use than existing programs (which mimicked complex professional accounting software) and 70 percent cheaper, Quicken not only became the market leader, it expanded the personal finance software market a hundredfold. In fact, Quicken produced a tipping point in the personal finance software industry, completely changing the criteria for what constituted a successful product. So the question is, Why is it that sometimes first movers win, and sometimes they don't?

A good place to look for answers is the next phase in the rise of the personal computer. The Altair's success, right up to the time it was sold, was largely due to its first-mover advantage. Other computers like the Sol and the IMSAI 8080 achieved as good or even better performance, but never caught the Altair in sales. And yet in spite of starting at the back of a highly competitive field, the Apple II, when it debuted, swiftly swept all before it. Few products in history leapt to a position of dominance as fast or as successfully. The story of the Apple II will not only resolve the first-mover issue. It will also show how emergent *fitness* between core elements of the intelligence embedded in key hubs is what creates the higher-level patterns that give rise to tipping points.

THE THIRD TIPPING POINT: THE APPLE II

Like Crick and Watson, the two Steves (as Jobs and Wozniak, the founders of Apple Computer, came to be known) were an odd couple whose very differences somehow produced extraordinary synergies. Woz, the son of a Lockheed engineer, was a full-time employee at HP, an inveterate tinkerer, and a technical wizard, perhaps one of the very best that Silicon Valley ever produced. Almost single-handedly, he was responsible for the brilliantly innovative hardware designs that gave Apple its initial technical edge.

Steve Jobs, whose adoptive father Paul was a crew-cut machinist and auto repo man with a penchant for fixing up old cars, had gone through a tinkering phase too. Unlike Woz, however, he possessed only a superficial knowledge of electronics and quickly grew bored with the technical talk that dominated Homebrew meetings. Although deeply drawn to the austerity and asceticism of Zen Buddhism, he also had a born entrepreneur's passionate desire to make money by creating a highly successful product for a broad market. His avowed aim was to design a product that would "make a dent in the universe."[3] What he shared with Wozniak was a zeal for "doing it right," and for bringing computers to ordinary people.[4] Their collaboration would lead directly to the creation of the Apple II, the best-selling personal computer ever made, and the machine that definitively effected the transformation of the hobbyist microcomputer into the personal computer.

After the Altair debuted, practically everyone at Homebrew started talking about building their own computers, and even about putting kits together themselves. Woz went to work, endlessly designing and improving schematics for motherboards, but it was Jobs who grasped the commercial opportunities.

Apple Computer was founded on April Fool's Day, 1976. The Apple I, sold in kit form like the Altair, was little more than a loaded circuit board based on a new chip from Motorola, 8 kilobytes of memory, plus hookups for power, a keyboard, and a television monitor, all to be supplied by the customer. The initial response to it at the Homebrew Club was tepid, especially since it was incompatible with programs and peripherals designed for the Altair. Technically, in spite of the elegance and simplicity of Woz's design, it really couldn't compete. The Altair, the Sol, and the IMSAI 8080 all offered superior features and easily outsold the Apple I, with the MITS machine leading the pack. In spite of this, largely because of Jobs's persistence in getting a deal to sell the kits through the newly established chain of Byte Shops (and in overcoming Woz's desire to sell it at cost), by the end of 1976 the Apple I had grossed $95,000, half of it profit.

When Jobs and Wozniak went to Atlantic City on Labor Day weekend to attend the Personal Computer Festival, the first industrywide trade show, they took with them the Apple I plus a working mock-up of Woz's new design, the Apple II, housed in a cardboard box. Their booth consisted of a card table framed at the back by yellow curtains and a cardboard sign announcing *Apple Computer.*

The computers being shown were for the most part second-generation designs. The sleek and improved machines on display included the IMSAI 8080, Polymorphic Systems' Poly-88, MOS Technology's KIM-1, Cromemco's Dazzler (which featured color), and of course the latest version of the market leader, the Altair. Perhaps most impressive of all, Processor Technology had a working version of the Sol featuring a stamped metal case, built-in keyboard, and the same chip as the Altair, making it compatible with programs written for the MITS machine. Furthermore, the Sol was fully assembled, ready to plug into a monitor. "By comparison," Jeffrey Young, Jobs's biographer wrote, "the crude mock-up of the Apple II was positively amateurish."

As the microcomputer began to definitively morph into the personal computer, few investors would have bet on Apple to lead the charge. Once again, they would have been completely wrong.

The swift rise of the Apple II to overwhelming industry dominance reveals a deeper phenomenon underlying the mechanisms that produce tipping points: the idea of *fitness.* In a complex, dynamic, highly competitive marketplace, fitness suggests the Darwinian notion of surviving and thriving, to the point of becoming the dominant species in the environment. In the context of dynamic networks of idea-spaces, however, fitness also refers to how things fundamentally cohere, make sense, *fit together*, in ways that enable the achievement of that kind of supremacy. Fitness (and the laws and principles associated with it) will help us understand how a series of links and connections in an idea-space can lead to the emergence of powerful new patterns of coherence and meaning. By the same token, it's deeply connected with the cognitive process in which intuition transforms into insight, creating a new space for the creative mind to work in. In short, fitness turns out to play an important role in invention, discovery, and innovation, particularly those creative leaps in which an idea suddenly crystallizes and takes off, sweeping competing ideas before it.

Things began to look up for Apple just over seven months after the debacle in Atlantic City. The West Coast Computer Faire opened in San Francisco on April 16, 1977, two years to the day after Steve Dompier demonstrated the musical abilities of the Altair. Both Woz and Jobs had returned to Cupertino determined to prove they could do better, and they decided the upcoming convention was the perfect opportunity. Jobs in particular felt humiliated by their first showing, and was committed to doing everything he could not to repeat the experience.

The Faire came at a crucial point. As Young notes, "By late 1976 the rush was on, and because no one had ever sold personal computers before, the entire field was filled with risk and opportunity."[5] In just eighteen months, the industry had moved from the debut of a crude, clumsy hobbyist computer kit to a full-blown microcomputer social-industrial complex with multiple players producing a whole range of second-generation machines, add-ons, and programs. Based largely in Silicon Valley, it had become a tightly knit community of practice in which most of the key figures (typically members of the Homebrew Club) knew one another, and companies collaborated as much as they competed, their shared goal to further the microcomputer revolution. Such communities, as we saw, are typically high on reciprocity but low on reach. And at this crucial stage of the industry's development, as it desperately needed to reach out to much larger markets in order to grow, that was a problem.

Most of the young microcomputer entrepreneurs sensed that a significant leap was needed to move the industry securely into the next phase—whatever that might be. Some focused on creating further technological dazzle. Others, like IMSAI, tried to make a breakthrough by concentrating their efforts on building up an effective sales force. But it was Steve Jobs, with a big assist from Woz, who got it right. The move Jobs made eerily parallels the one Ed Roberts crucially used at MITS to jump-start the hobbyist computer business. He reached out to the mainstream, in the process enlarging and transforming the industry's value network.

With hindsight, it looks like an obvious move. If you're going after the mainstream consumer, then look to conventional business to guide your thinking about such fundamentals as appropriate business models, investment, organizational structure, marketing, and so forth. But the industry was too new, and its mostly engineering-trained management too raw to see it that way. As no less an expert than Bill Gates, looking back on that chaotic period, put it: "Nobody really knew what was going on. So many things would have obviously needed to be done if you'd had the vision back then. Nobody had the view of the market."[6]

Well, almost nobody. Between the debacle in Atlantic City and the coming triumph in San Francisco, Jobs tapped into serious investment capital; appointed an experienced former Fairchild Semiconductor executive as president of Apple; hired a brilliantly innovative marketing agency headed by Regis McKenna, who promptly transformed Apple's clunky logo into the now familiar rainbow apple; and began giving serious thought to what consumers wanted in a home computer, including coming up with his own design for a stylish beige plastic case.[7]

None of this would have seemed particularly radical to the strategy team of a mainstream company trying to break into new markets with an innovative product, but it still represented a fairly sharp break with the existing precepts and practices of the hobbyist/microcomputer firms. But in at least one major respect, Jobs and Wozniak drew on an insight that had special relevance to the computer industry itself: the importance of third-party developers. This was something Ed Roberts grasped from the outset when he built multiple expansion slots into the Altair. Over Jobs's initial resistance, Wozniak insisted the Apple II have at least eight such slots, designed to make it easy for other companies to add value by manufacturing circuit boards that shared the main microprocessor. Meanwhile, Jobs recognized that good documentation in the form of a clearly written technical reference manual, in addition to making the Apple II more user friendly, would be a boon to outside software developers. This single addition helped ensure that for the next several years the majority of third-party-designed software would be developed almost exclusively for the Apple II. Another key touch to making the Apple machine more user and developer friendly was the chip Woz designed to hold BASIC, thereby obviating the hassle of inputting the language via cassette every time the machine was turned on.

To all this, Woz added his own signature touches. Mimicking the Sol, he designed an internal power supply and connections for a keyboard and television monitor, as well as an elegant system for minimizing the circuitry needed for color. The motherboard itself, the most advanced of any personal computer, was a masterpiece of elegant, highly integrated design that also helped shave costs. Finally, the whole machine came preassembled. The clear lesson of the Atlantic City show was that kits were out. The hobbyist phase of the home computer industry was now definitively over.

By the time the San Francisco show opened, Apple was ready with a booth to rival that of the best at the Atlantic City event and, more important, a computer both Jobs and Wozniak were convinced was superior to the competition. Jobs, certain the Apple II was trouncing the opposition, roamed the convention floor picking up every piece of literature he could on competing products. Suddenly he found himself staring at a leaflet about MITS' latest offering, the Zaltair, promising a far more powerful machine than the Apple II:

> *Imagine the computer surprise of the century here today. Imagine Z[ilog]-80 performance plus. Imagine BAZIC in ROM, the most complete and powerful language ever developed. Imagine raw video . . . autoscroll text, a full 16 lines of 64 characters . . . eye-dazzling color graphics . . . a blitz-fast 1200 baud cassette port . . . an unparalleled I/O system with full Altair-100 and Zaltair-150 bus compatibility . . . Imagine Zaltair, available now from MITS, the company where microcomputer technology was born.*[8]

Aghast at being leapfrogged again, Jobs raced back to the Apple booth to tell the rest of the crew the bad news. There was no way the Apple II could compete with those sorts of specifications. Determined to see this wonder machine for himself, Jobs wandered over to the MITS booth, only to find the staff frantically stamping FRAUD on every leaflet they could lay their hands on. It wasn't until months later that Jobs discovered the truth—Woz, ever the prankster, had written the whole thing. From now on, Apple would basically be competing with itself.

The West Coast Computer Faire admitted over thirteen thousand paying customers. As Young notes, "It was far beyond the organizers' wildest hopes, and it heralded the beginning of the personal computer age."[9] It also ushered in a period of industry dominance for Apple that it would not relinquish until 1983, when the IBM PC overtook it in sales. Initially, the Altair and Altair-compatible IMSAI continued to outsell the Apple II, which because of its reliance on a Motorola chip was regarded as largely confined to the home market while being shut out of the potentially more lucrative nascent business segment. But now two things happened, one planned, the other not, that would push the Apple II far ahead of its rivals.

At Markkula's urging, Woz came up with a truly innovative and elegant design for a disk controller card that vastly simplified the job of programmers who were producing software for personal computers. As a result of its superior disk drive, plus its technical manual and BASIC chip, the Apple II began to accumulate a significant amount of software (mostly games, easily the most popular application at this point) written expressly for it. Other computer makers, notably Commodore (which might otherwise have easily begun to dominate the market simply on the basis of size), had enormous trouble duplicating the drive's performance, and sales of the Apple II began to climb rapidly (at one point in 1978, there was a twenty-six-month backlog).

Almost by accident (Markkula's daughter was learning grade-school math and he thought some supporting software would be neat), the Apple II got into the education market, which sustained its rapidly growing sales. By 1979, in part because of its dominance in education, "Apple *was* personal computers . . . The company had all but destroyed the competition."[10] By year's end, sales topped 35,000, up from 8,000 the previous year, while gross revenues were approaching the $50 million mark. But as Regis McKenna understood perhaps better than anyone, the really big untapped market was business, and nothing Apple offered had much appeal.

Then the lightning of a killer app, the first in the history of personal computing, struck. Two Boston-based programmers, Dan Fylstra and Dan Bricklin, came up with VisiCalc, the first spreadsheet application. Jobs and Markkula were unimpressed, and balked at the $1 million price tag, but when it shipped in the fall of 1979, it ran only on the Apple II. Now the business market was wide open, and sales raced ahead yet again (by 1981, VisiCalc was selling 12,000 copies a month, and though by then available on other computers, was still providing a huge boost to Apple).

When Apple went public on December 12, 1980, the *Wall Street Journal* enthused that "not since Eve has an apple posed such a temptation."[11] Its stock, the largest IPO since Ford Motor Co. went public in 1956, gave the company a valuation of $1.778 billion. The twenty-six-year-old Jobs's share was $217 million—not too bad a return on his original investment five years earlier of $1,500, raised by selling his VW bus. By comparison, a software company in Redmond, Washington, by the name of Microsoft was barely a blip on Wall Street's radar. In 1982 Apple became the first personal computer company to exceed $1 billion in annual sales. By the early 1980s it would become the fastest-growing company in Wall Street history, with the Apple II's installed base reaching one million in 1983 and topping two million the following year. In May 1983 Apple was listed in the *Forbes* 500 at 411, the fastest ascent in business history. As sales climbed into the stratosphere, the February 15, 1982, *Time* featured Jobs on the cover under the headline, "Striking It Rich." Even the military were buying Apple. In a 1985 *Playboy* interview, Jobs claimed that "at least as of a few years ago, every tactical nuclear weapon in Europe manned by U.S. personnel was targeted by an Apple II computer."[12]

In the end, of course, Apple would be unable to withstand the sheer power of IBM's name and marketing power. Starting in 1982, it steadily lost market share to its East Coast rival. But if the IBM PC finally made the arrival of the personal computer official, it was the Apple II that created the personal computer in the form we know. The Apple II succeeded in converting what started out as a hobbyist machine designed for a highly enthusiastic but essentially niche market into a computer that would appeal to the mainstream.

In exploring the microcomputer's third and most powerful tipping point, we'll find that two puzzles command most of our attention. First, how did Apple, lacking the advantage of being first mover, come from the back of the field to dominate the industry? And second, what underlies the creative process capable of putting a "dent in the universe," otherwise known as an "insanely great" act of imagination?[13] On the surface, the questions appear unrelated. Nevertheless, as we'll see, the laws of fitness that shape network topography will provide substantial insight into both questions.

PREFERENTIAL ATTACHMENT, OR HOW THE RICH GET RICHER

When the Apple II debuted, it entered an extremely competitive market that other well-established and highly talented firms were working flat out to dominate. The Altair, despite being known for poor reliability and inferior performance, had maintained its position as industry leader. Products such as the Sol and the IMSAI 8080 closely followed the Altair, but though technically superior, were unable to overtake it. Chalk up another victory for the advantage of being first mover. So how did Apple manage to overcome this seemingly well entrenched principle?

Albert-László Barabási has reformulated the first-mover advantage as what he terms the *law of preferential attachment*, which states that we tend to connect "at a higher rate to those nodes that are already heavily linked."[14] This induces "a *rich-get-richer* phenomenon that helps the more connected nodes [such as those of a first-mover] grab a disproportionately large number of links at the expense of the latecomers."[15] As we saw in the preceding chapter, the Altair quickly became a very well-connected hub with links to the emergent market of hobbyists, the Homebrew Club, suppliers, magazines, user groups, and so on. As the market grew, along with the industry as a whole, new competitors had to vie with MITS for both established and new links in its value network. The law of preferential attachment worked in the Altair's favor, ensuring that it remained the market leader until it was sold to Pertec in May 1977.

Clearly, the principle of first-mover advantage (and by extension, the law of preferential attachment) is not inviolable. Intuit overcame it. Similarly, Google came late to a crowded search-engine market led by AltaVista, Lycos, and Ask Jeeves, but quickly vanquished its competitors. In both cases the programs qualitatively and quantitatively transformed the way people use the type of software application in question—in other words, the idea-spaces of personal accounting and Internet searching tipped as a result of their appearance. If the principle of the rich get richer, driven by the law of preferential attachment, didn't account for these tipping points, what did? The lightning-fast rise to industry dominance of the Apple II can point us to the answer.

WHY THE FIT GET RICH

As a late entrant, the Apple II, like Intuit and Google, found itself having to go head to head with successful, well-entrenched competition. It not only became the industry leader in a matter of months, but over the next several years achieved a level of exponential growth and market ascendancy that has remained unmatched in the industry to this day. How did this come about? Since the market was expanding rapidly, why did so many firms go under, instead of all benefiting from a larger pool of customers? Why was it the Apple II and not its competitors that finally made the personal computer revolution a reality, giving rise to the industry's most powerful and enduring third tipping point?

The answer is to be found in a second law that under the right circumstances prevails over the law of preferential attachment. Instead of the rich get richer, what we find is *the fit get rich*.[16] This essentially Darwinian principle comes into play when a company is able to offer consumers a product with truly significant advantages over the competition. Fitness, in other words, represents a product's capacity to satisfy core customer concerns. Intuit, for example, offered customers a far more user-friendly product at a significantly lower price. Similarly, Google vastly increased the accuracy of searches.

We can state this principle as follows:

THE LAW OF THE FIT GET RICH

In an open, dynamic network, the fit get rich.

According to Barabási, fitness "is a quantitative measure of a node's ability to stay in front of the competition."[17] In formal network terms, fitness measures a node's ability to compete for links: nodes with higher fitness are linked to more frequently. In this case, preferential attachment is driven not by richness alone but by the product of a node's fitness and the number of links it has. In plain English, what all this says is that—using the example of search engines—a user is more likely to choose Google (i.e., link to the Google hub) if it has more links and/or its links are more fit than competing search services.

You may be wondering at this point if we really need all this theoretical machinery. Why not simply say that the best product quite naturally rises to the top? The trouble with that idea is that it leaves unexplained why some products produce tipping points—qualitative transformations accompanied by explosive growth—while others don't. We need to understand how increasing fitness triggers tipping points, and what light network theory can throw on this. Let's see what the Apple II's extraordinary success has to teach us.

By the time the Apple II debuted in April 1977, the microcomputer industry looked to be in healthy condition. Excitement about the microcomputer revolution was sweeping the nation, and sales among leading brands were blazing hot. Basic models now included an effective operating system; built-in monitor, keyboard, and power supply; sleek looks (the Sol actually sported solid walnut side panels); and genuinely useful applications such as accounting and word processing. The Apple II's design was undoubtedly superior in certain respects, but hardly to the point where it could have been expected to sweep away the opposition so conclusively. The decisive factor was the exponential growth of fitness within the Apple II's value network. As we'll see, this was driven not by individual features themselves or by their aggregate impact, but rather by *the set of powerful feedback loops* that emerged between major hubs in the web of communities that constituted the heart of Apple's expanded value network.

In reaching out to the idea-space of mainstream business, Jobs established weak ties (weak because they extended far beyond the relatively closed social-industrial complex the industry had become) to two communities largely ignored by other microcomputer firms: investors and mainstream consumers. Apple made itself attractive to investors by putting together an enterprise that got right many of the key components of running a successful business, from bringing in professional management to marketing to a youthful mainstream male audience (McKenna took out ads in *Playboy*) to having sufficient capital to grow. For a market of increasingly nonhobbyist consumers, the Apple II offered sleek style, ease of use, good documentation, and reliability. For his part, Wozniak strengthened existing links to the software development community. The Apple II's disk controller and technical reference manual made it much easier for third-party programmers to design software for it, resulting in a flood of game and educational software developed uniquely for the Apple II that further increased its consumer appeal.

In effect, Jobs and Wozniak established or strengthened ties to three groups that would prove essential to the future growth of the industry. In doing so, they enriched the idea-space of the microcomputer with the intelligence—much of it new to the industry—embedded in the idea-spaces these groups represented, creating the conditions for the hobbyist machine to finally metamorphose into the personal computer. As figure 5-1 shows, each of these groups preferred to link to the Apple II hub because of its higher fitness—that is, its ability to compete based on desirable features.

Each group's needs represent core embedded intelligence—those elements that are the key to establishing effective links between the hubs/idea-spaces, and thus the groups themselves. The map thus represents Apple's core value network.

Reach enlarges and enriches. What happened at Apple is a perfect example. By the end of 1977, there was a growing belief that professional management might have its advantages; however, scarcely anyone considered it the time to put such a radical idea into practice. The chief users, designers, and company presidents were still hobbyists at heart.[18] It was Apple that, overcoming the Homebrew Club/counterculture dislike of corporate America, first grasped the benefits to be reaped from creating a connection with mainstream business practices. After the Apple II's meteoric rise, what was once regarded with suspicion became standard. In fact, a brief glance at figure 5-1 reveals that many of the elements listed characterize the PC industry to this day. Such was the tipping point the Apple II created.

If reach enlarges and enriches, reciprocity integrates. Here is where the second part of the fitness dynamic kicks in. The heavy double-headed arrows in the figure represent positive feedback loops between the main hubs. A rapidly growing customer base made the Apple II more attractive to both investors and third-party developers. Additional rounds of capital investment and a growing flood of programs accelerated sales growth, starting the cycle over again and increasing still further the Apple II's overall fitness relative to its competitors. The first-mover advantage of the Altair and its closest competitors was quickly overcome by the Apple machine's greater fitness, and as the law of the fit get rich kicked in, its market and industry dominance

FIGURE 5-1

A network map of three central external groups' linking preferences

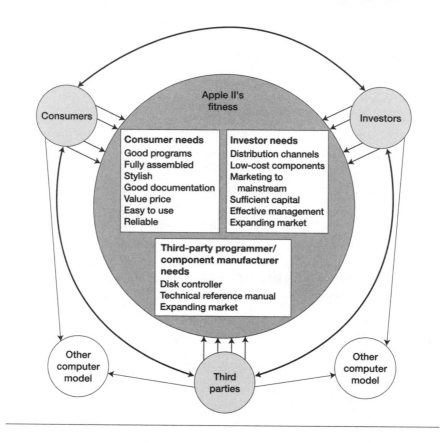

increased dramatically as the microcomputer finally morphed into the full-blown personal computer.

More is different—but not always. The Altair's main competitors were technologically superior but the overall idea-space of the microcomputer didn't change dramatically, and the Altair initially remained the sales leader. Two key factors underlie the tipping point the Apple II created. First, two of the three hubs in its value network were linked to Apple via weak ties. The investor community and mainstream consumers, both standard elements of the conventional business world, represented previously unconnected hubs that at the time lay largely outside the value network of the microcomputer industry. When novel embedded intelligence flows between hubs across weak ties, it produces a powerful transformative effect. Key amounts of the energy, connectedness, and ideas contained in one world are transferred to another, *resulting in a significant expansion of the network as a whole*. As might be expected, there is risk here as well as opportunity, the risk being that the transfer will end up having more of a disruptive than constructive impact. One need only recall the disastrous attempts in the late 1990s to create "convergence" between television and the Internet.

This brings us to the second key factor relating to the Apple II as an industry tipping point. The initial fitness that Jobs and Wozniak established between Apple and the three hubs shown in figure 5-1 triggered the law of the fit get rich. By itself, however, this was insufficient to create the almost total industry dominance by Apple that finally established the personal computer in the mainstream. This was the result of a different law: *the fit get fitter*.

The feedback loops between the three main hubs and the Apple II in the Apple value network drove a self-organizing process in which the fit between investor, external developer, and consumer needs and the product itself became ever tighter and more integrated. Once this self-organizing dynamic of increasing fitness had been achieved, producing internal stability and strength and thereby obviating the danger of disruption, the major network expansion produced by the weak links Jobs forged to external hubs could work in Apple's favor. As the Apple II's fitness in relation to its value network rose, so its market dominance increased, now driven by an accelerated law of the fit get rich.

TIPPING POINTS AND THE LAWS OF FITNESS

The law of tipping points, as formulated in the preceding chapter, states that in a dynamic network, more becomes different *under certain critical conditions*. We can now define what those conditions are. When external intelligence is first brought into an idea-space by means of weak ties, it enriches and expands that space proportionately. But to be effective, this potentially destabilizing event must be followed by a phase in which the new intelligence is fully integrated into the space. Such integration is achieved dynamically by means of increased fitness resulting from feedback loops between key hubs in a value network. This self-organizing process (once in place, the fitness loops operate more or less autonomously) gives rise to the higher-level pattern, in the form of a highly integrated network, that constitutes the tipping point's transformative shift and that drives further growth.

In short, tipping points arise as the result of *balancing reach and reciprocity* (i.e., weak and strong ties) within a dynamically linked network of idea-spaces. We can see this in the rise of both the hobbyist microcomputer and the Apple II personal computer. Ed Roberts successfully integrated elements imported from the mainstream computer industry into the Altair, whose rapid growth was driven by a series of feedback loops between technical design, alliances with external developers, and customer needs. The emergence of the Homebrew Club, with its ties to electrical engineering, Silicon Valley entrepreneurialism, and the counterculture, set off a new cycle of integration driven by fitness loops. The outcome was the well-oiled machine of the microcomputer's social-industrial complex.

Excessive reach produces instability and even disintegration. Witness the overly ambitious attempts of the dot-comers to invent a new economy based on largely untried network models of commerce. Correspondingly, too much integration (i.e., reciprocity) leads to complacency and possible stagnation or demise. The minicomputer industry was doing extraordinarily well when it failed to see the challenge posed by the microcomputer. Similarly, by late 1976 the rapidly expanding microcomputer industry, though certainly aware of the challenges it faced, largely fell back on tried-and-true tactics in order to keep growing. Jobs reached out to the mainstream industry, chose well, and set off a new cycle of integration and growth driven by fitness loops.

As should by now be clear, tipping points created by weak ties that import external intelligence and by fitness loops that integrate it account for the ability of certain products and services to overcome the first-mover advantage. The laws of fitness trump the principle of the rich get richer. More generally, this dynamic balancing of reach and reciprocity, network expansion and integration, explains the seemingly mysterious process whereby new order emerges from relative disorder. The creative leaps that tipping points represent arise through integrating imported intelligence into an existing space, transforming its internal coherence in the process.[19]

WEBS WITHOUT A SPIDER

The fit get fitter, producing an integrated idea-space whose strength and resilience is even able to tolerate and correct major mistakes—the system itself autonomously solves the problem. The success of VisiCalc is a case in point. Jobs and Markkula both initially rejected it. Bricklin's finance professor at Harvard ridiculed it as "a complete waste of time." Bricklin himself thought VisiCalc's main application might be for real estate transactions.[20] When it finally came out (with little help from Apple), it was available only for the Apple II. Why? Because the Apple II's superior disk controller and technical reference manual made it far easier for third-party developers like Bricklin to design software for a microcomputer. The Apple II's exploding sales only increased the attraction. And its increasing segment of mainstream business users quickly decided what the program's true domain of application was. As a result, the Apple II's value network, which was rapidly becoming the basis of the emerging personal computer industry itself, was able to enlarge itself while maintaining overall coherence. Within two years, sales of VisiCalc rose from 500 copies per month to 12,000, further accelerating the transformation not only of Apple, but the industry as a whole.

The VisiCalc example points up a novel but crucially important aspect of fitness: in networked systems fitness is *emergent*—in other words, it arises as a result of the interplay of elements within the system as a whole. The emergent nature of this fit is evidenced by the fact that in the case of VisiCalc, not one of the major players involved, including the program's inventor, correctly foresaw the impact it would have on the nascent personal computer industry. The intelligence that drove VisiCalc's success was embedded in the self-organizing dynamics of the network itself—that is, in the capacity of its fitness loops to generate stability, integration, and growth.

This blindness to innovation pervaded the computer industry. Repeatedly, both those involved and those on the outside remarked how little they understood at the time what was going on. Intel's Gordon Moore didn't get what all the fuss was about: "I personally didn't see anything useful in [the PC], so [Intel] never gave it another thought."[21] There was much talk of "toy computers." Estimates of numbers were invariably way off. No one could reliably judge whether this was a passing fad for a highly restricted market, or the initial churnings of a profoundly important industry. As Young notes, "No one had any idea how computers would be used, let alone what the market would respond to," a view evidently shared by Bill Gates.[22]

The phenomenon of fitness that builds on itself lies at the very core of the process whereby new order emerges unexpectedly out of disorder. Its inherently emergent nature helps explain why creative leaps are so hard to predict, design, or control.[23] As Steven Johnson explains in his lucid and enlightening book, *Emergence*, in certain kinds of complex adaptive systems, patterns emerge from the bottom up: "In these systems, agents residing on one scale start producing behavior that lies one scale above them: ants create colonies; urbanites create neighborhoods . . . The movement from low-level rules to higher-level sophistication is what we call emergence."[24] Emergent, self-organizing, bottom-up behavior, undirected and uncaused by any type of higher-level agents, is to be found everywhere: not only among ants and city dwellers, but also in Adam Smith's invisible hand, in the operation of Pareto's 80/20 law, on the Web, in certain types of video games such as *SimCity*, and even in our brains.[25]

The emergence of the microcomputer and its transformation into the personal computer was no exception. Some people were more blind than others, but no one had a clear enough view of where things were headed to act on the basis of purely linear analysis. Most of the time confusion reigned.

Scores of firms came into existence virtually overnight, only to go under just as quickly. Chips came and went. There was endless debate about what features and business tactics (color, more memory, reliability, keeping dealers happy) really mattered. Major mistakes were made, often leading to a firm's demise. Such failures were not contingent but inevitable, since it is a defining characteristic of emergent networks that participants *are blind at any given moment to the pattern that is emerging at the next higher level.*

Yet somehow the industry as a whole not only grew exponentially, but achieved a structure where it became self-sustaining. The twin laws of the fit get rich and the fit get fitter played a fundamental role in this extraordinary trajectory. But if emergent fitness is central to the creation of new order, then it follows that creative leaps cannot be entirely agent-driven, since the agents involved are of necessity partly blind to the new pattern they are helping to make at a higher level.

Belief in the necessity of centralized control dies hard. Steven Johnson refers to it as the "myth of the ant queen: the assumption that collective behavior implie[s] some kind of centralized authority."[26] We still find it very hard to tolerate situations where things are seemingly out of control or don't really make sense, and where unanticipated outcomes are the norm. But this is exactly what an emergent situation is: that is, one where the major elements and the principles governing their alignment are not being formulated from a centralized authority, but are an outcome of the *self-organizing dynamic of the space as a whole.*

An emergent network is, to use Barabási's term, "a web without a spider," built without anyone at the center directing things. "In the absence of a spider, there is no meticulous design behind these networks . . . [They] are self-organized."[27] Our modern faith in a strictly linear relationship between cause and effect and the efficacy of analytical reasoning makes it hard for us to accept the fundamental idea Barabási is propounding here: that it's the space itself—*the network topography*—operating under the principle of self-organization, that does the most important designing.

Agentless design may be puzzling enough, but there's an even deeper paradox awaiting us. A self-organizing system grows fitter over time. Since the fit get rich, such a system, typically driven by hub-dominated feedback loops, will grow very rapidly. In the process the system will undergo one or more tipping points, resulting in a major qualitative transformation, and that poses an intriguing problem. A tipping point marks the full emergence of a higher-level pattern built from the activity of lower-level elements. In an adaptive system (i.e., one that is becoming fitter), learning—the system's capacity to change effectively—thus takes the form of the alignment of lower-level elements *with what lies in the future*—a growing but as yet unseen pattern. This is the reverse of normal learning, which is based on reasoning from past experience.

Insofar as human agents play a role in creative leaps, this paradox applies to the mind also. Reason, proceeding cautiously, *looks backward*: rational argument on which learning can be based is valid only insofar as its founding premises and previous logical moves are sound. It builds from the simple to the complex, one step at a time, and so is virtually blind and powerless in the face of an emergent situation. The imagination and its allied capacities, however, look *forward*. The imagination is the mind's supreme faculty for dealing with the future, for intuitively sensing and insightfully grasping patterns that do not yet exist but are still forming themselves and coming into being. It is the entrepreneur's (and scientist's, and inventor's, and artist's) most precious gift.

GENIUS, IMAGINATION, AND NETWORK DYNAMICS

If the early development of the personal computer can lay claim to genius, it was undoubtedly embodied in Jobs and Wozniak. And that genius was never more on display than in the aftermath of the humiliation they suffered at the East Coast conference, an experience that undoubtedly led to much soul-searching. Let's put ourselves in their shoes for a moment. For all the hype and razzle-dazzle, no one had a clear idea of where things were headed, or what consumers really wanted in a home computer. As the sheer variety of models on display testified, there was no consensus on such matters as basic software, operating systems, color, style, or applications, let alone what it would take to run a successful computer company. Most companies were poorly managed and chronically underfunded, lacked a coherent marketing plan, and had little idea about which technical components were crucial to get right.

Jobs's intuitions regarding the need for a combination of adequate investment capital, sound business organization, and outstanding marketing proved, of course, to be remarkably prescient, as did Wozniak's idea of encouraging and supporting third-party developers by designing a superior disk controller. At the time, they were anything but obvious. And the two Steves themselves seem to have operated blindly much of the time, more or less blundering into the huge education market by accident, failing to see VisiCalc's killer-app potential, and being endlessly surprised by how fast Apple was growing.

So how did they do it? Once again, emergent fitness is the key. When Jobs and Wozniak began thinking about the Apple II, they entered a game that was already going on, and it was changing in each of the three areas they identified as the key to Apple's future success: investment, software development, and the market. Undoubtedly, many of the young entrepreneurs thought about these things, but only Apple got it right.

Jobs in particular seems to have had the ability to step back and take in the whole picture, recognizing the main idea-spaces involved and the links between them. Desperate to envisage what the future would look like, the pair set their imagination to work, mentally trying out this and that combination of elements. At first, it was intuition, mostly on Jobs's part.

Gradually, a pattern began to emerge. Certain things *made sense*, they hung together, in some cases setting up powerful feedback loops. If mainstream consumers were the next big market, then well-designed software would be crucial. Marketing would require adequate capital, and so forth. The fit grow fitter. As this initial apprehension of reciprocal fitness increased, intuition suddenly tipped into insight. *Of course, that's it!* The complex became simple, and the new idea-space of the personal computer and the social-industrial complex to produce it was born. Now the imagination could go to work once more—further expanding the space, trying new possibilities that seemed to fit—and the cycle could begin again.

The truly great intelligent imagination does two things. It grasps the game being played, and figures out how the key elements fit together—the major idea-spaces, the elements of embedded intelligence, and the network dynamics driving their evolution. Above all, it homes in on areas of emergent fitness indicated by feedback loops. The paradox of emergence is still there, however. As the mistakes Apple itself made on the way to unprecedented growth and market dominance show, even the most powerful imaginative faculties cannot divine the future with much accuracy. In the end, the imagination must surrender to the network dynamics of space itself, trusting that the way ahead will be revealed and increasingly make sense as things unfold. To produce an insanely great product, you need to let the space do much of the thinking for you.

How do you see the future before it arrives? How do you make the guesses that have the best fit with what is still in the process of emerging? Rational analysis, which looks backward, won't tell you, so you have to rely on your imaginative faculties instead. The trick is to tune in to the dynamics of key networked idea-spaces.

I've argued that there is a basic symmetry between the individual mind and the networked idea-spaces of the extended mind—that the same laws drive the dynamics of both. This claim, which will be elaborated and supported by further evidence in future chapters, may initially appear counter-intuitive. After all, the MITH tradition has long drawn a sharp line between the organization of the mind and that of culture and society at large. These may interact and influence one another, but are hardly supposed to be run by the same laws.

In abandoning the MITH thesis, however, we're finally breaking down the age-old firewall that's been erected around the mind. Once we begin to think in terms of network dynamics, there's no need to draw such a sharp distinction between the workings of the inner and extended mind. This is not a matter of psychologizing the latter, but rather of de-psychologizing the former: inside or outside, it's networked idea-spaces all the way down. Just as the conventional wisdom now sees individual computers as an integral part of the greater network of interconnected machines, so we can interpret the individual mind as an integral part of the extended mind. What the rise of the personal computer shows us is that some minds are far better than average at tuning into the extended mind's elegant and powerful pattern-forming dynamics.

The central point of chapters 4 and 5 is that creative leaps can largely be understood in terms of the dynamics of network topography. Barabási's pioneering research, which has transformed network science, has revealed among other things the key role hubs play in these dynamics. If in the present context hubs may be interpreted as idea-spaces seen from the point of view of their network connections, then we now possess a powerful new way of modeling creative leaps in both the extended mind and the individual human mind.

Technically, a network with large hubs is known as scale-free, meaning that unlike the distribution of points in a bell curve, no node is typical. With this in mind, we can now modify the statements of the laws posited earlier:

THE LAW OF TIPPING POINTS

In an open, dynamic, scale-free network,
at some critical point *more is different.*

Change in lower-level elements prompts a self-organizing process that gives rise to a new pattern of elements that is both self-sustaining and qualitatively distinct from its original state. A scale-free network is always tipped.[28] Emergent fitness, driven by the law of the fit get fitter, plays a key role in triggering a tipping point.

THE LAW OF THE FIT GET RICH

In an open, dynamic, scale-free network, the fit get rich.

Preferential attachment is driven by increased fitness. The probability that a given node will link to another is expressed by the formula $\kappa\eta/\sum\kappa_i\eta_i$, where κ is the number of links and η the relative fitness.[29]

THE LAW OF THE FIT GET FITTER

In an open, dynamic, scale-free network with positive
feedback loops between hubs, the fit get fitter.

What these abstract but rigorous formulations reveal is the central fact that *breakthrough creativity is inherently an emergent process governed by laws of network dynamics.* Analytical reason, because by definition it looks back to established facts and premises, is blind in such situations. On the other hand, the intelligent imagination—that is, imagination intuitively attuned to sensing emerging fitness—is capable of producing adaptive intelligence, new thinking that grasps the direction in which the future is unfolding.

Steven Johnson has noted that emergent systems themselves "can be brilliant innovators . . . more adaptable to sudden change than more rigid hierarchical models."[30] Emergent systems, in other words, have their own autonomous dynamics on which the human imagination piggybacks. Crucial to this process is the emergence of new, higher-level patterns. To really grasp how such patterns form, we need to bring to bear a further law derived from network science: the law of spontaneous generation.

Chapter Six

THE MATHEMATICAL ECOLOGY OF CREATIVITY

Order for free . . . will change our view of life.

—Stuart Kauffman[1]

In the beginning was the space, and the space was alive with possibilities . . .

In 1973, a Xerox PARC engineer named Robert Metcalfe proposed an architecture for local area networks that rapidly became the standard for networked computer communication. In the course of helping to develop and promote the Ethernet, as it became known, Metcalfe came up with an interesting observation relating to the growth of digital networks: "The power of the network increases exponentially by the number of computers connected to it. Therefore, every computer added to the network both uses it as a resource while adding resources in a spiral of increasing value and choice."[2]

The technology guru George Gilder subsequently dubbed this *Metcalfe's law*, which he reformulated as follows:

The value of a network is $N(N-1)$.[3]

Metcalfe's law was appealed to repeatedly to explain the explosive growth of digital telecommunications in general during the seventies and eighties, and of the World Wide Web and other core aspects of the new economy during the nineties. To grasp Metcalfe's essential insight, consider an evolving group of Web sites, each of which agrees to provide links to the others' home pages. The value each new Web site adds in terms of the total number of additional links grows *exponentially*, not linearly (see figure 6-1).

FIGURE 6-1

Links grow exponentially

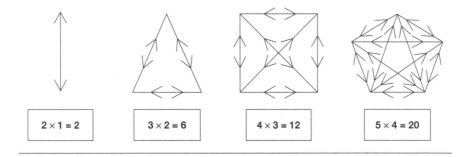

| $2 \times 1 = 2$ | $3 \times 2 = 6$ | $4 \times 3 = 12$ | $5 \times 4 = 20$ |

What the law says is that the addition of even a single node to a network *creates a much larger set of potentially meaningful links*. Metcalfe's law applies to the value dimension of networks in general, not just computer networks. A telling illustration of this is the often unanticipated outcome when parents decide to have a third child. Many parents will view this as simply a relatively minor increase in family size from four to five (i.e., 25 percent), with a concomitant increase in the expenditure of resources. Only later do they realize how much more is involved, both positively and negatively. In terms of relationship pairs (the ones that matter with regard to family unity, emotional balance, conflicts, expenditure of time, etc.), adding a child represents an increase from twelve to twenty—a whopping 67 percent! Moreover, in larger families certain groupings (e.g., a pair of siblings who are especially close) may emerge, creating a new set of relationships with the rest of the family and thereby exponentially increasing the total number of relationships still further.

Knowingly or not, Metcalfe seems to have stumbled across a version of the important principle underlying Cantor's theorem. Cantor, a Russian-born German mathematician, arrived at the principle as part of his effort to demonstrate the counterintuitive truth that some infinities are larger than others. Stated informally, the principle says that *there are always more* sets *of things than things.*[4]

A *set* is a collection of things that all share some common property, such as the set of all unmarried men or the set of Winston Churchill's grandchildren.[5] No matter how large or how small the total number of elements in the set is, there is always a still greater number of subsets of elements. Churchill had only three grandchildren—Cecily, Nicholas, and Winston. But this set of three elements has *seven* subsets (including those with just one member): [C], [N], [W], [C, N], [C, W], [N, W], and [C, W, N]. Similarly, the set of married men contains subsets that include those who like baseball, those who vote for Ralph Nader, those who own SUVs, and so on.

The central point is that the members of any set *simultaneously belong to many other sets*, and these sets *always* outnumber the members themselves. This is so not in practical terms but as a matter of mathematical necessity. We might, for example, arbitrarily carve from the set of unmarried men a subset [A], Fred, Ron, and Jim, who have nothing in common other than the fact that they belong to this particular set. Repeating this tactic demonstrates the truth of Cantor's principle.

This principle (and subcases of it like Metcalfe's law) reveals the way in which relationships between groups of things (some real, some arbitrary) *are spontaneously generated*. Furthermore, this growth is not linear, but exponential. Adding one thing to a set immediately creates a multitude of subsets. Could such spontaneous (i.e., self-organizing) generation turn out to be the source of the raw material for the laws of fitness and tipping points, and by extension creative leaps? If so, then we will have found the fundamental cause of the process whereby order arises out of disorder. For this to be the case, the spontaneous emergence of relationships must somehow give rise to new meaningful *patterns*, that is, to the kind of novel coherence that represents the qualitative change produced by tipping points. Let's look and see.

THE LAW OF SPONTANEOUS GENERATION

Let's start by noticing that a set is simply a collection of related elements—in other words, it's a network. Now we're back on familiar territory. Cantor's principle translates as follows: in any network there are always more links (including potential links) than nodes. This is precisely the basis of Metcalfe's law, a fact which may not seem very interesting until we look at some actual examples.

Consider the cardinal number system. Conceptually this system, or network, of numbers is incredibly simple. All we need to generate any number is two elementary concepts: unity (1) and iterative addition. Let's imagine starting at 1 and adding numbers as we go. As the network of numbers grows, all kinds of new meaningful relationships spring up. Not just "odd," "even," "divisible by 5," "cube root of 27," and so forth, but the whole mysterious system of prime numbers, the phenomena underlying Fermat's last theorem, the Goldbach conjecture, and all the other fascinating properties that form the subject matter of the branch of mathematics known as number theory.

Interestingly, when we think of the cardinal number system in this way, we see that it is *emergent*: as the system itself unfolds, higher-level patterns emerge spontaneously from the interaction of lower-level elements that do not contain those patterns or their properties analytically. Consider prime numbers, for example. Most numbers are the product of two smaller numbers (e.g., 21 = 3 × 7, 108 = 9 × 12), and so their occurrence may be said to arise from relationships between existing elements in the system. This is not the case for primes, however, which are exclusively the product of 1 and the prime itself. Twenty-three, for example, equals 1 × 23, and cannot be factored any other way. Within the cardinal number system, therefore, primes occur at unpredictable intervals (we can't tell if a number is going to be a prime until we get to it).

An interesting discovery in prime number theory demonstrates with striking clarity how even a minor configurational change in a network can unpredictably give rise to an avalanche of new relationships, revealing in this case important patterns that previously lay hidden. The intervals at which primes occur has for centuries resisted precise formulation. Laid out in simple linear sequence, the intervals appear to be virtually random:

1 **2 3** 4 **5** 6 **7** 8 9 10 **11** 12 **13** 14 15 16 **17** 18 **19** 20 21 22
23 24 25 26 27 28 **29** 30 **31** 32 33 34 35 36 **37** 38 39 40 **41** 42 **43**
44 45 46 **47** 48 49 50 51 52 **53** 54 55 56 57 58 **59** 60 **61** 62 63
64 65 66 **67** 68 69 70 **71** 72 **73** 74 75 76 77 78 **79** 80 81

When this conventional ordering is replaced by an outwardly coiling square known as Ulam's spiral, a pattern of diagonals suddenly surfaces (see figure 6-2).[6]

Ulam's spiral of prime numbers

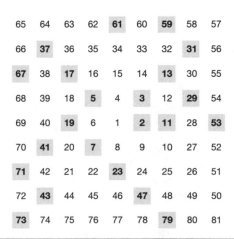

Even the gaps in the diagonals are relatively systematic: in virtually every case they represent an odd number that can only be factored into two primes: 21 (7, 3); 57 (3, 19); 33 (3, 11); and so on. Again, the meaningfulness of the pattern is emergent: absent from the original inputs (i.e., the cardinal number system itself), it increasingly manifests as the system (Ulam's spiral) unfolds.

These examples are instances of the third law of networks:

THE LAW OF SPONTANEOUS GENERATION

In an open, dynamic network, the creation of potentially meaningful relationships or patterns is spontaneous, emergent, and self-transforming.

Notice that the law differs from Cantor's principle in the following crucial respect. Implicitly, Cantor's principle says that for any set of elements, an exponentially larger set of subsets can automatically be generated. Cantor, however, makes no claim that such subsets of relationships are necessarily *meaningful*—some groupings may be entirely arbitrary. Conversely, the law of spontaneous generation, in focusing on meaningful patterns, doesn't claim their emergence is necessarily exponential. Rather, what is implied is that given the automatic explosion of virtual relationships between the elements of a dynamic set, at least some will be meaningful. As we'll see, this outcome will have significant consequences for generating new embedded intelligence and hence new idea-spaces.

This last idea, which has profound consequences for creative leaps, is a form of what the mathematical biologist Stuart Kauffman calls *order for free*. Before investigating that principle in more detail, however, let's look at a couple of real-life examples.

NAPSTER, THE STOCK MARKET BUBBLE, AND SPONTANEOUS GROWTH

Metcalfe's law is a natural outcome of integrating Cantor's principle and the law of spontaneous generation. A good illustration is a telephone network. When you get a new telephone number, it can potentially access and be accessed by all the other numbers in the network, thus instantly creating a huge number of virtual relationships (in Cantor's terms, sets of binary pairs). Of course, in practice, only a small subset of these relationships is meaningful: just those phone numbers that you are likely to call or whose owners might call you.

The workings of Metcalfe's law were seemingly to be found everywhere in the new economy. A classic example was Napster, a file-sharing system that made available an index of hundreds of thousands of digitally formatted songs and other types of music that could be downloaded for free in a matter of minutes. Napster was unofficially launched on June 1, 1999, when a nineteen-year-old Northeastern University dropout named Shawn Fanning sent a copy of a distributed-search software program he had developed to thirty chat-room friends. Despite his requests for confidentiality, some of them promptly leaked it on the Internet. In a matter of days, ten to fifteen thousand people had downloaded the program, and the eighty-year-old, $15 billion recording industry found itself beginning to stare into what *Time* presciently called "the dark void of a post copyright economy."[7]

Over the next eighteen months Napster grew to include an astounding 38 million users, a rate of expansion that led some 130 universities to ban students from using the service—not because it was illegal, but because it was overwhelming entire campus networks. Shortly thereafter, the service was sued by the Recording Industry Association of America, eighteen individual recording companies, and the heavy-metal band Metallica, the beginning of a legal odyssey that resulted in its eventual shutdown.

There were many reasons for Napster's runaway growth—ease of use,[8] access to high-bandwidth connectivity on the part of college students, a huge market segment, a certain *coolness* factor, widespread anger at the record companies for charging high prices for CDs, and a generally anarchic attitude on the part of the young toward centralized control. And, of course, free is always hard to beat. But at the core of its phenomenal expansion rate lay the very factor Metcalfe pointed to: the growth of a network via "adding resources in a spiral of increasing value and choice"—classic conditions for triggering a tipping point that would result in self-reinforcing epidemic growth. Each new user brought his or her own collection of files to the service, thereby increasing the value of using it for everyone else. The incentive to join thus increased exponentially relative to the total pool of users.

Nor was this value enhancement simply a matter of numbers. As the *New York Times* noted at the time, "Napster's transfer screen shows both the files arriving at your computer, and the files that other people are siphoning from your hard disk. Are you lonesome tonight? With the click of another button, you can enter a public chat session with other Napster users on your server—up to about 6,000 people per server—or send an instant message to anyone connected to Napster at the time."[9] The virtual communities such chat-room service enabled generated a strong sense of shared value among their members, creating a further dynamic for the network to expand itself.[10]

Interestingly, a similar dynamic appears to have been at work in the infamous stock market bubble of 2000. As Gary Wolf has perceptively noted in his recent book, *Wired—A Romance,*

> *a bubble feeds upon skepticism. Today's skeptics are tomorrow's buyers. People who decline to purchase shares at five hundred, who laugh at them at a thousand, and revile them at fifteen hundred eagerly snatch them up at two thousand when the spectacle of friends and neighbors celebrating their profits becomes too much to bear. As the bubble grows, the story [behind the bubble] becomes more and more popular, for it is the buyer's indispensable justification and excuse. Only when the story's truth is more or less universally acknowledged do prices plateau and then plummet. Skepticism, a key ingredient, has run out.*[11]

In other words, the conversion of former skeptics adds value to the story, leading to a further increase in the share price that in turn triggers more skeptics to convert. In effect, in the case of both Napster and the stock market, we are dealing with a system that, powered by Metcalfe's law, could drive its own transformation.

Napster (and similar Web services such as Hotmail that underwent dramatic growth during the latter part of the nineties) and the ballooning stock market are cases of exponential growth that led to a *qualitatively* new state of affairs. In other words, they represent forms of tipping point. Napster is a classic instance of a disruptive innovation in the form of a new product that essentially has no competition initially (downloading music over the Internet was so difficult prior to Napster that it was restricted to a small community of hackers).[12] In the course of its explosive growth it transformed itself into something new and different: it became a genuine threat to the music industry, and also took on a community-creating dimension. Both these qualitative transformations were emergent, broad patterns arising from millions of purely local acts of downloading.

In similar fashion, as the stock market grew and grew, it too morphed into something qualitatively different—the infamous new economy with its equally infamous *new rules.* Once again, this was an emergent phenomenon. No one sat down and planned the new economy. The pattern of beliefs, hopes, behavior, and actual economic trends that came to characterize it at its height emerged as the result of millions of local actions: buying stocks, sending e-mails, and engaging in conversations, bolstered by thousands of articles in the print media, specialist newsletters, and hundreds of radio and television talk shows.

The law of spontaneous generation completes the quartet of laws representing the fundamental forces that underlie the network dynamics of creative leaps. Let's be clear what we mean in this context by the phrase *network dynamics*. Like the other laws, the law of spontaneous generation applies to dynamic—that is, changing or growing—networks. When we speak of networks, we are referring to sets of elements seen from the standpoint of the *relationships* among them. Relationships are what create meaning among and between sets of elements. The law of spontaneous generation, then, is the first law—the root law—dealing with how meaning (significant pattern) arises and is organized. In essence, it says that meaning arises spontaneously, because although not all relationships are meaningful, all meaning is relational, and some subset of the relationships in a network is bound to be meaningful. Meaning, in other words, is naturally emergent in dynamic networks, because as relationships multiply, they inevitably create meaningful patterns. This is what we saw, for example, in the number system with the emergence of primes and other properties.

The other laws—the twin laws of fitness, and the law of tipping points—similarly deal with the emergence of meaning. What these laws say is that as meaningful relationships emerge, they tend to increase, grow more coherent, and eventually self-transform qualitatively. It's important to note that the human mind is not a necessary component of this process. Evolution, for example, equally manifests the operation of these laws, leading some to suggest that nature "thinks."[13] Napster and the new economy both illustrate in full this process of emergent meaning, growth, and transformation, as does the rise of the microcomputer and the social-industrial complex that produced it. While not stating it in quite the same terms, some economists have begun to take notice of this phenomenon.

PAUL ROMER'S NEW GROWTH ECONOMICS

Classical economists, those dismal prophets of scarcity, have long maintained that because of limited material resources and the law of diminishing returns, economic growth must eventually slow down and perhaps even cease altogether—a kind of economic version of the second law of thermodynamics.[14] Paul Romer, an economist at Stanford University, profoundly disagrees with this view. Updating and modifying theories originally developed by Peter Drucker and Nobel laureate economist Robert Solow, Romer postulates that essentially there are no limits to growth, because in the knowledge economy it is *ideas*, not material resources, that are the fundamental drivers of economic expansion. Ideas, Romer notes, unlike things, are *nonrival goods*—their use by one person or group doesn't diminish benefits for others, nor do they deplete or wear out. In fact, the more they are used the more they grow in value, thereby offering not diminishing but increasing returns.[15] Appropriate investment in the production of creative ideas can thus potentially lead to radical economic transformation, freeing us from the economics of scarcity, and opening up new vistas of exponential growth and development.

Romer relates this view directly to growth produced by discovery: "Every generation has perceived the limits to growth that finite resources would pose if no new ideas were discovered. We consistently fail to grasp how many ideas remain to be discovered. Possibilities do not add up. They multiply."[16] In other words ideas, unlike things, have limitless potential for exploitation: "On the ideas side you have combinatorial explosion. There's essentially no scarcity to deal with."[17]

As an illustration, Romer cites silicon, whose material value was virtually nil until human ingenuity turned it into computer chips, launching the digital revolution. He also points to the vast untapped potential in the system of chemical elements for producing new laboratory-synthesized materials such as superconducting compounds. Employing mathematical techniques that lead to even more exponential output than those underlying Metcalfe's law, Romer estimates that for the roughly one hundred known atomic elements, there are approximately 330 billion ways of combining just four elements in varying proportions.

New growth theory, as Romer's work came to be known, became the basis for much of the new economy's wildly optimistic predictions of exponential expansion. Inevitably, Romer's reputation suffered somewhat from the dot-com/technology bust. His central ideas have taken on a new lease on life, however, following the publication of Richard Florida's *The Rise of the Creative Class*, which builds on Romer's economic theory.[18] Citing Romer, Florida claims that creativity will increasingly become the main factor driving economic growth, and that those cities and/or regions that have the right mix of lifestyle and other factors to attract creative people will be the dominant growth areas of the future.[19] For a variety of reasons, he contends that the virtuous cycle effect of the creative economy is now reaching critical mass, so that we find ourselves "embarking on an age of pervasive creativity that permeates all sectors of the economy and society."[20]

The dot-com bust notwithstanding, Romer and Florida are surely fundamentally right in the following sense: we are now living in the *idea economy*, and the economics of ideas implies that such an economy is capable of producing sustained, potentially exponential growth. If valid, as it appears to be, this is surely an important insight into the relationship between growth and creativity. Underlying this are the multiplication of possibilities and the growth of value, which appear to be Romer's terms for spontaneous generation and emergent fitness. Like economists, biologists have also begun to recognize how fundamentally important these processes are.

DARWIN'S ERROR: COMPLEXITY AND ORDER FOR FREE

The Santa Fe Institute in New Mexico was founded in the early 1980s, and first came to the attention of the general public as a result of James Gleick's 1987 best seller *Chaos: Making a New Science*. The new science Gleick is referring to has turned out to be not so much chaos theory per se as the emerging science of *complexity*, which deals with the rather abstruse subject of the nonlinear dynamics of nonequilibrium physical and biological systems. The reader may be forgiven for thinking that the connection between this subject and the dynamic laws underlying human creativity is less than immediately obvious!

Etymologically, *nature* derives from the Latin word for "to be born," which in turn is linked to the Indo-European *gena-*, a root that also shows up in *generate, engender*—and *genius*. In spite of this suggestive linguistic association, however, we rarely link creativity in the natural world with its human counterpart. Nature, we assume, has little to teach us about the noblest efforts of the human spirit.

The source of this belief is not hard to figure out. In making his celebrated distinction between body and mind, Descartes argued that, as a strictly physical entity, the body was a *res extensa* governed by the laws of physics. The mind on the other hand, as an incorporeal *res cogitans* or thinking entity, was not, obeying instead the laws of reason. Lopping off the mind from the body in this way created all kinds of difficulties (e.g., How does my purely mental intention to move my arm cause me to do so?), but the divide between the mental and the physical has endured. Ask any practicing psychologist how much his or her discipline is based on strict principles of physics and biology, and the answer comes back, "Not much."

Enter Stuart Kauffman, member of the Santa Fe Institute, MacArthur fellowship recipient, and mathematical ecologist. Like Crick, Kauffman is interested in the baffling problem of how the architecture of the extraordinary biological complexity of our world comes about, in this case as seen from the standpoint of evolution.

As I look out of my living room window, the stunning order wrought by the twin miracles of evolutionary speciation and ontogenetic unfolding is everywhere in evidence. I see lightly wooded terrain populated by white birch, alder, pine, oak, and a variety of other species, all well adapted to the peculiar stresses of the Maine summer and winter climate, all making use of the same process of photosynthesis to convert sunlight to energy, and yet each with its own graceful beauty, shapes, and patterns. Exploring outside, I can find a whole range of plants, insects, and animals—pumpkins, flowers, ferns, voles and raccoons, chickadees and cardinals, crickets, flies, and worms, all living together in a miraculously harmonious and stable ecosystem.

Whence this order? The standard answer, of course, has been that it arose as a result of Darwinian selection working on the outcome of random genetic variation, or what Kauffman sardonically refers to as "design by elimination."[21] Essentially we, and the remaining organisms around us, are nothing more than "nature's Rube Goldberg machines," tinkered together by pure chance. Without natural selection, Kauffman notes, according to the standard account, "there would be nothing but incoherent disorder. I shall argue . . . that this idea is wrong."[22]

Kauffman suggests that it is just too much of a stretch to imagine that the infinitely varied forms of order we find in the natural world all arose as a result of natural selection. But if the standard Darwinian account, updated with the idea of genetic mutation, doesn't explain the order of nature, then what does?

Before looking at Kauffman's ingenious answer, let's be clear about its relevance. Simply put, there appears to be a *direct congruence* between the problem of the source of life itself and the problem of the nature of breakthrough creativity. This equivalence resides in the basic fact that in dynamic systems, *the creation of order is the fundamental phenomenon to be explained.* In any open thermodynamic system (one that has a constant external supply of energy), *order is always less probable than disorder*, for the simple reason that there are far more possible states of disorder than order. Thus the emergence of order requires explanation in terms of some kind of work. But exactly the same is true of human creativity: the emergence of new order—structure, organization, meaningful patterns and relationships, harmonious design— in a constantly changing world requires explanation, because it is far less probable than the emergence of disorder. Kauffman's deep and powerful explanation of how order emerges in the natural world turns out to throw light on how it arises in acts of human creativity as well.

Kauffman's solution is stunningly simple. He calls it "order for free." The order we observe in both the unfolding of individual organisms and in evolution requires neither a central directing force (divine or otherwise) nor the astronomical improbabilities of mere chance. Instead, it arises quite naturally and spontaneously in any reasonably diverse dynamic system. Far from being improbable, it is the *expected* outcome. Life, however improbable its particular configurations, just happens. Creativity is an automatic, spontaneous, inevitable outcome of the unfolding of the system itself, and furthermore is law-governed: "The emerging sciences of complexity begin to suggest that the order [of the natural world] is not all accidental, that vast veins of spontaneous order lie at hand. Laws of complexity spontaneously generate much of the order of the natural world. It is only then that selection comes into play . . . the range of spontaneous order is enormously greater than we have supposed."[23]

Kauffman explains the emergence of order for free with an ingenious illustration. Imagine that you are constructing a random network consisting of nodes and links. In figure 6-3a, the network of twenty nodes is imagined as a set of buttons randomly connected with threads.

As the ratio of threads to buttons increases, a series of clusters begins to emerge. Picking up one button would lift several more with it. As the ratio passes .5 (i.e., 10/20; see figure 6-3b), a *phase transition* begins to occur, manifesting a qualitative shift to relative order.

Suddenly, a giant cluster emerges (see figure 6-3c), the result of most of the subclusters becoming connected to one another. A new pattern not present in the original structure has spontaneously emerged: *order for free*. Further linking will increase the degree of connectedness, but the overall quality of the new state—that of being a cluster in which most or all nodes are interlinked—will not change significantly.

Notice that the phase transition occurs at a relatively *low* level of interconnectivity. The total number of links is $N(N/2) - 1$, or 199, but the qualitative change occurred with just fifteen connections.[24] Notice also that although at a certain point (typically after the link/node ratio surpasses 1) the giant cluster stabilizes (practically all nodes are connected to one another), smaller subclusters will continue to emerge at an exponential rate—*more order for free*.

Kauffman goes on to argue that the phenomenon of emergent order for free is not just some curious property of networks, but *underlies the emergence of life itself*, the crucial transition from collections of purely chemical molecules to biological systems, capable not only of sustaining but also of reproducing themselves. This has deep implications for the biological sciences:

> The existence of spontaneous order is a stunning challenge to our settled ideas in biology since Darwin. Most biologists have believed . . . that selection is the sole source of order in biology, that selection alone is the "tinkerer" that crafts the forms. But if the forms selection chooses among were generated by laws of complexity, then selection has always had a handmaiden. It is not, after all, the sole source of order, and organisms are not just tinkered-together contraptions, but expressions of deeper natural laws.[25]

FIGURE 6-3a

Links/nodes = 5/20

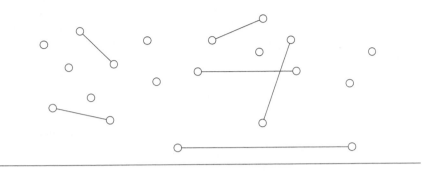

FIGURE 6-3b

Links/nodes = 10/20

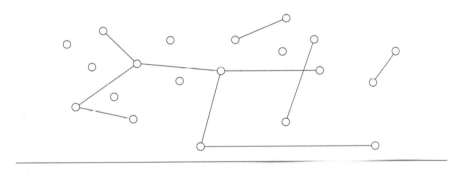

FIGURE 6-3c

Links/nodes = 15/20

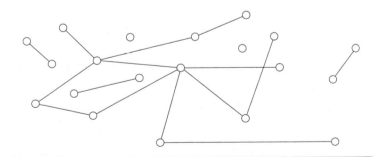

Source: Adapted from Stuart Kauffman, *At Home in the Universe* (New York: Oxford University Press, 1995), 55. By permission of Oxford University Press, Inc.

A deep student of complexity theory, Kauffman is quick to recognize the possibility of extending this radical conception of how order arises to dynamic systems in general:

> The natural history of life may harbor a new and unifying intelligent under-pinning for our economic, cultural, and social life . . . I suspect that the fate of all complex adapting systems in the biosphere—from single cells to economies—is to evolve to a natural state between order and chaos, a grand compromise between structure and surprise. Here, at this poised state, small and large avalanches of coevolutionary change propagate through the system as a consequence of the small, best choices of the actors themselves, competing and cooperating to survive.[26]

Kauffman is expressing two ideas here of deep import for the study of cre-ativity. First, the emergence of spontaneous order in complex adaptive sys-tems (including cultural and economic ones) points to the existence of "deeper natural laws." Second, these laws cooperate with biological agents in creating order. Rather like Adam Smith's famous "invisible hand," the laws underlying order for free play a role in creating order out of chaos.

Kauffman's model affirms the role played by the law of spontaneous gen-eration in biological, cultural, and social systems, just as Romer's does in eco-nomics. Could it be that such a law-governed model will turn out to pose no less dramatic a challenge to our settled ideas about human creativity? I have argued from the start that the standard view of breakthrough creativity as exclusively a product of genius is misguided. Rather, the creation of qualita-tively new order arises partly as a natural, spontaneous outcome of the unfolding of dynamic systems of ideas themselves. Just as whole avalanches of new and meaningful concepts are created as the system of cardinal num-bers unfolds, so too does the sudden drama of human creativity appear to be shaped by more than human agency alone. The role of genius is not to be denied, certainly, but it may need to be reinterpreted as operating in cooper-ation with preexisting laws and the emergent, self-organizing order already latent in cultural, social, cognitive, and economic systems.

As a test case, let's look at one of the most extraordinary and influential eruptions of creativity in the twentieth century, the invention of cubism.

CUBISM, GENIUS, AND THE STRENGTH OF WEAK TIES

In the first decade of the twentieth century, art and science both underwent profound revolutions. In 1905, Albert Einstein published his paper on the spe-cial theory of relativity that forever changed our conceptions of space and time. In 1907, Picasso painted the picture that irrevocably set painting on a different course. *Les Demoiselles d'Avignon*, with its fractured planes, was the immediate precursor to cubism, the movement that in many ways constituted the powerhouse for twentieth-century art. As we'll see, the two events were hardly disconnected. In looking at cubism, our main focus will be not on the rise of the movement itself, but rather the way in which it constituted an idea-space in which the law of spontaneous generation began to play a key role in enabling the viewer of cubist paintings to discover meaning in them.

Cubism's status as a revolutionary art movement is hardly in doubt. As the art critic Robert Rosenblum notes, cubism "altered the structure of Western painting to a degree unparalleled since the Renaissance," achieving this goal by means of its "drastic . . . shattering and reconstruction of traditional representations of light and shadow, mass and void, flatness and depth."[27] To grasp how radical a break with the past cubism represents, consider for a moment a typical impressionist painting such as Renoir's *Le Moulin de la Galette* (painted in 1876—but almost any post-Raphael/pre-Cézanne painting would do). The scene shows several figures seated at a table outside a café, while dancers swirl in the town square behind them. Although impressionism of course effected its own important innovations, particularly in regard to the treatment of color perception, it otherwise generally conforms to the classical canons of figurative art. The rules of perspective and foreshortening are obeyed, with more distant figures drawn significantly smaller than those in the foreground and receding along lines radiating from a single focal point. Similarly, light and shadow are treated in a natural and realistic fashion, and the conventional relationship between form and space (i.e., that forms fit the spaces they would occupy in real life) is rigorously observed.

Now let's look at a typical cubist painting, Picasso's *Landscape with Poster* (1912). (See figure 6-4.) Immediately we recognize we are in *a completely different kind of pictorial space*. Classical perspective has been banished, along with the rest of the grammar of figurative painting.

FIGURE 6-4

Pablo Picasso: *Landscape with Poster* **(1912)**

Source: National Museum of Art, Osaka, Japan.
© 2007 Estate of Pablo Picasso/Artists Rights
Society (ARS), New York. Used with permission.

The unity of the picture space has been fragmented into multiple planes representing varying points of view simultaneously, as though what is being captured is the result of someone walking about. The static snapshot viewpoint of Renoir has thus given way to a *dynamic* configuration—suggestive of movement—in which, as in relativity theory, space and time have merged. Conflicting light sources, suggesting multiple perspectives, are presented within a color scheme that verges on the monochromatic. Figuration, although not abandoned altogether, has been severely subordinated to the abstract geometry of rectangles, trapezoids, and semicircles. The painting, far from attempting to create an illusion of an actual scene, constantly moves in and out of being an autonomous object in its own right, creating its own level of reality and obeying its own internal aesthetic logic. A crucial dimension of this logic, which is representative of the intelligence embedded in the idea-space of cubism as a whole, is the way in which the painting is structured so as to enable the viewer to spontaneously generate patterns of meaning. The viewer shifts from being a passive spectator to an active participant in constructing the painting's interpretation.

Looking at the painting more closely, for example, we notice, in addition to various schematically depicted objects (exteriors walls, doorways, windows), several words displayed quite prominently: *Pernod* across the top of a bottle, *Leon* inscribed on a billboard in bold cursive script, and near the bottom of the painting, *Kub 10c*. Words in fact appear repeatedly in cubist paintings—brand names, numerals, shop signs, and various parts of newspapers. As in the case of other forms of figuration, words and letters move in and out of representing something and becoming aesthetic objects in their own right, integrated into the remaining abstract forms.

This use of letters in cubist iconography, as Rosenblum points out, bears directly on the central issues of how painting relates to the real world and the role of the viewer in shaping how the artwork is experienced.[28] In the case of Renoir's painting, life is depicted with sufficient realism to give the illusion of actuality, leaving the viewer with little to do except passively gaze at it. In Picasso's painting, on the other hand, objects are not so much depicted as *denoted by means of a visual sign*. A flat rectangle with writing on it stands for a billboard, a line in the shape of an inverted J for an archway. Cubist forms thus point to objects in roughly the same way that words do—not by means of realistic figural representation but via visual signs. We are left to read their meanings into them, aided by motifs such as bottles, glasses, archways, and musical instruments that are used over and over. The viewer, in other words, actively shapes the meanings of the painting.

What are we to make of all this? From one perspective, cubism looks like an enormous impoverishment of the rich language of classical figurative painting. "What a loss to French art!" a Russian collector remarked on seeing *Les Demoiselles d'Avignon.*[29] Yet in breaking decisively with the five-hundred-year-old tradition of depicting the illusion of real life, cubism inaugurated a new era. As one critic put it, "This is the moment of liberation from which the whole future of the plastic arts in the Western World was to radiate in all its diversity."[30]

Cubism shifted from realistic representation to the spontaneous generation of implicit meanings for viewers themselves to discover, play with, and even elaborate. Far from being an impoverishment of art's expressive powers, cubism in fact *opened up a vast new array of possibilities*. In the process, it changed forever the idea-space in which art evolves. Its new grammar of abstraction, flattening, fragmentation, analytical decomposition of objects, simultaneous perspectives, and multiple ambiguities made possible an immense enrichment of meaning along manifold dimensions, as well as a deepening and broadening of art's metaphysical content.

The constant interplay between elements on different levels, allowing simultaneous meanings (visual and verbal puns) to coexist and multiply, enriched art with irony, humor, and ambivalence. By the same token, it radically undermined any simple reliance on a literal, unitary interpretation of perception. Time and space became integrated in a single flattened plane. Paintings seemed to flip back and forth between semiabstract objects creating their own reality and semifigurational works pulling the viewer back into the real world. Indeed, a typical cubist painting seemed quite profligate in the levels of reality it engendered: almost completely abstract, geometric denotation (a cube for a building), semiaccurate figuration (bottles, buildings, doorways), accurately drawn symbols (letters/words), and finally the intrusion of real objects (collage).

Cubism's witty permutations of these levels and elements and its deliberate use of commonplace objects may seem playful, but it effectively initiated a complete metaphysical reframing of art from the ground up, raising questions destined to shape the progress of art for decades to come: How does a work of art relate to the real world? How is perceptual space organized? What is the role of the viewer—passive spectator or engaged participant, continuously constructing and reconstructing an artwork's meaning? What are a painting's borders, where does art stop and the real world begin, what is inside versus outside the frame?

The depth, range, and power of the revolutionary cubist aesthetics and metaphysics, embodied visually in the radically new space it created for the artistic imagination to unfold in, lies in its discovery of a universal truth about the fundamental calculus of creativity. In effect, cubist art exploits a version of the law of spontaneous generation. Identifiable elements in a painting form a network of related elements (visual resonances and analogies, verbal puns, etc.) that invite the viewer to construct out of them a series of meaningful patterns. Furthermore, as each pattern emerges, it subtly shifts the relationships among the remaining patterns, giving rise to still larger patterns (consider how the recognition of a sexual pun in the middle of a painting might change the interpretation of other elements). Thus in a cubist painting, what shapes the viewer's aesthetic experience is the ongoing generation of meaning that is spontaneous, emergent, and self-transforming. By cocreating with the viewer multiple layers of meaning, this new grammar of painting enabled art to express more authentically the multidimensionality and complexity of human experience.

Cubism vastly enriched the idea-space of twentieth-century art—for artists and viewers alike. In the process it launched a highly energized wave of change that continued to sweep through art over the next seventy years, from constructivism and the Dutch De Stijl movement to conceptualism and pop art.

As any art history textbook will tell you, cubism was invented by Braque and Picasso. The workings of genius in this achievement are not to be denied. But let's ask Kauffman's intriguing question: Whence this order? Did it spring fully formed from the heads of Braque and Picasso? Are they alone responsible for one of the greatest revolutions in the history of art? Or were there, in Kauffman's phrase, "vast veins of spontaneous order" lying at hand that Braque and Picasso discovered and mined? In short, was the new order cubism represented in reality an example of *coevolutionary change*, the spontaneous and emergent result of two painters of genius interacting with the laws of self-organization?

The foregoing analysis of cubism suggests precisely that. The break cubism made with the past was above all a break with realistic representation in favor of abstraction. Not the purely nonrepresentational abstraction of Kandinsky, but a much more analytic, formal, *geometric* abstraction. That this occurred at the very same time that Einstein was overthrowing Newton by reintroducing geometry into physics, while simultaneously undermining our commonsense faith in the reality depicted by falling apples, is no mere coincidence, as Arthur I. Miller has brilliantly demonstrated in his recent book, *Einstein, Picasso*.[31]

It was part of Picasso's genius to have intuitively recognized very early the significance of this historic scientific shift. Furthermore, once the basic move to abstraction had been made, much else followed almost automatically. Abstract form, like mathematics itself, proved to be a rich generative engine. *There are always more sets of things than things.* Picasso and Braque, influenced by radical new theories in mathematics and physics that destroyed the unity of a single perspective, discovered this for themselves, and then created an art that allowed the viewer to discover it too. In an abstract space, relationships come to the fore and spontaneously multiply.

Each new element adds value well beyond its intrinsic content, interacting with all the other elements in the picture. The result could be chaos, of course, subjecting the viewer to a dizzying calculus of forms, only a small subset of them meaningful. In reality, Picasso and Braque avoid that pitfall for the most part (though some of Picasso's late cubist paintings flirt dangerously with it) by carefully educating the viewer's eye to notice certain fairly obvious sets of relations first. This has the effect of progressively building a *model* of meaningful relations in the viewer's mind that can then be used to seek and recognize more subtle visual and linguistic plays while disregarding meaningless ones. The mind seems innately programmed to seek the same patterns over and over. *The fit get fitter.*

Cubism broke with a five-century-old tradition of figurative art by reaching out to a science that was becoming radically more abstract and geometric, and in the process overturning our commonsense view of the world. This move created a *weak tie* that connected art with a whole domain of thought that was far removed from it. And just as weak ties turn out to be better at getting you a new job than your immediate circle of friends, so they are better at producing creative breakthroughs. Connecting to the hotspot of early-twentieth-century physics and the focus on abstract geometric form that it triggered released an avalanche of new ideas into the art world, ideas that spontaneously multiplied and are still playing themselves out. Creative ideas frequently lead to exponential growth. What hasn't always been grasped is that, conversely, under the right circumstances *the exponential growth of ideas can lead to creative breakthroughs.*

THE EXTENDED MIND AND NETWORKED IDEA-SPACES

We began the chapter by asking whether there might be a connection between spontaneous generation and the emergence of order out of disorder that leads to creative leaps. The law of spontaneous generation, supported at a theoretical level by the insights of Cantor, Metcalfe, and Kauffman, suggests that there is. In dynamic networks of relationships, meaningful order arises freely and naturally. The laws of fitness ensure that such order both increases in internal coherence (i.e., becomes still more meaningful) and expands externally. Creative individuals ranging from Picasso and Braque to Jobs and Wozniak to Shawn Fanning and other architects of the new economy have intuitively found multiple ways to exploit this, ingeniously creating webs of structures related in such a way that the laws of the extended mind enable them to drive their own further transformation.

The focus of this chapter has been on how the law of spontaneous generation, abetted by the laws of fitness, can be seen as operating in the emergence of new order within idea-spaces such as art, computing, and so forth, even at the level of an individual painting. But there's also a broader—and *parallel*—point to be taken in here. Just as viewers of a Picasso cubist painting are aided in their creative interpretation of the work by the dynamic structure of the space they are contemplating, so Picasso and Braque weren't exclusively responsible for the creative leaps they made. Like Jobs and Wozniak, they made use of weak ties to idea-spaces whose embedded intelligence helped drive their thinking. The Apple duo connected to mainstream business. The cubist pioneers (particularly Picasso) discovered a weak tie to the new science of space-time being developed by Einstein and Poincaré. Relativity says that there are multiple ways of analyzing an event in the physical universe, depending on the position and speed of the observer. Using their imaginative intelligence, Picasso and Braque adapted this insight to the world of painting, producing the greatest revolution since the discovery of perspective. With great insight, they recognized the connection between the way the new physics was transforming commonsense notions of reality and the way art could similarly transform our conventional conception of realistic figurative art. In geometric abstraction they found the source that could feed their own (and the viewer's) imagination with endless new meaningful forms and patterns. Once again, it was the space of ideas itself that was doing most of the thinking, spontaneously producing new space for the human imagination to engage with creatively.

In similar fashion (as we'll see in greater detail in chapter 10), the pioneering entrepreneurs of the new economy did not invent their ideas from scratch, but found in other idea-spaces—notably computer networking (Metcalfe's law), chip manufacture (Moore's law), and economic theory (Romer's principle of increasing returns)—the intelligence they needed to create novel idea-spaces of their own. As these ideas combined and recombined in varying ways, a vast array of new possibilities began to emerge that eager, ambitious twenty-somethings and their VC backers developed into a plethora of new kinds of business.

The spaces of the extended mind are alive with possibilities. Creative breakthroughs arise through the law-governed, emergent, self-organizing unfolding of the extended mind itself, coevolving with the best choices of the inspired, gifted, or accidentally fortunate. Emergent order for free lightens the burden of creativity. Interestingly, cubism succeeded; the new economy largely failed. As the fate of many of its hopeful enterprises (and twenty years earlier the rapid demise of Apple's competitors) showed, only certain combinations of elements work. Not every possible configuration turns out to be a game that makes sense. But how to find just those that are meaningful? That, as they say in network science, is the all-important issue of *navigation*.

Chapter Seven

SEX AND THE SINGLE DOLL

Barbie, Ruth Handler,
and the Navigation Problem

The acts of finding and creating are exactly identical;
there is no conceptual difference.

—Kevin Kelly[1]

That Barbie is a genius.

—Jane Smiley[2]

What does it take to see the potential in a pornographic doll based on a risqué cartoon about a German tart, and transform her into the very embodiment of the All-American Girl? How do you turn an 11.5-inch piece of polyvinyl into one of the most successful toys of all time, in the process making her into an icon of American popular culture? Against the odds, Ruth Handler and her design team at Mattel successfully pulled off this difficult trick. Their creation, Barbie, has delighted children for decades while infuriating her many critics. Feminists have derided her, angry artists have pounded nails into her, and anxious mothers have refused to let their daughters play with her, but Mattel has laughed all the way to the bank. The diminutive doll is now a $3 billion-a-year business.

Barbie's vital statistics are impressive. The average American girl owns ten. She and her plastic friends are now sold in one hundred fifty countries—significantly more than McDonald's Big Mac—although she's been banned in

Saudi Arabia for indecent attire and condemned in Iran. Globally her brand recognition is right up there with Mickey Mouse and Coca-Cola. Largely on the basis of sales of Barbie and her myriad accessories, Mattel, founded in a Los Angeles garage in the late 1930s, is now one of the largest toy companies in the world—the doll's clothes alone make Mattel the fourth-largest manufacturer of women's garments in the United States. After Barbie was launched at the New York American Toy Fair in March 1959, in the first year of production alone, sales topped 350,000. Ten years later, they approached 80 million, and today they are well over 1 billion.

Barbie started life as a teenage fashion model, and still adds over a hundred items to her wardrobe annually. But even though she owns more shoes than Imelda Marcos, she's no mere fashion plate. Since her debut she's had more than eighty careers, including nurse, paleontologist, pilot, astronaut, and veterinarian. In spite of this busy life, she still found time to win a gold medal in the 1976 Innsbruck Winter Olympics. In 1992 she ran for president on a platform of opportunities for girls, educational excellence, and animal rights.[3]

It's easy to laugh at her, but the fact is Barbie is one of the great business and cultural success stories of the past fifty years. When Ruth Handler died in 2002, she earned a front-page obituary in the *New York Times*, as well as a full-page one in *The Economist*. How did Handler and her colleagues at Mattel pull off such a masterly piece of innovation? How did they make the initial breakthrough, and how did they manage to sustain a near exponential rate of growth over the next four and a half decades? Was it luck, being in the right place at the right time with the right product, management savvy, marketing brilliance, Ruth Handler's sheer genius, a combination of these? Or, underneath all this, were some deeper principles at work? The answers will help address a central question in any exploration of creative breakthroughs: How does an agent of any kind—a scientist, entrepreneur, company, even an emerging trend—somehow find the path to success in a maze of possible alternatives? Simply put, this is the navigation issue.

THE LAW OF NAVIGATION

Creative people deal in future possibilities. We can think of this set of possibilities as a network, with each node representing a possible product, service, invention, or discovery, in effect a tiny idea-space with its own embedded intelligence. Links constitute the various relationships between nodes (e.g., similarity and difference, closeness and distance), as determined by their varying characteristics.

As Kevin Kelly, *Wired* magazine editor at large, astutely notes, creating and finding are the same thing. (Kelly has etymology on his side: the root meaning of *invent* is "to find," from Latin *invenire*.) Thus if we think about possibilities as nodes in a network, then success entails dealing effectively with the *law of navigation*:

THE LAW OF NAVIGATION

In an open, dynamic network, identifying a potentially useful pattern (form of intelligence embedded in an idea-space) increases in difficulty as a function of the size of the search space of possibilities.

Most innovation is incremental. In business, for example, a new product or type of product is often simply a fairly linear extension of an existing one. Recently, for instance, my daughter Elizabeth, formerly an avid Barbie fan, has switched allegiance to Bratz dolls, the first line to seriously challenge Barbie's market supremacy. While Bratz dolls reveal a number of interesting new features, including large heads with expressive and ethnically diverse faces, small torsos, and an intense focus on fashion (not to mention a sassy attitude), in the final analysis they represent a fairly typical case of competitive incremental innovation.[4] In such cases (and examples can be found in most industries), the overall search space for innovation is relatively small. The navigation problem—finding just that node or set of nodes in the network of possibilities that will translate into success—can typically be solved through step-by-step tinkering, trying one thing after another until the right formula is found. The set of possibilities is restricted by its strong ties to what has preceded it.

Genuine creative leaps, involving a clear break with the past typically followed by explosive, sustained growth, are quite different from a navigational perspective. The entrepreneur dreams that somewhere out there, in the realm of possibilities, is a very different world, a new idea-space characterized by its own distinct form of embedded intelligence. Like Columbus setting sail for what he thought were the Indies, the entrepreneur is often not quite sure what or where this new world is, and may eventually wind up in a different place from the one he or she was aiming for.

In network terms, the problem is that creative leaps characteristically involve weak ties, and these multiply possibilities to the point where the linear approach used in incremental innovation would become a tedious and hopelessly ineffective strategy. The law of spontaneous generation ensures that, as more possible weak ties are included in the search space, the set of possibilities, even when restricted to those that are at least meaningful, threatens to become unmanageably large.

The conventional wisdom is that successful breakthroughs arise from a combination of luck and talent. Luck is almost invariably an element in one form or another, but talent raises the troubling issue, talent for what? We're in danger here of falling back on the Longinian/Romantic notion in which genius somehow draws forth the new from its own inner creative resources. The mystery of creativity becomes all the greater when, as in the case of Barbie, the creative leap turns into enduring success in the marketplace. Even *The Economist* professed puzzlement at such durability. Noting that Barbie (now well into her fifth decade) had long outlived her original competition, it commented: "No one has been able to say why, not even Ruth Handler . . . Longevity in toyland is as much a mystery as it is in real life."[5]

So how did Barbie's creators, faced with myriad possibilities for revolutionizing the doll industry, find just the right path through the maze? How does anyone with a bright idea navigate their way to success in a crowded, highly competitive marketplace? The answer throws further light on the interactions of the imaginative faculties with networked idea-spaces: skill in finding weak ties between distant spaces; identifying areas of emergent fitness; looking for feedback loops between elements of embedded intelligence; and more generally, letting the space of ideas and network dynamics do the hardest thinking. Let's look at Barbie's development in a little more detail.

A REAL DOLL

The story has been told many times, and the details vary, but basically it goes like this. Like many a born entrepreneur, Ruth Handler was forever imagining possible new products. During the mid-1950s she repeatedly urged executives at Mattel (founded by herself and her husband Elliot) to expand their product range in the toy business. One day, spotting her daughter Barbara playing with her paper dolls, she thought she saw a good way to do this.

Dolls are probably the most ancient playthings. Painted wooden ones dating from 3000–2000 BC have been found in Egyptian graves, and a fragment of a Babylonian alabaster doll even possessed movable arms.[6] Dolls that could speak, walk, and move their eyes all date from the nineteenth century. Traditionally, dolls had always been tiny replicas of adults, but in the 1820s, the French started making baby dolls.[7] Adult dolls continued to be produced, but the majority of dolls sold to American children after World War II were babies. Popular models included the Kewpie doll, Betsy Wetsy, Ginny dolls, Vogue fashion dolls, and the ubiquitous Madame Alexander dolls. Typically measuring eight to twelve inches, they had baby faces, thick bodies, flat chests, fat legs, and cute period costumes.

Barbara Handler wasn't much into baby dolls. Instead, she and her friends liked to act out stories with paper dolls. Unlike their three-dimensional counterparts, these could quickly change clothes and hence roles. Furthermore, the paper dolls they preferred invariably represented *adult* characters, not children or babies. Observing Barbara and her friends at play, an idea took shape in Ruth's watchful mind:

> They were using these dolls to project their dreams of their own futures as adult women. So one day it hit me: Wouldn't it be great if we could take that play pattern and three-dimensionalize it so that little girls could do their dreaming and role-playing with real dolls and real clothes instead of the flimsy paper or cardboard ones? It dawned on me that this was a basic, much needed play pattern that had never before been offered by the doll industry to little girls.[8]

After mulling things over, she floated the idea of making an adult doll to Mattel's male executives, but they reacted coolly, claiming that such a doll would be too costly to make. Ruth was convinced that in reality they were all horrified by the idea of making a doll with breasts.

The breakthrough came on the family's first vacation in Europe, during the summer of 1956. Barbara, then fifteen, became fascinated with a set of adult dolls, all wearing different outfits, in the window of a toy store in Lucerne. Ruth instantly recognized in them a model of the doll she'd been imagining, and decided to buy one. It turned out the dolls didn't come with changeable outfits as she'd hoped, so when Barbara saw another one she liked in Vienna, Ruth bought that one too.

It was only later that Ruth found out what she had brought home . . .

LILLI

The *Bild* Lilli, as the doll Handler purchased was known, started out life as a cartoon by Reinhard Beuthien in the German newspaper *Bild Zeitung* (see figure 7-1). Begun on June 24, 1952,

> Lilli's cartoon antics fit right in with the *Bild Zeitung's* sordid, sensational stories. A gold-digger, exhibitionist, and floozy, she had the body of a Vargas Girl, the brains of Pia Zadora, and the morals of Xaviera Hollander. Beuthien's jokes usually hinged on Lilli taking money from men and involved situations in which she wore very few clothes. Male wealth was of far greater interest to Lilli than male looks; she flung herself repeatedly at balding, jowly fat cats.[9]

In August 1955, the veteran Bavarian toymaker Greiner & Hauser GmbH issued Lilli as an 11.5-inch doll, to be sold mainly in smoke shops. The target

FIGURE 7-1

Bild Lilli

The caption reads: "Your impatience is unbearable—I've been saying for half an hour I'll be ready in a second."

Source: Axel Springer AG, Bild Zeitung, Hamburg, Germany. http://zenzo.de/homepage/cartoons. Used with permission.

market certainly wasn't young girls. Men hung Lilli on their dashboards, leered at her, and even gave her to their girlfriends.

Chance favors the prepared mind. Less than a year after the Lilli doll appeared, Ruth Handler saw one and took it home with her, and a radical idea that had been germinating for years emerged into full bloom. As a marketable product, Barbie has four differentiating characteristics. First, she is a *posable* doll. Although her range of movement increased dramatically with the introduction in 1967 of the Twist 'N Turn doll, Barbie was from the outset intended as a doll to be bent into various attitudes, rather than cuddled or taken to bed. Second, she is designed as a *mannequin*, a diminutive piece of plastic specifically intended to model multiple outfits to their best advantage. This makes her far more dynamic and interactive, allowing her to switch roles or even identities in no more time than it takes to undo a few tiny buttons and zippers. Third, she is an *adult*, connecting the child's fantasy to a world she interacts with constantly, but rarely if ever controls.

In themselves, none of these first three characteristics is especially revolutionary. Most baby dolls had limbs that allowed at least some movement. And costume dolls had always represented little mannequins, so making their outfits interchangeable wasn't such a big step. Furthermore, the Miss Revlon doll produced by Ideal Toy and Novelty Corporation in 1956 was intended as an adult fashion doll, as signified by its "incipient breasts,"[10] although it retained a babyish face and thick limbs. Possibly a competitor to Miss Revlon was what Handler initially had in mind. But then Lilli showed up. Enter factor number four.

Sex isn't all that Barbie is about, but it's a sizable chunk of it. M. L. Lord, in her engaging and insightful book, *Forever Barbie: The Unauthorized Biography of a Real Doll*, remarks that to children, including herself, Barbie's body looked "terrifying yet beguiling; as charged and puzzling as sexuality itself."[11] Yona Zeldis McDonough confesses that "at six, I inchoately understood Barbie's appeal: pure sex. My other dolls were either babies or little girls, with flat chests and chubby legs . . . Barbie was clearly a woman doll, and a woman was what I longed to be." She adds that in play with other girls' Barbies, "mostly they stripped, showing off their amazing, no-way-in-the-world human bodies."[12]

In this jaded, sex-saturated age, it's hard to realize just how big a risk Handler was taking.[13] Sears at first wouldn't touch the doll, considering it too sexy (though it later repented, even selling a genuine mink Barbie stole for $9.99). Mattel executives continued to drag their feet. At the New York Toy Fair in the spring of 1959, Barbie essentially flopped. Only 25 percent of Mattel's usual buyers ordered the doll in any quantity, and 50 percent would have nothing to do with her. In classic fashion, the mainstream, faced with a brilliant entrepreneurial breakthrough, was barefacedly dismissive. "Ruth, little girls want baby dolls. They want to pretend to be mommies," one executive exclaimed. But as Handler herself notes, like Mattel's designers nearly a decade earlier, "the buyers' biggest objection to Barbie . . . was her most prominent feature: 'Ruth, mothers will never buy their daughters a doll that has . . .'—cough, cough."[14] The *New York Times* predicted that Mattel's hottest item would be "a yard-long, two-stage plastic rocket which soars to about 200 feet" (an item, incidentally, that represented navy missile designer Jack Ryan's main effort that year—shortly thereafter he would switch his attention to Barbie herself). Barbie, the *Times* noted, was mostly intended by Mattel to "balance the heavy male emphasis in toy guns."[15]

Barbie succeeded anyway. Retail sales were slow at first, but by summer when school was out, the dolls flew off the shelves, racking up over a third of a million sold in the first twelve months.

BARBIE'S MAGIC GIRDLE
AND THE GRAMMAR OF GLAMOUR

When Ruth Handler saw Lilli, she could have played it safe, turning her into a three-dimensional version of paper-doll nurses, teachers, and mothers. Instead, she took her for what she was—a glamorous sex symbol—and began integrating her into the idea she'd had all along for a young adult doll. In serendipitously finding and then exploiting a weak tie to a complex, highly volatile idea-space about as far away from the world of baby dolls as you could get, she took a huge risk that paid off brilliantly. What was her intuition in touch with that made her so confident she could succeed? Did she consciously or unconsciously recognize some pattern of embedded intelligence that eluded others (Mattel continued for a time to resist the idea)? There's a tiny but significant clue to Barbie's enduring, universal appeal to be found in the doll's very first wardrobe.

Among the twenty-two pieces of clothing Barbie was launched with on that warm March day in 1959 were three items of underwear: two strapless bras and a girdle. Given Barbie's miniature thirty-nine-inch bust and preference for dresses that showed off her boyishly broad shoulders, the bras are understandable. But a *girdle*? If ever there was a girl who didn't need one, it was Barbara Millicent Roberts (to give the doll her full name). Moreover, it's unlikely most three- to ten-year-old girls (the target market) ever put the girdle on her.[16] But it wasn't little girls Mattel had in mind when they included it. *It was their mothers.*

When Ruth Handler was asked many years later what the secret of her success was, she simply said, "I was a marketing genius."[17] She was. But she had the sense to back up her intuitions with the best professional market research available, and in the late 1950s, that meant Ernest Dichter, head of the Institute for Motivational Research in Croton-on-Hudson, New York. Dichter, in case you've forgotten, was the man excoriated by Betty Friedan in *The Feminine Mystique* for manipulating housewives (he also plays a central role in Vance Packard's 1957 classic, *The Hidden Persuaders*). Dichter, whose six-month study for Mattel included watching children play from behind a one-way mirror, confirmed Ruth's intuition: kids loved Barbie, but mothers *hated* her. As one mother of an eight-year-old put it:

> . . . *my daughter would be fascinated. She loves dolls with figures. I don't think I would buy this for that reason. It has too much of a figure. (SHE STARED AT THE DOLL FOR A LONG TIME.) . . . I'm sure she would like to have one, but I wouldn't buy it. All these kids talk about is how the teachers jiggle . . . Maybe the bride doll is O.K., but not the one with the sweater.*[18]

Since mothers were the ones doing the buying, Mattel had a real problem on its hands. But Dichter devised a deviously clever answer: convince the mother that the doll's beautifully designed, intricately detailed costumes would teach the child to be well groomed. Marketing should focus on "awakening in the child a concern with proper appearance."[19] Mattel took Dichter's advice, hired Max Factor's advertising agency, and launched Barbie as a fashion model.

Although Lord professes to be puzzled by Barbie's need for a girdle, as she herself notes earlier, part of Ruth Handler's genius lay in her recognition that "if any one character trait distinguishes the American middle class, both today and in 1959, it is an obsession with respectability."[20] Respectable mothers wore girdles, and made sure their daughters—in training to be, as Dichter put it, "a poised little lady,"—did too.[21]

As any reader acquainted with classical Greek mythology knows, however, the girdle has resonances that go far beyond the need to compress the flesh. Writers aiming to invest Barbie with a mythological dimension often connect her with Venus, but the Roman goddess of love and beauty suffers from a supreme flaw in the place she has come to occupy in the Western mind: she is almost invariably depicted *naked* (Botticelli's famous picture being the primary source and representative of this tradition), making her physical beauty the overwhelming point of focus. Venus is in fact (or perhaps more accurately, has become) a much reduced version of her more complex Greek incarnation, Aphrodite.[22]

Ruth Handler may not have been that well versed in classical mythology, but she was too good a marketer not to have recognized the reemergence in the late fifties of the double aspect of the feminine the Greek goddess offered. Feminist critics have often attacked Barbie as an embodiment of the beauty myth, but in doing so they miss other dimensions of her character that in one form or another can be traced back to Aphrodite. In fact, the list of connections is surprisingly long. Aphrodite, goddess of love, beauty, desire, marriage, and fertility, was parentless: she was born when Kronos (Time), at the urging of his mother Ge (Earth), castrated his father Uranus (Sky/Heaven) with a sickle and cast his severed genitals into the sea (*Aphrodite* means "foamborn").[23] She has a cripple, the lame Hephaestus, for a consort, and a "bad" side that blatantly exploits her beauty and sex appeal in the successful pursuit of her own sensual gratification and love affairs. Through her priestesses, she is associated with sacred harlotry. As one popular book on Aphrodite (part of the new age *goddess* vogue) puts it, the goddess is "alchemical," possessed of magical powers that "promote growth, change, and transformation" through the seductive capacity of love and beauty.[24] She "always had the freedom of choice," and "promotes curiosity [and] generosity of the heart." She "makes others feel wonderful in her presence . . . encourages change and development all around her," but is often "misinterpreted as frivolous and shallow."[25] Aphrodite's most famous characteristic is of course her allure—her seductiveness and capacity for enticement—whose powers reside in her magic girdle.[26]

Ruth Handler was blessed with having been born before the new age goddess cult took off. But the instant she laid eyes on Lilli, she must have been struck by the immense attractive power of a figure—as yet only dimly perceived in her mind's eye—that could incorporate glamorous sexual appeal alongside more conventional feminine virtues. The ancient Greeks imbued

Aphrodite with precisely this double nature, and intentionally or not, Barbie reflects it. Consider the parallels (see table 7-1).

The girdle that came with Barbie forms a resonant (if on Mattel's part probably unwitting) link between the doll and the goddess, both of whom in their own ways represent an ambivalent view of woman. If Barbie's success and popularity are any indicator, then the Aphrodite myth (or at any rate the cultural and social intuitions underlying it) is alive and well, reincarnated in 11.5 inches of well-dressed plastic. On that fateful day in Lucerne when Ruth Handler first saw Lilli, she recognized the doll's power to enormously expand her initial idea-space, and the tremendous opportunities this opened up. The task now was to make her vision real.[27]

Aphrodite rose from the waves naked but fully formed. Barbie, however, took some years to reach her mature, iconic form and character. The various stages of development she went through reveal how skillfully Mattel, with the help of its marketing team, zeroed in on the formula for success in a vast space of myriad possibilities. Professional marketers such as Dichter, whatever their actual familiarity with Greek mythology, were no slouches when it came to figuring out how archetypes such as Aphrodite manifested in mod-

TABLE 7-1

Parallels between the Aphrodite myth and Barbie

	Aphrodite	Barbie
Positive qualities	Goddess of beauty, love, desire	Icon of beauty, desirability
	Promotes transformation	Role model for girls to have choices, pursue their dreams
	Generous heart	Helps her friends
	Alluring, charismatic, adored by men and women	Little girls adore her
Negative qualities	Goddess of sacred harlotry	Modeled on a sluttish German cartoon figure/doll
	Seen as frivolous, changeable, unfaithful, promiscuous	Seen as frivolous, changeable, shallow
	Constantly changes	Addicted to variety, constantly changes outfits, shops for new ones
Other	Parentless	Parentless (famously has no navel; no parent doll figures)
	Combines female qualities with male ones (bold, independent, free, born of castrated male genitalia); has an androgynous child with Hermes	Seems to embody male, as well as female, characteristics: bold, independent, "her own person," free
	Husband is a cripple, weak	Main squeeze is dorky, emasculated
	Lover is Ares, god of war	Has a serious flirtation with G.I. Joe
	Has a magic girdle	Has a girdle

ern culture, and it seems clear that they used this idea-space as a guide as they progressively solved the navigation problem.

FITNESS, FEEDBACK LOOPS, AND THE INTEGRATION
OF EMBEDDED INTELLIGENCE

In the world of toy dolls, Barbie represents a huge tipping point that permanently changed the industry. As we saw in previous chapters, such transformations occur in part as the result of increasing fitness built by feedback loops. These operate between elements of intelligence embedded in separate idea-spaces that have been linked by one or more weak ties. In more everyday language, this process is the *integration* of idea-spaces, the natural outcome of the law of the fit get fitter. Picasso integrated African art into his own; Crick and Watson fit empirical data drawn from highly diverse fields into a unified model of DNA; home computer pioneers successfully incorporated various aspects of the mainstream computer industry within the design limitations of a mass-market microcomputer. Mattel's challenge was to achieve, step-by-step, an integration of the two wildly opposed poles of Barbie's emerging character: her wholesomeness and her sex appeal.[28] One of the first steps in this process of integration was to design her face.

Fitness rarely comes into being instantaneously. Picasso, for example, made hundreds of drawings in the process of arriving at the arresting faces of the nude figures in *Les Demoiselles d'Avignon*, faces that jointly integrate the stern indifference of the African mask with the western tradition of the staring figure that engages the viewer directly (see figure 1-1).[29] It's instructive to see how Mattel, in navigating their way to the fully evolved form of Barbie familiar today, similarly worked their way through various different forms of her face. Originally, this was closely modeled on Lilli's (see figure 7-2).[30]

Notice the Marlene Dietrich arched eyebrows, the flirty, sideways-glancing eyes exaggerated by their white irises and heavy makeup, and the pouting red mouth. Jack Ryan, chief designer for Barbie's patented joint mechanisms, Raytheon Hawk missile engineer, and one-time husband of Zsa Zsa Gabor, described the first Barbie as looking like a "hooker or an actress between performances."[31] No wonder the mothers Dichter interviewed were ambivalent at best about giving Barbie to their daughters!

Over the next few years, Mattel progressively modified the face. By 1963, Barbie's eyes were significantly larger and looked straight ahead, and the coquettishly arched eyebrows were drawn more naturally. The face was gradually softened with bangs and eyelashes, and the nose made more child-like. By 1977 Barbie was given her so-called Superstar face, featuring very large, sparkling eyes and a broad smile.

FIGURE 7-2

Barbie's original face

Source: Patricia R. Smith, *Modern Collector's Dolls*
(Paducah, KY: Collector Books, 1995), 50. Used with
permission.

Barbie's face conveys a passage toward innocence, filling out the "good" side of the Aphrodite archetype. The slightly decadent sophistication of the Lilli-like original has been replaced by a childlike prettiness. The eyes in particular have the guileless look of a very young girl (see figure 7-3).[32]

In the mid-1960s, Mattel further fleshed out Barbie's wholesome, All-American-Girl image with a series of stories about Barbie helping her friends solve problems and resolve their upsets. One story even has Barbie trying to reconcile estranged parents with their children. Barbie embraced domesticity sufficiently to have a furnished apartment (though there's no evidence of her ever stooping to doing household chores). She acquired a steady if dorky boyfriend, Ken, although some girls seemed to follow Aphrodite's preference for Ares, the god of war, and set her up with G.I. Joe. And she went through a series of careers explicitly designed, as Ruth Handler put it, so that "little girls could have choices about their futures."[33]

FIGURE 7-3

**Sparkle-eyed Barbie (1991) with
Superstar Barbie face**

Source: Kitturah B. Westenhouser, *The Story of Barbie*
(Paducah, KY: Collector Books, 1994), 26. Used with
permission.

Alongside this goodness and innocence, however, Barbie was and still is a sex goddess (it is of course ironic, probably intentionally so on Mattel's part, that the most innocent face given to Barbie was introduced as the Superstar Barbie, connoting all the celebrity trappings of Hollywood sex goddesses). Barbie's feet are permanently molded for high heels. She frequently wears skimpy outfits that show off her curvaceous figure and long, slender legs. Naked, she is everything a prepubescent girl might dream of. As one early fan put it, "When, in 1962, I was presented with my first Barbie doll, I did what all the other little girls did with their Barbies: I took her clothes off. Wow! I could hardly wait to have a pair of my very own."[34]

Mattel may have gotten rid of Lilli's knowing, flirty face, but they kept her sexy body and a wardrobe that ranged from Chanel suits to lacy black negligees. Lilli also passed on to Barbie some of her promiscuity and gold-digging. In the early 1990s, Mattel authorized Western Publishing to produce a series of games, including Queen of the Prom and Barbie's Dream Date. Queen of the Prom has players competing on the basis of cars, clothes, looks, and boys. Collecting female friends slows a player down, while having a boyfriend is essential to winning. In Barbie's Dream Date, the point of the game is to get Ken to spend as much money as possible on his date before the clock strikes twelve. As Lord notes, "So similar is players' behavior to that of a call girl that it might more aptly be termed 'The Hooker Game.'"[35] Nor are games the only venue that give a glimpse of Barbie's darker side. In one aborted story for the 1984 Barbie magazine, a giggling Barbie tries to run over Ken in her pink Corvette![36]

From the start Mattel used the perceived polarities of the feminine, embodied in the Aphrodite myth but also in modern American culture, to narrow the search space to the point where a concrete, highly specified model of Barbie could emerge. It filed off the nipples her less prudish Japanese manufacturers placed on the prototype models, but made sure her ample bust was displayed to advantage. It created her as a career girl to empower little girls to dream of something beyond domestic drudgery, but also gave her a wardrobe and accessories (including a Porsche and a Ferrari) that made her the original Material Girl. It dressed her as a teenager moving into her twenties, clearly distinguishing her from the tradition of baby dolls, but then gave her a child's innocent face.

The success of Mattel's model as a navigation strategy can be judged by the dismal failure of its competitors. Who now remembers Bizzie Lizzie, Tammy, Tressy, or Dawn? Even though these toys had Barbie as a model to imitate, they largely failed to connect to any powerful or compelling cultural idea-spaces. Bizzy Lizzy, "clutch[ing] an iron in one hand and a mop in the other, was a drudge."[37] Tammy, brought out by Ideal Toy and Novelty Corporation in 1962 as a direct competitor to Barbie, came with parents and a brother, but no boyfriend. Even though she was marketed as a fashion doll with interchangeable clothes, and came with a car and other adult goods, she possessed the body of an eight-year-old. "Boring, sexless, and shackled to the moribund nuclear family," Lord notes, "Tammy bit the dust in the mid-sixties when the divorce rate took off."[38] Similar factors limited the market longevity of the others.[39]

But of course the best evidence of the creative power that lies in connecting to the right idea-spaces is surely to be found in Ken, Barbie's official consort. The simplest measure of Ken's failure is his price in the collectibles market—typically around $75, as compared with up to $10,000 for a Barbie of the same period. Many commentators have advanced explanations for Ken's failure, but the most basic reason is that he doesn't draw power from any clearly identifiable idea-spaces. Neither warrior nor prince, dorky, dull, and emasculated, Ken has had to content himself with existing as a minor node in Barbie's vast web of connections.

Looked at more closely, Mattel's method of navigation boils down to allowing the reciprocal fitness between the opposite elements of Barbie's personality to gradually emerge. Each positive element balanced a corresponding negative one, and as a pair they influenced each other by limiting one another's scope. This is true of both Barbie and her mythical model. Aphrodite is good, but not so good that she never strays from the path; she is powerful and independent but can still fall head-over-heels in love. In the same way, Barbie is sexy and glamorous, but not loose to the point where she becomes hard and cynical like Lilli. She is innocent and generous, but not so much so that she loses her independence. Mattel may have used this positive-negative tension (a form of reciprocal emergent fitness—the basic dynamic of the law of the fit get fitter) to create and progressively refine their product, but they did not need to invent it. In effect, it was already present in the culture as a well-developed, iconic idea-space.

If Barbie's inner coherence as a character was driven by the reciprocal effects of the law of the fit get fitter, then like the Apple II, her early exponential growth and ability to trounce her competition was largely driven by the law of the *fit get rich*, manifested in her capacity to satisfy a wide range of customers' needs in the context of emerging social trends. While feminist critics have rightly pointed out the unfairness of encapsulating messages about what it means to become a woman in the somewhat constrained framework of the Barbie icon, we must bear in mind that the late fifties and early sixties were marked by broad cultural and social changes that are both reflected and to some extent challenged in the Barbie model.

One was the redrawing of gender boundaries after World War II. Women were being encouraged, as the troops came home, to become housewives again, ceding the role of breadwinner back to the man of the house. This resulted in a significant loss of the power and independence working women had enjoyed during the war. At the same time, this was an era (contrary to our popular image of the repressed fifties) of burgeoning sexuality, manifested above all in clothes. Starting with Dior's New Look, which introduced the tight sweaters and cinched waists made memorable by Doris Day and Jayne Mansfield, women were encouraged to get rid of the drab forties look and start embracing glamour again. Such fashions granted women a measure of freedom, but within a male-dominated, sharply delineated model of gender roles. This attempt to get the sexual toothpaste back in the tube—women were allowed to look sexy, but only within the confines of marital bliss—had limited success, of course, and by the mid-1960s the divorce rate started climbing.

A second emerging trend of the period was consumerism, driven by prosperity and television advertising. Consumerism encouraged women to find an outlet for the frustrations of their domestic taming through shopping, not only for themselves but for their daughters. Mothers were encouraged to see in Barbie's glamorous outfits the means to train their female offspring to lay claim to their gender's inviolable birthright: to spend, spend, spend on glamorous clothes and accessories, and thus attract a husband who could afford to pay for this devil's bargain of supporting his wife's consumption in exchange for accepting a diminished gender role. The 1950s also saw the rise of the child as consumer. Mattel cleverly jumped on this trend, advertising Barbie and her glamorous accessories directly to children via Disney's television show, the Mickey Mouse Club.

Against this seeming exploitation of the negative side of the Aphrodite/femininity myth must be set Ruth Handler's insistence on giving little girls choices about their futures. In hindsight, feminist critiques notwithstanding, Handler seems to have been remarkably prescient in making Barbie a young woman who could do what she wanted, and who from the outset was a career woman. As scholars have noted, this freedom is a central characteristic of Aphrodite. Alone among the female goddesses, she was never violated, and even Zeus was afraid of her allure and persuasive powers. For young girls, as Handler seems to have recognized from the outset, Barbie was a connection through fantasy play to adulthood: independence from parents, glamorous careers that could bring financial independence, and above all, the alluring world of sex.

Ruth and Elliot Handler, Charlotte Johnson (her first fashion designer, and a Seventh Avenue veteran), Jack Ryan, Bud Westmore (Universal Pictures' makeup czar hired to give her face a makeover), Ernest Dichter, and the many other highly talented people who helped design Barbie and hence create the icon, didn't need to study the Aphrodite myth in detail to intuitively grasp its resurgent manifestation in postwar America. Mattel carefully built its model of Barbie over the formative period of the late fifties to midsixties, when she went from prototype to best-selling doll. Long before Dick Morris thought up triangulation for Bill Clinton, Mattel was using it to entice both daughters and their anxious mothers, cleverly exploiting the zeitgeist while also finding ways to transcend it. In choosing to let Barbie encapsulate the positive/negative aspects of the Aphrodite/femininity myth and its various contemporary manifestations, Mattel connected to a set of culturally embedded idea-spaces powerful enough to navigate by as the company progressively developed the doll's model.

NETWORKED BARBIE

Let's take a look at the overall network of idea-spaces from which Barbie emerged. Figure 7-4 identifies relationships between Barbie, her customers, and some of the embedded intelligence of the main idea-spaces to which Barbie is connected. The multiple dimensions of the model Mattel progressively discovered for developing Barbie clearly endowed her with many more ways of appealing to mothers and girls than her competitors. Furthermore, these dimensions possessed a high degree of fitness with the emerging late-fifties zeitgeist and its social and personal concerns. Again as in the case of the Apple II, this fitness clearly was accelerated by a series of feedback loops (indicated by the heavier lines) between the main hubs/idea-spaces. Thus the greater the emphasis on Barbie's sexuality and power, the more need there was to stress her innocent side, and vice versa. Correspondingly, the more Barbie embodied this dynamic polarity, the more she appealed to her two key market segments of young girls and mothers, and so the more sales rose, promoting a further round of development on Mattel's part.

The law of the fit get fitter ensured that over a period of years, Barbie became extremely well adapted to her core market, easily vanquishing the competition. By the same token, the reciprocal relationships driving the fitness loops in figure 7-4 had the effect of progressively narrowing the development space for Barbie. Each side of the polarity at the heart of Barbie's character acted as a delimiting context for the features that fell under the other, thus excluding certain sets of possibilities while subtly reinforcing others. The outcome was a highly specified design that successfully solved the navigation problem. This suggests a corollary to the law of navigation: the more sets of reciprocal relationships there are among hubs in an idea-space,

FIGURE 7-4

Idea-spaces from which Barbie emerged

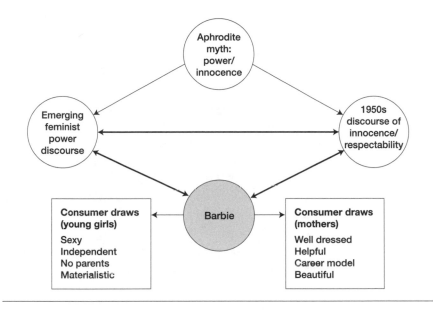

the more the set of possibilities defined by the space is limited and hence rendered more determinate.

Because Barbie is deeply embedded in a scale-free network (i.e., one in which large hubs predominate), her development and promotion were tipped from the start. Particularly in the early 1960s and again in the 1990s, her growth, driven by the twin laws of fitness, was exponential, with sales reflecting a kind of Barbie epidemic. For precisely inverse reasons, her competitors failed to tip, and so lasted just a year or two.

Entrepreneurs are natural navigators. Guided by intuition—especially for space-expanding patterns and emergent fitness—and with the measure of luck that belongs to the bold, they leap into spaces full of new possibilities in which their imagination can really go to work. Ruth Handler was no exception. After finding Lilli, she began aligning Barbie with one of the great female archetypes of Western culture, one whose polarized dynamics were once more being put in play by the social and cultural changes of the late fifties and early sixties. From that point on, the path Barbie would take would be determined less by Handler's innate genius than by the law-governed interplay among the nodes of intelligence embedded in that vibrant space of possibilities.

Idea-spaces that are deeply and pervasively embedded in the culture are enormous sources of energy and creativity. They spew forth myths, art, literature, social trends, ideas, products, movements—and still more idea-spaces. At times, their dynamic interplay becomes the hinge of history. Mattel's development of one of the most popular and profitable toys of all time certainly owes a measure of its success to the conventional elements of entrepreneurial achievement: hard work, attention to detail, hiring outstanding talent, quickness in recognizing an opportunity, willingness to take enormous risks, unshakable self-confidence, and innovative marketing. But the breakthrough itself and subsequent exponential growth are primarily the result of hooking up, partly by chance and partly by intuition and imagination, to a series of immensely powerful idea-spaces whose interaction was creating profound rifts and shifts in the zeitgeist of postwar America.

More than anything, what Handler and the Mattel designers, engineers, and marketers did was tune their intuition and imagination to the resonances of the web of ideas in which they found themselves. The true measure of their success is the doll's current status. Interminably derided (and praised) by feminists and other cultural critics, painted by artists ranging from Andy Warhol to William Wegman, Maggie Robbins, and Dean Brown, made into books and movies, Barbie has achieved the ultimate goal for a consumer product—more than a trusted brand or even an icon, *she has become her own idea-space*.[40]

SOME OTHER WAYS TO SOLVE THE NAVIGATION PROBLEM

Luck, and progressive model building guided by emergent fitness. That was how Crick and Watson navigated too, finding their way through the maze of possible structures for DNA to just the right one. Sometimes luck alone, a single happy accident, is sufficient. Sometimes the chances of getting lucky are increased by tinkering. Analogy and the pull of cultural or intellectual hotspots also act as guides along the mazelike path to invention and discovery. Before giving the law of navigation its final formulation, let's explore some of these other path-finding strategies.

Accidents

The myth of the heroic genius inclines us to believe that great acts of creativity arise from the sheer inner force of intellect and will. History tells a different story. One of the great turning points in modern art, for example, can be traced back to a chance occurrence that might easily not have happened. Returning from some outdoor sketching one day in 1908, Wassily Kandinsky opened the door to his studio: "I was suddenly confronted by a picture of indescribable and incandescent loveliness. Bewildered, I stopped, staring at it. The painting lacked all subject, depicted no identifiable object and was entirely composed of bright color-patches." Kandinsky had in fact merely failed to recognize one of his own paintings, left standing on its side. Mulling the incident over, however, Kandinsky was struck by an apocalyptic insight: "Objectiveness, the depiction of objects, needed no place in my paintings, and was indeed harmful to them."[41] Thus by chance was abstract art born.

The history of creativity in the arts, science, and technology is littered with such moments. Repeatedly, a new space of possibilities opens up as the result of an accident. Alexander Fleming discovered penicillin after a petri dish containing *Staphylococcus* became accidentally contaminated, probably by a stray airborne mold spore from another lab.[42] In the early 1940s, Russell Ohl, a Bell Labs engineer, was experimenting with silicon to improve radio reception when he observed a piece with a crack down the middle. This particular piece had a curious photovoltaic property that none of his Bell colleagues had observed before: exposed to light, the current flowing between the two sides of the crack jumped significantly. Further research revealed that the crack was the dividing line between two impurities in the silicon, one with an excess of electrons, and the other with a deficit. The crack became known as the p-n (for positive/negative) junction, and led to the development of the first modern solar cells and the transistor.

On a more commonplace level, the annals of invention are replete with opportune mishaps, among them Coke, vulcanized rubber, and the Slinky toy. In nature, biologists now recognize that the contingencies of chance lie at the very heart of natural creativity, through the mechanism of random mutation. When it comes to human discovery, however, we tend to give them short shrift. Notice the key role played by intuition-driven insight in exploiting fortunate accidents. Kandinsky, for example, was open to finding a hidden pattern of significance in what he saw, a new way of making sense of what at first appeared merely random. Similarly, Fleming stopped to think about the meaning of the pattern of mold contamination he was looking at. Intuition, a core characteristic of those who achieve breakthrough creativity, is a deep capacity to seek and perceive patterns where others see only disorder.

Analogy

A purely linear, node-by-node search through a maze of possibilities is tedious and slow, and typically moves in straight lines, missing the "knight's jump" (to use a metaphor from chess) into a new space. Being open to exploiting providential accidents (representing the fortuitous linking together of elements embedded in previously unconnected spaces or networks) short-circuits the navigation process. So too does recognizing potent analogies—finding similarities in two otherwise unrelated areas. Gutenberg recognized in cheese and oil presses a mechanism for improving the cumbersome printing process of his day. After spotting a Holt Caterpillar tractor at work, Ernest Swinton invented the tank, solving the difficulties traditional wheeled vehicles encountered moving over trenches during World War I. In rolls of canvas lying around San Francisco harbor, Levi Strauss saw a solution to gold miners' pants that wore out too quickly. Velcro was invented by a Swiss engineer who, finding cockleburs clinging to his pants after a walk through the fields, put them under a microscope and saw tiny hooks that acted as remarkably efficient fastening mechanisms.

Using a horse-drawn plow to turn over a potato field, Philo T. Farnsworth, who had been thinking hard about a new concept electronic hobbyists were calling *television*, was struck by an idea: "An electron beam could create moving images by zipping back and forth across a phosphorescent screen—just as his plow was cutting furrows, only 1 million times as fast."[43] The sports bra was invented when two entrepreneurially minded women, horsing around with a couple of male jockstraps, suddenly recognized the basic design and need for a female athletic support.

Analogies can connect elements existing at a distance from one another, and are thus ideal mechanisms for exploiting the strength of weak ties. Again, the pattern-recognition powers of intuition are crucial. With the help of a little imagination, the similarities (i.e., fitness) uncovered allow the embedded intelligence of one space to solve a problem in another.

Tinkering

Associated with any given idea-space (including not just ideas themselves but products and their uses, services, etc.), there invariably exists a community of tinkerers who, both individually and collectively, grope their way to inventing something new. In effect, tinkering is a low-level navigation strategy, randomly testing different combinations of links spewed out by the law of spontaneous generation. Success often depends as much on chance—suddenly stumbling on the right combination—as any inherent skill. Watson tinkered with different combinations of bases before he suddenly found himself looking at one that worked. Tinkering can also be dangerous, however. Mattel carefully developed a market research–based model in designing Barbie. Their competitors, lacking such a model, tried tinkering with the basic idea and failed.

When tinkering does produce genuine breakthroughs, it is often as a result of chancing to wander into what Kauffman calls the *adjacent possible*—a nearby space of unexploited possibilities.[44] Consider mountain bikes. Three decades ago, they were used only by a handful of small fringe groups who had developed them in piecemeal fashion in an effort to design an off-road bike. They now account for 50 percent of all bikes sold in the United States. The development of the basic design and its subsequent progressive modification illustrate how an innovative new product can emerge spontaneously as the result of *mass tinkering* by a loosely connected community of users.[45] If market conditions are just right (in this case, the emergence of mountain bikes coincided with the onset of the jogging/fitness craze), then the law of the fit get rich will kick in, the market will tip, and exponential growth will follow.

Tinkering is basically an ongoing source of new input into an open network of idea-spaces. In one way or another, the laws governing the dynamics of such spaces will apply, leading to the emergence of an inherently unpredictable new combination of elements.

Sometimes tinkering applies not so much to the invention or innovation itself as to its application. The zipper, for example, was originally invented as a means of sealing bales of grain for shipment. It took another twenty years for someone to adapt it for use in clothes—the first such breakthrough in the fashion industry in centuries. Similarly, Edison expected the phonograph to be used to record people's dying words and teach spelling. The idea of using it for recorded music barely figured on his list of possible applications.

Many inveterate tinkerers, of course, waste much of their time until they get lucky. The U.S. Patent Office is full of the names of chronic inventors with dozens or even hundreds of patents to their name who are now known for a single breakthrough. Hewlett and Packard, a couple of bright Stanford engineering students, were working on a self-flushing urinal and various other unlikely devices before they managed to sell some of the oscillators they were developing to Disney.

Breakthrough thinking typically requires moving into a new, often conceptually distant space. If creating is often indistinguishable from finding, then navigation skills are the key. The trouble is, the law of spontaneous generation ensures that the search space itself keeps getting larger. Linear thinking travels one link at a time. Accidents, analogy, and tinkering can all be exploited to break free from such bounds. They can directly link two widely separated areas of a web of ideas without any concern for the myriad lower-level intervening links, thereby short-circuiting the connecting process and so saving creative energy. Once the weak tie has been established, the process of downloading intelligence from one space to another can proceed, and the laws of fitness can begin to further narrow the search space.

We can now restate the law of navigation as follows:

THE LAW OF NAVIGATION

In an open, dynamic network, finding a path to a successful creative breakthrough increases in difficulty as a function of the size of the search space, as measured by the power set (i.e., set of all possible subsets) of its component nodes.[46]

COROLLARY

In a search space dominated by sets of reciprocally interacting (i.e., context-determining) hubs, the size of the search space diminishes as a function of the delimiting conditions each hub places on the others via feedback loops.

Effective strategies for dealing with the navigation issue include exploiting weak ties in a network by being receptive to paths opened by accident, analogy, and tinkering; and progressively constructing a model shaped by the laws of fitness.

As we've seen, constructing a model is typically facilitated by connecting to a highly dynamic idea-space or set of such spaces via weak ties. Crick and Watson built theirs using physics and genetic geometry as their source. Ruth Handler and her team at Mattel implicitly used the Aphrodite myth as manifested in contemporary, culturally embedded idea-spaces relating to femininity. It's time to take a more detailed look at how idea-spaces act as both inspirational hotspots and overarching contexts for breakthrough developments.

Chapter Eight

THINK DIFFERENT

Frank Gehry and the Law of Hotspots

The utilitarian end aimed at by most contemporary architects is responsible for the great backwardness of architecture as compared with the other arts. The architect, the engineer, should have sublime aims: to build the highest tower . . . to throw across a harbor or a river an arch more audacious than the rainbow, and finally to compose a lasting harmony, the most powerful ever imagined by man.

—Apollinaire[1]

I'm being geniused to death.

—Frank Gehry

"The word is out that miracles still occur, and that a major one is happening here . . . 'Have you been to Bilbao?' In architectural circles, the question has acquired the status of a shibboleth. Have you seen the light? Have you seen the future? Does it work? Does it play?" Thus began Herbert Muschamp's breathless review in the *New York Times Magazine* of what was to become the most widely celebrated new building in more than half a century—Frank Gehry's Guggenheim Museum in Bilbao:

The miracle taking place here . . . is not Gehry's building, wondrous as it is. The miraculous occurrence is the extravagant optimism that enters into the outlook of those who have made the pilgrimage. What if American art has

161

not, after all, played itself out to its last entropic wheeze? What if standards of cultural achievement have not irretrievably dissolved in the vast, tepid bath of relativity, telemarketing and manipulated public opinion? Has it even become possible, once again, to think about beauty as a form of truth?[2]

The giddy, almost ecstatic enthusiasm with which Muschamp celebrated Gehry's achievement may have seemed outlandish back in 1997, but time proved him right in claiming that "an architectural intelligence of unequaled stature" was now among us.

My own first encounter with Gehry's genius back in the early 1980s was rather less of a Saul-on-the-road-to-Damascus revelation. Strolling around Santa Monica after dinner, an old friend and I came across a strange sight at the corner of Washington and 22nd Street. In a quiet, tree-lined neighborhood full of snug 1930s stuccoed bungalows, we found ourselves looking at what appeared to be just such a house whose exterior had been wrapped with weirdly nonorthogonal frames made of chain-link fencing, ridged concrete, unfinished plywood, and similar industrial materials. It was possible to see through openings and windows in this outer frame into the interior of the old house itself, giving one an immediate sense of being a voyeur. The overall impression was one of peering into a giant chicken coop with an outsized dollhouse in the middle. This, my friend explained, was the Frank Gehry residence.

Gehry's neighbors had been enraged with his remodeling, carried out in 1978–1979, describing the house as "offensive," "antisocial," a "monstrosity," "a dirty thing to do in somebody else's front yard."[3] One threatened to sue, and on at least two occasions shots were fired through the windows. And to cap it all, for this achievement along with others of similar ilk, in 1989 the man was awarded the Pritzker Prize, the Nobel of architecture.

To say that I was astonished to see a picture of the Guggenheim Museum in Bilbao on the cover of the September 7, 1997, edition of the *New York Times Magazine* would be an understatement. The building, with its swooping, soaring curves and titanium sheath, was itself sufficient cause for amazement. To discover that the creator of this gorgeous building was none other than the designer of the chicken-coop house I'd seen in Santa Monica fifteen years earlier was shocking. Even for an L.A. architect, going from unfinished plywood to titanium, cuboids of hurricane fencing to airy steel-framed curves, was quite a jump.

That Gehry's architecture represents an outstanding example of a major creative leap is no longer arguable in the way it might have been fifteen years ago. He has lately added to his long list of extraordinary buildings yet another acknowledged masterpiece, the Disney Concert Hall in Los Angeles.

His work has come to be recognized not only as a sharp break with previous architectural styles, but also as enormously influential on professional practice as a whole, inspiring an entire generation of young architects. He has succeeded in freeing architecture from the stifling grip of both modernism and postmodernism, in the process establishing a new standard for what a successful building is and how it should relate to its surroundings. He has also radically transformed the technology used to design, develop, and execute buildings. As a result of all this, he has opened up a huge new space in which architecture can develop, giving new life to a field that by the last quarter of the twentieth century was showing distinct signs of having run out of ideas.

What forces shape a bold and expansive imagination like Gehry's? How do you know when to follow your intuition and make a risky leap that takes you far from the mainstream? What factors determine the trajectory of your eventual success—or failure?

Gehry's story suggests some intriguing answers that will take us still deeper into the calculus of creativity. Dissatisfied to the point of boredom with the state of architecture, Gehry found himself pulled by the attractive force of two powerfully hot idea-spaces, one cultural, the other technological. As the interplay between these began to energize and drive his imagination, he discovered a way to build a bridge, to let the intelligence embedded in them start to flow into architecture and transform it, producing a vastly expanded space to think with. In short, he discovered how to make architecture interesting again.

FROM THE BAUHAUS TO GEHRY'S HOUSE: HOW ARCHITECTURE STALLED

At the start of the twentieth century, cubism sent shock waves through the art world and beyond. Walter Gropius's 1925 design for the new Bauhaus at Dessau, Germany, for example, featured steel frames and glass walls sharply angled along cubist lines. With the exception of Le Corbusier, however, cubism found little sustained response in architecture.[4] Gropius's successor, the engineering-trained Mies van der Rohe, embraced cubism's rectangular geometry, but insisted on realizing it within an industrially oriented means of production based on a utopian-inspired acceptance of modern technology and the virtues of machine-made things.[5] This faith in technology's ability to solve problems and reduce production costs by using standardized parts became embodied in the so-called International Style. Famously exemplified in the soaring skyscrapers of the great American cities, it came to represent the epitome of modernist architecture. Deliberately deprived of all ornament and local historical reference, and shackled inescapably to the steel grid, it proudly made *form follows function* its universal mantra.

For nearly four decades, while art, sculpture, drama, music, literature, and science were convulsed by a series of revolutions, mainstream architecture's predominant style and underlying philosophy remained essentially unchanged. Finally, in the midsixties, Robert Venturi and Aldo Rossi, breaking the prohibition on historical and local reference, attempted to free architecture from "the strangulating orthodoxies of the modern movement."[6] In retrospect, the AT&T building designed by Philip Johnson, who began his career as an ardent modernist, seems emblematic of the whole postmodern enterprise: a curving eighteenth-century rooftop façade ironically perched atop an otherwise unremarkable modernist tower. In the end, the postmodernist movement in architecture lacked the energy and radical appeal it developed elsewhere in the arts, literature, and philosophy, and gradually ran out of steam. Having started out as a rebellion against the mainstream, it wound up hidebound by its own codes and rules about what was permissible. The late seventies saw the beginning of a period when, as Herbert Muschamp succinctly put it, "American architecture spectacularly lost its way."[7]

Architecture's essentially conservative interpretation of modernism is at odds with the radical changes the modernist ethos produced elsewhere in the arts and sciences. By the last quarter of the twentieth century, a gaping opportunity had opened up for someone with enough boldness and imagination to catch architecture up with the rest of the culture. Someone who, in the words of the Apple ad, could "think different."[8]

A DUMB LITTLE HOUSE WITH CHARM

Coming to grips with Gehry's achievement is not exactly easy. How can we take the measure of a man whose career now spans over fifty years, yet who didn't achieve success until he was sixty? Whose roster of buildings stretches from Los Angeles to Berlin, but who for decades couldn't get a decent commission in his own town? Who is currently lionized but whose 1981 design for an addition to a residence was sniffily rejected by the Bel Air Fine Arts Commission on the grounds that it didn't look like a house?[9]

A good place to start might be the asphalt paving on Gehry's dining room floor.

Of all the strange things Gehry did with the remodeling of what he affectionately termed "a dumb little house with charm," none appears at first sight more idiosyncratic or opaque than this. But of course, the choice of asphalt—seemingly out of place even given Gehry's long-standing use of industrial materials—wasn't senseless at all. On the contrary, it was, characteristically, a gesture loaded with meaning.

The architect Philip Johnson once remarked that he liked the sense of confusion in the Gehry dining room. "I asked myself when I was there: 'Am I in the dining room or in the driveway?'" Sitting down to dinner in the new outer segment of the house, guests would glimpse someone inside the old house, creating the illusion that they themselves were outside. When this person then entered the dining room, the illusion was shattered. Gehry elaborated the point: "I intended to walk around the house and each opening, each event, in the house would be something different and I would explore a different idea."[10]

Each opening—a door, window, or other aperture—while reinforcing the inside/outside confusion, also became an opportunity for Gehry to create a new vision of the old house, depending on which space one was occupying in the new house. This virtual decomposition, preserving the house while simultaneously fragmenting it, "creat[ed] a tension that results in a continual oscillation between interiority and exteriority."[11]

Playing with inside/outside is a theme that runs throughout Gehry's architecture. In the Norton Residence, a beach house in Venice, California, built between 1982 and 1984, the study is separated from the main building. Designed in the shape of a lifeguard shack with a direct view of the ocean, it poses the question directly: Am I on the beach or in the house? Am I at work or at play? Another residential design went so far as to decompose the house completely by making the rooms into individual buildings scattered down a hillside, "separate objects sitting together on the site, playing off one another," as Gehry himself described it.[12]

What is going on here? At first sight, we seem to be encountering a highly idiosyncratic quirk of Gehry's style, bordering on a series of private jokes. In reality, in playing his inside/outside games, Gehry was connecting with a theme that could be traced back at least as far as the turn-of-the-century Austrian architect Adolf Loos. To quote Muschamp again: "The interplay between in and out has been a recurring theme of architecture for the past century . . . Twentieth century architecture has unfolded as a series of variations on the relationship between the interior and exterior of buildings, bodies, minds—between public and private realms."[13] No doubt Gehry was aware of this. But he enriches this theme by connecting it to others—fragmentation/recomposition, plays on meaning, the deliberate involvement of the spectator in the creative act of interpretation—that came from a very different source. In order to reinvent architecture, he had to go outside it.

THE LAW OF HOTSPOTS

Picasso changed his whole approach to painting after encountering African art. Crick turned to genetic geometry and the speculative model building of physics in uncovering DNA. Mattel found inspiration in the social and cultural embodiments of the Aphrodite myth. In each case, the path to a breakthrough within a maze of possibilities required a bold leap to an external *hotspot*.

In common parlance, a hotspot is something that both radiates and attracts energy. In the world of tourism, London is a hotspot. The new economy in the 1990s and "China Rising" in the current decade similarly exemplify the phenomenon. In cell biology, epigenetics (the study of how genes are turned on and off) is rapidly becoming a hotspot.[14] On the Internet, Web services are so hot that even Microsoft has made them the center of its entire software development strategy.

In terms of the extended mind, hotspots are highly energized, densely interconnected hubs (idea-spaces). They represent the natural outcome of the extended operation of the laws of fitness, which jointly produce two core characteristics of hotspots: rapid growth through attracting links, combined with a high level of integration. Once again, we find these laws acting reciprocally on one another. Fitness triggers preferential attachment—the fit grow rich. As new nodes link up to a hotspot, possibilities for meaningful relationships and feedback loops increase. The law of the fit get fitter progressively gives rise to a central set of nodes that are well integrated with one another, thereby creating a stable core of embedded intelligence. This core fitness triggers still further growth, and so on.

In many cases, the result of this process is the emergence of a massive idea-space like the counterculture, a social and cultural hotspot that drew everything from music to politics to computers into its orbit during the 1960s and 1970s. More recently, the new economy became a huge, if doomed, multidimensional hotspot during the late 1990s. Sometimes, however, in the process of increasingly attracting links while building an ever more integrated core, a hotspot turns into a natural exporter of its own core embedded intelligence as its vibrant energy and expansiveness spills over into other domains. As it matures and becomes more structurally stable and organized, an expanding hotspot is able to act as a catalyst, turning into a transforming agent for other idea-spaces while remaining largely unchanged itself.

This was what happened in the spread of the scientific method, the core embedded intelligence of the sciences. In part because of the tremendous prestige physics acquired during the first third of the twentieth century, disciplines outside of the hard sciences—including psychology, philosophy, economics, linguistics, sociology, anthropology, and business management—began to emphasize the importance of adhering to rigorous scientific procedures and modes of inquiry. On a more mundane level, the Apple iPod (on Internet time already a mature, highly integrated product) has leapt beyond shaking up the music world. Not only has it helped to launch the idea of podcasting, but also to reframe the whole concept of portable digital content, from family photos to TV to education programs. In other words, both the scientific method and the iPod have become hotspots, able to act as transforming agents in other domains.

Often, the idea-spaces that are most impacted by hotspots turn out to have achieved long-term stability verging on stagnation. They have become so integrated—in other words so internally fit—that innovation is stifled. It takes the violent energy of an expanding hotspot to break through the barriers of conventional thinking, but once it has done so, the wave of new ideas typically encounters little resistance.

In Crick's day, mainstream biology had become a mature field wedded to strictly empirical methods of inquiry that were rapidly being replaced by a more theoretical approach in physics. Crick mastered the speculative, model-building methods he'd learned from Pauling and Bragg, helping to complete the revolution they'd begun. In similar fashion, printing was able to sweep away an entrenched scribal industry that had changed little in the preceding thousand years. During the last two decades, Detroit's long-established ways of mass-producing cars has been forcibly replaced by the far less wasteful "lean thinking" pioneered by Toyota and other Japanese firms.[15] Again, the music industry's century-old copyright system has been brought under severe pressure to change because of Internet-based file sharing pioneered by Napster.

Hotspots are culture's and society's way of avoiding stagnation. They succeed in creating a strongly integrated core while continuing to attract weak links from external nodes. As a result they thrive and grow through maintaining the right balance between strong and weak ties or, in other words, reciprocity and reach.

Boldly imaginative minds are instinctively pulled toward the energy radiating out of hotspots. Intuitively, radical thinkers recognize that the intelligence embedded in a hot idea-space has the power to remake their own too-stable world. Newly fired up, the questing imagination becomes imbued with novel patterns and forms that both shape and enlarge its own creative powers. As these patterns are imaginatively transplanted to a new domain, they transform its structure, giving it new meaning and enlarging its boundaries. Sometimes slowly, sometimes in a single illuminating flash, insight comes, the space tips, and something new is born.

The role of hotspots in creative leaps can be stated in terms of the following law:

THE LAW OF HOTSPOTS

The potential transformative power of a hotspot
relative to another idea-space is a function
of fitness combined with distance.

As you may have noticed, there is an apparent contradictory tension here. Distance is measured in terms of the number and strength (i.e., degree of meaningful connectivity) of the links between two idea-spaces. The fewer or weaker the links, the greater the distance. Violin making and law, for example, have little in common, and are thus in network terms quite distant from one another. Fitness implies a degree of coherence and hence connectedness. The greater the degree of fitness between two hubs (idea-spaces), the closer they are likely to be in terms of the links between them. Thus there is a fairly close fit between business and law: there is business law, and the business of law, for example, and correspondingly they share many common links, including to other nodes and hubs.

What the law of hotspots tells us, then, is that the richest rewards come when we discover a distant idea-space whose embedded intelligence nevertheless bears a recognizable fitness with the space of our own creative endeavors.

When a comparatively remote hotspot is found to fit with an idea-space in some way, the initial distance increases the likelihood of a breakthrough by ensuring there will be little overlap with the past while simultaneously generating a host of new potential connections. This, of course, is precisely *the strength of weak ties*.

BACK TO THE FUTURE: FROM POP ART TO CUBISM

Art was Gehry's hotspot. When he was at the University of Southern California, he started out as an arts major and only later switched to architecture. Over the next few decades, long before he became famous for building museums, he developed close friendships with well-known artists, including Claes Oldenberg, Ron Davis, Ed Moses, Richard Serra, Donald Judd, Robert Rauschenberg, and others. "I have always felt that living artists are working on the same issues I am," he remarked.[16] Several of his Southern Californian artist friends were making use of industrial materials in their painting, and Gehry, liking the rawness and energy of this practice, decided to bring it into architecture. His remodeled house was just one in a long line of residences and buildings that incorporated everything from the infamous chain link to corrugated metal cladding, unfinished plywood, and even tunnel cement.

The sixties and seventies were a period of tremendous ferment in the art world, with the L.A. art scene acting as the major West Coast hub. Feeling the strong attractive pull of one of the period's major cultural hotspots, Gehry instinctively saw in art the possibility of freeing architecture from the dual straitjackets of modernism and its weakly rebellious successor post-modernism, both of which had become too rule-bound to allow much fresh thinking. Using highly unorthodox materials was clearly one means of achieving a breakout. "I wanted to prove you could make an artwork out of anything. This is being done, of course, in sculpture," he once remarked. "Art gives you a sense of freedom. There were rigid rules in architecture and there don't need to be. Architects should be able to free associate."[17] But if Gehry sought to transform architecture by more closely associating it with art, in the end it was not so much artists' use of utilitarian and industrial materials that left an enduring mark on his thinking. Rather, it was their handling of the altogether more conceptual themes noted earlier—inside/outside, plays on meaning, and so forth—that holds the key to understanding the revolution Gehry was in the midst of creating.

Nothing illustrates this better than one of the most celebrated examples of Gehry's embrace of art, the entrance to the Chiat/Day building in Venice, California. For this Gehry collaborated with pop artists Claes Oldenburg and Coosje van Bruggen, modeling it on a huge pair of binoculars originally developed for a performance piece in Venice, Italy. As Thomas Krens (director of the Solomon R. Guggenheim Foundation, who collaborated with Gehry on the Bilbao project) put it, this building was especially important

because it was here that he took hold of art—obviously and aggressively—by enthusiastically embracing another artist as a collaborative ally in a joint project . . . In art, Frank saw a huge potential for architecture—as inspiration, as counterpoint, and as content . . . he opened a door to the rich world of artistic collaboration as a process and as an end in itself, from which he would never turn away.[18]

In other words, just as Handler found sex and glamour in Lilli, it was in this project that Gehry finally became fully connected to the first of two powerful hotspots that would bring about a far-reaching transformation of his profession. If the binoculars are a forceful, dramatically realized assertion that art can be integrated into architecture, however, they are nevertheless (despite appearances) perfectly functional, containing two large conference rooms on the second floor.

The conceptual, minimalist, and pop artists of Gehry's generation progressively rejected "a purely visual . . . experience of art" (which in turn coincided with the view that works of art constituted real objects in their own right) in favor of explicitly bringing the audience's own response into the field of the artwork itself.[19] Muschamp similarly remarks on "the increasing awareness that art resides only partly within individual artworks . . . Art has spilled out of its classical containers . . . at least since the advent of conceptual art, the task for many artists has been not only to create objects but also to escape their confining dimensions."[20]

From the outset Gehry picked up on contemporary art's concern with how we experience art, especially how we find multiple meanings in it, and imported this theme into architecture. Seen from the outside, his Santa Monica residence prompts the viewer to ask, Is this a building or a work of art? Once inside, however, the visual becomes integrated with the mental (Am I inside the house or outside it?) and the bodily. By forcing the viewer to see the old house in a series of fragmented views gained only by walking around it, Gehry makes the *body's participation* a direct and integral part of the aesthetic experience. The viewer can construct and make sense of the whole only by recomposing the parts. By the same token, time and space merge: space—the visual dimension of our experience—can no longer be grasped instantaneously, but only over an extended period.

The Chiat/Day binoculars are a further well-constructed play on these various themes. Spectators can literally walk inside what looks from the outside like a giant piece of art in the shape of an everyday object, only to find themselves in a functioning office building. The point is sharpened by the fact that the binoculars bring to the fore the whole question of *how we look at things*, whether art, architecture, or life itself. The fact that the client is an internationally known advertising firm merely compounds the irony.

The integration of space and time, the deliberate undermining and fragmentation of the visual, inside versus outside, the establishing of a new metaphysics concerning the relationship of art objects to reality, plays on meaning—we have been here before, but in a very different era. As we saw earlier, cubism, energized and inspired by the new physics, created a radical new idea-space for art characterized by these same concepts at the very beginning of the twentieth century. Einsteinian relativity and cubism jointly initiated one of the most revolutionary and extended periods of change in art, science, philosophy, music, and literature since the Renaissance. But somehow, architecture was bypassed. In the midst of all this intense transformation, the art of designing and putting up the buildings in which we all, in one way or another, live out our lives was left behind.

The idea-space of modernist architecture, with its focus on rigid geometries, material purity, the primacy of function, and the economics of industrial production, allowed the architect's imagination little freedom to produce truly innovative designs. By the same token, it put a greater distance between art and architecture than at any time since the Renaissance. Postmodernism made an attempt to close the gap, but it was a half-hearted gesture, too lacking in real connectivity to tip. Gehry's genius was to have apprehended the transforming power that lay at the heart of cubism, the originating force that drove much of the cultural radicalism of the twentieth century.

Cubism's most fundamental move was to trade the straitjacket of creating an illusion of reality for the freedom of playing with meaning, now humorously and ironically, now at a metaphysical level. Directly or indirectly (through pop art, conceptualism, etc.), Gehry absorbed cubism's lessons regarding the primacy of meaning and the involvement of the viewer in cocreating it—the idea postmodernism also developed, though mainly outside architecture. In the Chiat/Day building he skillfully incorporated these into what was essentially a pop art piece of architecture. Shortly thereafter, however, he would begin to use his insight into the core intelligence of cubism, not (as might have been expected) to rejuvenate a waning postmodernist movement, but to create a thoroughly reinvented modernism.

CATIA AND THE FISH

Take a look at a typical modernist office tower—the Metropolitan Life Building in Manhattan, for example, or the more recent Canary Wharf complex in London. Not much humor, irony, or ambiguity there. If anything, these buildings are painfully serious, literal, and monolithic.

To postmodernism's own attempts at irony and ambiguity—"the postmodern game," as he called it—Gehry offered an ironic, highly ambivalent gesture of his own: a fish. "I said, 'Okay, if you're going to go back, fish are three hundred thousand years before man, so why don't you go back to fish?'"[21] In typical cubist-inspired Gehry fashion, the gesture played on multiple layers of meaning. As a boy, he had watched his Jewish grandmother bring home a live carp to be made into gefilte fish. "We'd put it in the bathtub, and I would watch this fish for a day, this beautiful object swimming around."[22] At school, Gehry was nicknamed Fish, evidently as a way of publicly marking his marginalized ethnic status. Like Picasso, Gehry exorcised this ugly taunt by making it into art. Among his numerous fish sculptures, the twenty-two-foot glass fish in the Walker Art Center in Minneapolis represents the very apotheosis of joyous movement, indeed of life itself, soaring upward like the exhilarating curves of his later buildings. Nothing could be further from the whole rigid modernist ethos: "I was looking for movement earlier, and found it in the fish. The fish solidified my understanding of how to make architecture move."[23]

In his quest to bring architecture to life through movement, Gehry didn't start with the fish—that was quite literally too difficult. The intersecting cubist planes of his early architecture, most notably in his own residence, brought a visual movement of their own, in sharp opposition to the four-square solidity of the old house. But the movement, as in cubism itself, was as much *conceptual* as visual. The constant shifting from outside to inside and back again, and the play with meanings (Am I on the beach or in the study? Is this a piece of pop art or an office building?) never let the viewer's mind settle down with a single perspective.

That was a good start, but it didn't go nearly far enough. To design *and construct* a building that could truly be said to move as gracefully and beautifully as a fish, Gehry, paradoxically, had first to embrace what appeared to be its very antithesis: *the modernist ethos of the machine.* Here, Gehry created a weak tie to a second hotspot that at the time was surprisingly distant from architecture—computer-aided design and construction. Le Corbusier famously said, "A house is a machine for living in." Gehry went one better, perfecting a machine for designing and building houses, not to mention art museums, concert halls, and other large civic structures.

As William J. Mitchell, dean of the School of Architecture and Planning at MIT, has observed, "Architects tend to draw what they can build, and build what they can draw."[24] Conventional techniques for making architectural plans were basically Euclidean, using compass, rule, dividers, triangles, and T-squares to create straight lines, angles, parallels, and simple curves. Richard Smith, a computer graphics expert who joined Gehry's firm in the early 1990s, has given a vivid description of one widely used drawing practice:

> The architects built a box that had a frosted glass window, and they set up an elevation. They'd shine a light from behind the box, which would cast a shadow on the frosted glass. Then they'd take tracing paper, trace the shadow, and they'd say, "Well, that's our elevation." I came in and asked, "How do you know that the dimensions are right?" And they told me, "Hey, Michelangelo did this. This is the way it's been done for centuries. Don't buck it."[25]

In short, even by the latter part of the twentieth century, architectural drawing remained a largely traditional art that had changed little in centuries.

Needless to say, such techniques imposed severe constraints on what could be designed and built. Straight lines and simple curves are easy to draw and translate into parts that can be manufactured using standard industrial machinery. Any kind of free-form curve, on the other hand, is a nightmare to draw and sends production costs skyrocketing. Jørn Utzon's original sail-like design for the roof of the Sydney Opera House (1956–1973), for example, had to be considerably simplified for it to be properly drawn and executed, resulting in a building that is "much stiffer and more classically geometric than the version that Utzon had originally imagined."[26] No wonder modern architecture became so hidebound. "Throughout the twentieth century," Mitchell observes, "the straightforward logic of industrial production seemed to provide an unassailable justification for the spare geometries of architectural Modernism."[27] Industrial production, in short, was an idea-space that severely limited new thinking in architecture, aided and abetted by the comparative primitiveness of drawing techniques.

It was Gehry who blew this system apart, opening up architectural design and manufacturing to a whole new world of vastly more elegant and complex curves. CAD (computer-aided design) systems had been introduced into architecture in the 1970s, but for the most part these had simply computerized existing drawing practices. Around the same time, highly sophisticated CAD/CAM (computer-aided manufacturing) systems capable of rationalizing and simplifying the whole design and production process, from drawing board to manufacturing to logistics and cost control, had begun to transform the aircraft, shipbuilding, automobile, and film animation industries, including those located in and around L.A. Architects, however, ignored the emergence of this major technological hotspot until Gehry's office set out to find a system capable of designing a giant fish sculpture for the 1992 Barcelona Olympics. James Glymph, a partner in Gehry's firm, finally settled on CATIA, a CAD/CAM system used in the French aerospace industry, and the fish sculpture, measuring one hundred sixty feet long by one hundred feet wide, was built.

Gehry now had the technical apparatus needed to turn his boldest imaginings into reality. The difficulties architects faced prior to the introduction of a highly sophisticated CAD/CAM system like CATIA wasn't just a matter of drawing complex curves (Utzon's problem), but of providing comprehensive sets of highly complicated specifications that could be fed directly into the computer-guided machinery of the companies that would manufacture a building's parts. CATIA not only made producing complex geometries and multiple nonstandard parts possible, but also brought their cost in line with those of the simple, mass-produced forms of modernist boxes.

In effect, CATIA's massive computer-embodied array of programmed intelligence represented an idea-space—quite literally a space to think with— capable of releasing the imagination of the architect bold enough to use it from the shackles imposed by modernism's orthodox ethos and techniques.

Gehry, having now grasped the relevance to his professional aims of not one but two hotspots—the liberating cubist-inspired precepts of modern art and the immensely powerful technologies of CAD/CAM—finally had the means at his disposal to build his first unquestioned masterpiece.

GEHRY'S CATHEDRAL

Even a glance at the gloriously undulating curves of the Guggenheim Museum Bilbao reveals that it could only have been designed and built—on time and on budget—using the kind of sophisticated technology the CATIA system made available. There is, quite simply, nothing like it in all of previous architecture.[28] Journalists and critics have been at a loss for words, variously describing it as "an exploded artichoke heart," "a giant whale," "a silver dream machine," "Marilyn Monroe's wind-assisted skirts," "silver balloons ready to float away," and (my personal favorite!) "an explosion in a sardine factory."[29]

The GMB, as the museum has come to be known, is strategically situated on a bend in the Nervión River, next to a bridge connecting the business and historic districts with the rest of the city. The route to the city center passes through the detritus of a former shipbuilding town left behind by globalization—slag heaps, disused smokestacks, and rusting gantries. One glimpse of the museum's shimmering profile brings with it the recognition that one is in the presence of something truly extraordinary. Gehry's magical ability to transform space, light, and scale are here manifested as never before, and the show is only just beginning (see figure 8-1).

The first impression, magnified by the heavy rectilinear frame of the street buildings, is one of shimmering metallic petals unfolding toward a blue, cloud-flecked sky. It's almost impossible not to interpret this as a bouquet of silver flowers, a peaceful gesture offered to a city lying at the heart of a deeply strife-torn region. In classic Gehry fashion, however, the building cannot be taken in at a glance, revealing itself only as the visitor walks around it. Once again, space and time merge. In fact, in the GMB, Gehry reworks every facet of cubism he learned to incorporate into the Chiat/Day offices—plays on meaning, irony, paradox, self-reference, incorporating the spectator into the process of visually constructing and interpreting the building, and producing a constant sense of movement—but now in the service of creating a thoroughly transformed modernism.

As the visitor approaches, the museum's titanium skin (just a third of a millimeter thick) appears to flutter slightly as the breeze moves across it, creating a secondary impression of billowing sails. From the opposite side, the museum's profile unexpectedly resolves into that of a ship moored to the riverbank, a silent reminder of the city's shipbuilding past. The gesture

FIGURE 8-1

The Guggenheim Museum Bilbao

Source: www.thomasmayerarchive.com.
Used with permission.

toward salient historical elements of the local context is in sharp contrast to the cultural emptiness of the International Style's eschewing of local reference in favor of the deliberate embrace of universalism.

On reflection, the museum's whole exterior seems to play, now ironically, now almost in homage, on modernist themes. In profile, the building consists of a series of large nonrepeating volumes whose smoothly undulating curves form a nicely balanced counterpoint to the entirely regular pattern of identical titanium tiles that make up the building's skin. Gehry's nod to modernism here is characteristically full of paradoxical tension: the tiles are industrially mass-produced, rectangular, and made of a pure metal (titanium is an element). But even as they embrace these modernist values, they simultaneously move against them, as Gehry surely recognized: "I'm a strict modernist in the sense of believing in purity, that you shouldn't decorate. And yet buildings need decoration, because they need scaling elements. They need to be human scale, in my opinion. They can't just be faceless things. That's how some modernism failed."[30]

The pun may or may not be intentional (the remark followed talking about studying fish to learn about movement), but the titanium tiles, as many observers have noted, resemble nothing so much as fish scales, elegantly integrating movement into the building while honoring modernism's ideals of geometric form, industrial production, material purity, and aesthetic simplicity. Just as the pioneers of the home computer were able to achieve a tremendous creative breakthrough by connecting the combined hotspots of the hobbyist and counterculture with key aspects of the existing mainstream industry, so Gehry was able to make a radical leap in architecture through integrating cubist ideals that still energized and shaped contemporary art into the modernist ethos.

This reciprocal interplay of art and architecture, cubism and modernism, continues in the building's interior. "The truism that nominates the museum as the modern cathedral" was never more compellingly embodied than in the atrium that lies just beyond the museum entrance.[31] Rising above the visitor's head to a height of 164 feet, the atrium leads the gaze ever upward past a crisscrossing array of soaring free-form arches and limestone- and plaster-covered walls, lit by a series of windows through which light pours from seemingly every angle. The space echoes cubism with its clashing planes and angles, decomposed vistas, vividly contrasting textures, and above all its ever-expanding play of multiple, often opposed meanings (see figure 8-2).

In spite of this astonishing visual and tactile tumult, a strange and harmonious logic, a concisely configured geometry of light, proportion, and shape seems to pull everything together into a dynamically unified whole. This unanticipated congruence of geometries could only have been achieved by some very sophisticated, computer-driven mathematical functions. Without CATIA, the Guggenheim Bilbao simply couldn't have been built.

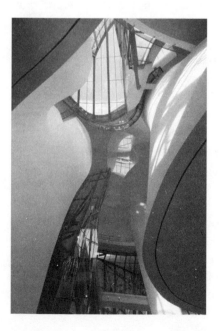

FIGURE 8-2

The Atrium, Guggenheim Museum Bilbao

Source: www.thomasmayerarchive.com. Used with permission.

As the visitor walks around inside, the plethora of materials—glass, metal, plaster, and limestone—continually slide across one another; voids are suddenly replaced by solids, shadows by light. Soaring planes and curves come into view only to be occluded a moment later. Like Gehry's house, the physical building simultaneously hides and reveals itself, decomposing and recomposing itself and yet never tumbling into visual chaos.

What Gehry has embodied in his design is the intelligence embedded in the idea-space of cubism: fragmentation, when properly handled, leads not to disorder but to the spontaneous creation of new forms and meanings as decomposed elements enter playfully into new relationships that build on one another. In place of Frank Lloyd Wright's modernist void at the center of the Guggenheim New York's spiral, he has created a space that, through the interplay and fusion of counterposed elements, constantly regenerates itself.

Gehry's whole art is founded on channeling the surging energy that flows from putting opposed, orthogonal, or previously unrelated elements into dynamic interaction with one another: art and architecture, inside and outside, fragment and whole, modernist grid and free-flowing movement, banality and beauty. The elements he sets in play create spaces and cultural meanings that in the end become both self-generating and self-transforming. Like Picasso and Braque, Gehry has *mastered the law of spontaneous generation*, allowing forms to multiply freely and yet, through the law of the fit get fitter, become progressively more integrated and hence more meaningful. For the viewer, the meanings that are built are emergent and self-transforming, shifting in interpretation as more and more patterns are observed and reconciled with one another in an astonishing exercise in contrapuntal harmony. Apollinaire would have cheered.

Gehry found in modern art and in CAD/CAM technology an energy and intelligence that fired his imagination. Intuitively, he recognized in them, and especially in cubism, patterns of embedded intelligence that had the power to transform modern architecture. But boldness in leaping to a new idea-space isn't sufficient to guarantee success. A bridge from the new to the old has to be built, turning the weak tie into a strong one. Distance, in other words, has to be balanced by fitness. The road to creative success is littered with the wrecked projects of those who became too intoxicated with the new to worry about whether the links to the present were stretched too thin, as the graveyard of dead dot-com companies amply testifies.

In Gehry's case, the fitness lay in a series of links to the very modernism he sought to transform. His early use of raw industrial materials is an ironic play on modernism's own belief in the purity of material elements. Correspondingly, his embrace of cubism's complex dynamic of fragmentation and recomposition became embodied in forms that gave new life to modernism's spacious geometries. And CATIA represents a new, more powerful, and flexible embodiment of modernism's machine ethos. Gehry reinvented modernism by connecting it, insightfully and with bold imagination, to two hubs—art and CAD/CAM—that, distant though they were, shared important common elements with it.

Gehry's acknowledged passion was to restore imaginative freedom, movement, and life to a profession that was in danger of rigidly ossifying. His fired-up imagination rode the huge wave of energy generated when the twin hotspots of art and CAD/CAM technology came into contact with a moribund modernist architecture. The law of the fit get fitter progressively brought about the harmonious integration of the diverse intelligence embedded in these idea-spaces, while the law of the fit get rich produced an explosion of forms, materials, and meanings that vastly expanded the thinking space available to architects. The Guggenheim Museum Bilbao was more than a personal triumph.[32] It proved to be a tipping point for architecture as a whole.

SUPERSIZING

Creative leaps aren't limited to the arts, science, and technology. They also occur in commerce, sometimes at the most mundane level. In the 1960s, David Wallerstein, now a senior executive with McDonald's, was wracking his brain to figure out how to expand sales of soda and popcorn (a major source of profit) in the chain of theaters he worked for.[33] Wallerstein tried everything—two-for-one deals, matinee specials, and many other ideas—but nothing worked. People would buy only one soda and one bag of popcorn. Then he had an idea that over time was to revolutionize the entire food service industry, altering virtually every aspect, from production to marketing. Instead of trying to get people to go back for "seconds" (or buy two servings to start with), he would make the initial serving much larger: Eureka . . . *supersize it!* The sheer success of the idea (the calories in a McDonald's serving of french fries went from two hundred to more than six hundred over the past four decades, with concomitant growth in profits) testifies to the brilliant psychological breakthrough Wallerstein made. In effect, supersizing (the term itself came later) legitimized the act of eating significantly larger amounts of food than is either natural or healthy.

Supersizing is a classic instance of what behavioral economists call *reframing.*[34] People can be shown to make choices based not on purely rational grounds of maximizing personal benefit (utility), but as a result of how they frame the decision by taking into account the social or cultural context in which it arises.

Think for a moment. Why didn't people buy a second container of food or drink? Not because they weren't hungry, or couldn't afford it, or even on health grounds, as the rapid success of supersizing clearly demonstrates. Rather, the evidence suggests that people generally regarded going for an additional helping as gluttonous. The apparent source of this taboo in American culture is the predominant influence, even among nonbelievers, of Christian ethics, since gluttony is one of the seven deadly sins.[35] Historically, Christian ethics has become an extremely fit idea-space integrated into multiple domains of our everyday lives. As a result it has grown increasingly rich, circumscribing ways of behaving at work, in school, at home, and so forth. It thus represents a deeply embedded, densely interconnected, highly stable cultural hotspot.

In network terms, we can picture the hotspot of Christian ethics as a hub that *controls connectivity*—that is, acts as a dominant context for action. The hub attracts a majority of links representing individual eating choices via preferential attachment (the outcome of the law of the fit get rich). In other words, most individuals allow their eating behavior in public to be conditioned by the prohibition on gluttony, which is generally regarded as ruling out acting like Oliver Twist—*publicly asking for more*. The genius of supersizing was that it allowed consumers to reframe eating significantly more in terms that no longer appeared to contravene Christian ethics, which does not specify how big a normal portion should be.

Behavioral economists have uncovered many similar examples in which a socially or culturally hot idea-space acts as a space to think with, leading to behavior that may flout commonsense norms. Consider the case of New York cabbies. Economic logic dictates that we should "make hay while the sun shines," or in the case of cabbies, keep driving when it's raining and fares are plentiful, even if this means extending the length of their shift. The majority, however, do just the reverse: they typically go home early when they're making money and drive long hours when fares are scarce. The reason appears to be that they operate by a rule of making a set amount each day, for fear of not being able to pay their bills at the end of the month. Most cabbies are recent immigrants, transients with little economic security, so this rule consequently has high fitness with their need to survive economically. As a result, the rule acts as a hotspot, in the form of a controlling thinking space, that governs their work practices, even when these fly in the face of common sense.

Economists Amos Tversky and (Nobel laureate) Daniel Kahneman have named this kind of behavior, where a powerful emotional context overrides rational analysis, *type 2 thinking*. These examples demonstrate how the dynamics of breakthrough creativity, far from being exceptional, are in fact grounded in laws that also govern everyday behavior. The attractive forces that shaped Gehry's architectural imagination in terms of the hotspot of postcubist art are driven by the very same principle of preferential attachment to hotspots that guides thinking about such mundane activities as buying french fries or driving a cab.

ERATOSTHENES THE GEOMETER

Those who are keenly attuned to the extended mind's dynamic topography are naturally drawn to spaces from which creative energy is radiating—to hotspots. A classic illustration of this is Eratosthenes' accurate estimation of the earth's circumference in the third century BC. Many previous thinkers had tried to figure this out, but with little success.

Imagine trying to measure how large the earth is without the benefit of modern technology. It's hard to even know where to begin. In spite of the obvious difficulties, however, Eratosthenes, a Greek scholar and scientist, was undaunted. When he heard that at noon on the summer solstice in the Egyptian city of Syene (modern Aswan) the sun is directly overhead, casting no shadow in a deep well, an interesting idea occurred to him. By measuring the shadow cast by a pole set vertically in the ground in Alexandria (which lies directly to the north), he would be able to compute the earth's circumference.

How did Eratosthenes arrive at an accurate solution when this had eluded so many before him? As an educated Greek and active scientist, he was fully aware of the lively debate concerning the size and shape of the earth: most thought of it as a concave disk, but there was a speculation by the late-fifth-century Pythagorean Philolaus that it was spherical.[36] As the librarian at Alexandria, he would have been well positioned to learn about the sun's position at Syene during the summer solstice. But this mix of fact and speculation had little significance in and of itself. It could become useful only when placed inside a framework capable of making sense of it all.

In spite of its name (*ge[o]* earth + *metros* measure), geometry—the most prestigious of the Greek sciences—had been applied by Greek mathematicians and astronomers in a practical way primarily to arrive at models of *heavenly* bodies and their relationships to one another. Eratosthenes' genius was to recognize that if Philolaus's speculation was correct, then geometry could also be used to calculate measurements too huge to carry out in a purely physical way on earth. What he realized was that because the sun is so far away, its rays fall on the earth in roughly parallel lines. A vertical pole can be thought of as lying on a line drawn from the center of the earth. As such it would at that point intersect a similar line drawn from a well. The angle the lines formed would determine the arc between the pole and well on the earth's surface, provided these were on the same longitude. If this angle could be calculated, then the distance between the poles would represent the same proportion of the earth's total circumference as the angle would be of a complete circle (i.e., of 360 degrees). Of course, it wasn't possible to travel to the earth's center to perform this calculation. Reframed within the hotspot idea-space of geometry, however, the problem reduced to a simple one about parallel lines, arcs, and angles that any fourteen-year-old Greek schoolboy could work out (see figure 8-3).

If the angle of the shadow cast by the pole at Alexandria was seven degrees, then so must be the angle at the center of the earth. Eratosthenes was thus able to calculate that the distance between the two cities constituted an arc representing 7/360ths of the whole, and from that proportion determine the total circumference of the earth.

Eratosthenes' calculation, which has recently been nominated as one of the ten most beautiful experiments ever conducted in physics, is thought to have been no more than 5 percent off.[37] His success came from recognizing that the intellectual hotspot of geometry had the power to transform what looked like an intractable puzzle into a simple piece of homework. Like the Arabic number system, it had the power to do some of the basic thinking for him.

The history of discovery repeatedly reveals that the bright ideas we so readily attribute to the creative genius of individuals are in fact inextricably bound up with, and partly generated by, whole webs of intelligence

FIGURE 8-3

Eratosthenes' geometrical calculation of the earth's circumference

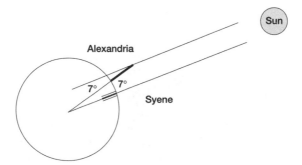

Source: Adapted from several conventional ways of graphically representing Eratosthenes' experiment.

embedded in external, publicly shared idea-spaces. The law of hotspots, the law of navigation, the law of spontaneous generation, the law of tipping points, and the laws of fitness, working in tandem, all actively shape and stimulate the human imagination, intuition, and insight in the process of making creative breakthroughs. The sixth law of network dynamics, which I discuss next, is one of the best known and most powerful, and at the same time one of the least understood in terms of its role in focusing these dynamics: the law of small-world networks.

Chapter Nine

THE NETWORKED DYNAMICS OF RISK

Printing and the Law of Small-World Networks

I don't have to invent anything . . . It's out there somewhere if I can just find it and integrate it . . . Inventing is frustrating, it's dangerous, it's expensive, and inventors should avoid it whenever possible. Be a systems integrator.

—Dean Kamen, inventor of the Segway[1]

In 1975 a popular television commercial depicted the trials and tribulations of Brother Dominic, a humble medieval scribe. The good monk, lit only by candlelight, has just finished copying by hand a lengthy ancient manuscript. He shows it to his superior, who promptly requests several dozen more copies. Dominic retreats, head bowed, promising to do the best he can. The following morning he returns, triumphantly carrying a large stack of paper. "It's a miracle!" his superior exclaims—failing to notice behind the door through which Dominic has just entered a gleaming new Xerox 9200![2]

Printing—the mechanical reproduction of texts that superseded scribes as a way of producing multiple copies—*was* a miracle. Francis Bacon grouped it with gunpowder and the compass as one of the three most important inventions of his era.[3] Jared Diamond, author of *Guns, Germs, and Steel*, goes even further, calling printing the best single invention of the millennium.[4] Without it we wouldn't have had the explosion of knowledge in the late Renaissance, the Reformation, the rise of science, the nation-state—in short, printing launched the modern world.

The invention of printing also happens to be a wildly improbable business story: a young man setting out to make a lot of money as the first wave of capitalism sweeps Europe, obsessed with his vision and with the technology that would make it happen; regulatory problems (the Church controlled the book market); intense secrecy; a first and then second round of financing; an excessive burn rate; worried investors pulling the plug at the last minute; subsequent failed attempts to monopolize the market, followed by growth so explosive it completely annihilates the entrenched competition. In short, to study the invention of printing is to study a classic case of early entrepreneurship, not to mention one of the most successful disruptive technologies of all time.

Most people know little more than the basic "fact" itself: Gutenberg invented the printing press. In reality, there were antecedents to Gutenberg stretching as far back as the seventeenth century BCE Minoa, followed much later by China and Korea. But even if Gutenberg wasn't the first person to come up with the core ideas underlying the development of printing, the key advances he made, achieved within a unique configuration of social and cultural conditions, caused printing to become a central technology of Western culture and one of its most enduring hotspots.

The invention of printing raises two important and intriguing questions concerning creativity. First, timing: Why is the history of invention, discovery, and innovation sometimes *discontinuous*, with long breaks between progress followed by sudden periods of explosive growth? For example, as John Man succinctly puts it in his highly readable and informative biography: Why Gutenberg? Why the Rhineland? Why the middle of the fifteenth century?[5] Second, the relationship of imagination to history: Does the imagination of an outstandingly creative person transcend social and cultural context, as the Romantics believed, or is it largely shaped by it?

Network theory provides real insight into these questions. As we shall see, the *law of small-world networks*, operating in dynamic interplay with several other network laws, helps explain instances of chronological discontinuity, showing why certain inventions and discoveries emerge only when a whole series of social and cultural factors aligns in just the right configuration. In addition, the law also reveals how such external factors act as a powerful framing device for the imaginative intelligence, creating the ideal space in which something new can come into being. The curiously spasmodic history of printing—*inventus interruptum*—turns out to be, as Jared Diamond observes, "the millennium's best window into how inventions actually unfold."[6]

THE PRECURSORS

Until the advent of Xerox machines and the digital revolution, printing basically required a precisely configured assemblage of individual letters (type), pressure, ink, and paper. Beneath these purely material details, however, lies the essential character of printing: the mechanical capacity to mass-produce a text effectively, efficiently, and uniformly. In this regard, the Minoans apparently got there first. In 1908 Italian archaeologists excavating a ruined 1700 BCE palace in Phaistos, Crete, discovered a strange-looking six-inch clay disk. The Phaistos disk is imprinted with some 241 images (122 on one side, 119 on the other) that spiral leftward from the outer edge toward the center.

The images themselves, which include a number of repeats, represent a total of forty-five syllabic signs denoting a form of Greek that predates Homer. Although their meaning remains enigmatic, a single fact leaps out from the rest: instead of being scratched on by hand, the standard method of marking clay objects, they were stamped out with wood or ivory punches of some kind. The evidence for this is the fact that whenever a sign is repeated, *it is exactly the same.* John Chadwick, an internationally renowned expert on Cretan scripts, called the Phaistos disk "the world's first typewritten document."[7]

Why would someone go to all the trouble of intricately carving a series of punches in order to impress linguistic signs on a piece of clay, rather than marking the clay directly with a stylus of some kind? Although no similar disks have been found so far, there seems to be only one reasonable explanation: to make a lot of duplicates. Although the signs on the disk have never been fully deciphered, the scholarly consensus is that the text is a brief sacred hymn or chant, which would account for the repeated phrases. Possibly the disk was meant to be carried around as a charm to ward off evil, or to be used as a memory prompt during religious rituals. In any event, the Phaistos disk demonstrates that over thirty-three centuries before Gutenberg, someone had figured out a central piece of Brother Dominic's problem: how to create multiple identical copies of a text without resorting to the labor-intensive technique of handwritten inscription.

The next step in the evolution of printing took place over two millennia later, on the other side of the world. Clay is fine for impressing short pieces of text, but it's hopelessly impractical for anything lengthy. The challenge of finding the appropriate medium for printing—easy to make impressions on, light enough for even long texts to remain compact and portable, yet strong enough to be durable—was solved in China in AD 105 by the invention of paper.[8] At first, paper, which was made from bark, hemp waste, and old rags, was used solely for calligraphy. But by the fifth century the Chinese were impressing letters on paper with ink by means of engraved stamps. Three centuries later the Chinese, Japanese, and Koreans were printing whole books created from signs carved into blocks of wood and stone. Incredibly laborious and cumbersome though this method was, it was used in China in the late tenth century to print the entire Buddhist canon, amounting to over 130,000 pages.[9]

By about 1041, a Chinese blacksmith and alchemist named Pi Sheng had found a way to make the whole process a lot more efficient. Pi Sheng's idea was to create individual reversed signs in clay, bake them, and then assemble them in a wooden form from which an inked rubbing could be taken. The process was soon improved by creating metal characters.[10] Somewhat similar methods were subsequently used by the Koreans.

It is thus Pi Sheng and his successors, not Gutenberg, who must really take credit for inventing printing with *movable* type—that is, using small pieces of type representing individual signs that could be composed in lines, broken down, and then reused. In spite of Pi Sheng's invention, however, printing in the East was to remain a culturally peripheral phenomenon. For centuries after, books continued to be produced in relatively small numbers, largely for the religious and governing elite, and thus had little impact on society as a whole.

THE LOGIC OF MECHANICAL INVENTION

This bare recitation of historical fact raises more questions than it answers. Why did printing take so many centuries to evolve? Why was it the Chinese and not the Greeks who took the next step after the Minoans? Why didn't printing take off and become firmly rooted in those cultures that developed a printing technology prior to Gutenberg, given the enormous economic, social, and cultural advantages such an invention could confer?

To answer these questions, it's helpful to keep in mind two key aspects of mechanical devices. First, by efficiently performing repetitive tasks they typically reduce the amount of time, labor, and cost involved in producing something. Second, in addition to this purely quantitative value, mechanization may bring with it *qualitative* advantages that result in work being done more effectively. Prime among these is increased quality control: a mechanical device is typically less error prone than purely manual labor, and is thus capable of achieving a higher level of uniformity and precision among the items produced. Repetition, then, is a key factor in both the quantitative and qualitative values of mechanization.

The Phaistos disk represents the first artifact we know of in which an extended piece of text was mechanically reproduced. Potentially, this opened the way to the development of printing as we know it. The punches used to create the signs would in fact continue to play a central role in printing technology right down through Gutenberg and on into the late nineteenth century. But having taken the first step, the technique used in creating the Phaistos disk could go no further. Historically it was a dead end, incapable in the Minoan culture of the time of evolving into a truly efficient, flexible, comprehensive printing technology. The reason is obvious. Since the Minoan language had thousands of different signs representing words and syllables, anything much longer than a brief prayer or chant (which most likely would contain repeats) would run into the problem of insufficient recurrence. Again, repetition is key to both the quantitative and qualitative values of mechanization. Without it, the labor of carving the hundreds or even thousands of punches needed for comprehensive coverage would have more than offset any potential advantages (including eliminating copying errors) to be garnered from mass production. Handwritten scripts would remain the best way to go. But what about the Greeks?

By no later than the seventh century BC, the Greeks had come up with the brilliant innovation of adding vowels to the Phoenician consonant-based system of signs, thereby creating the first true alphabet. Since Greek script didn't employ capitals, punctuation, or even breaks between words, in principle just twenty-four punches would have sufficed to churn out hundreds of copies of the plays of Aeschylus and Sophocles or the dialogues of Plato, for use in school or as a means of exporting Greek culture. So why didn't the Greeks develop printing?

Aside from the machinery of war—all those brilliantly engineered triremes and devices for burning distant objects by mirroring the sun's rays—the ancient Greeks weren't an especially technologically adept or innovative race. Quite apart from that, however, two major factors blocked further development of the Phaistos technology. First, the Greeks used papyrus as the universal medium for writing, and that was too fragile for imprinting. Second, even with the exponential increase in repetition afforded by the Greek alphabet, mechanized mass production of text based on punches still couldn't compete with the existing system of handwritten copying.

Imagine that you're a smart young Greek, laboring away in a scriptorium and already bored with the work. Suddenly the proverbial light bulb goes on. Why not adapt the age-old techniques used by potters and goldsmiths for stamping out letters on clay vessels, tablets, medallions, coins, and the like? Perhaps you already see a way around the papyrus problem. You borrow a couple of dozen punches, hive off to the chariot shed, and start in on your alpha-version prototype for a revolutionary new means of mass-producing written scrolls. But of course it doesn't work. Every letter has to be impressed individually, a thousand or more per page. By the time you've completed the first line, picking up and putting down a different punch for each letter, a trained scribe would already be on paragraph three. Whoops! Oh, well, back to the scriptorium . . .

The invention of paper by the Chinese solved the papyrus problem. Wood-block printing using paper made it possible to create a page at a time. The next step in the evolution of the technology was again a small and rather natural one. Even in a syllabic system consisting, as Chinese did, of thousands of signs, there are repetitions, so why not improve efficiency by creating reusable type? One small step for Pi Sheng, one giant leap for mankind.

The Chinese, then, must take full credit at the technological level for inventing printing in the modern sense—movable type, paper, ink, pressure, all finally pulled together into a single technology. But we aren't there yet. The syllabic writing system with its thousands of signs still made printing even relatively short texts hopelessly labor-intensive. From the standpoint of pure productive efficiency, printing at this stage still couldn't compete with traditional calligraphy as a means of mass-producing texts. As in the case of the Phaistos disk, the main reason for printing books most likely had to do with eliminating scribal errors, an important consideration for religious and government documents (constituting the great majority of early printed texts) where accuracy was of prime importance. Once more, it was the qualitative issue of uniformity that was the dominant motivator.

The Chinese didn't attempt to simplify their writing system by adopting an alphabet until modern times. The Koreans, however, who were fully conversant with Chinese printing techniques, started using an alphabet in 1444, when the Emperor Sejong published *The Correct Sounds for the Instruction of the People*. This set out an alphabetic script known as Hangŭl that, having only twenty-eight letters, could be learned rapidly. Although 308 books were published during Sejong's reign, half of them using movable type, only the emperor's pet projects, plus some Buddhist literature, were printed using Hangŭl. The change was strongly resisted by the elite, whose status was very much connected to knowing how to write Chinese. Use of Hangŭl, which could have revolutionized printing, lapsed, and wasn't taken up again until 1945 in the north and the 1990s in the south. As they say in Silicon Valley, never underestimate the influence and staying power of an entrenched technology. Finally cracking the problem of how to mechanize the mass production of books and documents so effectively that scribes could no longer compete would take a very differently organized set of social and cultural conditions.

THE ENTREPRENEUR FROM MAINZ

We don't know exactly what Gutenberg said to Johann Fust, a wealthy Mainz goldsmith and merchant, when they met in 1449, although we do know Gutenberg's aim was to persuade Fust to become his business partner. Did he get him excited about the business itself, like Steve Jobs telling John Sculley there were more interesting things to do than selling sugar water? Did he emphasize the vision: together they could change the world, transform education with mass literacy, jump-start the Renaissance? Or did he run the numbers by him? In retrospect the upside turned out to be awfully good. When Gutenberg got started, you could have put all the printed books in Europe (mostly produced using the cumbersome wood-block method) in a single wagon. Fifty years later there were between 15 and 20 million.

Whatever the pitch was, it convinced Fust to make an initial investment of 800 gulden (about $125,000) at 6 percent interest in an enterprise centered on a new, largely untried technology Gutenberg had been working on for about a decade. And so, the great revolution finally got started. But once again, Why Gutenberg? Why Mainz? Why the 1550s? And what did Gutenberg need that kind of money for anyway?

Johann Gutenberg was born in Mainz around 1397. The younger son of a patrician father who was a Companion of the Mint, he was blocked from entering the ranks of patricians himself by the fact that his father had married a shopkeeper. With little prospect of inheriting property, money, or position, Gutenberg quickly realized he was going to have to make his own way in the world. Smart, well educated, ambitious, and resourceful, in 1429 at the age of thirty-two he set out from Mainz, "striving to be the first to cash in on the Continent-wide market offered by the Catholic Church."[11]

The market Gutenberg was so eager to cash in on was, in a word, *pilgrims*. In fifteenth-century Europe, going on a pilgrimage, for anyone who could afford it, was the thing to do. Aachen, for example, two hundred fifty kilometers to the north of Mainz, drew crowds of up to ten thousand pilgrims a day when, once every seven years, the city's famed relics—collected in the cathedral city Charlemagne had made his capital—were put on display. What this crowd wanted, apart from food and lodging, were basically two things— trinkets and indulgences (Church documents granting remission of temporal punishment for sin)—and Gutenberg aimed to make money in both.

The trinkets included small convex handheld mirrors for catching the invisible healing rays that were thought to stream from the relics of saints. Gutenberg put together a plan to make up to thirty-two thousand mirrors to be sold at the 1439 pilgrimage for half a gulden each. Bearing in mind this equaled about $80, Gutenberg was aiming to set up a $2.5 million business!

For that he needed cash, which he duly raised from three local Strasbourg investors.

This was Gutenberg's first real entrepreneurial venture, and like many such schemes it failed. The Aachen pilgrimage that year was postponed due to the return of the plague—the infamous Black Death—and the investors wound up losing most of their money. But Gutenberg was already at work on another money-making scheme, a "secret art" as it was described in the trial Gutenberg's first investors unsuccessfully brought against him. This art, which could only have been printing, appears to have been aimed at mass-producing indulgences, which typically promised the buyer forgiveness of sins for anywhere from three months to a lifetime, depending on the price. The Church would have taken in most of the cash, but there would still have been profit in helping it produce documents that could cost up to four gulden ($640) apiece.

THE IDEA

It is a peculiar irony that the man who did more than anyone to make producing copious written records of the past possible left almost none relating to his own. We know very little about Gutenberg's life from the time he left Mainz around 1429 to 1448, when he returned, most of it gleaned from scraps of documents such as legal and court papers. This much at least is clear. First, by the time he was back in Mainz, he still hadn't made much money. Second, he brought with him a team of six assistants, whom he promptly set up in a workshop in the family home. This suggests that he had either a fairly complete prototype or a working press that he had perhaps already used to print indulgences.

No doubt he showed it to Fust. Venture capitalists love nothing better than a demo of a viable technology, and Fust would have been well qualified to assess the potential of what he saw. For one thing, he was no stranger to the book business. His adopted son Peter Schöffer, who also became one of Gutenberg's partners, was studying calligraphy in Paris, and Fust himself traded in books. Furthermore, he was a goldsmith, so his eyes wouldn't necessarily have glazed over when Gutenberg got into the finer points of type-casting. Whatever Fust saw, he was impressed enough to insist the equipment be used as collateral for the loan.

So what did Gutenberg have to show him after years of hard work? The secret of papermaking had come to Europe via the Arabs and was now being made in several places in Germany. Paper made strictly according to Chinese methods was too soft for use with a quill pen and had to be strengthened with animal glue. This turned out to be strong enough for use with metal type, and could also be printed on both sides, but was now too hard to take a good impression and had to be dampened. Ink was also a bit of a problem. The water-based ink used by scribes wouldn't adhere to metal, and so a special oil-based ink, probably borrowed from painters or textile makers, had to be developed.[12] Then, of course, there was the famous press. Screw presses had been in use since ancient times for crushing olives and grapes and for making cheese, and currently they were also being employed to squeeze the water out of wet paper and to stamp patterns on fabrics.[13]

All of this was highly ingenious, of course, but in the end it's just the sort of tinkering you'd expect an entrepreneur with a hot new technology to engage in from the outset. The core of the business, quite obviously, was the movable type itself.

When Gutenberg got started, probably some time in the mid-1430s, there were two methods of mass-producing books in Europe: scribes and woodblocks. In other words, the state of the art was about where it was before Pi Sheng started cutting out and baking clay signs some four centuries earlier. In fact, the woodcuts were a lot cruder than anything the Chinese produced, consisting mostly of drawings with a few words attached. Carving alphabetic letters in wood would have been an excruciatingly slow business for a text of any length. Not that the scribes were exactly fast. It took an experienced scribe two to three days to turn out a page. A book produced by several hands in a scriptorium might take a couple of months, and would cost up to two months' salary for the average church or state official, depending on the quality of the rubrification (the colored, decorated margins and highly embellished capital letters at the beginnings of paragraphs). But the quality was outstanding, producing books of extraordinary beauty and workmanship. Besides, there was no shortage of scribes, and the market, though growing, wasn't exactly huge. In short, no one was looking for a breakthrough technology. No one, it seems, except a young entrepreneur from Mainz.

Which brings us back to the nub of the matter, the type—small slugs made of lead alloy about four centimeters long, each carrying the reverse image of a letter. Where did Gutenberg get *that* idea? It's the wrong question, of course. Anyone who had learned the alphabet as a child was already aware of the fact that a written text is composed of reusable, endlessly repeated elements. So, as in the case of Pi Sheng, recognizing that the next step in productivity beyond woodcuts was to break the page down into its reusable component elements wasn't exactly a huge leap. The more appropriate question is, Why didn't more people think of it sooner?

In all probability, more than one other person did have the idea. But having an idea is one thing; being able to translate it into a viable technology of mass production, never mind go on to set up a business that can turn a profit and put the competition out of business, is entirely another. In this sense, Gutenberg was ideally suited to the job.

Gutenberg's father and uncle were both Companions of the Mint. The mint itself, controlled by the archbishop of Mainz, was located in the market square a short distance from the Gutenberg house, so as a young man, Johann must have repeatedly watched highly skilled craftsmen carve the tiny heads of steel punches used for making dies for coins and commemorative medals, including the lettering on them. It would take even the best carvers a day to carve the punch for a single letter or design, in some cases doing so to an accuracy of a twenty-five-thousandth of an inch (i.e., one micron).[14] Fortunately, the invention of the alphabet meant that in principle only a few dozen punches were required to cover all upper- and lowercase letters plus a few punctuation signs, rather than the fifty thousand needed for Chinese. By the time Gutenberg moved to Strasbourg, he was listing his profession as goldsmith. The huge pilgrim market for indulgences must have set his mind thinking about how to adapt his goldsmith's knowledge to the task of mass-producing text.

Punches had been part of the history of printing since the Minoans, and were to remain so for centuries to come. But the trick to effectively *mechanizing* printing lay not in these per se, but in using them to mass-produce type that could in turn be used to mass-produce books and other documents. Here coin making provided just the model the young Johann needed. First a punch was carved in tempered steel. The intricate design would include a suitably meaningful image of some kind, plus tiny lettering. The punch, known as the *patrix*, was then used to stamp the design in a softer metal (typically copper), known as the *matrix*, thereby creating a die for one face of the coin. The two dies were then assembled in a handheld mold into which molten metal was poured. When the metal had cooled, the mold was broken apart, revealing the finished gold or silver coin.[15]

Patrix, matrix, mold.[16] That had been the basic technique for mass-producing coins and medals since ancient times. All the next step in printing took was to imagine replacing coins with metal type.

Don't invent; what you need is already out there. Just find it and integrate it.

In Gutenberg's case, what he needed had been right under his nose, ever since earliest childhood. But it would take him well over a decade to perfect and integrate it all—paper, ink, type, and press. The paper had to be of exactly the right strength and thickness to go through a mechanical process and yet remain bindable into books that would run to hundreds of pages. The ink, made from soot derived from pitch, linseed oil, and a mix of dangerously volatile, foul-smelling chemicals, had to be black enough to be clearly legible, and of just the right consistency to coat the metal type without smudging.

The type itself had to be cast to accuracies of a hundredth of a millimeter, and not just for clarity's sake (imagine the precision needed to carve the letters you are looking at as you read this). If a piece of type protruded by even a hair's breadth, other letters wouldn't print evenly. The handheld molds had to be easy enough to manipulate that a skilled typecaster could produce up to four slugs of type a minute—composing the type for a book would require hundreds of identical copies of each letter. By the late 1440s, Gutenberg was ready for something bigger than indulgences. Timing is everything. Unlike the Aachen fiasco, on this occasion history would be on his side.

THE FIRST BOOK

Printing indulgences, not something demanding the most exacting production standards, may well have been part of the beta test, but when Gutenberg met up with Fust, he already had another project in mind.

It didn't take a genius to recognize that there was a growing market for books all across fifteenth-century Catholic Europe, both among an increasingly literate public and within the Church itself. Grammars and other instructional materials were in strong demand for the wave of new schools and colleges founded from the fourteenth century on, while missals, Psalters, breviaries, and Bibles were needed for an expanding clergy. Two major problems, however, faced anyone trying to break into this market. The Church had an unbreakable monopoly on it—you had to get backing, if not explicit official approval, from the ecclesiastical hierarchy to produce and/or distribute a book; and you had to compete with a deeply entrenched industry: whole armies of scribes producing books of exceptional quality and beauty.

To succeed, a disruptive technology has to exploit some fatal weakness of the current competition. Neither cost (books were expensive but the Church was rich) nor capacity (despite increasing demand, scribes could handle it) presented an opening. A printed book, however, offered one potential advantage the scribes couldn't match: *uniformity*. In the process of copying the same work over and over by hand, scribes inevitably made mistakes, and since these flawed volumes were then in turn copied, an endlessly multiplying chain of errors arose. Gutenberg's disruptive technology wasn't so much aimed at putting the scribes out of business (which it did, twenty years later) by virtue of being cheaper or faster (which it was), but rather at supplying the Church with a significantly better product: a printing press doesn't make mistakes. The key to making money in the book market was significantly improved quality.

Here we come to one of several key cultural factors that simultaneously aligned in Gutenberg's favor. If the Church had simply been dealing with the medieval equivalent of getting rid of a few irritating typos, the matter might have rested there. But the whole issue of eliminating error in the service of uniformity was at bottom a *doctrinal* one. Christian Europe in the mid-fifteenth century was rife with religious conflict—spiritual schisms that as often as not were settled primarily on the battlefield. Germany, especially in the Rhineland, was the scene of endless sectarian religious turmoil, often pitting patricians against the rising and increasingly prosperous class of guildsmen, and Mainz found itself at the very epicenter of all this. The main reason Gutenberg set up shop in Strasbourg for over a decade while he was working on his invention was that Mainz was far too dangerous a place to be.

In this strife-plagued era, the call for Christian unity was finding increasingly receptive ears. The rapid rise to power of Nicholas of Cusa—destined to become cardinal of all Germany—was in no small measure due to his being on the stump all over Europe advocating an end to conflict and the restoration of peace and unity. One Church, one united congregation of the faithful ministered to by priests using one Bible, one Mass, and educated with one set of instructional materials. The trouble was, the scribal production of books was a cottage industry, with no central control. Local prelates had the power to order the scriptorium in the diocese to produce whichever of several competing versions of the standard religious texts—missals, breviaries, even the Bible—they preferred. In short, the Church-dominated publishing industry of the time mirrored exactly the error-prone, strife-ridden state of the Church itself.

Gutenberg, attempting to break into the publishing industry, would have been very aware of these issues and the potential of his new technology to solve them. Was this part of the dog-and-pony show Gutenberg put on for Fust that persuaded him to risk what was in those days a staggeringly large sum on a largely unproven technology in a highly regulated market? Quite possibly. Nicholas of Cusa had arrived in Mainz in December of 1448, a matter of months before Gutenberg and Fust met, and continued his campaign to get agreement on a single version of the missal and breviary to be used throughout Catholic Germany. But Fust would have been aware that discussions had bogged down, so going ahead with a printed version of such texts would still have been premature. In fact, if Fust was to be convinced, the initial product would have to meet a rather complex set of requirements.

The first book to be printed would have to be a text that existed in a standard version not subject to doctrinal debate—no point in halving the potential market by having to pick sides in a rancorous ecclesiastical conflict. It would have to be widely used, or there was no potential for profit, and be capable of "demo-ing" the technology convincingly without being so complicated that it risked cost overruns or even outright failure before the inevitable bugs in the production process could be worked out. It would also need to be a book where accuracy was an issue, but one the scribes wouldn't see as a threat to their age-old craft.

Given this rather daunting array of regulatory, entrenched industry, and competitive marketing conditions, Gutenberg's choice was tactically nothing less than brilliant. The book in question, Aelius Donatus' *Ars Grammatica*, might be mind-numbingly dull, but it solved at a stroke the whole raft of problems facing anyone attempting to introduce printing at the time. As the standard Latin grammar for schools, it was free of doctrinal controversy but constituted a huge market where uniform reproduction was an issue. Furthermore, at a mere twenty-eight pages, it was, like indulgences, short enough to be something the scribes would be more than willing to job out, and by the same token relatively straightforward to produce.

Whether Gutenberg explained this stealth strategy to him or not, Fust put up the money, and the grammar duly rolled off the presses. It appears to have been a modest success (eventually, Gutenberg would print some twenty-four editions), but the initial run didn't make enough to cover all of Gutenberg's costs. In fact, Gutenberg wasn't even able to pay the 150 gulden he owed in interest on the original loan, and in 1452 he was forced to go back to Fust for more money. Fust may at first have demurred, but whatever initial doubts he may initially have had about coming up with a second round of financing apparently vanished when Gutenberg told him what he wanted the money for, and he promptly advanced another 800 gulden. He was now in for well over a quarter of a million dollars.

GUTENBERG'S MASTERPIECE

In 1452 Nicholas of Cusa finally succeeded in his campaign to establish a uniform set of liturgical texts. With the pope's backing, he settled the conflict over which texts were to be used in German churches and monasteries, including approving a new missal and standard edition of the Bible. Gutenberg, recognizing an unparalleled opportunity, seized it.

What Gutenberg was now pitching to Fust was not some ugly, utterly pedestrian school grammar, a work so dull and unloved that not a single complete copy has survived, but the very capstone of Church literature, a book capable of showcasing Gutenberg's new technology to all of Christendom while simultaneously serving the purposes of powerful princes of the Church, all the way up to the pope himself. The idea was outrageously ambitious, but with the technology now proven, and the regulatory path cleared, definitely doable. The marketing fallout from producing a widely used Bible certainly wouldn't have been lost on Fust, as canny and daring an investor as we are likely to find in this first era of capitalism. But still, what about the numbers?

The Donatus grammar was short. The Bible, in the two-volume, forty-two-line format Gutenberg was proposing, would be 1,275 pages long. Printing it was going to require a significant investment in supplies alone: 5,000 vellum calfskins for the thirty to thirty-five luxury vellum copies, each taking a month or more to prepare; 200,000 pages, handmade in Italy, for the remaining 150 paper copies; six additional presses; ink; typecasting metals; rent for a second workshop. And of course, wages.[17]

A prodigious amount of labor was involved in creating such a product. Because Gutenberg didn't want his revolutionary technology to put off potential buyers by appearing to be too radical a break with current practice, he chose to make his typeface look as much like the best scribal handwriting as possible. Which meant not only imitating all the different versions of a letter that scribes used, depending on its place in the manuscript, but all the ligatures indicating an abbreviation to save space. In all, Gutenberg needed 290 different characters, each requiring a separate punch that would take a day to carve. Each page of the forty-two-line Bible contained on average 500 words, or about 2,600 characters, including about 275 individual types of the letter *e*.[18] Six compositors, each working on three pages at a time (composing one, printing another, dismantling a third), would have required at least 46,000 characters, each a tiny piece of type that had to be cast by hand. In all, they would have to compose some *3 million* characters.

The German book historian Leonard Hoffmann has estimated that Gutenberg's expenditures for printing the Bible would have totaled 2,120 gulden, or about $340,000. The bill for the paper alone was 400 gulden, nearly a fifth of the total.[19] It took a team of between twenty and thirty highly skilled craftsmen two years to complete, printing some 230,000 pages in all.

The design was extraordinary. Following scribal tradition each page was set out in two columns that together made up an area based on the "golden section," a ratio of about 5:8 that is particularly pleasing to the eye, and that can be found in many buildings in antiquity, including the Parthenon. The Gothic typeface, even today still sharp and black, was virtually indistinguishable from the finest handwritten manuscripts. In only one detail did it vary: the right-hand margin was justified (i.e., even), something that was impossible to do in handwritten manuscripts. If anything, it added a final touch of elegance.

To jump from twenty-eight pages to 1,275, from the pedestrian to the sublimely beautiful, was an act of extraordinary daring. To paraphrase Steve Jobs, another entrepreneur with a passion for beauty and technological innovation, the Gutenberg Bible was an *insanely great product*. It was also Gutenberg's downfall.

Fust must surely have suspected when he made the second loan that Gutenberg would only go deeper into debt, and he was right. By the time the Bible was ready, in 1454, Gutenberg still hadn't managed to pay any interest on either loan. And so Fust made his move. He went to court, demanding repayment in accordance with the contracts Gutenberg had signed. The court decided in Fust's favor, and he walked away with not just the presses but the Bible as well. To add insult to injury, he then hired away some of Gutenberg's best people, including Fust's own adopted son, Peter Schöffer, and the father-son team went on to produce a whole stream of books for the Church. Later, Schöffer, who was to become the first international printer and bookseller, would even endeavor to claim that the invention was his, too.

Gutenberg was by no means destitute. He still had the original printing works he'd set up in the family home, and he continued to turn out other texts, including two thousand indulgences ordered by Nicholas in 1452 to help raise cash for mercenaries to resist a possible Turkish invasion of Cyprus. By the time he died in 1468, the technology of printing was already beginning to spread across Europe, radiating out from Mainz to Strasbourg, up and down the Rhine Valley and into the Danube basin; then on to Basel, Antwerp, and Venice; by the 1470s it had reached Paris, Lyon, and London. Print shops were springing up at the rate of eight per year; by 1500 there were some one thousand printing works spread across 236 towns throughout the continent and employing up to twenty thousand people. Venice alone had over one hundred fifty presses, and could boast of being the printing capital of Europe. Perhaps even more astonishing was the number of books published—between 15 and 20 million, amounting to 28,360 titles! In a move any modern venture capitalist would have appreciated, Peter Schöffer, who inherited his father's business, tried to monopolize this tidal wave of expansion by making his trainees promise not to reveal their trade secrets. He might as well have played King Canute.[20]

In just two decades Gutenberg had brilliantly reinvented and improved a technology that, unknown to him, dated back centuries. If strictly speaking the Chinese got there first, it was Gutenberg who succeeded in cracking the problem of making the mass production of books economically viable, transforming forever how books and other texts are produced. The scribes lasted another twenty years or so and then vanished forever. One statistic tells all. On average it took several scribes one to two months to produce a single copy of a book. By the time Gutenberg died, five hundred could be printed in a single week, an increase in productivity on the order of 30,000 percent or more. This hard-won gain is the true miracle of Gutenberg's method of printing. No craft or industry, no matter how entrenched, could withstand that kind of onslaught.

But the most earth-shattering and deeply ironic change wrought by printing lay nearly a half-century ahead. Luther's ninety-five theses, whether they were actually nailed to the door of the castle church in Wittenberg in 1517 or (as most scholars now suspect) leaked via Luther's letter to the archbishop, were to lead directly to a deep and permanent schism in the Church. As in the American revolution, printing played a fundamental role in fanning the flames of revolt. It has been estimated that between 1518 and 1525, over three hundred thousand copies of Luther's works were in circulation, representing perhaps as much as a third of the books printed in Germany during that period. Gutenberg, with his dream of contributing to the Church's reunification, could only have regarded this as a tragedy.

The rise of the European novel, the rapid and reliable dissemination of scientific discoveries, the American and French revolutions, and the advent of nationalism, among many other significant turning points in Western history, were yet to come, all undreamed of by Gutenberg yet all deeply influenced by his invention. No subsequent invention—not steam power, not the telegraph, not the automobile, not even the computer—comes close to having the same impact, if only because these later developments themselves depended in part on the mass distribution of knowledge that had become possible as a result of printing. Gutenberg's press was a massive tipping point, for printing and more broadly for Western culture as a whole.

CULTURE, HISTORY, AND THE INDIVIDUAL IMAGINATION

As every investor and inventor knows, timing is a huge factor in successful risk taking, especially when it comes to pursuing the Next Big Thing.[21] Both the development of the personal computer and the Barbie doll, as we've seen, owed much to their close fit with emergent social and cultural factors of the period. A major part of the successful venture capitalist or entrepreneur's genius is to recognize the convergence of such factors, and to creatively exploit the dynamic patterns that are in the process of emerging—in other words, to let the space of ideas do some of the thinking. Thus are culture, history, and imagination yoked together in the creative act.

But just how do you get the timing right? How do you learn to "read the world" as it were, to correctly discern the emergent opportunity? And what do the dynamic laws of networked idea-spaces reveal about how to do this successfully?

As we've seen, for printing to reach its fully evolved form and finally take off, a whole array of elements had to align themselves: the physical technology (stamping, metal molding equipment, and paper); the cultural technology (an alphabet); market access (initially via winning the backing of religious and cultural elites); rising literacy rates (to produce a mass market); a strong need for uniformity (to give printing a competitive advantage over the scribes); and investment capital.

The Minoans developed a primitive printing technology and gained the backing of the priestly elite because of its capacity to eliminate copying errors, but failed to get beyond a few brief texts in clay for want of an alphabet, a more appropriate medium, and a more literate culture. The Greeks had the basic physical technology, an alphabet, open market access, and a literate culture, but lacked paper. The Chinese, whose governing elite also appreciated printing's guarantee of uniformity, had the technology, the medium, and the market access, but lacked an alphabet and a broad literate market. The Koreans had practically all of it, even an alphabet, but their entrenched scholarly elite wasn't about to give up its privileges even to please the emperor. In the end, achieving success in printing was like aligning a Rubik's cube, with now this set of elements, now that coming together in different combinations. Not until the middle of the fifteenth century did everything finally line up.

The key new element in Gutenberg's day was *capital*. The rise of early forms of capitalism fueled the growth of trade and technology (e.g., global exploration, shipbuilding, wind power, architecture), resulting in further demand for investment. This economic growth in turn both stimulated and was stimulated by rising education and the mounting demand for knowledge. Partly in response to economic expansion and partly to meet its own needs, the Church, which at the time was responsible for education, acted to promote learning through building more schools. This common interest with capitalism, however, was counterbalanced not only by Church control of schooling, but also by the fact that the market for goods and services, though expanding rapidly, was still partly regulated by the ecclesiastical authorities. The Church thus had considerable influence over the growth of capitalism, creating significant tension between itself and proponents of a free market.

Where does Fust's investment fit into this picture? Put yourself in his shoes for a moment. With hindsight, we recognize Fust cannily put up the first and second rounds of investment for the biggest Next Big Thing of all time. But what was the view of the future in 1449? The smart money was going into building faster trading ships. The existing market for books, while growing, was still relatively small, highly regulated, subject to the tumult of Church politics, and well served by an entrenched cottage industry of scribes. And the entrepreneur's track record already included going bankrupt in some madcap scheme to make money selling mirrors to pilgrims.

Whatever form Gutenberg's pitch to Fust took, the underlying logic of the situation, which he must have exploited, looked like this. Rising literacy clearly represented both a threat and an opportunity for the Church. Potentially it could increase doctrinal schisms (a fact that Luther would later brilliantly exploit). If the Church could succeed in circulating uniform texts, however, then control over education could be reasserted. The new metal-based technology of printing would make such uniformity possible. Moreover, high-volume metal type fabrication (which was capital intensive) would make mass production of books cost effective. This in turn would fuel the emerging market for books, improve mass education, and thus further stimulate an expanding capitalist economy.

In persuading Fust to invest in his new press, Gutenberg created a weak tie between money and the production of books whose strength manifested in a pair of highly synergistic feedback loops connecting capitalism, printing technology, uniformity, mass literacy, and Church desire for control, as figure 9-1 shows.

FIGURE 9-1

Printing lies at the center of a series of interlinked hubs/hotspots

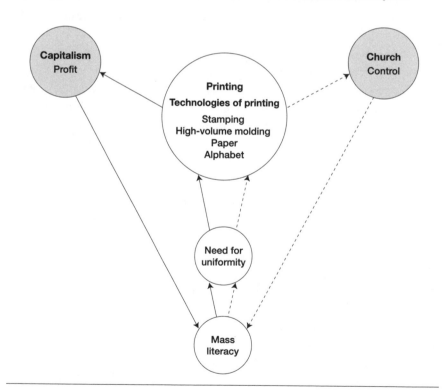

The Church supported the growth of literacy through expanded schooling, but wanted to end doctrinal schisms via uniform texts. Since printing supplied these, the Church sanctioned the new technology. As more uniform texts became available, the Church could feel secure in further expansion of education, thereby renewing the cycle. Correspondingly, capitalism needed mass literacy to satisfy increased demand for knowledge and an educated workforce. This could best be supplied by the economically viable mass production of texts, which could be achieved via the uniformity (stamping/high-volume type molding) that lay at the heart of Gutenberg's mechanization of printing. Increased production of texts not only provided a huge potential source of profit, but also furthered capitalism's expansion via education, again triggering the cycle.

As John Man has aptly observed, by Gutenberg's time, printing was "an invention waiting to happen."[22] Gutenberg's press created a highly dynamic fit between the quite distinct interests of the Church and an emergent capitalism in regard to rapidly expanding literacy. The intelligence embedded in two relatively antagonistic idea-spaces could now become linked in a highly positive, self-reinforcing network. Fust may have lacked a formal understanding of the network laws of fitness, but he intuitively understood how such interlocking relationships were creating a huge opening. No wonder he didn't hesitate—the timing was perfect, and the prospects for exponential growth excellent.

If Fust's decision—to invest or not—was relatively straightforward, the imaginative challenge facing Gutenberg in finding exactly the right mix of technologies to make printing economically viable certainly was not. To understand how he solved it, we need to probe more deeply into the network dynamics of the situation.

PRINTING AND THE PARADOX OF THE LAW OF SMALL-WORLD NETWORKS

As we know, in network science a web of linked hubs is termed a small-world network. The interconnected hubs/idea-spaces (including their constituent elements of embedded intelligence) mapped out in figure 9-1 clearly represent such a network. Since in a small-world network, every node is connected to every other by just a few links ("six degrees of separation"), navigation should be simple: the would-be starlet in Kansas has a friend who knows an indie film maker in New York who worked for a producer in Hollywood who has the ear of a director . . . Such connectors, reaching out through a web of weak ties, make connecting easy—*when the overall path is more or less known*. But what if it isn't?

Paradoxically, contrary to what the name implies, in this situation small-world networks turn out to be a major source of the navigation problem. In a network in which nodes have on average k links, a hub with k links has k^d nodes d links away.[23] Thus a hub with just 7 links has 49 nodes just 2 links away, 343 just 3 links away, and so on. This is a form of Cantor's principle (there are always more sets of things than things), which as we saw, makes navigation harder. The law of spontaneous generation (in a hub-dominated network, meaningful new sets of relationships will inevitably emerge) points to the massive generativity inherent in small-world networks. In other words, small-world networks are huge *virtual network expansion machines*, spawning multiple new, potentially meaningful idea-spaces and connections between them.

Solving the navigation problem, as we've seen repeatedly, is the key to successfully making a creative leap. The question is, How do you find the route to a successful breakthrough when faced with so many possible paths? How do you ensure you wind up with the double helix, the Apple II, or Barbie, rather than Pauling's three-stranded model of DNA, the North Star computer, or Bizzy Lizzy? Gutenberg had to make the leap from extremely crude woodcut prints all the way to a fully functioning press capable of efficiently mass-producing text. Solving this severe navigation problem would require—in addition to mechanical genius and sheer hard work—entrepreneur's luck and a powerful imaginative intelligence, alternately guided by and refashioning the enormously rich web of ideas in which he found himself.

It was Gutenberg's good fortune to stand at the very nexus of the hotspots and feedback loops that gave birth to printing. The product of excellent schooling, Gutenberg was a devout Catholic, a follower of Nicholas of Cusa (the main proponent of uniformity), the son of a Companion of the Mint familiar with sophisticated metalsmithing skills, and an inveterate tinkerer driven by strong entrepreneurial instincts. That connected him closely to virtually all the intelligence embedded in the idea-spaces that jointly gave rise to printing.

Gutenberg seems to have intuitively sensed the power that lay at the center of this configuration and the immense opportunity that it portended. But that didn't solve Gutenberg's own navigation problem: finding a technology capable of cost-effectively printing millions of books. Like Crick and Watson, he had to make several imaginative leaps, connecting things until *everything clicked*.

Does the lens of network dynamics afford some glimpse into how the central ideas evolved in his mind, or when the tipping point was reached and everything fell into place? Let's take another look at the key technologies of printing, focusing in particular on the relationship between stamping, high-volume molding, and the alphabet.

A key part of figuring out how to mass-produce books cost effectively lay in recognizing that written prose is made up of endlessly varying combinations of the same basic set of twenty-odd alphabetical letters. The point may seem utterly obvious now, but as Paul Needham insightfully observes, this wasn't necessarily how a scribe would see things. Gutenberg's invention, he notes, "required a fresh look at the question of how to create text. When writing, scribes thought in terms of one word or phrase at a time, not one letter at a time. As they created words using successive strokes of a quill pen, individual letters often took on slightly different shapes, according to the influence of the letters that preceded or followed it [sic]."[24]

Scribes were also inclined to see each text, and even each page and line, as a unique object, both aesthetically and in terms of content. Every element of a book bore its own individual pattern of decoration, not just in the binding, but in the rubrification that adorned each page and paragraph. Gutenberg followed scribal practice in creating multiple variants of the same letter, the better to match their standard of beauty, but not the scribes' mode of thinking. Even while creating up to twelve different versions of some letters, he nevertheless saw them as *standard elements* that could be stamped out in large batches of uniform pieces of type. And of course, as we know, he was an advocate of doctrinal uniformity as well.

There's a fascinating matrix of ideas here that resonate with one another, and that go to the very core of Gutenberg's imagination. We speak of putting the stamp of authority or approval on something, and of minting new ideas. Uniformity, achieved by stamping out dissent, is also the result of the stamping process used in making coins. And coins, mass produced in this way, are an excellent means of achieving a form of centralized control through standardizing money. We also speak of putting ideas in circulation.[25] And of course, minting money is exactly what an entrepreneur like Gutenberg aimed to do, as his initial foray into the pilgrim trinket and indulgences market revealed. Somehow all this seems to have settled into a new gestalt in Gutenberg's fertile imagination. The twin ideas of doctrinal unity through uniform texts and the process of stamping out identical metal coins seem to have played off one another in his mind, reciprocally growing fitter until they fused into a single new idea—a printing technology based on high-volume production of standardized type. Scribes couldn't think in terms of standardized products—their whole craft was oriented toward producing unique objects of beauty. It took a goldsmith, the devout entrepreneurially minded son of a coin-making family, to enter that space of ideas and make the connection.[26]

Here indeed, as both Gutenberg and Fust recognized, was an idea (surely the irony couldn't have been lost on either of them) capable of making money. All it would require now was Gutenberg's mechanical genius and a decent infusion of capital. But the tipping point had been reached, the great insight achieved. As Crick might have said, *there were no more jumps to be made* . . .

The space of ideas thinks for you. Gutenberg's imagination seems to have been deeply interpenetrated by the configuration of external idea-spaces in which he operated. To get from woodblock printing to printing with movable type involved following a path largely configured by the dynamic interaction of existing culturally embedded ideas, practices, skills, and intelligence. In this highly networked space, the same basic laws were operating *inside and outside*, at the level of both Gutenberg's imagination and the culture as a whole. In particular, the fundamental dynamic, a fascinating if seemingly paradoxical oscillation between potentially exponential expansion and focused contraction, was a product of the law of small-world networks.

As the number of hubs in the overall space increased through the emergence of hotspots such as capitalism, mass literacy, and the religious imperative of doctrinal unity, the size of the small-world network created by these hubs increased dramatically. The more hubs there are, the greater the number of ways there are of creating links between the nodes they dominate. This expansive, potentially destabilizing dynamic, however, was constrained by the law of the fit get fitter, which because it produces *increased coherence*, has a corresponding narrowing effect on the space of possibilities. In the case of printing, increasing fitness took two main forms: necessary conditions, and sets of reciprocal relationships.

The cultural/historical space in which a fully viable form of printing could emerge was defined by an array of hubs/idea-spaces and the intelligence embedded in them, with each component in the network playing a necessary role. The greater the number of necessary conditions, the more narrowly the space is defined. By Gutenberg's day, that space was uniquely *fit* for the emergence of printing. Correspondingly, the core insight that led to Gutenberg's printing press resulted from the focusing effect produced by the reciprocal interplay between the hubs of entrepreneurial capitalism, doctrinal standardization, and the technology of minting, each delimiting the other like overlapping Venn diagrams. The space defined by their intersection was again uniquely appropriate, its high fitness serving to eliminate other possible paths through the maze of possibilities.

Once the hotspot of printing was in place, the various feedback loops illustrated in figure 9-1 enabled the law of the fit get rich, now accelerated by the high connectivity of the law of small-world networks, to kick in. This led to vast new cycles of expansion—otherwise known as the emergence of the modern world.

I've described the law of small-world networks informally. Stated formally, including the effect of its interaction with the laws of spontaneous generation and of fitness, it looks like this:

THE LAW OF SMALL-WORLD NETWORKS

In a large scale-free (hub-dominated) network, the distance between any two nodes is small, typically less than six. While each additional hub potentially increases the total size of the network exponentially, increasing fitness (in the form of reciprocal relationships) will lead to the emergence of narrow, even uniquely defined worlds, thereby concretely specifying navigation pathways. Conversely, such worlds, once configured, expand rapidly as the law of the fit get rich is accelerated by closely linked hubs.

THE NETWORKED DYNAMICS OF RISK

The inventor and the investor are alike in that both are seeking to find their way to future success in a maze of possibilities. The greater the maze, the greater the risk of failure. Success is a matter of effective navigation through a networked search space. The law of small-world networks embodies the heart of the paradox of risk: the very growth and expansion that both the inventor and investor dream of make the navigation problem harder. The more dynamic hubs there are in a small world, the greater the generative potential, but the bigger the search space.

The tools required to deal successfully with risk associated with breakthroughs are imagination, intuition, and insight, and the intelligence that drives them. Intuition recognizes the particular small-world network—the cultural/historical pattern of hubs—and the power residing there. In particular, in "reading the world," it is sensitive to hotspots, the most dynamic hubs from which heat is currently emanating. These trigger the search for reciprocal fitness, coherence, and the sudden insight that will tip the space, swiftly transforming relative disorder into a new order that narrows the search space to just a few promising possibilities. Now the imagination can go to work, trying different paths, making jumps, tinkering, refining, until finally it all comes together in a new gestalt, and a new paradigm is born. A hotspot in its own right, the new space creates feedback loops to the surrounding hubs, increasing the overall fitness of the small-world network as a whole and allowing the generative/expansive phase to resume once more.

This cycle of expansion/focused contraction/renewed expansion of the possibility space is a function of the law of small-world networks, operating in conjunction with the laws of spontaneous generation, navigation, hotspots, the fit get fitter, and the fit get rich. Coming to a better understanding of its dynamics will provide a whole new perspective on the risk this involves, both for inventors and discoverers, and for those who want to be the first to invest in an emergent breakthrough.

In successful risk taking, timing is everything, and the only thing worse than being behind the curve is being too far ahead of it. Pi Sheng's invention of movable type fell short because other necessary conditions like the alphabet, mass literacy, and capital investment were missing. The Xerox Alto was a technological marvel, but failed catastrophically because neither the industrial nor social environments were ready for such a sophisticated machine: the drivers weren't in place for lowering the cost to the price point the market was looking for, and the appropriate applications and programs that could make full use of its complex functionality hadn't been developed, any more than had public awareness of what to use a PC for. Brown and Duguid list any number of other technological breakthroughs that died because social practices invariably lag well behind the pace of technological development.[27]

So how do you know when the timing is just right? Again, intelligent intuition, insight, and imagination. You let your mind dwell on the dynamic interplay of hubs, and be drawn to emerging hotspots. You ask yourself what's new here, what could be new, what the pattern is that would make sense of the swirling confusion. Gradually (or perhaps suddenly), things simplify, the elements reorder themselves, move into a novel alignment, and something new begins to take shape in your mind's eye. Now you see it, and the puzzle is, why doesn't everyone else? Why, it's obvious—architecture enriched and transformed by the revolutionary thinking of modern art; sexy, glamorous teenage dolls in place of baby dolls; a computer you can use at home and configure yourself. *It all fits.*

It all fits. The fool on the hill always has a better view, can see earlier than others precisely where power and energy are concentrated in certain arrays of networked idea-spaces, and can quickly grasp new alignments and ways of linking things.

Business analysts speak of synergies and convergences in talking about how the future is going to look. Mostly these predictions fail, because they're using the wrong model. The new new thing never lies on a straight linear path, but comes into view unexpectedly. Why didn't we see it coming? Network dynamics, and the laws of self-organization that govern them, are beginning to lay bare why the way the future unfolds is so often nonlinear, and why only certain gifted individuals have the capacity to grasp the opportunities that are emerging. We've examined seven laws so far. It's time to look at the eighth, the law of integration, which shows how things all pull together.

Chapter Ten

THE TRIUMPH OF THE IMAGINATION

New Art, the New Economy, and the Law of Integration

More light . . .

—Goethe

The best mathematics is serious as well as beautiful . . . The "seriousness" of a mathematical theorem lies . . . in the significance of the mathematical ideas which it connects. We may say, roughly, that a mathematical idea is "significant" if it can be connected, in a natural and illuminating way, with a large complex of other mathematical ideas.

—G. H. Hardy, *A Mathematician's Apology*[1]

When Wordsworth chanced upon one of J. M. W. Turner's pictures in the Royal Academy show of 1830, he remarked to a journalist, "Did you ever see anything like that? . . . It looks to me as if the painter had indulged in raw liver when he was very unwell."[2] If Wordsworth's appreciation of contemporary art was not his strongest gift, the professional critics were scarcely any kinder in appraising Turner's paintings:

A strange jumble . . . thrown higgledy-piggledy together, streaked blue and pink and thrown in a flour tub. (John Eagles on Juliet and her Nurse*)*[3]

This is madness. (James Boaden on Falls of the Rhine at Schaffhausen*)*[4]

[He has] disgraced the high powers that dwell in him by caprices more wild and ridiculous than any other man out of Bedlam would indulge in. (The London Times *on* Falls of the Rhine*)*[5]

And all this was in reference to Turner's more conventional *exhibited* paintings. Such critics had never even laid eyes on his most original works, which Turner understandably held back and were never shown during his lifetime. Among these, constituting three-quarters of his paintings, were about fifty canvases discovered in the cellars of the National Gallery in 1939, rolled up and thought to be old tarpaulins. Representing Turner's late, most abstract style, having no identifiable subject, "depend[ing] for their effect entirely on light and colour,"[6] they were judged by Sir Charles Eastlake, director of the National Gallery and one of Turner's executors, to be "unfit for public exhibition."[7]

Modern critical opinion has shifted significantly. The distinguished art historian Sir Kenneth Clark judged that Turner "was a genius of the first order—far the greatest painter that England has ever produced . . . *Turner painted in a style absolutely outside his own time*—perhaps the first great artist to do so. Even exhibited pictures like *Rain, Steam, Speed* have no relation to anything that was being done in Europe, or was to be done for almost a century. In 1840 they must have looked absolutely crazy . . ."[8]

The space of ideas can blind you. Turner's contemporary detractors quite simply possessed no adequate framework within which to understand his achievement. In the early part of the nineteenth century, landscape painting was still judged in terms of seventeenth-century Italian idealist and Dutch naturalistic models. By these standards, even Turner's more conventional paintings look poorly executed and disorderly. Lacking a structured idea-space within which to make sense of what Turner was trying to do, the critics simply decided he was mad.

A glance at just two paintings suffices to show how far Turner traveled and how revolutionary a painter he became, especially in his later years. The first, *Dido Building Carthage*, consciously imitates seventeenth-century landscape painting that Turner modeled himself on in his early period. The second, *Sunrise, with a Boat Between Headlands*, is a work, entirely characteristic of his late period, "which could be shown with the canvases of any Abstract Expressionist."[9] (See figure 10-1.)

No painter except Picasso advanced so far from the painting styles he inherited, or bequeathed to those who came after him such a radically new vision of what painting could be. Turner's influence largely skipped over the art of the next five or six decades, but the revolution he wrought anticipated some of the most profound characteristics of twentieth-century painting.

FIGURE 10-1

J. M. W. Turner
(1775–1851): *Sunrise, with*
a Boat Between Headlands

Source: © Tate, London 2006. Used with permission.

His late paintings, of which *Sunrise* is a characteristic example, constitute an art in which light and color predominate over form, kinetic force replaces classical stasis, abstraction undermines faith in the reliability of visual representation, and (in seeming anticipation of relativity theory) space and time merge. To put it simply, Turner is the first truly *modern* painter.[10]

Great painters do more than produce beautiful or inspiring images. They succeed in *transforming the context of painting itself*, the space in which it can unfold in the future. This act of artistic paradigm creation is the work of the imaginative intelligence par excellence, transporting the mind to as yet unexplored regions where reason cannot go.

Turner possessed an imaginative intelligence of the highest order. His most radical achievements—liberating color, reducing figural representation to the point of pure abstraction, and making the process of painting meaningful in its own right—were, in modern business parlance, *game-changing moves*, representing a huge creative leap whose influence we can still recognize in the art of our own time. But the impulses that led him along this path flowed less from his own abundant artistic talent than from his passionate engagement with and integration of two of the most powerful emergent idea-spaces of the nineteenth century: Romantic art and empirical science. The very antithetical tension between them seems to have set his imagination on fire.

Turner's development as an artist affords a window into how the imagination does some of its most radical and exciting work: creating a new idea-space by integrating intelligence embedded in widely separated existing or emergent spaces. The unfolding of Turner's thinking as an artist shows how he allowed key ideas from Romanticism and science to play off one another until they finally—and powerfully—fused.

Integration is fundamental to breakthrough creativity. Without it, the linking of ideas and idea-spaces, no matter how novel, will fail to achieve the aimed-for tipping point and lapse into disorder. As we will see later, it was in no small measure the failure to recognize the imperatives of integration, embodied in the eighth law of network dynamics, that led to the demise of that most recent glorious attempt at game changing, the half-finished revolution of the new economy.

CULTURE, PAINTING, AND DOMINANT IDEA-SPACES

All cultures operate, with varying degrees of awareness, within some overarching framework, a dominant idea-space (or set of such spaces) that organizes and integrates pervasive sets of ideas, assumptions, practices, traditions, social institutions, economic conditions, and religious beliefs—that is, other idea-spaces—relating to the nature of the lived-in world, human beings' place in it, and what truly matters in the general scheme of things. The Hawaiians who greeted Captain Cook clearly lived in a quite different dominant idea-space from the one he and his fellow sailors inhabited. Similarly, it's not hard to recognize that we ourselves, with our profound faith in the powers of science and technology, global commerce, and the modern corporation, live in a quite distinct space from, say, fourteenth-century Florentines.

Artists of all stripes—poets, novelists, musicians, dramatists—are often peculiarly sensitive to the dominant idea-space of their age, and painters are no exception: think of Michelangelo and Picasso, and the very different ways in which they both typified and helped create the social, cultural, and aesthetic milieus of which they were part.[11] Art is deeply interwoven into the web of concepts, ideas, assumptions, practices, and institutions that make up our world, and is connected, both passively and actively, in their ongoing transformation.

Turner's chosen artistic genre, landscape painting, though it has roots in medieval art, did not come into its own until the seventeenth century, reaching its climactic point of development with impressionism in the latter part of the nineteenth century. It thus affords a unique window into the extraordinary series of revolutions in dominant idea-spaces that swept through European culture following the Renaissance, culminating in the birth of modernism. These included the decline of classical idealism; the rise and fall of both Enlightenment rationalism and Romantic subjectivity; the progressive decay of conventional religious belief combined with a new interest in pantheism, transcendentalism, and other unorthodox spiritual movements; and the emergence of an empirically based scientific methodology leading to the monumental paradigm shift of Einsteinian relativity.

Turner (1775–1851) occupied a critical place in all this, being witness during the sixty or so years of his working life to "the period of the most profound social, economic and scientific change that the world had ever seen."[12] When Turner began painting seriously at the age of fifteen, the century of the Enlightenment—intellectually rationalist, economically agrarian—was drawing to a close. By the time of his death, the Great Exhibition at the Crystal Palace in London was showcasing the results of the Industrial Revolution, railways had been laid across much of England, steam power was rapidly replacing sail, and the Royal Society was weekly convulsing the scientific world with new empirically based theories about light, heat, electromagnetism, chemical elements and compounds, geological formation, astronomical bodies, and more generally the underlying unity of the sciences. Turner was supremely sensitive to multiple aspects of this extraordinary period of upheaval, uncertainty, and transformation, and vividly registered his response to them in his painting—not passively, as a seismograph records passing tremors, but with the active, shaping force of an extraordinarily imaginative intelligence. As we examine the development of Turner's artistic vision, we will see in particular how he integrates the opposing idea-spaces of Romanticism and science. This became his crowning achievement, creating a new idea-space for art that would gain its fullest resonance more than a century later.

Like all great painters, Turner was a close student of art history, and his own painting has its origins in both Italian idealism and Dutch realism, the two principal movements that characterized the rise of landscape painting in the early 1600s. Italian idealism, with its roots in the art of the Renaissance, is typified by the expatriate French painters Claude Lorrain and Nicholas Poussin, both of whom lived in Rome. As a young painter Turner worshipped Claude, and his *Dido Building Carthage* is explicitly—and visibly—based on Claude's *Seaport with the Embarkation of the Queen of Sheba*.

Claude's painting shimmers with light, its golden hues reflecting the mythic Golden Age that painters of the Italian idealist school so often depicted. Nature is certainly represented, in the form of sea, sky, clouds, sun, and trees, but its depiction remains remarkably urbane. The overall architecture of the painting is composed, in accordance with the idealist dictates of the period, of carefully balanced masses marked off by a series of horizontals, verticals, and a strong diagonal that leads the eye to the center of the canvas.

If the harmonious order of Italian idealist landscapes appeals to the mind, the realism of Dutch naturalist landscapes engages the senses. We have only to think of Vermeer's almost photographic *View of Delft*, or Rembrandt's wonderfully detailed landscape sketches, to see we are in a very different world, one that prizes true-to-life color, realistic detail, and the depiction of natural vistas largely for their own sake.

Dutch naturalism was the artistic expression of a vast cultural and social shift taking place in northern Europe. Rapidly expanding global trade and rising prosperity, particularly in the Netherlands and England, was weakening the influence of the Renaissance on these non-Mediterranean countries. An increasingly wealthy commercial class had little use for worshipping an idealized past. At the same time, empirical science entered the cultural mainstream. The latter's objective, fact-based ethos was quite inimical to the idealism of Italian post-Renaissance painting.

An early seascape by Turner reveals how much he had learned from his Dutch predecessors. In *Calais Pier*, we can see the extraordinary skill with which Turner is able to depict every curl of the surging surf, the billowing sails, and the shifting light of a gathering squall. In his realistic depiction of the sea and ships, and especially the beautifully modulated light, Turner is not only drawing on but in fact surpassing his Dutch predecessors.

By the time Turner painted this picture, however, a second post-Renaissance dominant idea-space was already beginning to emerge, this time in England. In 1798 Wordsworth published *Lyrical Ballads*, and the emotion-laden *weltanschauung* of Romanticism was born. We can already see signs of this shift in *Calais Pier*. Turner brings the water right up to the edge of the picture plane, so that the viewer not only feels part of the scene, but indeed may suffer the vertigo-inducing illusion of being about to tip right into the churning sea below. This engagement of the viewer's emotions is heightened by the depiction of the wild forces of nature threatening to produce a disaster. At the same time, Turner lightens the drama by means of the painting's humorous narrative. As Walker notes in his commentary, Turner, himself a skilled sailor, had little respect for French seamanship:

> The skiff trying to get away from the jetty will surely be dashed to pieces, blown against the dock by the gale; yet the man in the stern is doing nothing to avert the calamity. Instead he is holding up a bottle of cognac, furious that his wife on the pier has kept back a second flagon. Another man grasps an oar, but the other oar seems to have gone overboard. No one is hoisting a sail. There is general confusion everywhere. By contrast, the English packet, which is beating up to the pier, shows how a boat should be sailed.[13]

Here Turner anticipates a theme that, in his later painting, he will elevate almost to the level of metaphysics: order in the midst of potential chaos.

By the opening decade of the nineteenth century, Turner had entered fully into the spirit of Romanticism, painting scene after scene in which the vast, unpredictable forces of nature threaten to overwhelm the puny efforts of human beings to survive and protect themselves. The titles of these paintings, created in Turner's mature middle period, speak for themselves: *Cottage Destroyed by an Avalanche*; *The Burning of the Houses of Parliament*; *Snow Storm: Hannibal and His Army Crossing the Alps*; *Slavers Throwing Overboard the Dead and Dying—Typhoon Coming On.* In Ruskin's words, Turner portrayed "the utmost anxiety and distress, of which human life is capable."[14] Looking at these paintings might convey the impression that Turner had now abandoned his earlier attempts to balance the Romantic spirit of wildness and excess with its antitheses, classical idealism and Dutch realism. But that would make him a far less interesting painter. The work of integrating idea-spaces would continue, but now at an altogether deeper level.

INTEGRATING THE TWO CULTURES

Claude Monet famously dismissed Turner "because of the exuberant romanticism of his fancy."[15] The label stuck, if not the disparaging implication of being a Romantic painter. Clark, for example, following Ruskin's lead, assures us that Turner "was an arch-romantic, recreating the moods of all the great romantic poets—Wordsworth, Byron and latterly Shelley—by an appeal through colour to our emotions."[16] Other critics have generally taken a similar interpretive stance.[17] Recent research nonetheless suggests that this view, at best a half-truth, misses the real core of Turner's revolutionary achievements, which is his integration of Romantic art with science.

Turner, who regarded painting as "the most truly great and least appreciated" of the arts,[18] was without question one of the most ambitious painters of the nineteenth century. In his early paintings he sought to surpass the masters of the two preceding schools of landscape painting. In his middle period he fully embraced Romantic worship of the sublime. And by the mid-1820s, he had begun to mine the intelligence embedded in yet another of the period's key idea-spaces: *science.* This set him on a path that would leap clear of the nineteenth century altogether. He began to create an incomparable series of paintings that constituted nothing less than a full-scale artistic assault on certain fundamental assumptions of European civilization that had persisted since Greek times. By the time Turner was done, he had developed a form of painting that could only be fully grasped and appreciated within the radically transformed culture of the twentieth century.

The period from roughly 1800 to 1850 saw the rise of steam power, factories, and railways. Blake might speak of the "dark Satanic mills" among England's "pleasant pastures," but Turner enthusiastically embraced the changes wrought by the Industrial Revolution. He repeatedly sketched and painted foundries with their huge furnaces and forges, cranes, gears, and other mechanical equipment, industrial towns such as Leeds and Dudley, locomotives, steamships, and even the famous if ill-fated Chain Pier at Brighton.[19] "I must go by steam," he wrote to a friend, and he frequently did, on both land and sea.[20]

Turner was also acquainted with several prominent nineteenth-century scientists. These included the astronomer John Herschel; Charles Babbage, inventor of the famous difference and analytical engines that prefigured the computer; Humphrey Davy, polymath and pioneering chemist; and above all Michael Faraday, whose experimental demonstration of the relationship between electricity and magnetism would later provide the basis for generating and storing electricity. Turner knew each of these men, and was a member of several close-knit social circles of which they were members. He was especially friendly with the mathematician and physicist Mary Somerville, who worked with Faraday on his research into magnetism and wrote a series of books explaining the latest scientific theories and discoveries to an eager lay audience.

There was nothing particularly unusual about such easy intercourse between scientists and artists. The Royal Academy and the Royal Society, the chief British institutions, respectively, of painting and science, were both located in Somerset House, and some individuals were members of both. Davy, for example, took an active interest in art, was consulted regarding how to preserve the moldering frescoes of Raphael at the Vatican, and gave a lecture on the chemical properties of artists' colors. In 1807 he wrote an essay entitled "Parallels Between Art and Science." Faraday collected art, and Mary Somerville was an accomplished painter. Turner himself kept up on the latest scientific theories and discoveries in diverse fields, including chemistry, geology, and physics. He discussed the nature of pigments and the effects of light in the sky with Faraday, followed his and Somerville's experiments in magnetism, and delved deeply into color theory. In his lectures on perspective he also demonstrated a clear grasp of Euclidean geometry.

Critical opinion has generally followed Ruskin in interpreting Turner as a quintessential Romantic painter. However, the pioneering research of James Hamilton into Turner's scientific interests, skills, and outlook have recently begun to cast some of his late paintings in an altogether different light. Consider, for example, one of Turner's finest canvases, *Snow Storm—Steam-Boat Off a Harbour's Mouth Making Signals in Shallow Water, and Going by the Lead: The Author Was in This Storm on the Night the Ariel Left Harwich*, exhibited in 1842.[21] Our first impression is that this is a continuation of Turner's Romantic phase. The "unrelieved chaos of the subject"[22] appears to be yet another terrifying representation of the sublime (see figure 10-2). As art critic Sam Smiles notes, "The spiralling smoke, surging waves and swirling cloud produce a centrifugal vortex that engulfs the spectator," who feels irresistibly sucked into the maelstrom.[23] During the height of the storm, Turner had the

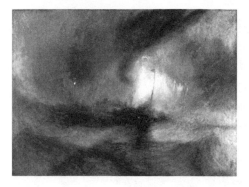

FIGURE 10-2

J. M. W. Turner (1775–1851):
*Snow Storm—Steam-Boat
off a Harbour's Mouth*

Source: © Tate, London 2006. Used with
permission.

crew lash him to the mast, so that he could sketch freely on deck. The image perfectly fits the heroic Romantic artist striving to capture the terrifying forces of nature.

However, the painting's subtitle—*Making Signals in Shallow Water, and Going by the Lead*—suggests a different, altogether more subtle and complex interpretation. The sailors are doing exactly what the rules of seamanship require in such extreme weather. The ship and its crew thus exploit rational practice (taking soundings by lead line) with the latest technology—steam-driven paddles and distress flares[24]—to make their way safely to port in the midst of a storm that might well have wrecked a sailing vessel.

Close inspection, as Hamilton demonstrates, uncovers a deeper point: "The flowing forms of the vortices, their rushing lines, curves, and peaks, reflect the forms of magnetic lines of force revealed by Michael Faraday and Mary Somerville when they placed magnets under sheets of paper scattered with iron filings."[25]

The similarity is no mere fancy on Turner's part. He was deeply interested in the two scientists' experiments on magnetism, which must surely have been a central topic of conversation in Somerville's visits to Turner.[26] In *The Connexion of the Physical Sciences*, Somerville theorized that since even fluids generate electrical currents under the influence of magnets,

> *it is probable that the gulf stream may exert a sensible influence upon the forms of the lines of magnetic variation, in consequence of electric currents moving across it, by the electro-magnetic induction of the earth. Even a ship passing over the surface of the water . . . ought to have electric currents running directly across the path of her motion.*[27]

Hamilton suggests that "with certain knowledge of Mary Somerville's words . . . and the extensive contemporary researches into magnetism, Turner subtly links the imagery of iron filings on paper in an invisible magnetic field with energized sea water surrounding and acting upon a magnetic iron ship." (See figure 10-3.)

Far from exclusively expressing the Romantic notion of human beings at the mercy of nature, the picture evidently suggests that by dint of rational practices, technological inventiveness, and scientific research, we can in fact not only learn to master the terrors of elemental forces, but come to a deeper understanding of them. At the same time, the Romantic interpretation remains valid. The depiction of the storm's fierceness is real enough, and executed in masterly fashion. Again, a central part of Turner's genius lies precisely in his ability to simultaneously portray two sets of contrary ideas— drawn from the diverging idea-spaces of science and Romanticism, objective knowledge and subjective emotional response, intellect and imagination— and successfully integrate them.

Turner placed himself at the very center of the picture. While some have interpreted this as an expression of the heroic, suffering Romantic artist, a different interpretation is again possible. Being lashed to the mast inevitably evokes associations with Ulysses, who did the same in order to outwit the Sirens luring him to his death at sea.[28] The reference to Ulysses, who survived by using his intelligence and practical knowledge, invites an implied comparison between the artist and the scientists whose knowledge and careful experiments he is seemingly praising. The suggestion may seem far-fetched on the surface, but further investigation appears to bear it out.

As a radically innovative painter, Turner is fully aware that he perceives such a scene quite differently from the way other people do. His compulsion

FIGURE 10-3

Magnetic experiment (iron filings) by Michael Faraday (1791–1867)

Source: © The Royal Institution, London, U.K./The Bridgeman Art Library International, New York. Used with permission.

is "to paint what he knows, despite the fact that others would be baffled."[29] The question is, what is the knowledge that he has *as an artist* that others don't? Part of the answer lies in a structure that recurs in many of his most Romantic paintings: the *vortex*.

Turner's innate classicism never let him abandon the idea of imparting to a painting a mathematically based order. In seventeenth-century Italian idealism, this took the form of symmetrically arranged, geometrically proportioned masses of light and shade. Turner's sensitivity to the kinetic forces of nature, especially wind and sea, led him, even in a relatively early masterpiece like *Snow Storm: Hannibal and His Army Crossing the Alps* (exhibited in 1812), to replace the classic Euclidean geometry of horizontals, verticals, and diagonals with a series of irregular intersecting arcs in the form of a vortex.[30] This was one of Turner's great formal innovations and he used it repeatedly from then on, particularly in the pictures of his middle, Romantic period. His later *Snow Storm* represents the apotheosis of this technique. Huge, powerful masses of alternating light and dark swirl around an incandescent center of white light, pierced vertically by the mast to which the artist is bound. It must have astonished Turner to discover that a technique he had been using for several decades apparently had a basis in recent scientific theories and experiments on electromagnetism. The effect was to reinforce his belief that the artist, no less than the scientist, could see beyond mere surface appearance to the truth.

At least one of Turner's contemporaries seems to have understood what he was up to. "No one else," Sara Taylor Coleridge (the poet's daughter) wrote, "gives me such a sense of the power of the elements, no one else lifts up the veil and discloses the *penetralia* [innermost parts, hidden recesses] of nature, as this painter does."[31] Turner himself notes: "He that has that ruling enthusiasm which accompanies abilities cannot look superficially. Every glance is a glance for study: contemplating and defining qualities and causes, effects, and incidents, and develops by practice the possibility of attaining what appears mysterious upon principle."[32]

Turner is suggesting that the artist does not view nature as most of us do ("superficially") but rather *analytically*, as scientists do. The result is to achieve a vision of what is normally hidden from view, "what appears mysterious upon principle." Far from enabling the artist to express his purely subjective vision (Monet's "exuberant romanticism of his fancy"), Turner's art, refined not only through artistic practice but with the theoretically and experimentally derived knowledge of current science, in fact presents us with a deeper *objective* truth about nature.[33]

William Hazlitt, the leading art critic of his generation, astutely grasped this when he objected that Turner, though "the ablest landscape-painter now living," painted pictures that represented "the triumph of the knowledge of the artist . . . over the barrenness of the subject."[34] Hazlitt might as easily have spoken of the triumph of the imagination. Not simply the ability to conjure images, but imagination in the sense Crick uses it, the faculty that allows us to progressively build and modify a mental model of reality that in the end discloses a deeper truth than that conveyed by immediate observation.

A central objective truth that Turner's vortex so powerfully conveyed was the primacy of energy. Faraday's study of electromagnetism suggested that at a sufficient level of abstraction, nature appears to be composed of a *continuum of interacting, dynamic fields of force* varying in intensity, duration, and location. His scientific partner Mary Somerville similarly spoke of perceiving in the domain of astronomy "the operation of a force which is mixed up with everything that exists in the heavens or on earth; which pervades every atom, rules the motions of animate and inanimate beings, and is as sensible in the descent of a raindrop as in the falls of Niagara; in the weight of the air, as in the periods of the moon."[35]

She observed that even the objects of the senses—light, heat, sound—are reducible to "mere modes of action." Taken together, the conception of nature conveyed by these scientist friends of Turner is at its most fundamental level that of a *purely kinetic world of endlessly interacting and shifting forces*.

By Faraday's time, a new dynamic geometry of parabolic arcs and vortices was giving novel form to this kinetic world, revealing the same patterns in magnetized iron filings and the curving lines of magnetic forces swirling around a ship. The rational parameters artistic idealism imposed on the material world of things—harmony, symmetry, universality, mathematical proportion—had now been successfully transferred by scientists to the *processes* underlying a purely kinetic world of invisible forces.

Turner was one of the first artists to intuitively grasp and respond to this enormous shift. In contrast to the static geometry of idealism, his vortex—a spinning circle that moves and yet repeats itself—was a brilliant visual embodiment of his intuition of the underlying stability of dynamic processes. But the true measure of how far he had advanced into this revolutionary new conception of a cosmos generated by the interplay of limitless forces lay in his liberation of color in the depiction of *light*.

COLOR AND LIGHT

In 1819 Turner made the first of two trips to Italy, visiting among other places Rome, Naples, and Venice. This journey was to change his life.

Turner was simply overwhelmed by the quality of light, above all in Venice, where it constantly shimmered in the balmy, vapor-filled air and reflected off the blue waters of the lagoon. From now on Turner's paintings would be imbued with an idea that seems to have been finally and irrevocably impressed on him in this timeless Adriatic port: the ephemerality of all things as the merely solid is dissolved in the ceaseless play of refracted light.

This loss of solidity (or *demassification*) marks a fundamental turning point for him, and indeed for Western painting as a whole. As Clark notes, "For centuries objects were thought to be real because they were solid . . . And all respectable art aimed at defining this solidity, either by means of modelling or by a firm outline."[36] In Turner, however, the traditional primacy of line and the rendering of light as a series of carefully modulated tonalities now give way to a full-blown use of color. It is color, not line, tone, or the symmetric disposition of massed volumes, that now defines form.

Clark (and he is not alone in this) chooses to see this "liberation of colour" as a key moment in art that leads directly to modern painting, the impact of which "is almost entirely due to colour."[37] Turner was "the first artist to realise that colour could speak to us directly . . . independently of form and subject matter,"[38] and his liberation of color, "like all romantic arts, was a triumph of the irrational."[39]

This interpretation of Turner's use of color, reflecting Clark's view of him as an arch romantic, is not without an element of truth. Turner had studied light incessantly since youth and unquestionably took deep delight in its varying hues and evanescent effects. He also experimented continually with ways to transpose these effects into pigment. But in the end, his radical departure from existing norms of color and tone in art has at least as much to do with his deep involvement in science as with his response to an emergent Romantic ethos.

After his two visits to Venice, Turner begins to enter into his own version of the paradox posed by contemporary science. For physicists like Faraday and Somerville, our visual perception was a fallacious guide to the true character of nature. At its most fundamental level, nature was composed of nothing more than the interplay of dynamic forms of energy (modes of action) that, despite their relative invisibility and unboundedness, were gradually being shown to be governed by universal and unifying laws of physics. Beyond that, chemists like Davy were continually discovering new elements and their combinations. For Turner, perception was equally misleading. The world is ultimately composed not of material objects but the endless interplay of light. And yet, as Turner's late paintings clearly reveal, at the heart of this radiant transience lay universal laws, harmonies, and symmetries that were all part of an underlying, pervasive unity.

No artist has ever depicted the purely ephemeral qualities of light more convincingly than Turner. In his most radically innovative paintings, objects dissolve into a vaporous, shimmering light in which outlines emerge from whole fields of color radiating through space. In a painting like *Sunrise, with a Boat Between Headlands* (figure 10-1), this sense of the insubstantial and transient has been taken to the ultimate extreme. Here the elements of earth, water, air, and the fire of the sun; light and its reflection; object and impression all fuse together in a single continuum of vibrating, radiant luminosity in which space and time are merged. For we know that even in a few moments these iridescent volumes of constantly changing light will have become something quite different.

If Turner cannot quite be said to anticipate Einsteinian relativity here in the strict sense, he nevertheless succeeds in vividly portraying the infinities that modern physics would continue to grapple with, for what we see here is a perfect visual representation of the boundless continua of space, time, and their interaction. As in the case of physics and chemistry, however, the boundless does not have to be purely chaotic.

Although Turner appears to have been endowed from birth with an extraordinary artistic talent that he constantly nurtured, the intensely scientific approach he took to the development of his art is reflected not only in his distrust of the senses as capable of transmitting the truth of nature, but also in his search for deeper theoretical principles that could accurately reveal it.

Turner carefully studied contemporary color theory. Ever the practicing scientist as well as artist, he filled his sketchbooks "full of completely abstract colour combinations in which he puts his theories to the test."[40] But Turner was not just aiming to incorporate scientific theory and practice into his own artistic procedures. His ambition was nothing less than to find a visual representation of the new dematerialized world of infinite force fields that contemporary scientific discoveries were laying bare.

Lawrence Gowing, one of Turner's most perceptive critics, speaks of "the infinite interpenetration of natural radiance" in his late paintings. One of Turner's Academy lectures

is a reverie on the indefinite transmission and dispersal of light by an infinite series of reflections from an endless variety of surfaces and materials, each contributing its own colour that mingles with every other, penetrating ultimately to every recess, reflected everywhere, "plane to plane, so that darkness or total shade cannot take place while any angle of light reflected or refracted can reach an opposite plane . . . We must consider every part as receiving and emitting rays to every surrounding surface . . ."[41]

Turner's *Yacht Approaching the Coast* is a breathtakingly beautiful illustration of these ideas. Light radiates out from an incandescent central axis in a calm spiral that is echoed in the yacht's billowing sails. Even a glance at a typical Constable, Pissarro, or Monet immediately makes clear that we are far from the conventions of nineteenth-century landscape painting, which placed a premium on picturesque asymmetry.[42] The finely wrought harmonies and modulations of color, organized by the subtle but dominant vortex of light, formally models the infinite yet still law-governed radiations physicists were theorizing about. Each detail of the painting is subordinated to the whole, suggesting under endless variation an underlying unity.

In his late paintings—one might almost call them his private paintings, for they were never exhibited—Turner seems to push analogy with scientific theory and practice even further, as though paint were some kind of parallel universe to the light-filled world of nature and the artist the discoverer/creator of its secret harmonies and symmetry.

Turner is without question the greatest watercolorist who has ever lived. He mastered the technique early and in later years began to apply aspects of it to oil painting, an innovation that would not reappear in Western art until Cézanne.[43] The technique, which involved laying semitransparent oils over a white ground, was brilliantly effective in conveying the rippling, flashing dance of light reflected on water, Turner's quintessential subject, but it appears to have symbolic value as well. Turner would start out with a plain white canvas—a *void*—over which he began to float thinned-down oils. Sometimes he would begin with just a series of bands of color, which he would then "drive about" until certain outlines began to emerge, the forms of things emerging from the colors themselves rather than, as in traditional practice, being first drawn and then colored.[44] As several critics have noted, because of the uncertainties of watercolor technique (the paint floats free of the brush), there is an irreducible element of chance in this practice, combined with the necessity imposed by the laws of color.

Turner was in the habit of mixing and grinding his own colors, and was quite knowledgeable about the chemistry involved. So if we follow things through, what we have is a picture of the artist starting from basic elements (Turner employed a palette of only the simplest colors), allowing them to flow together in an empty space according to the dictates of chance and necessity, and then gradually working them over until certain forms and masses begin to emerge. The parallel with how scientists viewed the formation of compound entities and forces in nature, not perfect but close enough, can hardly have escaped Turner's notice.[45]

Inevitably, the technique puts us in mind of Shelley's famous lines from his long poem *Adonais*:

> The One remains, the many change
>   and pass;
> Heaven's light forever shines, Earth's
>   shadows fly;
> Life, like a dome of many-coloured glass,
> Stains the white radiance of Eternity,
> Until Death tramples it to fragments.

Turner may or may not have been familiar with the poem, written in 1821, but his art, in both technique and content, resonates profoundly with its sentiments. For Turner the white radiance that so often figures as the central axis of his late paintings is unchanging. In terms of color theory, white is the coolest of colors, representing the cessation of all motion. As day breaks, the rising sun, white at first through the mist, begins to enliven the forms of nature with ever warmer, more active colors. Eventually, these become the bright reds and oranges of the sunset, followed by increasing darkness. In this cycle, the very colors that are the most active, depicting the play of the setting sun on water, are also the most ephemeral and fleeting. Like Shelley, Turner is fully aware of the paradox here, life at its most vivid being closest to its own extinction. But beneath it all, shining through the semitransparent glaze of oil paint, the white light remains, a reminder of that unifying medium that is unmoved and, free of transience, ever renews itself.

It does not seem too strained an interpretation to see in this Turner's artistic version of Romantic pantheism. Turner worshipped light. Throughout his life he rose to see the sunrise and by old age had several houses in London from which he could view the changing light across water. He loved its ephemeral, evanescent quality, which he painted as skillfully as any artist in history.[46] According to Ruskin, a few weeks before he died, Turner said, "The sun is God." Some have doubted the quote, but the mixture of Romantic pantheism and Platonic heliocentrism perfectly fits Turner's outlook.

SCIENCE, ART, AND THE LAW OF INTEGRATION

In our own jaded age, we have long accepted C. P. Snow's dictum that the two cultures, art and science, are separated by a virtually unbridgeable gulf. Even in Turner's day, when the boundaries between them were more fluid, the emergent sciences of electromagnetism and the new chemistry of elements and compounds would appear to have little in common with the Romantic obsession with natural beauty, the sublime, and spiritual pantheism. And yet Turner found a way to integrate vital aspects of the intelligence embedded in these seemingly antithetical idea-spaces, creating a new paradigm for art that was still unfolding well over a hundred years later.

Like Gutenberg, Turner was fortunate enough to find himself at the very nexus of powerful emergent worlds whose interplay was producing a series of profound shifts in the dominant idea-spaces of the age. Even as he espoused Romanticism, he brought to bear a sensibility drawn from earlier ages of landscape painting that inclined him toward a more scientific outlook: realism taught him an acute ability to observe nature, while idealism prompted the search for underlying universal laws and harmonies.

Even at the height of his embrace of Romanticism, Turner combined a fascination with nature's vast elemental forces with a search for deeper controlling principles and symmetries such as those exhibited by the vortex and color harmonies. But it was undoubtedly Venice that created the tipping point in Turner's path toward true integration. Here Turner, in thrall to color, would begin to paint some of the most incomparably beautiful paintings of the effects of light ever set down on canvas. And it must have been here that a profound revelation struck him with the force of a thunderbolt. If light can be so beautiful, then it must be divine, and therefore infinite and eternal. But light changes constantly. Science also seeks in nature the infinite, the universal, and the unchanging in the midst of change. Staring at the stones of Venice, even then slowly sinking into the Adriatic, it must have come to him as they shimmered in the morning haze: it is matter that decays![47] Light, streaming from its solar source, constantly renews itself. Its radiant energy, governed by the hidden symmetries of color harmony, is a visual manifestation of the invisible kinetic forces that Faraday, Somerville, and other scientists were beginning to discover. It is out of this that the world is created and endlessly remade.

In Turner's late paintings we can see the process of integration completing itself, driven by an ever-increasing sense of harmony and unity (i.e., fitness). Slowly, all trace of solidity evanesces, until what we are left with is the incandescent play of light on light. Now the Romantic quest to find in natural beauty an immanent manifestation of the divine has fully become one with science's search for the unities underlying nature's manifold diversity.

Embedded intelligence that flows from one hotspot to another across a weak tie is especially powerful. Its impact is measured by the law of hotspots: fitness times distance. Romantic art and the emerging sciences of the early nineteenth century appeared to have little in common, but Turner's intuition that they could be connected fired his powerful imagination to integrate them to the point where something new, beautiful, and profound emerged. His liberation of color opened the way for impressionism, fauvism, and ultimately color field painting. But it was his insight that the abstract, intangible, demassified world of kinetic forces proposed by scientists like Faraday could be made one with the spiritual dimensions of Romanticism that created nothing less than a new space for art to unfold in.[48] Nothing of similar importance to this freeing of Western art from the depiction of solid objects was to happen until the cubists, who in their own very different way again took up the task of addressing the challenge science poses to our conception of reality by endeavoring to integrate its most profound insights into a visual medium. Only in the era of the abstract expressionists, however, would Turner's extraordinary insight achieve its fullest development.[49]

Paraphrasing Hardy (quoted at the beginning of this chapter), we may say that the significance of a cultural achievement can be measured by the importance of the ideas it connects. By this standard, Turner's achievement was very significant indeed. To produce an enduring creative leap, however, the linked ideas (i.e., the intelligence embedded in major idea-spaces) must become fully integrated. This is because only integration has the power to produce something qualitatively new and different, a new unity that is distinct from the elements that gave rise to it. Put this way, we can see that integration provokes a tipping point. As in Turner's case, such a point arises as the result of ever-increasing fitness (the fit get fitter). Elements of embedded intelligence connect and begin to reciprocally alter one another's meanings until suddenly a new gestalt emerges. The dynamic interplay of radiant light in Turner's late paintings is neither a scientific theory nor a further modification of Romantic art's worship of nature, but a new aesthetic space in its own right.

We can capture this conception formally in the law of integration:

THE LAW OF INTEGRATION

The integration of intelligence embedded in major idea-
spaces is an essential component of creative breakthroughs.
This integration, driven by the law of the fit get fitter,
leads to a tipping point whose magnitude is a function
of the law of hotspots.

The new paradigm of art Turner created evolved discontinuously over the century following his death, reaching its apotheosis in abstract expressionism. In 1966 the revolution he began was given unprecedented recognition: a one-man show at the Museum of Modern Art in New York, the only artist dead for more than a century so honored. Thirty years later, another revolution involving the law of integration would get under way, this time in high technology—and with somewhat less staying power.

THE NEW ROMANTICS

Everything we ever said about the Internet is happening.

—Andy Grove (August 2003)[50]

Never mistake a clear view for a short distance.

—Paul Saffo[51]

Turner would have instantly recognized the dot-com entrepreneurs for who they were: a bunch of brash, highly ambitious young men and women bent on reenvisioning the world in terms of the new order of things they were convinced was about to emerge. Wildly in love with the latest efforts of science and technology, they were nevertheless in spirit the true heirs of the Romantics, writing software programs instead of verse, drawing wiring diagrams instead of nature, but no less giddily excited about the future that was rushing toward them. It was an era when it was a joy to be alive, and to be young was heaven—especially if you happened to have a business plan for an Internet start-up in your back pocket.

Turner might also have empathized with the ridicule heaped on most of these young entrepreneurs when the bubble finally burst. As any reader of Philip Kaplan's splendidly entertaining *F'd Companies: Spectacular Dot.com Flameouts* appreciates, the collective foolishness of the VCs, investors, and dreamy-eyed entrepreneurs who gave birth to the dot-com revolution would be hard to equal.

With hindsight it's all too easy to laugh. Let me admit that I, too, was involved in the early 1990s in two failed start-ups. And even as I write this, there are signs aplenty that part of this hypercritical reaction to the dot-com revolution was overblown, premature, and even wrong. In spite of Webvan's catastrophic failure (running through nearly a *billion* dollars of venture capital funding before flaming out), the online grocery business is alive and beginning to turn a profit. So are parts of the infamous "clicks-and-mortar" trade. Venture capital investment is finally starting to show signs of life again, and successful IPOs like Google's, while not coming close to Netscape's or Yahoo!'s megalaunches, are once again happening.

So where does the truth lie? Is there a new economy or isn't there? Are there truly new rules, or do the old ones still hold sway? Was the creativity of this notorious era the genuine article or just a mirage? As we'll see, the answer will bring us face to face with some negative implications of the law of integration.

First let's dispose of the blindingly obvious:

Every period of radical invention since the inception of the Industrial Revolution went through an initial period of exponential growth followed by a bust, and the dot-com boom was no exception.

The sheer availability of venture capital, totaling hundreds of billions of dollars, plus stock market valuations of several trillion, was bound to produce a profoundly distorting effect on a nascent industry trying to feel its way to stable profitability.

Just because the first wave of breakthrough innovation failed doesn't mean that its entire foundations were erroneous.

With hindsight, many analysts have concluded that the inability of so many dot-com entrepreneurs to achieve long-term success in following the now-infamous new economy business model was a nightmare mixture of youthful ambition and inexperience combined with an unprecedented outbreak of short-term greed. A level-headed reaction at this point would be to assume that the world has largely gone back to the way it was, signaling a welcome—if slightly boring—return to conventional modes of doing business, accompanied by incremental innovation. Sensible, comforting even, but *wrong*.

Turner knew for sure that the world was changing irrevocably, moving headlong into a new order of things, a new dominant idea-space that presaged a deep and lasting transformation. That was what the more visionary entrepreneurs of the so-called new economy saw too—and in truth, history may yet prove them right.

Forget metrics for the moment, and focus instead on the essential *topography* of the space that's still very much in the process of emerging and will probably continue to do so for the next several decades. No one articulated this topography better than Kevin Kelly in his 1998 bestseller, *New Rules for the New Economy*.[52]

Kelly writes so well that it's tempting to quote him at length, but for brevity's sake I'll try to summarize the main lines of his argument.[53] Kelly's fundamental claim is that that we are witnessing the emergence of a radically new form of economy, resulting from the convergence of three sub-economies: the *digital*, the *networked*, and the *demassified*. The first is generated by "the collapsing microcosm of silicon," the second by "the exploding telecosm of connections."[54] The third, more subtle but no less crucial, represents a profound, irreversible shift in business, industry, and society from hard to soft; tangible to intangible; things to information, ideas, and knowledge; atoms to bits—an across-the-board transformation that is the inevitable outcome of Peter Drucker's knowledge economy becoming integrated into a globally interconnected world.

Kelly insists that the emergence of the new economy, far from being some run-of-the-mill shift, is in fact revolutionary. The economy of material goods and resources, born of the Industrial Revolution, is now being totally transformed. Interestingly, however, it's not the advent of digital technology per se that was crucial:

> *This vanguard is not about computers. Computers are over. Most of the consequences that we can expect from computers as stand-alone machines have already happened. They have sped up our lives, and made managing words, numbers, and pixels quite extraordinary, but they have not had much more effect beyond that. The new economy is about* communication, *deep and wide.*[55]

Here we come to the nub of Kelly's whole argument. "Communication—which in the end is what the digital technology and media are all about—is not just a sector of the economy," Kelly insists. "Communication *is* the economy . . . This is why networks are such a big deal. Communication is so close to culture and society itself that the effects of technologizing it are beyond the scale of a mere industrial-sector cycle." In effect, digitally based communication networks "have produced a sector of an economy that is transforming all the other sectors."[56]

Kelly completes this case for what amounts to a kind of technological exceptionalism by noting that the ubiquity of such networks, which now globally connect chips embedded in everything from computers to tractors to toasters—"a trillion objects and living beings, linked together through air and glass"—is rapidly creating an entirely new kind of economic logic. Universal digitized connectivity (which is what Kelly means by communication) is leading directly to an economy where most value is created in the intangible realm of knowledge, information, and ideas, all converted into streams of bits. Because of so-called *network effects*—the deep generative powers residing in networks themselves—the new economy will be based on abundance rather than scarcity, and generate far more opportunities than it destroys.

New Rules for the New Economy, which elegantly synthesizes the ideas of a number of leading techno-gurus, including George Gilder, Nicholas Negroponte, Paul Romer, and Hal Varian, became a kind of manifesto for the dotcom era, the book that launched a thousand would-be killer apps. Kelly's insights, together with a talent for exuberant if succinct hyperbole, led to a series of claims and predictions that inevitably influenced many a hopeful dot-com business plan. The flaws in Kelly's logic are sometimes subtle, and sometimes obvious (especially with hindsight). But because they were an integral part of the great crash of 2000, it's worth briefly reviewing some of the more prominent ones.

First and foremost, every significant technological advance since the Industrial Revolution began has been about the mechanics of communication—that is, *more effective and efficient connectivity*. Steam, electricity, the telegraph and telephone, automobiles, and mass media all linked people, places, goods, and information and increased interaction between them. The technologizing of communication on a massive scale started long before the arrival of the Internet.

Second, the demassification (i.e., shift to reliance on digitized information) of the economy, while certainly significant, is not as widespread as it seems. Certain companies have undeniably been highly successful in exploiting the value embedded in the intangible soft part of business. Wal-Mart, with sales exceeding those of Target, Sears, Kmart, JC Penney, Safeway, and Kroger combined, has been relentless in exploiting its advances in network technologies to maintain its highly profitable growth.[57]Amazon.com has prospered in part through exploiting highly innovative customer relations technology that supplies book buyers with a plethora of information about other customers' views and preferences.

The problem is, first, that other firms have found it notoriously difficult to duplicate these companies' successes, and second, that in many industrial and business sectors, it's hard to see how much more value can be extracted from the soft, networked side of the business than present constraints allow. To take two of Kelly's own examples: Will agriculture and food distribution really be revolutionized by putting a chip in every lettuce? Will the fact that hotel doors are now opened with digital cards linked to the front desk change anything except the convenience of not lugging metal keys around?

Third (and here we get close to the heart of the matter), Kelly speaks throughout the book as though the new economy is creating its own all-embracing context: "The net is moving irrevocably to include everything of the world," he confidently asserts. "Bit by bit, the logic of the network will overtake every atom we deal with."[58] Well, no. In particular, the new economy did not suspend the rules of the old economy, such as making a profit, buying for less than the selling price, and so forth. Nor did it succeed in invalidating Brown and Duguid's telling insights into the social life of information, including the fact that new technology is successful only to the degree that it meshes with existing social practices.

Kelly seems to operate throughout with a fatal assumption that the high-tech net can either be isolated from other external factors, including social, political, and economic ones, or that its logic is sufficiently powerful to overcome them. It's as though, while cheerfully admitting that networks saturate society, he grants only electronic networks any real power of transformation. Thus, for example, Kelly boldly declares that while the classical economic theory of diminishing returns predicts ever-increasing prices, "by now, the oil industry is so invaded by chip technology that it is beginning to obey the laws of the new economy . . . Diminishing returns are halted. The oil flows at steady prices, as the oil industry slides into the new economy."[59] As I write this, the price of oil is close to $55 a barrel and climbing. The reason is a whole slew of powerful geopolitical factors from which no amount of network technology can isolate oil prices.

In short, Kelly failed to grasp the corollary to the principle of integration: *In order to survive and prosper, breakthrough innovations must be integrated into the mainstream* (i.e., achieve external fitness). This is precisely what the dot-commers failed to do, of course, with fateful consequences.

The fourth and perhaps most serious problem of all, however, isn't really Kelly's fault. Kelly makes certain factual assumptions about the nature of networks that subsequent research has shown to be false. In particular, Kelly assumes that "the net[work] has no center, no orbits, no certainty. It is an indefinite web of causes. The net is the archetype displayed to represent all circuits, all intelligence, all interdependence, all things economic, social, or ecological, all communications, all democracy, all families, all large systems, almost all that we find interesting and important." Elsewhere, he adds that "the distinguishing characteristic of networks is that they contain no clear center and no clear outside boundaries. Within a network everything is potentially equidistant from everything else."[60]

We now know, thanks to Barabási and his colleagues, that this isn't so. Because of the laws of dynamic networks—tipping points, the fit get rich, hotspots—the net is not one continuous, smooth, all-embracing web. On the contrary, it is distinctly *clumpy*, forming huge hubs that deeply influence everything around them, and often prevent other nodes from linking up effectively except by routing through them.

Curiously, Kelly here fumbles one of his best insights. Increasingly, he notes, the economy is taking on a biological structure.[61] One of the most fundamental aspects of biology, however, is the concept of the cell, an organism defined by a membrane that regulates its transactions with the external world. Similarly, the whole of ecology is built on the notion of niches, each with its own unique character, structure, and mode of interaction with its surrounding ecological context. Yet the all-important notion of a *controlling context* is almost completely absent from Kelly's book. This is hardly a minor omission. Because of the lack of boundaries, Kelly assumes that the network economy is capable of the kind of runaway growth sometimes to be found in nature. Once network logic has begun to infect an area, nothing can stop it from taking over. The result is abundance, with the law of increasing returns triumphing over the diminishing returns of the old, resource-scarce economy. And it's precisely in this growing abundance that Kelly sees the opportunity for endless growth, prosperity, and, yes, wealth.

The trouble is that biological networks are no less subject to the laws of networks Barabási uncovered than any other kind. In reality, almost everywhere we look, we find that nonlinear growth, when it occurs, inevitably returns to equilibrium as other ecological factors come into play. Yet Kelly not only ignores this, he uses the new logic of networks to pour scorn on the time-honored concept of economic equilibrium.[62] Instead, he argues, endlessly provoked by network logic into disequilibrium, the economy will enter an era of constant disruptive innovation, producing permanent plenitude. Unfortunately, as we now know, the faultiness in this logic produced the megadisruption of the dot-com crash.

THE THIRD WAVE

When, after careful reflection, we make due allowances for Kelly's various mistakes of analysis and prediction, his tendency to overinflate the importance of the trends he is describing, and his lack of access to future research on networks, we must still admit that in one crucially important sense *he was right*. Kelly recognized earlier and more clearly than most of his peers that the rules were indeed changing to the point where we have a new game, and that game is called *networked space*.

Kelly is fully aware that networks per se are nothing new—in fact, our entire culture and history are saturated with them. What's different about the networks he's so excited about is not, contrary to what he in places implies, that they're now global (think spice trade) or even global and electronic (think telephone, or mass media). It's that they operate *in a space rather than a place*: "Place still matters, and will for a long time to come. However, the new economy operates in a 'space' rather than a place, and over time more and more economic transactions will migrate to this new space."[63]

Kelly isn't talking about the familiar, overused half-truth about the "death of distance." What is at stake here is *multidimensional connectivity*, of a kind that exists only abstractly, as in a mathematical space. Such a space has unlimited dimensions in which "entities (people, objects, agents, bits, nodes, etc.) can be adjacent in a thousand different ways and a thousand different directions."[64] Of course, in theory such a space has always existed, for instance mentally. But the advent of the World Wide Web—a space in which "anything could connect to anything"—actualized this possibility concretely and in real time. The myriad connections made possible by the Internet gave birth to a type of space, demassified yet utterly real, that was *qualitatively* distinct from anything that had preceded it. *More is different.*

So is there still a new economy? In one sense, it's too early to tell. Much depends on how much value really migrates over to the soft side. Overall, though, it's likely that much of the consumer economy at least, constituting a good two-thirds of the whole, is still going to be about solid stuff that has to be hauled around by truck, train, and plane from one place, rather than space, to another. Even Amazon.com had to offer free shipping for orders over $25 to ensure profitable growth.

But if we take *economy* to mean the broader sense of an organized system of transactions, financial and otherwise, then surely there is a new game, with new rules, whose overall transformative potential remains vast, albeit mostly in the future and hard to predict with precision. The availability to the general public of huge amounts of medical and health-related information via WebMD, Medline, and similar online Web sites, for example, is beginning to shift the expert/patient relationship of conventional medicine as more and more people show up at the doctor's office knowing as much or more about their condition as their physician. As Kelly astutely notes, "When information is plentiful, peers take over."[65] Similarly, as college librarians bemoan, the Internet combined with laptops has transformed how student research is done. In a very different sphere, in the 2004 presidential election, online entities such as MoveOn.org began playing a significant role in shaping the outcome and may one day become a dominant force.

As these examples show, many of the changes wrought by the advent of an electronically mediated space of networks will produce *qualitative* rather than quantitative changes, and thus lack direct financial impact, at least in the short term. This much is virtually guaranteed by the law of tipping points. The sheer number of possible points of interconnection (the mega-multidimensionality of networked space) is bound to prompt numerous such shifts. Furthermore, in certain cases these shifts, operating under the law of the *fit get rich*, will inevitably grow rapidly, spreading far beyond their point of origin and achieving a dominant position in their domain of influence. Such cases are by definition disruptive and so constitute instances of breakthrough creativity. The instantaneously responsive, multidimensional nature of connectivity in the space suggests that the pace and volume of such breakthroughs will inevitably increase, perhaps exponentially. The nonlinear will more and more command attention over the merely linear; creative opportunities (as Kelly correctly notes) over efficiency; the knight's move over mere bishop's work.

The advent of this new demassified space, which Kelly was among the first to recognize and celebrate, is likely to prove in the long run no less revolutionary than the one Turner similarly made the central subject of his art. As in Turner's case, the radically new emerged from the novel integration of existing or emergent idea-spaces: conventional cultural, social, and economic networks, stand-alone digital technology, broadband networks, and the Internet. For a time these coexisted, but at some point during the middle to late 1990s they began to converge. If the hoped-for tipping point didn't arrive when expected, this is largely because the task of integrating all these idea-spaces is enormous and may take decades to complete. And we should not forget that the laws governing dynamic networks are multiple and interact in complex, hard-to-predict ways. Even so, the overall transition to some form of new economy seems assured.

In this sense it's possible to see the development of electronically mediated networked space in terms of three waves. The first was the advent of the computer, the machine that could mimic any other machine. Inevitably, that was bound to signal a radical break with the purely mechanical regime begat by the Industrial Revolution. The second wave was the deployment of narrow and broadband communications networks, together with the concomitant standards, software, and content of the Internet and the World Wide Web. The outcome of this advance was significant, but inevitably slowed down by the need for integration into existing social and economic practices and organization.

The third wave, yet to come but already on the horizon, will see the full integration of an electronically mediated, demassified space of knowledge, ideas, and information within the overall space of the purely physical world of organisms, objects, and forces. The value inherent in that wave, in terms of the creative opportunities it enables, will be measured by the extent to which we come to better understand the laws and principles of network dynamics that govern it.

No doubt other laws besides the eight formulated so far will be found to govern the new dominant idea-space whose existence Kelly so presciently and enthusiastically announced. For the moment, we will have to content ourselves with revealing just one more: *the law of minimal effort.*

Chapter Eleven

ROBOTS, POETS, AND
THE LAW OF MINIMAL EFFORT

Natura non facit saltus [nature doesn't make jumps].

—Linnaeus

The true entrepreneur has no time to stop and perform calculations. Instead, in love with the beauty of his idea, he rushes imprudently forth, gambling all he has on the chance to create something new.

—George Gilder[1]

Robots are hot these days. No longer the lumbering metallic androids of science fiction, they have burst out of the AI labs of leading universities, popping up all over the place. They propel themselves around on legs, wheels, rollers, even cushions of air, waving antennas, arms, electronic and mechanical sensors, and video cameras. They can probe, sniff, sense heat and cold, go around obstacles, fetch and carry, climb stairs, open doors, race across flat or bumpy terrain, vacuum the carpet, and even reproduce themselves. They play soccer, paint, disarm bombs, patrol environments too dangerous for humans, and—inevitably in this age of violent video games—engage in gladiatorial contests of mutual destruction.

The classic way to build a robot is to design it around a highly sophisticated central processor, a complex electronic brain that analytically sifts through incoming data, makes sense of it, and fires off commands for action. However, Mark Tilden, an engineer at the Los Alamos National Laboratory, insists that no such central processor is needed. He has repeatedly demonstrated that robots can be designed to perform many quite complex tasks employing a series of simple interlinked analog devices that respond directly to stimuli from the external world, in exactly the same way that animal nervous systems do. A similar approach is taken by Professor Robert Full of UC Berkeley, who has enormously increased the mobility and action repertoires of robots by modeling them on cockroaches, scorpions, and even geckos.[2]

If all this seems a rather dry technical dispute, there is nevertheless a deep philosophical point at stake. Are we living in a Cartesian world—one in which the world is rendered intelligible through reasoned inference—or not? The central processor advocates, believing that intelligent behavior can emerge only from the digital equivalent of a classic logical, mind-inside-the-head type brain, clearly think we are. The analog biomimicry enthusiasts evidently do not. In their view, the capacity to respond appropriately in dynamically changing environments and novel situations can be engineered without resorting to the installation of any such top-down executive controller.

As we have seen, many neuroscientists, AI researchers, and cognitive psychologists are increasingly coming round to the view that in trying to both understand and mechanically mimic the human mind, we have given far too little importance to the contribution to human mental functioning made by the environment itself. Just as relatively sophisticated patterns of behavior can arise from virtually brainless insects through their direct sensory coupling with the external world (how do those pesky cockroaches know where to run?), so humans have mastered the trick of exploiting the intelligence embedded in the technical, cultural, and social webs of knowledge and practices they live in. The Hawaiians who greeted Captain Cook didn't need to think up a whole new set of meanings to account for this totally novel event. They simply noted its alignment with certain existing features of their myths and rituals: all their subsequent beliefs and actions were then guided by these.

In *Being There*, Andy Clark suggests that this type of cultural "scaffolding" enables us to enormously reduce the computational load on our individual brains, which can accordingly function with a lot less cognitive machinery than is traditionally supposed: "We use intelligence to structure our environment so that we can succeed with *less* intelligence."[3] Most of us can probably recognize the truth of Clark's point about our tendency to offload cognitive processing onto the environment, at least at the level of everyday experience. Don't we use color coding to make shopping easier, looking for green packaging when buying environment-friendly products, bright yellow when purchasing Kodak film? However, we still resist the idea that this day-to-day reliance on external conventions extends to acts of high creativity.

In 1920 T. S. Eliot, anticipating Clark's approach by nearly three quarters of a century, set out to expose the myth of the individual creative genius. In a series of essays entitled *The Sacred Wood*, Eliot warns against succumbing to the erroneous belief that the individual genius works alone, pointing out that solitude is not the same thing as isolation. Attacking the Romantic idea of art as a manifestation of personality, he advances the view that in certain ages of extraordinary creativity, the artist lives in "a current of ideas in the highest degree animating and nourishing to the creative power," immersed in a social environment "permeated by fresh thought, intelligent and alive."[4] It is precisely this intellectual and cultural milieu that is in Eliot's view the true basis of creative power. Eliot insists that this context of ideas constitutes a kind of collective cultural "mind" that the great artist is very much aware of and comes to see as *"much more important than his own private mind"* (emphasis added).

As an example, Eliot points to the Elizabethan dramatists: "The Elizabethan Age in England was able to absorb a great quantity of new thoughts and new images . . . because it had this great form of its own which imposed itself on everything that came to it." The other Elizabethan playwrights, as well as the great dramatists of ancient Greece such as Aeschylus, Sophocles, and Euripides, owe much of the richness, subtlety, and sophistication of their plays to the web of ideas, forms, and cultural practices of the era in which they lived.

Extending this conception of the artist as but one element interacting with an overarching cultural context, Eliot suggests that we must inevitably recognize "how *little* each poet had to do." Dramatists such as Jonson, Marlowe, and even Shakespeare himself could exercise an "economy of effort" that allowed their art to fully flourish.

We are only now beginning to catch up with Eliot's extraordinarily bold and prescient insight into the creative process. Clearly, Eliot was bent on shifting much of the burden of creativity from the individual artist to a pre-existing external order of ideas, forms, and customs—in other words, a complex idea-space rich in embedded intelligence. Eliot in effect formulated not only his own version of the *mind out there*, but also a primitive version of the ninth law of dynamic networks, the *law of minimal effort*:

THE LAW OF MINIMAL EFFORT

Creative leaps come from imaginatively harnessing
the generative powers of the networked intelligence
embedded in the extended mind.

Kauffman's principle of *order for free*, embodied in the law of spontaneous generation, points up a basic property of complex adaptive systems such as the extended mind: even very small changes in input can result in large changes in output. In short, *it's the system itself that does most of the work.* The most effective way to be creative is therefore to let the system think for you. Edison's still-popular notion of genius as mostly hard work (99 percent perspiration) remains blind to how much work is done by the dynamic interaction of existing social and cultural structures, patterns, and practices. Like well-adapted organisms, creative artists and scientists see the virtue of conserving energy so as to fully devote their efforts to the challenges of future survival. Intuitively sensing both the energy latent in the external mindscape and its small-world geometry, they prove highly adept at maximally leveraging their own unique contribution by imaginatively integrating it into the larger system of ideas in which they find themselves immersed.

THE EXTENDED MIND AND THE LAWS
OF DYNAMIC NETWORKS

Eliot's insight into the source of the enormous creativity of the Greek and Elizabethan dramatists has brought us back full circle, then, to where we began: to the creative powers latent in the extended mind. Again and again, as we have seen, cultural and scientific hotspots have played a crucial role in the emergence of creative breakthroughs. The list is a long and distinguished one, from Crick to Tim Berners-Lee to Ruth Handler to Gutenberg.

This brings us back to the central issue: How *does* the space of ideas think for you? Notice first of all that this concept is related to one of Kevin Kelly's central claims: that most value and opportunity reside in the network itself—the so-called *network effect.* In Silicon Valley, for example, as AnnaLee Saxenian has famously pointed out, value (in terms of career opportunities, information flow, skill availability, etc.) is located more in the region itself than in any one firm.[5] Paradoxically, however, the network effect stems from the fact that networks are best viewed as *spaces*, not places. As Kelly goes on to note, the term *space* is used here in the mathematical sense of a complex abstract entity characterized by very high dimensionality and therefore connectivity. In a networked space, nodes can individually and collectively find literally thousands of ways to connect that have nothing to do with their proximity.[6] The World Wide Web is the perfect illustration of this fact.

The law of spontaneous generation ensures that in a dynamic network like the extended mind, this connectivity constantly increases nonlinearly. Even though the majority of these connections are likely meaningless, statistically a number will make sense, ensuring a net surplus of novel value.[7] The law of minimal effort simply acknowledges this fact. Networks are inherently value-creating spaces, so the trick for an artist, scientist, or entrepreneur bent on making a creative breakthrough is first and foremost to locate a suitably fertile space. Creative leaps are fundamentally a navigation problem (*don't waste time inventing—it's out there somewhere; just find it and integrate it*).

Hotspots are by far the most fertile spaces of the extended mind. In a dynamic network, the law of spontaneous generation ensures that hubs constantly emerge and grow, sometimes simply as the result of first-mover advantage (the Altair computer, Federal Express, Catholicism), but more likely by means of tipping points (the hobbyist computer industry in general, viral marketing), and the law of the fit get rich (Apple II, Google, Western market capitalism, molecular genetics).[8] Generally speaking, tipping points produce *qualitatively* distinct idea-spaces (more is different) involving the sudden emergence of novel order, while the law of the fit gets rich produces exponential growth. Notice, then, that networked space itself, if sufficiently large and aristocratic (hub dominated), naturally produces leaps in creativity. In other words, it produces sharp breaks with existing structure that lead to nonlinear growth.

We can even find this in nature (Linnaeus notwithstanding), demonstrating that the emergence of hubs that produce tipping points is not exclusively confined to human culture. Consider, for example, the Cambrian explosion. For the first two and a half billion years, life on Earth was a pretty uncomplicated affair, consisting basically of single-celled bacteria, blue-green algae, and a few rudimentary worms. Then, seemingly without warning some 535 million years ago, life erupted in the biological equivalent of the Big Bang. Elaborate creatures with heads, shells, gills, backbones, skeletons, arms, legs, antennas, mouths, anuses, eyes, even brain-pans, suddenly began to proliferate. The myriad bioforms that emerged laid the basis for all future evolution, from microbes to mammals. The Cambrian explosion went on for approximately 35 million years—a mere eye-blink in geological time—and then just as suddenly ground to a halt.

We tend to think of evolution as a long, slow, step-by-step business. So what could possibly have caused this dramatic tipping point, a never-to-be-repeated inflationary expansion in the basic forms of living things that vastly multiplied the number of existing species? Scientists now think they have finally come up with a plausible answer. Biologists have recently discovered that a single change, the development of *hox* genes, may have ignited the explosion in forms of organism.[9] These so-called map-making genes basically tell the embryo's cells where they are on the body's front-to-back axis, so that the embryo knows exactly what to build—legs, eyes, wings—where. As a result, if changing environmental conditions put pressure on an evolving organism to develop legs, for example, it could do so via an adaptation that was entirely *local*, leaving the rest of the biological system intact. The sheer simplicity of existing organisms ensured there was plenty of room for experiment, leading to an exponential increase in both the elaborateness and number of new species. At the same time, the essentially *modular* type of growth dictated by hox genes ensured that the huge diversity of organisms was nevertheless constrained by a few integrated principles of development, thus preventing the growth in species from spinning chaotically out of control.

In effect, hox genes acted as hubs, both controlling and at the same time expanding connectivity. In the virtual web of possibilities, only certain types of development were permitted (antennas on the head but not the thorax). Within those local constraints, however, a huge proliferation of forms became possible. Furthermore, just as hubs allow otherwise distant or unrelated nodes to be linked, so hox genes allowed species to multiply by connecting unrelated changes in organisms and combining them into new wholes (exoskeletons with legs, without legs, etc.). The outcome was that relatively minor inputs from random mutation and environmental conditions, interacting with the highly generative machinery of webs of hox genes, produced the biggest explosion of creativity nature has ever undergone. Without such genes, each genetic change could have resulted in utterly chaotic forms with little potential for survival. Instead of this extremely slow, wasteful approach, nature harnessed the generative power of the intelligence embedded in hox genes to produce a huge creative leap with minimal effort.[10]

A very different example of how the law of minimal effort is grounded in the generativity of intelligence embedded in existing idea-spaces is to be found in the sudden appearance of the phenomenon of *perimenopause*. This syndrome was virtually unknown to medical science until a 1996 World Health Organization report made a minor reference to it, noting that certain symptoms often associated with menopause itself can occur a year or two before the actual cessation of menstruation. Since then, perimenopause has taken on a life of its own. Dozens of books and scores of articles and reports have fanned public awareness and anxiety, capped by Oprah Winfrey dedicating an entire show to the subject. Hundreds of herbal and drug-based products are now flooding the market to alleviate alleged symptoms, which may include acne, allergies, leg cramps, anxiety, memory loss, sleeping problems, and weeping, not to mention the more usual suspects of hot flashes and mood swings.[11]

How did the idea that perimenopause is a serious medical condition tip so rapidly and with such minimal input? The answer reveals much about the generative power of existing idea-spaces. In the early 1990s, a flood of attention had been focused on menopause itself. Books like Gail Sheehy's *The Silent Passage* and *The Change* by Germaine Greer helped raise public awareness, accompanied by a multitude of new pharmaceutical and herbal products. What the WHO report did by focusing on premenopausal indicators was to link a set of previously amorphous, largely unrecognized physical symptoms to the existing hub of menopause, with its multiple links to medical, social, pharmaceutical, and media institutions and markets. As a result, perimenopause became an organized, coherent idea-space connected to a huge audience that was previously hard to reach. With the baby boomers beginning to turn fifty, information and products relating to perimenopause had a very high fitness rating, resulting in an explosion of interest. Had the WHO report come out a decade earlier, before the formation of the menopause hub, it's likely that perimenopause would have remained an obscure, narrowly defined term confined largely to medical textbooks. As things turned out, the law of minimal effort ensured that it exploded into female consciousness.

The sudden emergence of perimenopause as a significant medical phenomenon is an instance of a rich complex of existing embedded intelligence interacting with a minor discovery to create something new. More typically, the reverse is true. An emerging social or cultural phenomenon transforms an existing, relatively stable space, resulting in a major creative leap. The trigger may be a single idea or event that serves as a catalyst. Consider, for example, the design process for the Vietnam Veterans War Memorial in Washington, D.C. When Maya Lin was putting together her proposal, most of the basic elements for which the memorial is now admired—its horizontal orientation, the contemplative mood, the recording of names—had been specified ahead of time. The flourishing sculptural movement known as land art provided the fundamental form for the site—a shallow furrow cut into the earth—while the famous V shape recalled both Vietnam and the peace sign used in antiwar protests. Minimalism, the reigning art ethos of the time, provided a reason to keep the design simple.

If all these elements were already present and available to everyone, why was entry number 1,026 the only one to fuse them all together into a brilliantly creative synthesis? As in the case of Crick and Watson, there was an element of luck. Most of the designs echoed conventional war memorials, which typically glorified the heroic deeds of brave fighters. However, Lin happened to have spent the previous summer in Denmark studying funereal architecture in a famous cemetery that is also used as a park. That single element in her experience seems to have spread its significance across the web of other elements, fusing them into a new, profoundly meaningful gestalt focused not on glory but the fact of death. In effect, as Louis Menand noted, what she created was "a gravestone in a park."[12]

It's not hard to detect the laws of fitness operating here to produce a tipping point. We can imagine how the idea of focusing on the sadness and loss produced by war must have come together with the various other elements of the design, each increasingly fitting with the others, until a final, fully coherent and meaningful form emerged. By itself, however, the design of the Vietnam Veterans War Memorial, outstanding as it was, couldn't have produced the lasting impact that it did—that is, permanently shifting the criteria for memorial architecture. To do this, it needed to align itself with the emerging spirit of the times, which was a widespread revulsion at the carnage of the war, as well as deep-felt grief. In many ways, Maya Lin's brilliant achievement gave those feelings concrete expression, becoming a potent symbol of antiwar sentiment. The powerful fitness loop this alignment created fed on itself. Even as the memorial achieved enduring national and international fame, it served as one of the primary cultural vehicles for channeling and solidifying the sea change in feelings about war that emerged in the aftermath of Vietnam. In the networked idea-spaces of the extended mind, fitness produces its own richness.

As should be clear by now, the law of minimal effort, encapsulating in network terms the recurring concept that *the space of ideas thinks for you*, is the natural outcome of the interaction of the laws governing the dynamics of the extended mind. Further evidence confirming this can be found in cases we've already examined in detail. The law suggests there will be conditions under which the relevant idea-spaces are sufficiently fertile for a radical innovation to be a likely outcome. This is exactly what we found in the case of Gutenberg's invention (or more accurately, successful reinvention) of printing with movable type. The sheer density of idea-spaces (each a dynamic hub) that became aligned made it highly probable that someone would come up with a good solution. We can be quite precise about why, in general, this is so. Hotspots are vast reservoirs of energy with numerous links through which this energy can travel to external nodes, including other hubs and hotspots. The laws of spontaneous generation and fitness, interacting with the law of small-world networks, ensure that in many cases when two or three major hubs become connected, a kind of self-reinforcing cycle is set up that leads to still more interconnectivity. Because of the context-determining effect of hotspots, such nonlinear growth in connectivity tends to become focused, with each hotspot reinforcing the fitness of the others in relevant respects. Thus in Gutenberg's case, capitalism's natural drive toward making a profit intersected with the drive for uniformity in the vast Catholic text market and the technology of mass-produced stamping, jointly giving rise to a highly efficient form of high-volume printing.

A similar self-reinforcing loop leading to a creative breakthrough is to be found in the astonishing early success of Napster. As noted, there was nothing terribly original about Shawn Fanning's programming, which amounted to little more than tinkering with well-established file-sharing programs. What produced the breakthrough and exponential growth was the structure of the space in which it evolved: the presence of a high level of broadband interconnectivity in a market with a high interest in music, limited budgets, and relatively anarchic morals (college students). The growth of the market fueled technological improvements and vice versa, and these jointly led to the emergence of a kind of self-justifying ethic that seemed to suggest that if enough people were downloading music for free, it couldn't be wrong.

Sometimes an emerging social phenomenon is propelled through a tipping point (the network equivalent of a creative leap) by a multistage series of law-governed interactions that again are triggered by inputs significantly smaller than the resulting output. (In this sense, the law of minimal effort captures the fact noted in chapter 4 that tipping points violate the normal symmetry of cause and effect.) Consider, for example, the progressive emergence of homeschooling. In the fall of 1992, David Guterson, the future author of the best-selling novel *Snow Falling on Cedars*, took leave from his job as a public school teacher to promote his new book, *Family Matters: Why Homeschooling Makes Sense*. The reception he met among television, radio, and magazine journalists, as well as the public attending his readings, was one of shock bordering on outrage. How could he, as a teacher, take his own children out of the school system? Wasn't homeschooling fundamentally elitist and undemocratic? Weren't homeschoolers basically either right-wing religious zealots or left-wing/libertarian eccentrics? And regardless, didn't homeschooling fail to prepare children either academically or socially to become responsible, well-adjusted adults?

"Everywhere," Guterson noted in 1998, "I met people who were adamant that homeschooling should be banned. This fall, six years later, something clearly has changed." It certainly had. Guterson was quoted in an October 1998 *Newsweek* cover story whose headline said it all: "More Than a Million Kids and Growing: Can It Work for Your Family?" Homeschooling, in a word, had *tipped*. Having moved into the American mainstream, it is now well on its way to becoming a significant hotspot in education theory. Current estimates suggest over 2 million children are now taught at home, and a whole industry (materials, conferences, personal tutors, advice services) has grown up in the past decade or so to serve homeschoolers' needs. It's instructive to consider the way in which this came about.

Homeschooling is in fact something we've always done. This was how most children, poor and rich alike, learned basic education skills before grade-school education began to become institutionalized in America in the 1880s. But homeschooling in the modern sense of the word really resulted from the sustained efforts of the man whom Howard Gardner calls "the chief theorist" of the homeschooling movement.[13] John Holt, who began life as a New England–based grade-school teacher, did not originally set out to be the main intellectual force behind the homeschooling movement of the seventies and eighties (he died in 1985). But in the course of a career that included writing a half-dozen or so books (including two perennial best sellers), teaching stints at Harvard and Berkeley, and frequent contributions to the *New York Review of Books*, he moved, almost reluctantly one senses, from being a school reformer to an advocate of what he called *unschooling*, his own term for what homeschooling ideally is about.[14]

Holt argued convincingly that teaching children in an institutional setting curbed the natural creative energies that were the foundation of their learning. Most teachers, he suggested, are trained primarily in class management, testing, and curriculum-setting, rather than in helping children to learn, a task parents from all levels of society could take on without fear of harm. Holt fought for the right of parents to remove their children from school and teach them at home (a right now granted in all fifty states), and insisted that learning is a lifelong task, not something that takes place solely in our school years. Above all, he argued passionately that education should be about learning how to live a worthwhile life, not absorbing a required amount of information.

Holt specifically acknowledges the influence of thinkers like Herman Kohl, A. S. Neill, Paul Goodman, and Ivan Illich, all of whom in one way or another challenged conventional thinking about education. More than that, however, Holt was clearly swept along by the political *zeitgeist* of the late sixties and early seventies that undertook systematically to question the whole foundation of institutional power and authority in conventional society. Those of us who similarly found ourselves caught up in that celebrated counterculture can vividly recall how it pervaded the imagination, fueled by energy that radiated out into every corner of society. Holt's genius was to have found a way to channel that energy—the core intelligence of a hugely dynamic hotspot—and allow its drive for fundamental social reorganization to thoroughly reshape the conventional educational beliefs and practices he had inherited from his training.[15]

As the counterculture began to lose steam after the end of the Vietnam War and the recession produced by the oil shock of 1973, homeschooling seemed in danger of going the way of the "back-to-the-land" movement and other endearingly quaint products of the sixties. What rescued it was the way it fit with the concerns and ideals of another emerging hotspot, the fundamentalist Christian movement. Growing concern with what they regarded as the corrupting influence of the public school system led many evangelicals to look for an alternative, and homeschooling fit the bill perfectly, giving rise to another cycle of growth driven by the law of the fit get rich. It wasn't until the mid-1990s, however, that the homeschooling movement really appeared to come into its own. Increasing distrust of the public school system among middle-class parents worried about quality issues was certainly a factor. But the tipping point undoubtedly came with the emergence of the Internet as a mass phenomenon starting around 1995.

As anyone who has looked even briefly into homeschooling knows, the World Wide Web is now central to keeping geographically dispersed groups of parents, teachers, and advocates in touch with one another and with the movement's ongoing development. A multitude of Web sites provides everything from introductory information for those who are new to the movement to a vast array of teaching materials to weblogs, online newsletters, and community groups. Homeschooling has now reached a point of development, in fact, where it is beginning to undergo a process of reintegration into the educational mainstream, with the establishment of standard curricula, working arrangements to use local public school facilities for gym and other activities only such institutions can easily provide, and a much more supportive mood of acceptance on the part of the general public. John Holt might well be surprised, though hardly disappointed, at the way in which the interaction of a variety of emerging social and technological hotspots has created out of his original inspired vision a profoundly alive, dynamic, and significant educational phenomenon that continues growing at an exponential rate.

The central underlying theme of this book is that *the space of ideas thinks for you*. In previous chapters, we've made use of this concept to gain new insight into the mystery of creative leaps. Two important general claims have emerged, both related to the law of minimal effort. First, many such breakthroughs result from the imaginative transfer of intelligence from one space to another. Second, the self-organizing dynamics of the extended mind itself give rise to order for free, creating vast pools of surplus value available to creative minds sharp enough to find and exploit them. Let's briefly review these ideas as a means of drawing together the various threads of thought we've been exploring as we've examined the various laws governing the networked idea-spaces of the extended mind.

Some of the most significant creative leaps occur as the result of imaginatively transferring powerful embedded intelligence from one idea-space to another across a weak tie—in other words, between worlds that previously were relatively distant from one another. Of special relevance here are the laws of hotspots, navigation, fitness, and tipping points. The law of hotspots says that the weaker the tie (i.e., the more distant the idea-space from which intelligence is downloaded), the bigger the impact of the creative leap. The difficulty lies, of course, in finding the right hotspot, one that in spite of its distance nevertheless has just the right relationship of fitness with the recipient space. This is the navigation problem, and it's resolved by intuition and insight.

As always, chance can play a role, as when Ruth Handler stumbled across Lilli, but it's no use being handed the solution to your problem if, unlike her, you don't grasp that's what it is. Intuition, aided by luck or not, recognizes the pattern of fitness that unites the two spaces, and goes to work. Crick sensed that genetic geometry, a Mendelian twist on Schrödinger's application of physics to biology, would be crucial to solving the DNA puzzle long before he figured out what that geometry looked like. Insight—the mental tipping point (often driven by emergent fitness) in which the complex suddenly resolves into something new and simple—came relatively late in the game, as the data from Franklin, Griffiths, and Donohoe finally came together in a way that made sense. Others used weak ties to hotspots with equal success, and in a similar imaginative manner: Gehry's hotspot was art; Eratosthenes', geometry; Turner's, the new science of electromagnetic forces. In certain cases, a weak tie is created to an idea-space that is anything but hot. Tim Berners-Lee, the creator of the World Wide Web, went to an esoteric part of graph theory in mathematics for the all-important seed concept of a space in which everything was connected to everything. Reframing the space of the Internet in these terms provided the context in which his specific breakthroughs, such as the development of the three basic protocols for the World Wide Web, could happen.

As we've seen, the reverse process is also true: failure to reach out to an external hotspot in a field where strong reciprocity has served to inhibit reach can lead to stagnation and even blindness. Mattel's executives were so mired in conventional thinking about dolls that they repeatedly resisted Handler's audacious innovation. Chargaff couldn't sufficiently free himself from standard biochemical methods and practices to grasp the geometric significance of his own data. Turner's critics ridiculed even his more conservative paintings because they were trapped inside the interpretive space of classical idealist and naturalist landscape painting. The highly innovative team at Xerox PARC came up with a series of brilliant technological breakthroughs in developing the Star and Alto computers, but operated in classic university R&D mode. Cut off from much of the extraordinary ferment going on right in their backyard, they failed to see the significance of the emerging hobbyist computer, which they openly scorned, and what it pointed to—the development of both an *affordable* personal computer and the kinds of uses to which it would be put. Bill Gates initially dismissed the World Wide Web as a revolutionary force in computing because Microsoft's success rested largely on the tried-and-true model of exploiting the business side of technology, and he and his immediate circle of advisers couldn't see the money in it. Creative leaps come not from endlessly reworking what one already knows, but from the new understanding provided by connecting to distant intelligence.

The intelligence capable of triggering a breakthrough is sometimes distributed across more than one idea-space. Here the laws of small-world networks, fitness, and integration come to the fore. Classic examples of such distributed intelligence are Gutenberg's press and the rise of the personal computer. Both involved multiple linked idea-spaces (i.e., small worlds) that in a specific place and time began interacting in ways that made these technological artifacts inventions waiting to happen. The laws of fitness, operating largely through a variety of feedback loops, produced both internal integration (an effective technology) and external integration (fit with the social and cultural environment, creating exponential growth).

A less obvious example is to be found in the origins of modern aviation. Orville and Wilbur Wright made their first successful powered flight at Kitty Hawk on December 17, 1903, an achievement that was immediately reported in the press. Yet it wasn't until their flight over Manhattan in 1909 that flying really began to take hold of the public's imagination. What had happened was that powered flight was being demonstrated to thousands of very well-connected New Yorkers gazing from the windows of skyscrapers. Collectively, they formed a giant human hub of highly influential connectors. Excitement grew and more people flew as word about the wonders of flying quickly spread from Manhattan to the rest of the world.[16] When the Wrights' technological breakthrough became linked with this vast hub of connectors and the small-world networks they formed, a form of viral marketing spread the news, and the aviation revolution finally tipped.

In reviewing the law-governed dynamics of the extended mind and their role in creativity, it's worth touching once more on the tension between knowledge and imagination. Crick spoke about scientific discovery as based on a combination of "accuracy and imagination." By accuracy he meant the scientific tradition of carefully applying theoretical principles to empirical data in order to establish new scientific results and insights. Accuracy involves step-by-step analysis and careful checking to ensure there are no gaps. The whole basis of scientific truth depends on achieving as great a degree of completeness as possible. This linear progression, extending known principles by showing that they apply to novel cases, is how most scientific discoveries are made.

It's what Thomas Kuhn calls *normal science*. Valuable though it is, however, it remains essentially bishop's work. It never quite escapes from the conundrum first posed in *The Meno*: if something is connected to the known, how can it be new, and if it is wholly new, then how can it be known? Sooner or later, going in a straight line, step-by-step, lands you on top of a peak. You may be able to see where you want to go next, but you can't get there from where you are.

This is where imagination comes in. The imagination can recognize congruent patterns that are neither spatially contiguous nor logically related, build a whole new world around a fortunate accident or chance occurrence, or intuitively grasp the deep structure of the energized forces radiating out of a hotspot—in short, it can *jump*. It can make the knight's move into wholly new territory, discovering there new truth, new forms of expression and organization, new inventions. Of course, as Crick notes, you need both. The imagination needs to be brought back down to earth by the steady, step-by-step progression of rational knowledge. In the end only knowledge can take the true measure of the arc traced by the imaginative mind.

Unlike many other forms of creative endeavor, creative leaps *by definition* need to make good use of the imagination. Making a break with the past necessitates making a jump to a place knowledge either can't reach or would arrive at altogether too slowly. Mostly, the leap is to a distant hotspot. The disruptive creativity of the extended mind is powered by leaps of the imagination attracted by the pull of densely interlinked hubs spewing forth endless new patterns of connectivity. The adventurous mind sallies forth, guided only by intuition—another function of the inherently nonlinear imagination—in its quest for the startlingly new. Only later will the work of integration begin, restoring via the sound use of knowledge some measure of linearity and stability to a world poised on the edge of chaos.

Chapter Twelve

LEADERSHIP, IMAGINATION, AND THE ART OF THE LONG BET

*I think it's sort of indecent to have things so worked out that they
end up like you thought they should . . . You just have to expose
yourself to more, and see what the consequences are.*

—Robert Rauschenberg[1]

*Logic will get you from A to B, imagination
will take you everywhere.*

—Albert Einstein

If there's one thing most business leaders would agree on, it's that we live in
an increasingly complex and volatile business environment. In *Confronting
Reality*, Bossidy and Charan pose a critical question: "How can you anticipate change before it's too late? Is it really possible to know, in Wayne Gret-
sky's famous phrase, not where the puck is but where it's going to be? The
answer is yes, but only if you learn how to look around corners by understanding the realities outside your walls in more breadth and depth than
ever before."[2]

Figuring out the future, never an easy accomplishment, is getting harder.
The conventional response: *Do more analysis.* The conventional wisdom
strongly suspects that isn't going to cut it, knowing how dangerous rational

extrapolations based on the past can be, but isn't sure what usable alternative might exist. Looking around corners requires imagination, intuition, and insight, but these have generally been regarded as vague and unreliable, and thus as likely to mislead as guide to success.[3]

Great artists, scientists, and entrepreneurs have always had deeper faith than most businesspeople, economists, and sociologists in the power of the mind's imaginative faculties to create radically new worlds of possibility. As we have seen, they have much to teach us. So too do philosophers, who after long being in thrall to the primacy of analytical reason, are finally coming round to giving the imagination its due.[4] Colin McGinn goes so far as to suggest we regard the mind "as centrally a device for imagining."[5] Only when we are first able to imagine possible alternatives to our existing world can the rational work of analyzing, comparing, testing, validating, asserting, and predicting begin. Reason itself is built on the imagination.[6]

Corporate leaders, long accustomed to relying on the lens of rational analysis to peer into the future, are going to have to develop their imaginative faculties far beyond what was required for the infamous 1990s "vision thing." In the past few chapters I've proposed some foundations for an emergent new *science of ideas* that promises to increase our understanding of breakthrough creativity and how it shapes the unfolding of the future. Now it's time to get practical and focus on how this new understanding can help you transform your own business or profession.

PUTTING CREATIVE LEAPS ON THE AGENDA: A BRIEF GUIDE TO ACTION

According to Bossidy and Charan, "confronting reality has to become a leadership priority of the highest order . . . most businesses will be required to change more and more often in the coming decade than they have in their previous histories."[7] In the new business environment, leadership will demand "unprecedented awareness of a greater range of external realities than ever before."[8] The latter include such factors as competitive intensity, shorter product cycles, regulation, the constant risk of virtually overnight commoditization, the drive for global cost parity, demographic shifts, and rapid technological advances spread across the globe. All these elements must be tracked and the linkages between them analyzed.

In the face of such an environment, Bossidy and Charan note, leaders will need to develop a comprehensive business model that will act as an early warning system for real-world changes that present threats and/or opportunities. Constructing such a model will require an ability to get to the root cause of things, making sense of a bewildering mass of information and events, identifying sustainable trends as opposed to passing fads, and remaining passionately yet critically curious about what is new and different and the ways it might affect your business.[9] Those who fail to achieve this level of understanding and the commitment to change it implies "risk being overtaken, outcompeted, and obsolete."[10]

Confronting Reality is the latest in a series of books, stretching back to Hamel and Prahalad's groundbreaking *Competing for the Future*, that encourage leaders to focus more urgently on the task of understanding how the future will unfold.[11] In *Leading the Revolution*, Hamel stresses that the new industrial order we are now living in is the result of a type of innovation built on leaps of human imagination: "Companies fail to create the future not because they fail to predict it but because they fail to *imagine* it . . . So it is vitally important that you understand the distinction between 'the future' and 'the unimagined,' between *knowing* what's next and *imagining* what's next."[12] In a similar vein, Bossidy and Charan, noting that looking around corners is a discipline of its own, insist that leaders will need to "visualize scenarios—opportunities and threats—like movies in their brains."[13]

The framework I've developed here suggests that creative leaps—simultaneously the greatest opportunity and the greatest danger to companies and their leaders—arise from the interaction of the imaginative faculties with the self-transforming dynamics of the global mindspace in which business finds itself operating. From now on, successful business models intended to address future development will need to include, in addition to a healthy dose of reality-based analysis, a component mapping out the relevant spaces of the extended mind.[14] Indeed, this is where the highest priority lies, since it is imagination, intuition, and insight that create the space within which rational analysis goes to work. Great failures and successes stem from this fact. Microsoft's lateness in catching on to the significance of the Internet, and Chargaff's glossing over the meaning of the one-to-one base ratios, were *failures of imagination* resulting from doing intense analysis in the *wrong space*. Correspondingly, Gutenberg's reinvention of printing, the rise of the personal computer, and Barbie's triumphant transformation of the doll market all flowed directly from intuitively locating major emergent idea-spaces and responding imaginatively to the creative forces inherent in them.

So how is the trick turned? What does the section of your business model entitled "The Imagined Future" look like? How do you visualize it—and think it through? It's important to get the model right, because it frames everything that follows. More precisely, what you imagine and commit to will (for good or ill) *create* what follows. As Hamel correctly points out,

> To even talk about "the" future is a misnomer. There is no one future waiting to happen. While certain aspects of the future are highly probable (the earth will still be spinning tomorrow), there is little about the future that is inevitable. IKEA didn't have to be. eBay didn't have to be . . . Was cubism inevitable in art . . . Perhaps yes, in some cosmic sense. But [its] appearance at a particular point in history was far from a foregone conclusion.[15]

Here are some brief guidelines for getting started.

Horace Judson remarked that Watson was "extremely sensitive to heat." It's an excellent characteristic of anyone bent on creating or anticipating breakthroughs. So the first rule for leaders is:

Sharpen your capacity to sense heat.

Easier said than done. Heat arises from energy, and in network terms, that comes from dense interconnectivity combined with dynamism. Plenty of hubs are massively interlinked to other hubs and nodes, but aren't particularly dynamic: mainstream Protestantism, for instance, or the newspaper industry. Sometimes, of course, the heat is built in. Sex, for example. Ruth Handler knew at a glance she'd connected to an eternal source of heat the minute she saw Lilli. Sometimes the dynamism is latent, waiting to become white-hot through *fitness*—in other words, by being connected to just the right idea-space. For example, no one would describe the obscure section of graph theory known as world-wide webs as dynamic. However, applied by Tim Berners-Lee to the problem of how to make the (at the time) archaic structure of the Internet universally and uniformly accessible, it proved to be one of the hottest ideas of the past fifty years, leading directly to the explosive growth of the Web.[16] The lesson is to keep scanning the global mindscape for spaces of embedded intelligence that, connected in the right way, could cause the energy level in another space to rise dramatically.

Sometimes, of course, you're lucky enough to be right in the middle of things as they're unfolding. The participants in the Homebrew Club's activities knew from the outset they were in a firestorm caused by the conjunction (geographically as well as historically) of the exploding counterculture, a highly enthusiastic hobbyist electronics community, and the arrival of processors like the Intel 8080. Turner found himself in a perfect storm of emergent idea-spaces: the new science of electromagnetism, Romantic pantheism, and a rising market for landscape painting still evolving from its roots in Italian idealism and Dutch realism.

More than anything else, it's the connections that generate the heat. Gehry linked art and architecture, transforming the latter. Gutenberg connected the Catholic Church's quest for doctrinal uniformity with the technology for stamping out coins. Crick integrated aspects of physics and genetics.

In the highly dynamic, technologically diversified world in which we now live, it's fascinating to watch hot new ideas pop up from unexpected linkages. The *New York Times* recently reported enthusiasm among visitors to the Museum of Modern Art for a new type of audio guide. Instead of paying $5 to rent MoMA's clunky audio device programmed with staid official interpretations, they can listen to an irreverent but insightful commentary on their iPods, spiced up with remarks about the sexual meaning of certain Pollack canvases, music ranging from hip-hop to the Stranglers' 1970 song "Peaches," and the sound of a woman moaning in pleasure.[17]

Created by David Gilbert, a professor of communication at Marymount Manhattan College, and a group of his students, it's the result of linking several hotspots: podcasting (generating free downloadable Internet audio content), the iPod's cool technology (though any MP3 player will do), the growing remix culture, and the public's increasing interest in on-demand media fed by TiVo and similar devices.[18] Described as a way to "hack the gallery experience,"[19] it's a perfect blend of hot technological developments and social trends, creating a classic fit-get-rich growth scenario.

Not even on the horizon when the iPod was launched, podcasting is becoming a major new market driver for the device. More significantly, podcasting's flexibility as a format and close fit with current consumer trends is already producing the kind of white-hot growth reminiscent (according to *BusinessWeek*) of the early days of the Web.[20] "Happening entrepreneurs" are already hard at work thinking up new applications that go well beyond causing museum directors sleepless nights worrying if their cultural offerings too are about to be hacked.

Podcasting also illustrates a second principle for future-obsessed leaders:

Learn to recognize early emergent alignments
manifesting high levels of fitness.

Fust must have had this ability in spades, or he'd never have put up two rounds of funding for Gutenberg. A negative example involves *Encyclopedia Britannica*. I happened to be present at the opening plenary session of the Electronic Books Conference and Exposition held in New York in late September 1994, when Joseph J. Esposito, president of *Encyclopedia Britannica*, rose to address the assembled delegates. His talk, entitled "The Publishing Challenge," was clearly intended to dampen the excitement and hype generated by the prospects digital books and magazines appeared to be opening up. *Encyclopedia Britannica*, he announced, was moving into digital publishing, but cautiously, somewhat reluctantly, and only as a complement to their main print business.

Less than four years after that speech, *Britannica*, facing collapsing demand for the printed version of the encyclopedia, sold its business at under half its book value to a Swiss banking conglomerate that would publish the encyclopedia primarily in digital form online. The strategic leadership at *Britannica* had failed to perceive that a tremendous cultural change was under way in American society, particularly among *Britannica*'s core market—parents. As two well-known analysts put it: "*Britannica*'s executives failed to understand what their customers were really buying. Parents had been buying *Britannica* less for its intellectual content than out of a desire to do the right thing for their children. Today, when parents 'Do the right thing,' they buy their kids a computer."[21]

In other words, following the PC revolution, *Britannica*'s real competition was the computer, which had rapidly growing fitness in the home education market. Children were increasingly doing their school projects and reports on a home computer. Parents were supporting their children in doing well at school by providing them with educational software. More generally, there was growing appreciation for the dynamism of the computer as an educational tool, including its multiple integrated capacities for communication, word processing, hypertext linking, interactivity, and animated graphics.

At the time, most PCs were bundled with *Encarta*, Microsoft's digital encyclopedia. *Britannica* simply couldn't compete, its sales plummeted, and it was forced to sell its business. Parents who had around $1,500 to spend on supporting their children's education at home opted to buy a computer that already contained an encyclopedia.

Another more current example of an emergent alignment manifesting high fitness—one of the central effects of the law of small-world networks—is the unexpected popularity of digital camera technology embedded in cell phones. Initially, executives at leading manufacturers were skeptical that adding photo and video capacity to cell phones would attract a broad market. Inevitably, prices of chip manufacturing fell even as performance rapidly increased, making the technology available for midpriced phones. That much was predictable analytically from Moore's law. But what primarily held executives back was a failure of the imagination resulting from framing things wrongly. Video phones had never caught on, so even with more advanced technology, why would they now? Most business users, for example, have little interest in viewing the person they're calling. The emergent factor that was missed was the teenage market. Modern youth's insatiable need to instantly share what is happening had already driven the development of cheap instant messaging on cell phones. Now that same imperative would drive cell phone camera use—not so much to send pictures of the caller as to provide a live image of the surrounding scene. A conventional digital camera couldn't do that, and anyway, why lug around two devices when one will do? As prices fell, sales took off. Currently (such is the power of the law of the fit get rich), cell phones equipped for digital photography are outselling digital cameras by a significant margin.

Heat. Fitness. Alignment. All manifestations of energy in the networked spaces of the global mindscape. Sometimes, however, the place to start is where the energy is distinctly low—where nothing's really happening. When Mattel decided to get into the doll business, fundamentally not much had changed since the French started making baby dolls at the turn of the nineteenth century. Sex, Japanese skill with injection-molded plastics, and a remarkably savvy use of the novel phenomenon of advertising toys to kids on television quickly turned the industry on its head. Architecture was still struggling to escape the fifty-year-old straitjacket of modernism when Gehry found a way to forge a hot link to the contemporary art scene. The lesson is, if you want to start a revolution, don't just look for heat; explore its opposite:

Look for cold—low-energy spaces ripe for transformation through long-distance linkage.

Cast your eye around. What looks like a mature industry stuck at the top of an S-curve? The retail bookselling business was as traditional an industry as you could find until Barnes & Noble changed it forever by adapting the superstore approach. Then Amazon.com went one better, bringing book buyers the biggest selection possible, combined with all kinds of search and evaluation tools available only digitally. Of course, this type of breakthrough is not quite as simple as it may look. To some adventurous souls, the pet food business, which had already gone through the superstore stage, looked ripe for further transformation as a dot-com. No less than four startups—Petstore.com, Petopia, PetSmart.com, and Pets.com—tried to make a go of it, but none succeeded in fulfilling the original high expectations of its backers. Incredibly, Amazon.com (of all companies) managed to burn through a purported $100 million invested in Pets.com before it went out of business in November 2000. Evidently Bezos and his advisers failed to recognize that the logic of the book market, which made books a natural for an Internet business, has virtually nothing in common with that of a pure commodity business like dog and cat food![22]

The great dot-com bust demonstrated forcefully how crucial *fitness* and *integration* are as fundamental components of networked system dynamics.

When they are absent, breakthroughs, no matter how dazzling they may appear at the start, have little chance of long-term success. The flip side of this is that their presence can produce stunning tipping points. Consider, for example, the food industry. Until recently it's been a relatively stable industry. The first signs of turmoil came with the revised Atkins diet in the mid-1990s.[23] Atkins strongly appealed to consumers who were tired of being told by the U.S. Department of Agriculture to follow a diet rich in grains while eating meat and fats sparingly.

In the old days, academic nutritionists talked to one another, or to the federal government. Mainstream nutrition advice was mostly the province of diet gurus. Atkins changed that by proposing a rationale for meat eating grounded in evolutionary science. Then came a major shift in expert and government opinion, signaled to the general public in a groundbreaking article in the *New York Times* entitled "What If It's All Been a Big Fat Lie?"[24] This official about-face, suggesting that perhaps Atkins had been right all along about the dangers of a high-carb diet, was shocking. It coincided with a series of federal reports indicating that obesity rates among American adults and children were skyrocketing.

The low-carb fad took off in 2003, catching most industry leaders flat-footed. Even as they scrambled to catch up, however, filling supermarket shelves with an endless succession of low-carb, carb-smart, no-carb products, word began to spread that the *real* danger was from *trans*-fats—or was it sugar, or . . . ?

The result of this integration of nutrition science and popular concern about dieting is that the food industry as a whole has reached a tipping point, entering a future of ceaseless volatility. As an increasingly overweight, unfit, and aging public focuses attention as never before on nutrition news, the industry is now at the mercy of whatever the latest scientific report says is good or bad for you.

So this is the fourth rule for leaders bent on imagining the future:

Identify and prepare for potential tipping points.

Following this principle could certainly have saved Sony a lot of grief. As creators of the Walkman, the first portable music device, Sony was well positioned to assume a leadership position as the MP3 format began to become the standard for downloading digitally compressed music from the Internet. Instead, they did virtually nothing. In addition to being a consumer electronics giant, Sony owned several leading record labels, including Columbia Records and RCA, and was therefore unwilling to market devices capable of increasing illegal downloads. As services like Napster began to face serious legal challenges, it looked like a sound, rational decision. What Sony failed to anticipate was what would happen if someone could persuade the record companies to back a legal download service. That person turned out to be someone who, as head of Pixar, had a lot of credibility with the media industry, and who also happened to own one of the coolest computer hardware and software companies in the business. Steve Jobs pulled the whole package together, the iPod was launched, and the industry underwent a major phase transition.[25]

The dazzling success of the iPod brings us to the fifth rule for leaders:

Read the world.

Business leaders, or at any rate their advisers, are supposed to keep up with what's happening. So how come they keep getting blindsided? Bossidy and Charan give a whole list of reasons why this happens, including a tendency to filter information to fit internal mind-sets, wishful thinking, and emotional overinvestment in maintaining the status quo.[26] Sony executives exhibited several of these. To a nonbiased rational observer, it was obvious that following Jobs's return, the shine was back on the Apple logo. The company was increasingly targeting the consumer electronics market, and had both the financial and R&D resources to make a breakthrough there. Meanwhile, Pixar's success was boosting Jobs's status in Hollywood.

But staying well informed, a very necessary but entirely insufficient condition, is only the beginning. What matters is not depth and breadth of information, but skill in *making sense of it*. I'm using *read* here with the meaning of reading someone's expression or body language. To turn Marx on his head, if you want to change the world, you'd first better interpret it.

Now we seem to be back in the treacherous territory of trusting your gut. As we have seen, viewed in terms of networks this really isn't that mysterious. We've all had the experience of suddenly finding things fall into place; what was puzzling before now makes sense to us, hangs together, becomes unexpectedly coherent. A new gestalt forms—a pattern emerges where before there were just dots. In more formal terms, there is a movement from complex to simple. Mentally, we reach a tipping point. In network terms, the transition is to a state in which a group of nodes *have more internal links, fitness, and integration than external.*

This move to coherence and simplicity is the basis of intuition and insight, and it's something the human mind does very naturally. We are pattern-completing animals. Of course, if we try hard enough, we can see patterns where none really exists. Plenty of people were convinced they could divine in the unfolding events and trends of the 1990s boom the template for future enterprise. They read the world as new rules, new leaders, new economy. What was missing, of course, were the acid tests of *external* fitness and integration.

The infamous new economy, conceived as such, never managed to evolve a fit with the broader and deeper economic truths inherent in the old. The soundest intuitions are those that create coherence over the widest possible webs of connections. So in reading the world, cast your net widely.

The final principle is inherent in all the others:

Trust your imaginative faculties as they surf
the webs of the global mindspace.

It takes time to free ourselves from the age-old habit of disparaging imagination in favor of rational analysis. Bossidy and Charan are right: looking around corners—making the knight's move into a new space—*is* a different discipline. What it takes above all is imagination. Not in Shakespeare's conceit—the fantasy imagination of the lunatic, the lover, and the love-stricken poet—but the supremely intelligent, world-constructing imagination of the scientist, the artist, and the entrepreneur. Fortunately, we don't have to do all the work ourselves. The spaces of the extended mind are already richly embedded with intelligence. Mostly what we have to do is find it. The spaces of ideas will do most of our thinking for us.

THINGS THAT KEEP YOU AWAKE AT NIGHT

Learning to free up the imaginative faculties takes time and practice. To be an imaginative leader you must hone your emergent skills by continually confronting reality. To that end, the following issues may provide further cause for reflection.

What If You're Trapped in the Wrong Space and Don't Know It?

Blindness is always hard to deal with. After all, how can you discover what you don't even realize you don't know? As an imaginative leader, your basic stance should be that there is *always* something you are blind to that is both a threat and an opportunity. Then the appropriate action is to read the world, to constantly scan the available information sources for even faint signals of emergent heat. Magnify anything that your intuition tells you might be interesting and begin inventing scenarios around it. Ask yourself: What might this look like if it continues to develop? What threat and/or opportunity does it pose to what we are doing now? What is the potential *fit* here? None of this is easy. The temptation to see the future in terms of the bishop's moves—all straight lines—is easy to succumb to. It takes real energy, determination, and commitment to make the knight's move by jumping into an altogether new space.

How Do You Assess the Potential of a Hotspot?

Let's say the normal turbulence of the business environment just got significantly worse for your particular industry. You've got your antennae out, and new hotspots start popping up all over the place. Maybe it's a new science that seems poised to revolutionize all kinds of industries, like nanotechnology, or genomics. Perhaps it's a new application of an emergent technology: interactive television looked awfully good to Time Warner back in the late 1990s. Or maybe it's a different way of doing business. Why not sell groceries or pet food online?

To some extent God is in the details. Pet food just isn't nearly as good an online business as books, which have far greater potential for producing customer value through digital technology. Nanotechnology does have real promise, but many applications are still years away. More important than such considerations, however, are crucial metrics such as alignment and fitness. The history of printing shows how in some cases a real breakthrough depends on a whole series of key elements lining up.

Interactive television looked like a good idea at the time. The Internet was providing every digitally equipped household with the opportunity to interact with media in ways that simply weren't possible before the advent of the World Wide Web, so why not mass media too? What executives at Time Warner (and they weren't the only ones dreaming about this) failed to realize was that at least two key elements were missing. First, launching interactive television successfully would require a mass deployment of broadband technology that simply hadn't happened. Second, most people didn't want it. In spite of what many enthusiastic executives thought, there really wasn't much basic fitness between the highly active world of navigating the Internet and the essentially passive one of watching television.

Incidentally, the reverse can be true: fitness can emerge in unexpected places. BitTorrent, a superfast form of peer-to-peer software, was originally developed to help Linux developers transfer multigigabyte files quickly. Almost from the get-go, however, it was adapted by users for transferring pirated movies and television shows, a kind of Napster for videos. The fit between the technology and the market was almost perfect, and it rapidly came to account for a major proportion of all Internet traffic![27] The fit get richer . . .

How Do You Map Your Extended Networks
So You Can See Where You Are?

Executives love to talk about thinking outside the box. We all know what this means, but it's misleading. You're never outside the box, though you can jump to a different one. Or, more pointedly, you're always deeply enmeshed in the networked spaces of the extended mind, whose boundaries exist (recall that the law of hotspots, among other things, controls connectivity) but are also porous. So the lesson is, the deeper your network maps extend into the mindscapes of networked space, the better position you'll be in to see ripples that could rapidly become game-changing waves. Peering into deep space can be intimidating and thrilling at the same time.

Mapping interlinked spaces of embedded intelligence is so novel that it's hard to give detailed advice for how to go about it. The most effective technique is probably to map out the major hubs that are connected to your business, no matter how distantly, paying special attention to those that appear to be heating up. Think of it in terms of one of those satellite pictures taken at night where the major cities show up as intense blobs of light in the surrounding darkness. Crick spotted the heat coming from biophysics, with its techniques of abstract theorizing and model building. Ruth Handler sensed the build-up of energy that would unleash the sexual revolution and rode the wave to enormous success, despite the fact that the baby-doll industry at the time couldn't even dream of such a connection.

How Do You Recognize a Tipping Point When It's Happening?

Or better yet, before it happens? *More is different*, but who's to know how much more, and when it will arrive, and in what form? The sandpile may collapse under the impact of a shock wave or the addition of just a single grain of sand falling in just the right place. No one, it seems, foresaw that VisiCalc would become the first killer app for the PC industry. Jobs turned it down, and even its inventors saw only limited applications for it. And yet with hindsight it's not unreasonable to imagine that such a tipping point could have been anticipated. Virtually from the outset it was clear to most of the main players that business was going to be a very large, if not the principal, market for the personal computer. The main reason the business market didn't take off faster was precisely the lack of applications that would appeal to a broad customer base. Word processing was still in its infancy, and legions of secretaries still handled most of the volume. Such financial applications as were developed tended to be highly specialized. A spreadsheet was different. Granted, unlike word processing, in this case there was no nondigital equivalent. But the usefulness of being able to *run the numbers*, altering them at will with a few keystrokes, was self-evident. The degree of fitness between the application and its intended market was very high, resulting in an inevitable outcome. The only reason it was a surprise was that no one had ever seen a killer app take off before.

As we saw in chapter 4, tipping points can arise from a variety of causes, ranging from simple to complex. In the case of printing, no less than eight hubs tightly connected by feedback loops had to line up. The iPod is a similar case in point. Its success, which transformed the portable music business, resulted from a whole array of events: Napster's popularization of downloading individual music files from the Internet, the emergence of the MP3 format, the development of very high capacity microdrives, plus Jobs's exit from Apple and move to Pixar. Without the credibility he had built with Hollywood media moguls, he would never have been able to get the major record labels to agree to license their music to Apple.

THE ART OF THE LONG BET

If I had to reduce what I have to say about creativity and imagination to a single schematic diagram, it would look like figure 12-1. The series of small arcs model incremental innovation, representing most instances of progress in science, technology, the arts, and not least, business. Each step builds on what has gone before, proceeding linearly and largely analytically. From time to time, however, the normal course of things is interrupted by a creative leap to a new space of ideas, as indicated by the large arc. Here the imagination comes into play, leaving linear reasoning far behind. In the majority of cases, the arc passes through a distant idea-space or linked set of such spaces, taking along with it key aspects of the embedded intelligence it contains (see figure 12-2). Only the imaginative faculties, including intuition and insight, can successfully find and transfer intelligence via a weak tie in this way.

For business leaders this is the holy grail, the long bet that pays off. Such bets invariably involve long odds. Sometimes the payoff comes quickly,

FIGURE 12-1

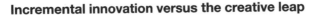

Incremental innovation versus the creative leap

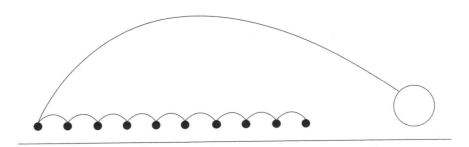

FIGURE 12-2

The arc of the imagination

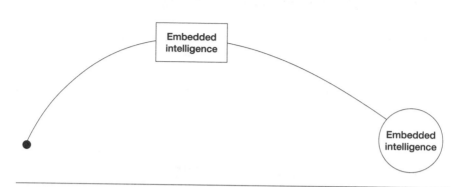

sometimes much later. In some cases the result fades, and sometimes it endures, producing consequences that stretch far into the future. Ed Roberts bet long when he accepted the challenge to build and market a home computer for under $500. The odds of doing so were very low, but Roberts was a man whose boldness was sharpened by the looming threat of financial ruin. The founders of Netflix also went up against significant odds when they founded a mail-order DVD business. Many predicted that this would be a niche business at best, because the looming advent of broadband access to movie libraries would surely condemn them, and retail outlets like Blockbuster, to an ever-diminishing share of the market. Instead, Netflix has transformed the movie rental business, successfully establishing a new business model for the industry that shows no signs of slowing its phenomenal growth.

Steve Jobs similarly took a long shot, risking the failure of his company, when at the end of the 1990s he resisted those who were urging Apple to turn itself around by quickly getting innovative new products to market. Instead, Jobs invested most of the company's available human, financial, and technological resources in building a new operating system that became the hugely successful OS X.

It was this move that later made possible the iPod, whose brilliantly designed interface depended crucially on the OS X. The example is especially interesting because at the time Jobs made the decision to invest in a new operating system, products like the iPod weren't even distant blips on Apple's radar. But Apple is a unique company. It is in effect its own hotspot. Apple's core intelligence (the famous Apple DNA, as it's sometimes called)—superb technology, sleek design, and dazzling marketing skills—is by now so well established that Jobs and his production design team appear to have supreme confidence that a risky investment like OS X will pay off in terms of new and as yet unimagined products. This is exactly what happened with the iPod, a creative leap tied directly to the company's own embedded intelligence.

So what is the art of the long bet? All the principles in this chapter—firmly based on the laws I describe throughout the book—are strategies for honing your ability to make creative leaps against the odds that lead to extraordinary success: learn to sense where the heat is, spot potential tipping points, "read" the world. Above all, trust your imaginative faculties as they surf embedded webs of intelligence near and far, and have the confidence that if you're up for the ride, the space of ideas, shaped by the laws of network dynamics, will do most of the hard thinking for you.

NOTES

Introduction

1. John Holt, *Teach Your Own* (New York: Delacourt, 1981).

2. See "Get Creative: How to Build Innovative Companies," *BusinessWeek* special report, August 1, 2005. The article notes that "increasingly, the new core competence is creativity." It cites a study by the Boston Consulting Group, Inc., in which 940 senior executives claimed that "increasing top-line revenues through innovation has become essential to success." See also Richard Florida, *The Rise of the Creative Class: And How It's Transforming Work, Leisure, Community and Everyday Life* (New York: Basic Books, 2002).

3. William Shakespeare, *Macbeth* I, vii, 25-28.

4. On long-term memory, see Eric R. Kandel, *In Search of Memory: The Emergence of a New Science of Mind* (New York: Norton, 2006); on early work in neural networks and the connection with recent research on analogy, see Keith Holyoak and Paul Thagard, *Mental Leaps: Analogy in Creative Thought* (Cambridge, MA: MIT Press, 1995), 240ff.; and on a networked approach to concept formation, see Gilles Fauconnier and Mark Turner, *The Way We Think: Conceptual Blending and the Mind's Hidden Complexities* (New York: Basic Books, 2002), to be discussed in chapter 3.

5. Cited in an interview with Brubeck in "Risk," vol. 8 of *Jazz*, DVD directed by Ken Burns, PBS Paramount.

Chapter 1

1. Fragment VII, translated by Charles H. Kahn, *The Art and Thought of Heraclitus: An Edition of the Fragments with Translation and Commentary* (Cambridge: Cambridge University Press, 1979), 31.

2. "Le rôle des voyages dans la constitution des collections ethnographiques, historiques et scientifiques," Congrès national des sociétés historiques et scientifiques, 130 e congrès, La Rochelle, 2005: Voyages et voyageurs; http://www.cths.fr/4DACTION/www_Con_Detail/34_176.

3. Pablo Picasso, "Discovery of African Art: 1906-1907," in *Primitivism and Twentieth-Century Art: A Documentary History*, eds. Jack Flam with Miriam Deutch (Berkeley, CA: UC Press, 2003), 32-33; excerpted from André Malraux, *La Tête d'Obsidienne* (Paris: Gallimard, 1974), 17-19. The interview with Malraux took place in 1937. As John Richardson notes in *A Life of Picasso, Volume II: 1907-1917* (New York: Random House, 1996), 32, the exorcism was of more than private demons (including possibly syphilis): ". . . it was also an exorcism of traditional concepts of 'ideal beauty.'"

4. In *A Life of Picasso: Volume I, 1881-1906* (New York: Random House, 1991), 519, John Richardson notes that Picasso later (in 1939) denied there was any African influence on *Les Demoiselles d'Avignon*. In *Volume II*, 24ff., however, Richardson states his reasons for giving this view little weight. Whatever Picasso's reasons for flip-flopping, both the visual evidence of the picture itself and the forcefulness of the original quote testify against his later denial.

5. Quoted in Richardson, *A Life, Volume I*, 488.

6. Joel Mokyr, *The Lever of Riches* (New York: Oxford University Press, 1990). Mokyr is referring to technological invention, but it is no less true of breakthrough creativity in general.

7. See especially Andy Clark, *Being There: Putting Brain, Body, and World Together Again* (Cambridge, MA: MIT Press, 1997) and *Natural-Born Cyborgs: Minds, Technologies, and the Future of Human Intelligence* (New York: Oxford University Press, 2003). This research, as Clark and others recognize, has its roots in earlier work outside these disciplines. Cultural anthropologists, and more recently postmodernists, have for decades insisted that in order to make sense of the world and to think creatively, the mind continually taps into vast reservoirs of intelligence embedded both culturally and socially in the form of myths, rituals, social conventions, institutions, traditions, and practices that, as the distinguished anthropologist Clifford Geertz put it, are "good to think with."

8. John Brockman, ed., *The Greatest Inventions of the Past 2,000 Years* (New York: Simon and Schuster, 2000), 177.

9. Clark, *Being There*, 180, emphasis added.

10. See Andy Clark, "Magic Words: How Language Augments Human Computation," in Peter Carruthers and Jill Boucher, eds., *Language and Thought: Interdisciplinary Themes* (Cambridge, UK: Cambridge University Press, 1998), 162.

11. See "Now You See It, Now You Don't" in "A Survey of Information Technology," *The Economist*, October 30, 2004, 7–8. The article cites the work of Joe Corn, a history professor at Stanford University.

12. Clark, *Being There*, 180.

13. Daniel Dennett, *Kinds of Minds* (New York: Basic Books, 1996), quoted in Andy Clark, "Reasons, Robots and the Extended Mind," in *Mind and Language* 16, no. 2 (2001): 121–145.

14. Both the slide rule and the African masks are instances of what Gilles Fauconnier and Mark Turner would call objects acting as "material anchors" for complex integrated networks, or what we would call idea-spaces. See their *The Way We Think: Conceptual Blending and the Mind's Hidden Complexities* (New York: Basic Books, 2002), 203ff.

15. For a fascinating account of the Roman and Hindu-Arabic number systems, see Peter L. Bernstein, *Against the Gods: The Remarkable Story of Risk* (New York: Wiley, 1996), chapter 2.

16. As we'll see, an idea-space is, more strictly, a world seen in terms of its basic elements and the relations (links) between them—in other words, seen as a network.

17. For a recent, cogently argued discussion of the importance of developing a sound business model, see Larry Bossidy and Ram Charan, *Confronting Reality: Doing What Matters to Get Things Right* (New York: Crown, 2004).

18. Quoted in Bossidy and Charan, *Confronting Reality*, 19.

19. In *Being There*, 194-195. Clark refers to this kind of external cognitive equipment as "scaffolding," which he explicates as follows: "We have called an action scaffolded to the extent that it relies on some kind of external support. Such support could come from the use of tools, or from exploitation of the knowledge and skills of others; that is to say, scaffolding (as I shall use the term) denotes a broad class of physical, cognitive and social augmentations—augmentations that allow us to achieve some goal that would otherwise be beyond us." There is an apparent connection here with Heidegger's notion of equipment.

20. Robert H. Frank, "Economic Scene: If firmly believed, the theory that self-interest is the sole motivator appears to be self-fulfilling," *New York Times*, February 17, 2005.

21. Picasso, "Discovery," 34.

22. See Clayton M. Christensen, *The Innovator's Dilemma: When New Technologies Cause Great Firms to Fail* (Boston: Harvard Business School Press, 1997); and Clayton M. Christensen and Michael E. Raynor, *The Innovator's Solution: Creating and Sustaining Successful Growth* (Boston: Harvard Business School Press, 2003).

23. Alice Calaprice, ed., *The Expanded Quotable Einstein* (Princeton, NJ: Princeton University Press, 2000), 317. She notes it's commonly attributed to Einstein, but does not know the source.

24. As Clark notes in the conclusion to "'Author's Reply' to symposium on Natural-Born Cyborgs," in *Metascience*, in press: "The time is ripe to begin to put together the many pieces of the puzzle of mind. That means, I firmly believe, seeing our unique cultural and technological scaffoldings as not just aids for understanding the mind, but as key parts of the minds we seek to understand." On the term *extended mind*, see Clark, *Being There*, 179ff, 213ff.

25. Mokyr (*The Lever of Riches*, vii–viii), for example, speaks of human creativity as "that rare and mysterious phenomenon in which a human being arrives at an insight or act that has never been accomplished before," depending among other things on "inspiration, luck, serendipity, genius, and the unexplained drive of people to go somewhere where none has gone before." In spite of his own efforts to explain technological genius (the particular focus of his research), he confesses that "[a]t some level we stand in uncomprehending awe before the miracle of human genius."

26. Robert S. Albert and Mark A. Runco, "A History of Research on Creativity," in *Handbook of Creativity*, ed. Robert J. Sternberg (Cambridge, UK: Cambridge University Press, 1999), 28.

27. William Shakespeare, *A Midsummer Night's Dream* V, i, 7–17.

28. See Alden M. Hayashi, "When to Trust Your Gut," *Harvard Business Review*, February 2001, 59–65, and Eric Bonabeau, "Don't Trust Your Gut," *Harvard Business Review*, May 2003, 116–123.

29. Malcolm Gladwell, *Blink: The Power of Thinking Without Thinking* (New York: Little, Brown, 2005). See especially chapter 2, "The Locked Door: The Secret Life of Snap Decisions."

30. See Charles Spinosa, Fernando Flores, and Hubert L. Dreyfus, *Disclosing New Worlds: Entrepreneurship, Democratic Action, and the Cultivation of Solidarity* (Cambridge, MA: MIT Press, 1997), and Terry Winograd and Fernando Flores, *Understanding Computers and Cognition: A New Foundation for Design* (Reading, MA: Addison-Wesley, 1987).

31. See James Gleick, *Chaos: Making a New Science* (New York: Viking, 1987), and Steven Strogatz, *Sync: The Emerging Science of Spontaneous Order* (New York: Hyperion, 2003).

32. See Albert-László Barabási, *Linked: The New Science of Networks* (Cambridge, MA: Perseus, 2002), and Mark Buchanan, *Nexus: Small Worlds and the Groundbreaking Science of Networks* (New York: Norton, 2002).

33. See Christensen, *The Innovator's Dilemma*, and Larry Downes and Chunka Mui, *Unleashing the Killer App: Digital Strategies for Market Dominance* (Boston: Harvard Business School Press, 1998), 61.

34. See Steven Johnson, *Emergence: The Connected Lives of Ants, Brains, Cities, and Software* (New York: Scribner, 2001).

35. See Stuart Kauffman, *At Home in the Universe: The Search for Laws of Self-Organization and Complexity* (New York: Oxford University Press, 1995), and *Investigations* (New York: Oxford University Press, 2000).

36. Few scientists have been more aware of the limitations of analytical reasoning in science, also known as reductionism, than the evolutionary biologist Stephen Jay Gould. See his "Humbled by the Genome's Mysteries," *New York Times*, February 19, 2001.

37. See Harold Evans, *They Made America: From the Steam Engine to the Search Engine: Two Centuries of Innovators* (New York: Little, Brown, 2004).

38. Bossidy and Charan, *Confronting Reality*, 29.

39. Ibid., 54.

40. Ibid., 169.

41. On this last example, see ibid., 171.

42. Peter Nichols, *Evolution's Captain: The Story of the Kidnapping That Led to Charles Darwin's Voyage Aboard the "Beagle"* (New York: Harper Collins, 2003), 286ff.

Chapter 2

1. Francis Crick, *What Mad Pursuit: A Personal View of Scientific Discovery* (New York: Basic Books, 1988), 78–79.

2. I'm grateful to Dr. John Bridge, Research Professor of Internal Medicine at the University of Utah, for making a number of useful suggestions regarding this chapter, several of which I have incorporated here. Some of his comments, while highly clarifying, would take us deeper into biological science than space allows in a book of this kind. The interested reader will find them posted on the Web site for this book.

3. Horace Freeland Judson, "Annals of Science: DNA III," *The New Yorker*, December 11, 1978, 181, quoting Crick. I have relied closely throughout this chapter on Judson's account of the discovery of DNA, set down in a series of three articles in *The New Yorker* and in his *The Eighth Day of Creation* (New York: Simon and Schuster, 1979).

4. The term is Crick's. The account that follows is closely based on his memoir (1988), chapter 3. For Watson's parallel decision to focus on solving the mystery of the gene, see his own memoir, *The Double Helix: A Personal Account of the Discovery of the Structure of DNA* (New York: Atheneum Press, 1968).

5. As John Bridge has pointed out to me, Mendel's extraordinary work essentially placed the whole of genetics on a quantal basis and led ultimately to the fundamental question: What molecular mechanism could possibly explain Mendel's laws of inheritance? It's interesting that Mendel was educated in physics at the University of Vienna, initiating a long tradition in which highly creative thinkers would draw on the idea-space of physics in order to make dramatic advances in their research in biology.

6. Horace Freeland Judson, "Annals of Science: DNA II," *The New Yorker*, December 4, 1978, 134.

7. Ibid., 133ff.

8. Crick, *What Mad Pursuit*, 60.

9. Ibid., 68; the phrase is Crick's.

10. Judson, "Annals of Science: DNA III," 134, citing Robert Olby, *The Path to the Double Helix* (New York: Doubleday, 1974), emphasis in the original.

11. Judson, *The Eighth Day of Creation*, 142.

12. Judson, "Annals of Science: DNA III," 136–137, citing Olby, *The Path to the Double Helix*, emphasis in the original.

13. Ibid., 150; for details of the incident, see Watson, *The Double Helix*, 159ff.

14. Luck played its part here. Part of the reason Crick was so quick to recognize the import of the symmetry in the DNA molecule was that the same symmetry also occurred in hemoglobin, the subject of his own PhD research at the time.

15. Quoted in Judson, "Annals of Science: DNA III," 181.

16. Ibid., 174.

17. Judson, "Annals of Science: DNA II," 133.

18. See Brenda Maddox, *Rosalind Franklin: The Dark Lady of DNA* (New York: HarperCollins, 2002).

19. What she got right were the all-important measurements of angles and spacing of the bases, the critical identification of the space group the DNA molecule belonged to, and the fact that the backbones were on the outside.

20. Franklin would have had to dwell on the importance of the basic paradox of genetic functioning: the need to somehow fuse the measureless variation of individual genetic inheritance coded into the gene with the implacable demand of exact cellular replication, a mind-bending conundrum of structurally fusing identity and difference together flawlessly in a structure a few billionths of an inch across. The paradox could be resolved only if you believed in helices, and were enough of a geometer to envisage how the two backbones could, if inverted, spiral around one another to form a mirror image. This line of reasoning in turn depended on allowing the dictates of genetic theory to shape the interpretation of data.

21. Judson, "Annals of Science: DNA III," 182.

22. Ibid., 164.

23. Three of the flaws were purely structural. First, the like-with-like hypothesis ignored Crick's argument, solidly grounded in Franklin's data, that the backbones must run in reverse directions. Second, even if Crick were wrong on this point, the fact was that the four bases were very different in size and shape. The result would be that the backbones would bulge and pinch, creating horrendously messy problems for packing all the atoms together in the tiny space of the cell. Crick's model with reversed backbones would solve that problem, although that wasn't obvious at this stage. Third, as Donohoe was to point out when the model was presented, Watson's form of hydrogen bonding wouldn't work.

24. Watson, *The Double Helix*, 194–196.

25. As Watson notes (ibid., 193, emphasis added), "Francis did not like the fact that the structure [Watson's like-with-like model] gave no explanation for the Chargaff rules. . . . I, however, *maintained my lukewarm response to Chargaff's data.*"

26. This assumes that the bases bonded end to end, not (flatly) side to side, but the latter variant had evidently been abandoned by this point.

27. Crick, *What Mad Pursuit*, 65–66, emphasis added.

28. Bold speculation goes back to the Greek cosmologists, of course; see Karl R. Popper, "Back to the Presocratics," chapter 5 of his *Conjectures and Refutations: The Growth of Scientific Knowledge* (New York: Basic Books, 1962). But model building was a distinctly twentieth-century phenomenon.

29. Crick, *What Mad Pursuit*, 60.

30. Pauling's apparent blindness to the logic of genetic geometry is all the more puzzling, given that in 1940 he had written a paper with Delbrück about the possibility of complementary replication in DNA. We must assume that his immersion in the details of the molecular structure of DNA was such that he simply put this in the back of his mind.

31. Crick, *What Mad Pursuit*, 13–14.

32. For an enlightening account of this capacity, see Arthur I. Miller, *Insights of Genius: Imagery and Creativity in Science and Art* (Cambridge, MA: MIT Press, 2000). Crick (*What Mad Pursuit*, 45) claims that in teaching himself X-ray diffraction analysis, he quickly found he was able to see the answer to many of the mathematical problems it posed "by a combination of imagery and logic, without first having to slog through the mathematics."

33. Crick, *What Mad Pursuit*, 53.

34. Ibid., 147.

35. J. D. Watson and F. H. C. Crick, "Molecular Structure of Nucleic Acids: A Structure for Deoxyribose Nucleic Acid," *Nature* 171 (April 25, 1953): 738.

36. Judson, *The Eighth Day of Creation*, 60.

37. Recall that even after Avery's groundbreaking work, biologists continued to vacillate as to whether the genetic material was DNA or proteins, but neither choice resolved the underlying problem of how to accurately replicate genetic heredity. Until Chargaff's brilliant work, DNA was thought to be composed of a set of four bases repeating in fixed sequence (the so-called tetranucleotide hypothesis), so generating specificity was the problem. On the other hand, if genes were proteins, then how was the sheer amount of specificity generated, since there appeared to be no rules for specifying their structure. See Judson's interview with Jacques Monod, *The Eighth Day of Creation*, 210ff.

38. Crick, *What Mad Pursuit*, 36, emphasis in the original; Crick notes that the basic idea "was not entirely new."

39. Judson, *The Eighth Day of Creation*, 203.

40. The quote is from a six-page letter Crick wrote to Watson in the spring of 1967 expressing his outrage at Watson's depiction of the discovery of DNA. Quoted in Judson, "Annals of Science: DNA III," 182.

41. Quoted in Judson, "Annals of Science: DNA III," 181.

42. Crick, *What Mad Pursuit*, 35.

43. As Crick explained to Judson, "There was a moment when it clicked as far as *I* was concerned. That was the moment when Jerry Donohue told us about the tautomeric forms. I realized immediately that you could do the thing by base pairing. Though I didn't actually say that we should now build this, that, and the other, *I thought it was obvious*. I recall it as something I saw very clearly and I thought they [Watson and Donohoe] saw it very clearly . . . that was the moment when . . . the final brick fell into place. It only needed—" He laughed. "From then on, you just had to try and see that it worked. But *there was no further jump to be made*" (Judson, "Annals of Science: DNA III," 181, emphasis added). Nothing conveys Crick's confidence in the solution so much as his spontaneous laugh at this point. Having figured out all the twists and turns of the genetic geometry, determining which base went with which was a cakewalk. Significantly, Crick then immediately goes on to explain his apparent hesitation: "The feeling we had on that occasion was, it's very curious, that it would be *too good to be true* if it worked. You see. And if you asked me why I didn't do it myself that evening—I don't know. Jim got there very fast."

Chapter 3

1. See Marshall Sahlins, *Islands of History* (Chicago: University of Chicago Press, 1985), and *How "Natives" Think, About Captain Cook, For Example* (University of Chicago Press, 1995). For an incisive summary of the many issues of interpretation Sahlins's approach raises, see Clifford Geertz, "Culture War," *New York Review of Books*, November 30, 1995. For criticism of Sahlin's approach, see Ganath Obeyesekere, *The Apotheosis of Captain Cook: European Mythmaking in the Pacific* (Princeton, NJ: Princeton University Press, 1992). For further critical commentary, see Ian Hacking, "The End of Captain Cook," chapter 8 of his *The Social Construction of What?* (Cambridge, MA: Harvard University Press, 1999). See also A. Grenfell Price, ed., *The Explorations of Captain James Cook in the Pacific, as Told by Selections of His Own Journals, 1768–1779* (New York: Dover, 1971). I'm grateful to Peter Kalajian for drawing Price's book to my attention.

2. Walter Truett Anderson, in his *Reality Isn't What It Used to Be* (San Francisco: Harper & Row, 1990), uses a telling example of what he terms "the theatrical dimension of life" that can only further undermine our smugness at the Hawaiians' beliefs about Cook. Ronald Reagan skillfully used images of himself dressed in western gear at his ranch to invoke the myth of the cowboy with its simple good guy/bad guy morality. This was effectively used during the invasion of Grenada during Reagan's first term as president. Code-named Operation Urgent Fury, this assault on the smallest nation in the Western Hemisphere convinced many Americans that the country's recently elected Marxist government posed a serious security threat to the United States. In the subsequent election, Republican admen helped sweep Reagan to victory on the slogan "America is back—standing tall." Like the Hawaiians, Americans at the time were in the grip of a larger web of myths and beliefs that played a major role in shaping how they perceived the situation confronting them.

3. Wordsworth, *The Prelude*, III.

4. Regarding possible veracity of the Newton/apple story and its probable interpretation, see James Gleick, *Isaac Newton* (New York: Pantheon, 2003), 54ff.

5. See Peter Kivy, *The Possessor and the Possessed: Handel, Mozart, Beethoven, and the Idea of Musical Genius* (New Haven, CT: Yale University Press, 2001). As Kivy points out, the likely author of *On the*

Sublime is actually not Longinus but pseudo-Longinus. But historical precedent has long determined that the theory be referred to simply as Longinian.

6. Quoted in Kivy, *The Possessor and the Possessed*, 74.

7. Kivy, *The Possessor and the Possessed*, 21.

8. Steven Pinker, *How the Mind Works* (New York: Norton, 1997), 361. In *Genius Explained* (Cambridge, UK: Cambridge University Press, 1999), Michael Howe argues at length that genius is mostly hard work.

9. Quoted in Kivy, *The Possessor and the Possessed*, 171.

10. Quoted in James Hamilton, *Turner* (New York: Random House, 2003), epigraph.

11. Quoted in Kivy, *The Possessor and the Possessed*, 170.

12. Kivy, *The Possessor and the Possessed*, 172.

13. Ibid., 217, emphasis in the original.

14. Ibid., 238, emphasis in the original.

15. Andy Clark, in *Natural-Born Cyborgs: Minds, Technologies, and the Future of Human Intelligence* (New York: Oxford University Press, 2003), 1, terms this engaging in "semantic good behaviors."

16. This human capacity to use a finite set of rules to generate a potentially infinite series of situationally appropriate responses is of course the basis of human creativity, as first recognized by the Cartesians and later developed by the linguist Noam Chomsky. See his *Cartesian Linguistics: A Chapter in the History of Rationalist Thought* (New York: Harper & Row, 1966).

17. Pinker, *How the Mind Works*, 14. I have largely relied here on Pinker's excellent exposition of the computational theory of mind. While I disagree with Pinker's treatment of the imagination (see note 52 below), it should be borne in mind that what he has to say reflects the consensus in the psychological literature of the time.

18. Pinker, *How the Mind Works*, ix, 24.

19. Ibid., 307.

20. As Pinker notes (ibid., 308), "Mental boxes work because things come in clusters that fit the boxes."

21. Ibid., 314–315.

22. Pinker (ibid., 304) cites research into "ecological rationality" by Tooby and Cosmides as one of the sources. See J. Tooby and L. Cosmides, "Ecological Rationality and the Multimodular Mind: Grounding Normative Theories in Adaptive Problems," unpublished manuscript, University of California–Santa Barbara, 1997.

23. Pinker, *How the Mind Works*, 23.

24. Ibid., 564, emphasis added.

25. Ibid.

26. Ibid., 360. This meshing of mind and nature appears to be a modern version of post-Cartesian faith in how a rational universe mirrors the logical structure of reason.

27. Ibid., 60.

28. Ibid., 362.

29. See Thomas Nickles, ed., *Thomas Kuhn* (Cambridge, UK: Cambridge University Press, 2002), especially Nickles's introductory essay, for a good overview of Kuhn's ideas, development, and background. See also Clifford Geertz, *Available Light: Anthropological Reflections on Philosophical Topics* (Princeton, NJ: Princeton University Press, 2001), chapter VII, "The Legacy of Thomas Kuhn: The Right Text at the Right Time"; and Richard Rorty, "Thomas Kuhn, Rocks, and the Laws of Physics," in Richard Rorty, *Philosophy and Social Hope* (New York: Penguin, 1999), for sympathetic and insightful evaluations of Kuhn's achievement.

30. Thomas S. Kuhn, *The Structure of Scientific Revolutions*, 2nd ed. (Chicago: University of Chicago Press, 1970), 208.

31. Ibid., 92: "Scientific revolutions are here taken to be those non-cumulative developmental episodes in which an older paradigm is replaced in whole or in part by an incompatible new one."

32. Nickles, *Thomas Kuhn*, 5.

33. Kuhn, *Structure*, 109.

34. Ibid., 62ff.

35. Ibid., 113.

36. Ibid., 111.

37. Ibid., 24.

38. Ibid., 116ff.

39. The German philosopher Martin Heidegger spoke in these terms regarding what he called a *clearing*, which roughly corresponds to our idea-space. Heidegger would of course have eschewed the mental-

ist overtones of *idea*, although as noted above, the term is not intended as used here to connote exclusively mental phenomena.

40. John Seely Brown and Paul Duguid, *The Social Life of Information* (Boston: Harvard Business School Press, 2000), 159.

41. Kuhn, *Structure*, 17ff.

42. Nickles, *Thomas Kuhn*, 3.

43. Kuhn, *Structure*, 111.

44. Based on Garrison Keillor's account in *The Writer's Almanac*, broadcast over PBS radio on March 8, 2005.

45. E. L. Murray, *Imaginative Thinking and Human Existence* (Pittsburgh, PA: Duquesne University Press, 1986), 235, quoted in Emma Policastro and Howard Gardner, "From Case Studies to Robust Generalizations: An Approach to the Study of Creativity," in *Handbook of Creativity*, ed. Robert J. Sternberg (Cambridge, UK: Cambridge University Press, 1999), 213–225.

46. See "Thought," *Encyclopedia Britannica Online*, http://www.search.eb.com.prxy5.maine.edu/eb/article?tocId+9108663.

47. Alice Calaprice, ed., *The Expanded Quotable Einstein* (Princeton, NJ: Princeton University Press, 2000), 22. See also Policastro and Gardner, "Case Studies," 217, who quote Einstein: "To raise new questions, new possibilities, to regard old problems from a new angle, requires imagination and makes real advance in science."

48. Judson, "Annals of Science: DNA III," 124.

49. Ibid., 182.

50. Quoted in http://www.llnl.gov/str/May02/pdfs/05_02.3.pdf.

51. See James Engell, *The Creative Imagination: Enlightenment to Romanticism* (Cambridge, MA: Harvard University Press), 1981.

52. This is in fact more or less how Pinker (*How the Mind Works*, 284ff.) deals with the imagination.

53. Fauconnier and Turner, *The Way We Think*, 15.

54. Ibid., 25–26.

55. Ibid., 217.

56. Fauconnier and Turner use the word *entrenched* in roughly the same way as I am using *embedded*.

57. See the pioneering work of George Lakoff and Mark Johnson on metaphor in their *Metaphors We Live By* (Chicago: University of Chicago Press, 1980; afterword 2003), and also their more recent book, *Philosophy in the Flesh: The Embodied Mind and Its Challenge to Western Thought* (New York: Basic Books, 1999). For recent syntheses of two decades of intensive research in cognitive psychology that has deepened our understanding of analogical thinking and its role in creativity, see Dedre Gentner, Keith J. Holyoak, and Boicho N. Kokinov, eds., *The Analogical Mind: Perspectives from Cognitive Science* (Cambridge, MA: MIT Press, 2001); A. Ortony, *Metaphor and Thought*, 2nd ed. (Cambridge, UK: Cambridge University Press, 1993); Keith J. Holyoak and Paul Thagard, *Mental Leaps: Analogy in Creative Thought* (Cambridge, MA: MIT Press, 1995). On the neglect of analogy, see Keith J. Holyoak, Dedre Gentner, and Boicho N. Kokinov, "The Place of Analogy in Cognition," in Gentner et al., *The Analogical Mind*, 7. On the role of analogy in creative thinking, especially in science, see Holyoak and Thagard, *Mental Leaps*, 186ff.; Kevin Dunbar, "The Analogical Paradox: Why Analogy Is So Easy in Naturalistic Settings, Yet so Difficult in the Psychological Laboratory," in Gentner et al., *The Analogical Mind*, 315.

58. See Fauconnier and Turner, *The Way We Think*, 131ff.

59. Ibid., 89, emphasis added. As they show, the mental operations governing the construction and integration of conceptual networks are not random, but governed by a series of principles having to do with compression, matching elements, topology, pattern completion, and so forth. Generally speaking, such principles, which (unlike those of conventional analytical reasoning) are largely nonlinear and holistic, facilitate the basic cognitive need of being able to create an open-ended array of novel ideas and meanings from a limited number of elements and relations.

60. Fauconnier and Turner allude continuously to the potential application of their approach to major creative breakthroughs, although they exemplify this with only one or two real cases; see, for example, their treatment of the invention of complex numbers. For the most part they do not address the issue of discontinuity, which is one of the key themes of *Smart World*.

61. Colin McGinn, *Mindsight: Image, Dream, Meaning* (Cambridge, MA: Harvard University Press, 2004).

62. Ibid., 5.

63. Gestalt psychologists took both topics seriously, especially the nature of sudden insight. But their methods and findings underwent a period of severe criticisms in the mid-twentieth century that continues

even today; see, for example, Robert W. Weisberg, "Prologomena to Theories of Insight in Problem Solving: A Taxonomy of Problems," in *The Nature of Insight*, eds. Robert J. Sternberg and Janet E. Davidson (Cambridge, MA: MIT Press, 1995), 157–196. As Roger L. Dominowski and Pamela Dallob ("Insight and Problem Solving," in the same volume, 33) note, "some psychologists consider *insight* to be a meaningless term." Many articles in this volume address issues of insight in relation to creativity. However, in a concluding summary article, "Epilogue: Putting Insight into Perspective" (584), Jonathan W. Schooler, Marte Fallshore, and Stephen M. Fiore note that "although the basic mechanisms of insight lend themselves to scientific scrutiny, we may still feel, when all is said and done, that something is missing."

64. K. S. Bowers et al. ("Intuition in the context of discovery," in *Cognitive Psychology* 22 [1990]: 72–110), define intuition as "a preliminary perception of coherence (pattern, meaning, structure) that is at first not consciously represented, but which nevertheless guides thought and inquiry toward a hunch or hypothesis about the nature of the coherence in question." Quoted in Mark A. Runco and Shawn Okuda Sakamoto, "Experimental Studies of Creativity," in Sternberg, *Handbook*, 68.

65. For further examples, see Rupert Lee, *The Eureka! Moment: 100 Key Scientific Discoveries of the 20th Century* (New York: Routledge, 2002).

66. See Ward, Smith, and Finke, "Creative Cognition," 194.

67. McGinn, *Mindsight*, 157.

Chapter 4

1. Paul Freiberger and Michael Swaine, *Fire in the Valley: The Making of the Personal Computer*, 2nd ed. (New York: McGraw Hill, 2000), xv.

2. On the influence of the counterculture on the development of the hobbyist and personal computers, see Jeffrey S. Young, *Steve Jobs: The Journey Is the Reward* (Glenview, IL: Scott, Foresman and Co., 1988), 78ff. See also John Markoff, *What the Dormouse Said: How the 60s Counterculture Shaped the Personal Computer* (New York: Viking, 2005).

3. I've drawn on several sources here, including http://opencollector.organization/history/homebrew/Chapter10.html, and Freiberger and Swaine, *Fire in the Valley*. As will become apparent, I have relied extensively throughout this chapter on the latter's indispensable book, by far the most detailed account of the early history of the personal computer.

4. Freiberger and Swaine, *Fire in the Valley*, 161, emphasis in original.

5. See Douglas K. Smith and Robert C. Alexander, *Fumbling the Future: How Xerox Invented, Then Ignored, the First Personal Computer* (New York: Morrow, 1988).

6. In *Apple Confidential: The Real Story of Apple Computer, Inc.* (San Francisco: No Starch Press, 1999), 52, Owen W. Linzmayer suggests that if the original Alto had been sold commercially, it might have cost as much as $40,000 (approximately $132,000 in 2004 dollars).

7. Freiberger and Swaine, *Fire in the Valley*, xii.

8. Malcolm Gladwell, *The Tipping Point: How Little Things Can Make a Big Difference* (New York: Little Brown, 2000).

9. The account of phase transitions given here, while indebted to Gladwell, relies heavily on Albert-László Barabási's *Linked: The New Science of Networks* (Cambridge, MA: Perseus, 2002). Barabási's groundbreaking research was the original inspiration for the network science–based approach to creativity that forms the basis of this book. On the rise of network science see also Mark Buchanan's engaging and highly accessible *Nexus: Small Worlds and the Groundbreaking Science of Networks* (New York: Norton, 2002).

10. See Steven Johnson, *Emergence: The Connected Lives of Ants, Brains, Cities, and Software* (New York: Scribner, 2001), 18ff. Johnson is also the source of the earlier reference to slime mold (11ff.).

11. Stated in this way, the insight may not seem like much, but figuring out exactly how the trick is turned, whether in nature or in human society, took a great deal of scientific sleuthing. In *Linked*, Barabási gives an excellent historical and explanatory account of the various key discoveries in mathematics, physics, sociology, biology, and economics.

12. Here and throughout the remainder of the book, the term *open, dynamic network* refers to a network dominated by large hubs, technically known as a "scale-free network"; see chapter 5 for details.

13. According to Freiberger and Swaine, *Fire in the Valley*, 135, by late 1976, "DEC was selling its LSI-11 bottom-of-line minicomputer for slightly over $1,000" (i.e., approximately $3,300 in 2004 dollars). However, even this development, which broke through a significant price barrier, failed to address the programming problem. This failure on the part of established firms to design and build the personal computer and its subsequent successful development and marketing by much smaller peripheral firms appears to follow the classic trajectory of what Clayton Christensen, in *The Innovator's Dilemma* (Boston: Harvard

Business School Press, 1997), calls a *disruptive technology*. Among those whose attempts to get their employer corporations to develop microcomputers for the home or (one step away) school market were Steve Wozniak at HP, David Ahl at DEC, and Robert Albrecht at CDC. See Freiberger and Swaine, *Fire in the Valley*, 25ff. Typical of the kind of mentality blocking such efforts was DEC president Kenneth Olson's comment that he could see no reason why anyone would want a home computer.

14. Freiberger and Swaine, *Fire in the Valley*, 35.

15. Freiberger and Swaine (ibid., 108) note that the nascent microcomputer industry was "a grass-roots movement of hobbyists fully conscious that they were ushering in not just a technological revolution, but a social one as well."

16. John Seely Brown and Paul Duguid, *The Social Life of Information* (Boston: Harvard Business School Press, 2000), 161, emphasis added.

17. Brown and Duguid (ibid., 141ff.) develop this distinction to differentiate between communities of practice and *networks of practice*, that is, ties between professionals who may stay in touch via journals, magazines, and professional associations, but typically don't work together or know one another on a personal basis. They claim that such networks (NOPs), in contrast with COPs, are good at sharing information but not at coordinating action or producing new knowledge.

18. Mark Granovetter, "The Strength of Weak Ties," *American Journal of Sociology* 78, no. 6 (1973), 1360–1380.

19. See Buchanan's comment, *Nexus*, 204: "To live within a cluster [Granovetter's equivalent of a COP] is to be protected from differing norms, and also from truly novel ways of thinking, patterns of behavior, or pieces of information."

20. Gladwell, *The Tipping Point*, 54.

21. Small-world networks will be explored in more detail in chapter 9. For discussion, including in relation to Granovetter's weak ties, see Buchanan, *Nexus*, and Barabási, *Linked*, 25ff.

22. Clayton M. Christensen and Michael E. Raynor, *The Innovator's Solution: Creating and Sustaining Successful Growth* (Boston: Harvard Business School Press, 2003), 44.

23. See Christensen, *The Innovator's Dilemma*, xiiiff. Christensen uses the terms *disruptive innovation* and *disruptive technology* in closely related ways. Usefully, he avoids a narrow definition of technology, instead embracing its wider social dimensions: "*Technology*, as used in this book, means the processes by which an organization transforms labor, capital, materials, and information into products and services of greater value" (ibid.). In regard to the minicomputer and personal computer industries as disruptive, see 108–110. He speaks of them as disruptive *technologies*, but as noted, uses the term disruptive *innovation* in a very similar way. I prefer the latter term, since it avoids the narrow construing of technology to exclude social dimensions.

24. Freiberger and Swaine, *Fire in the Valley*, 137.

25. Ibid., 44ff, 149, and 247ff. Such a tactic would become familiar in both the hardware and software industries—design your product so that others can add value. Among the companies that both supported and/or competed against the Altair were Processor Technology (4k memory boards, and later the Sol microcomputer), Cromemco (the Dazzler video interface board), IMSAI (8080 microcomputer), Commodore (the PET microcomputer), Tandy (the TRS-80 microcomputer), Atari (microcomputer), Texas Instruments (TI-99/4), and Northstar (microcomputer). On the role of complementary technologies in general, combined with parallel complementary organizational innovations, see Brown and Duguid, *The Social Life of Information*, 161ff.

26. Freiberger and Swaine, *Fire in the Valley*, 81.

27. Ibid., 386.

28. It's worth noting that MITS, based in Texas, was also out of the loop to some extent. Not being closely involved in Homebrew meetings, it failed to pick up the latter's information-sharing ethos. This led to a series of disastrous attempts to protect its turf through proprietary designs and distribution arrangements. It also lacked close relationships with Silicon Valley companies that were producing ancillary products for the Altair, with the result that those companies eventually built computers of their own.

Chapter 5

1. Owen W. Linzmayer, *Apple Confidential: The Real Story of Apple Computer, Inc.* (San Francisco: No Starch Press, 1999), 11.

2. See W. Chan Kim and Renée Mauborgne, "Creating New Market Space," *Harvard Business Review*, January–February 1999, 86.

3. Linzmayer, *Apple Confidential*, 55.

4. On bringing computer power to the people, see Jeffrey S. Young, *Steve Jobs: The Journey Is the Reward* (Glenview, IL: Scott, Foresman and Co., 1988), 6–7.

5. Ibid., 120.

6. Paul Freiberger and Michael Swaine, *Fire in the Valley: The Making of the Personal Computer*, 2nd ed. (New York: McGraw Hill, 2000), 69.

7. The investment capital was initially provided by Mike Markkula, a former Intel engineer; the new president was Mike Scott, who had been trained at Cal Tech before going to Fairchild; the new logo was designed by Robert Janov, of the McKenna agency.

8. Young, *Steve Jobs*, 140.

9. Ibid., 139.

10. Ibid., 160.

11. Freiberger and Swaine, *Fire in the Valley*, 297.

12. Linzmayer, *Apple Confidential*, 14.

13. See Steven Levy, *Insanely Great: The Life and Times of Macintosh, the Computer That Changed Everything* (New York: Penguin, 2000), 27.

14. Albert-László Barabási, *Linked: The New Science of Networks* (Cambridge, MA: Perseus, 2002), 86.

15. Ibid., 88.

16. Ibid., 103ff.

17. Barabási, *Linked*, 95. He goes on (96) to note: "Each new node decides where to link by comparing the *fitness connectivity product* of all available nodes and linking with a higher probability to those that have a higher product and are therefore more attractive. Between two nodes with the same number of links, the fitter one acquires links more quickly." The probability that a given node will link to another is expressed by the formula $\kappa\eta/\Sigma\kappa_i\eta_i$, where κ is the number of links and η the relative fitness.

18. Freiberger and Swaine, *Fire in the* Valley, 149.

19. There is a (loose) parallel here with Schumpeter's concept of creative destruction. Notice how crucial it is that reciprocity and reach, innovation and integration, be kept in dynamic balance. Part of the problem with the dot-com boom was that an excess of cheap money broke the normal reciprocal link between investment and profitability. Too many bad products were financed, leading to an inevitable crash. A similar reciprocity holds between technological innovation and user requirements. As Clayton Christensen (*The Innovator's Dilemma: When New Technologies Cause Great Firms to Fail* [Boston: Harvard Business School Press, 1997]) has pointed out, there is a tendency for companies at some point in the development cycle of a successful product to disconnect these, leading to an excess of bells and whistles the user is reluctant to pay for, and opening the way for a disruptive technology to gain market share.

20. Freiberger and Swaine, *Fire in the Valley*, 289ff.

21. John Seely Brown and Paul Duguid, *The Social Life of Information* (Boston: Harvard Business School Press, 2000), 157.

22. Young, *Steve Jobs*, 120.

23. This spells trouble for those who advocate dealing with the ever-present threat of disruptive innovation through managing the innovation process better. Suggestions range from setting up a skunk works to using different financial yardsticks for innovative new products to scouting for products that can inexpensively enter underserved markets. (See Clayton M. Christensen and Michael E. Raynor, *The Innovator's Solution: Creating and Sustaining Successful Growth* [Boston: Harvard Business School Press, 2003], and Alexander Kandybin and Martin Kihn, "Raising Your Return on Innovation Investment," http:// www.strategy-business.com/ resiliencereport/ resilience/ rr00007). These are surely all useful advice. The problem is, these solutions, practical and effective though they may be for many typical cases of disruptive innovation, all fall into the standard model of organizational theory that prizes intelligent *control* as the surefire path to success. Unfortunately, control is exactly what emergent processes resist. This is one reason why the NBT rarely if ever originates in corporate environments, as the failure of the Xerox Alto vividly illustrates.

24. Steven Johnson, *Emergence: The Connected Lives of Ants, Brains, Cities, and Software* (New York: Scribner, 2001), 18.

25. On Smith and Pareto as examples of emergence, see Mark Buchanan, *Nexus: Small Worlds and the Groundbreaking Science of Networks* (New York: Norton, 2002), 198. Buchanan defines emergence as "the idea that meaningful order can emerge all on its own in complex systems made of many interacting parts."

26. Johnson, *Emergence*, 168.

27. Barabási, *Linked*, 221ff.

28. A non-scale-free network will tip provided the link-to-node ratio is greater than one. See Barabási, *Linked*, 18.

29. See endnote 17.

30. Johnson, *Emergence*, 223.

Chapter 6

1. Stuart Kauffman, *At Home in the Universe: The Search for Laws of Self-Organization and Complexity* (New York: Oxford University Press, 1995).

2. Quoted in "George Gilder's Telecosm: Metcalfe's Law and Legacy," *Forbes ASAP*, September 13, 1993. Gilder considered Metcalfe's law to be as important in the *telecosm* (i.e., the realm of communications technologies) as Moore's law has proved to be in the *microcosm* (the realm of microprocessor technology).

3. Quoted in http://searchnetworking.techtarget.com/sDefinition/0,,sid7_gci214115,00.html. Some scholars have questioned the validity of Metcalfe's law as formulated; see, for example, Bob Briscoe, Andrew Odlyzko, and Benjamin Tilly, "Metcalfe's Law Is Wrong," *IEEE Spectrum Online*, July 2006, http://www.spectrum.ieee.org/jul06/4109. I'm grateful to Lloyd Nirenberg for drawing this article to my attention. While one may argue the details, there appears to be no reason to doubt the overall validity of Metcalfe's point regarding the increase in value of networks as new nodes are added.

4. For a beautifully lucid account of Cantor's theorem and the proof he used, see Jim Holt, "To Infinity and Beyond," *The New Yorker*, November 3, 2003, 85–87. See also A. W. Moore, "How to Catch a Tortoise," *London Review of Books*, December 18, 2003, 27–28.

5. As Moore, "How to Catch a Tortoise," 27, points out, this informal definition wouldn't have satisfied Cantor, who used what is termed an *iterative* conception of a set. For present purposes, however, the informal definition is sufficient.

6. See George Johnson, "From Here to Infinity: Obsessing with the Magic of Primes," *New York Times*, September 3, 2002.

7. "The Free Juke Box," *Time*, March 27, 2000, 2. On the rise and fall of Napster, see Charles C. Mann's highly entertaining account in "The Heavenly Jukebox," *The Atlantic*, September 2000.

8. The basic software Fanning designed was not in itself particularly innovative. Peer-to-peer file-sharing technology for swapping music files existed well before Napster showed up.

9. Peter H. Lewis, "State of the Art; Napster Rocks the Web," *New York Times*, June 29, 2000.

10. Regarding Napster's role in promoting peer-to-peer file sharing in general by demonstrating that people were willing to open their computers and share files with complete strangers when they saw value in doing so, see *The Economist Technology Quarterly*, June 23, 2001, 21.

11. Gary Wolf, *Wired—A Romance* (New York: Random House, 2003), xiii–xiv.

12. Technically, this is known as competing against nonconsumption. See Clayton M. Christensen and Michael E. Raynor, *The Innovator's Solution: Creating and Sustaining Successful Growth* (Boston: Harvard Business School Press, 2003), 103ff.

13. See, for example, David Perkins, *Archimedes' Bathtub: The Art and Logic of Breakthrough Thinking* (New York: Norton, 2000). Karl Popper made a similar suggestion.

14. Both Ricardo and Keynes held this view regarding long-term economic growth. See, for example, Keynes' 1930 essay, "Economic Possibilities for Our Grandchildren," cited in Kevin Kelly, "The Economics of Ideas," *Wired*, June 1996.

15. Romer has expounded his basic ideas in both technical and popular articles and interviews. See, for example, "Economic Growth," in *The Fortune Encyclopedia of Economics*, ed. David R. Henderson (New York: Warner Books, 1993); "Increasing Returns and New Development in the Theory of Growth," in *Equilibrium Theory and Applications: Proceedings of the 6th International Symposium in Economic Theory and Econometrics*, eds. William Barnett et al., 1991; interview with Paul Romer in *Reason Magazine*, December 1, 2001. For discussion of Romer's ideas, see Kevin Kelly, "The Economics of Ideas," *Wired*, June 1996, and Bernard Wysocki Jr., "For Economist Paul Romer, Prosperity Depends on Ideas," *The Wall Street Journal*, January 21, 1997.

16. Romer, "Economic Growth," 2.

17. Quoted by Kelly, "The Economics of Ideas."

18. Richard Florida, *The Rise of the Creative Class: And How It's Transforming Work, Leisure, Community and Everyday Life* (New York: Basic Books, 2002); see, for instance, 36 and 319.

19. Romer, Florida, and before them Drucker and Solow, are all essentially concerned with the *idea economy*. In varying measures they also explore what might be termed the *economics of ideas*, which

addresses the issue of how ideas, as a major economic resource, are generated, distributed, and used. This book is intended in part as a deeper-level contribution to this emerging discipline.

20. Florida, *The Rise of the Creative Class*, 56.

21. Kauffman, *At Home in the Universe*, 7.

22. Ibid.

23. Ibid., 8.

24. Generally speaking, the generalization about when the phase transition occurs holds more reliably of larger networks containing at a minimum several hundred nodes.

25. Kauffman, *At Home in the Universe*, 8.

26. Ibid., 15.

27. Robert Rosenblum, "Picasso and the Typography of Cubism," in *Picasso in Retrospect*, by Daniel-Henry Kahnweiler et al. (New York: Praeger, 1973), 49.

28. Rosenblum, "Picasso and the Typography of Cubism."

29. Quoted in "Western Painting: Cubism and Its Consequences," *Encyclopedia Britannica Online*, February 4, 2004, http://www.search.eb.com/eb/article?eu=115377.

30. Herbert Read, *A Concise History of Modern Painting* (London: Thames and Hudson, 1959), 96.

31. Arthur I. Miller, *Einstein, Picasso: Space, Time, and the Beauty That Causes Havoc* (New York: Basic Books, 2001), 3ff. Miller argues that both men were deeply influenced by Poincaré's work on non-Euclidean geometries.

Chapter 7

1. Quoted in John Schwartz, "New Economy: How Reality Fits with Fantasy in Cyberspace," *New York Times*, December 11, 2000.

2. Jane Smiley, "You Can Never Have Too Many," in *The Barbie Chronicles: A Living Doll Turns Forty*, ed. Yona Zeldis McDonough (New York: Simon and Schuster/Touchstone, 1999), 192.

3. See "Ruth Handler," obituary in *The Economist*, May 4, 2002, 85; "Barbie Fun Facts" by Denise Van Patten, http://collectdolls.about.com/library/blbarbiefacts.htm; and Kitturah B. Westenhouser, *The Story of Barbie* (Paducah, KY: Collector Books, 1994), 149.

4. Bratz dolls were launched by M.G.A. Entertainment in June 2001 and have since attained global sales of $2 billion. For an interesting comparison between Barbie and Bratz dolls, see Margaret Talbot, "Little Hotties: Barbies's New Rivals," *The New Yorker*, December 4, 2006, 74–83.

5. "Ruth Handler," obituary in *The Economist*, 85.

6. See "Doll," *Encyclopedia Britannica Online*, http://www.search.eb.com/eb/article?eu=31331.

7. M. G. Lord, *Forever Barbie: The Unauthorized Biography of a Real Doll* (New York: Morrow, 1994), 16. As the many references indicate, I have relied heavily on Lord for much of the material in this chapter, including the chapter title. If there is one book on Barbie that must be read, this is it.

8. Ruth Handler with Jacqueline Shannon, *Dream Doll: The Ruth Handler Story* (Stamford, CT: Longmeadow Press, 1994), 3. See additionally the remark (in Westenhouser, *The Story of Barbie*, 7), seemingly attributed to Handler herself watching Barbara and her friends play with paper dolls, that play of this kind "was a way of experimenting with the future from a safe distance."

9. Lord, *Forever Barbie*, 25–26.

10. Ibid., 40.

11. Ibid., 13.

12. Yona Zeldis McDonough, "Sex and the Single Doll," in *The Barbie Chronicles*, ed. Yona Zeldis McDonough (New York: Simon and Schuster, 1999), 112.

13. Stephanie Coontz, in "Golden Oldie: Barbie in the 1950s," in McDonough, *Barbie Chronicles*, 48, suggests that "sexual display, even for 'nice girls,' was not a stretch for 1950s culture, nor a rebellion against its basic values. Neither was the targeting of young girls' sexual fantasies and yearnings." Some commentators see in Barbie's sexiness a covert challenge to the mores of the day. Lord, for example (*Forever Barbie*, 51), sees Barbie's similarities to Helen Gurley Brown's Cosmo girl as making her "an undercover radical."

14. Handler, *Dream Doll*, 12.

15. Ibid., 11.

16. Even Lord, who has perhaps written more insightfully about Barbie than anyone else, throws up her hands at this point (*Forever Barbie*, 34), mystified as to why Barbie would need this item of clothing.

17. "Ruth Handler," obituary in *The Economist*, 85.

18. From "A Motivation Research Study in the Field of Toys for Mattel Toys, Inc.," unpublished report prepared by the Institute for Motivational Research, Inc., Croton-on-Hudson, NY, June 1959, quoted in Lord, *Forever Barbie*, 39 (emphasis added).

19. Lord, *Forever Barbie*, 41.

20. Ibid., 9.

21. Ibid., 40.

22. Lord (ibid., 74ff.) calls Barbie "the Venus of Hawthorne, California." Lord claims that Barbie's form "gives her mythic resonance. Barbie is a space-age fertility symbol: a narrow-hipped mother goddess for the epoch of cesarean sections." She backs up this argument by pointing to Barbie's small feet, which are like the mythic prong legs of Stone Age Venuses, to be thrust into earth. Barbie, she suggests, is "both relentlessly of her time and timeless," both toy and mythic object, modern woman and Ur-woman, "archetype of something ancient, matriarchal, and profound." While I am in agreement with the central thrust of this argument—Barbie is indeed both mythical figure and toy—to me it makes much more sense to associate Barbie with Aphrodite than with a mother-goddess fertility symbol. As will be noted, the one thing consistently ruled out of Barbie's life is having babies.

23. For a general account of the myths surrounding Aphrodite, see Robert Graves, *The Greek Myths*, 2 vols. (London: Penguin, 1960), and Mark P. O. Morford and Robert J. Lenardon, *Classical Mythology*, 2nd ed. (New York: Longman, 1977).

24. Manuela Dunn Mascetti, *Aphrodite—Goddess of Love, Goddess of Wisdom* (San Francisco: Chronicle Books, 1996), 12. The reference to the alchemical properties of the goddess is due to Jean Shinoda Bolen's *Goddesses in Everywoman* (New York and San Francisco: Harper & Row, 1984), which did much to launch the fashion in goddess books for women.

25. Mascetti, *Aphrodite*, 31.

26. See Graves, *The Greek Myths*, vol. 2, 271.

27. Having an actual physical model of what she had in mind must have energized Handler, giving her scheme dramatic new life. Additionally, it must have helped the whole business of prototyping Barbie. On the value of model building and prototyping in general, see Michael Schrage, *Serious Play: How the World's Best Companies Simulate to Innovate* (Boston: Harvard Business School Press), 1999.

28. Lilli compactly embodied a whole world far removed from the genteel realm of paper-doll nurses, teachers, and mothers: sex, glamour, clothes, money, and manipulation of relationships with men—in short, the entire dark side of the Aphrodite myth. Oddly, however, there was an analogy between these worlds that Handler must surely have intuitively perceived, a fitness that opened the way to further integration: men did with Lilli dolls what children do with paper dolls—*they used them to fantasize about a different world from one they lived in.*

29. Each of the four standing figures represents a variation on these two dimensions. The seated figure in the foreground achieves an apotheosis of these traditions, a masklike face that stares at the viewer with all the directness of Manet's *Olympia*.

30. Lord, *Forever Barbie*, 32. On changes in Barbie's face in general, see Westenhouser, *The Story of Barbie*, Chapter 4.

31. Lord, *Forever Barbie*, 9.

32. From the very beginning, in fact, Mattel continually produced versions of Barbie that embodied either her "good" or "bad" image. Lord, *Forever Barbie*, 48, notes that in 1960, Mattel launched a Dietrich-like Barbie, "Solo in the Spotlight," but also "'Friday Night Date'—an outfit Pollyanna might wear to a church social—a blue corduroy jumper with a birdhouse appliqué that came with two aggressively wholesome glasses of milk."

33. Quoted in "Barbie Meets Bouguereau: Constructing an Ideal Body for the Late Twentieth Century," in *The Barbie Chronicles*, ed. McDonough, 81.

34. Mariflo Stephens, "Barbie Doesn't Live Here Anymore," in *The Barbie Chronicles*, ed. McDonough, 193.

35. Lord, *Forever Barbie*, 153. She continues (154): "Forget the new professions on Barbie's résumé; in this game, she practices the oldest one." In the end, Barbie never sheds the part of her she inherited from Lilli. As further evidence that Mattel wants to keep the connection alive, note that in the 1980s they began reissuing the original Barbies, with their slightly sluttish faces, in porcelain (Westenhouser, *The Story of Barbie*, 140ff.).

36. Lord comments (*Forever Barbie*, 154) that "even in the vast contradictory morass that is Barbie history, the idea of We Girls Can Do Anything and the Hooker Game occupying adjacent shelf space is dumbfounding." But this seems to miss the point. By that juncture, thirty years after Barbie's debut, Mat-

tel had long since figured out the advantages of emphasizing Barbie's double take on being a woman. For the record, I want to make clear that I don't mean to imply any endorsement here of Mattel's particular interpretation of what it means to be a woman. The point I'm trying to make is that the elements of such an interpretation are deeply embedded in the culture, and that Mattel chose to exploit them.

37. Lord, *Forever Barbie*, 90.

38. Ibid., 56.

39. Tressy, for example, introduced by the American Characteristic Doll Company in 1963, again as a Barbie competitor, had weird hair but little else to recommend her. Dawn, launched in the early 1970s by Topper Toys, was characterized by a "glitzy lifestyle . . . devoid of social responsibility, a precursor, as collector Beauregard Houston Montgomery has put it, of the 'disco consciousness of the 1970s'" (Lord, *Forever Barbie*, 90). To the best of my knowledge, no other doll from the sixties, seventies, or eighties is still in continuous production, including Mattel's own non-Barbie efforts such as Chatty Cathy, a baby doll featuring sleepy eyes and two front teeth.

40. As Gaby Wood notes in "Dream Doll," *New Statesman*, April 1, 2002, Barbie "was, from the very beginning, a cultural artifact or allegory. She was a doll with a 'philosophy.'"

41. Herbert Read, *A Concise History of Modern Painting* (London: Thames and Hudson, 1959), 119.

42. See Eric Lax, *The Mold in Dr. Florey's Coat: The Story of the Penicillin Miracle* (New York: Henry Holt, 2004), 16ff. Contrary to the popular myth, in all probability the dish did not become contaminated by being left near an open window.

43. Hardy Green, review of *The Last Lone Inventor: A Tale of Genius, Deceit, and the Birth of Television*, by Evan I. Schwarz, in *BusinessWeek*, June 30, 2003, 20.

44. Stuart Kauffman, *Investigations* (New York: Oxford University Press, 2000).

45. On this kind of customer-based innovation, see Eric von Hippel, *Democratizing Innovation* (Cambridge, MA: The MIT Press, 2005).

46. The law of navigation is essentially a corollary to the law of spontaneous generation. However, that law, as stated, deals with the generation of potentially meaningful patterns, a subset of the set of all possible patterns. The latter is a function of the power set of the set of nodes in a given space. Since the search space doesn't distinguish between potentially meaningful and meaningless patterns, its size is determined by the power set.

Chapter 8

1. Guillaume Apollinaire, *The Cubist Painters: Aesthetic Meditations*.

2. Herbert Muschamp, "The Miracle in Bilbao," *New York Times Magazine*, September 7, 1997.

3. John Dreyfuss, "Gehry's Artful House Offends, Baffles, Angers His Neighbors," *Los Angeles Times*, July 23, 1978, part VIII, 1, 24–25, quoted in Beatriz Colomina, "The House That Built Gehry," in *Frank Gehry, Architect*, ed. J. Fiona Ragheb (New York: Guggenheim Museum Publications, 2001), 304.

4. Eve Blau and Nancy J. Troy, eds., *Architecture and Cubism* (Princeton, NJ: Princeton University Press, 1997).

5. On the theme of utopia in modernism, see Alan Riding, "Machine Dreams and Utopias: Selling Britons on Modernism's Heyday," review of "Modernism: Designing a New World 1914–1939" at the Victoria and Albert Museum, April–July 2006, *New York Times*, April 4, 2006.

6. Muschamp, "The Miracle in Bilbao," 72.

7. Ibid. Readers who may wish to supplement this indecently compressed survey of modernist and postmodernist architecture can consult Kenneth Frampton, *Modern Architecture: A Critical History*, 3rd ed. (London: Thames and Hudson, 1985); Charles A. Jencks, *The Language of Post-Modern Architecture*, 6th ed. (New York: Rizzoli, 1984); and David John, "History of Western Architecture: 20th-Century Architecture: The Modern Movement," *Encyclopedia Britannica Online*, http://www.search.eb.com/eb/article?eu=119576.

8. Gehry in fact appeared in one of the ads.

9. Mildred Friedman, "Architecture in Motion," in *Frank Gehry, Architect*, ed. Ragheb, 291.

10. J. Fiona Ragheb, "Sites of Passage," in *Frank Gehry, Architect*, ed. Ragheb, 345.

11. Ragheb, "Sites of Passage," 341.

12. Ibid.

13. Muschamp, "The Miracle in Bilbao," 82.

14. See "Life Story, the Sequel," in *The Economist*, December 24, 2005, 108.

15. James P. Womack and Daniel T. Jones, *Lean Thinking: Banish Waste and Create Wealth in Your Corporation* (New York: Simon and Schuster, 1996).

16. J. Fiona Ragheb, "Sites of Passage," 340.

17. Colomina, "The House That Built Gehry," 311.

18. Thomas Krens, "A Personal Reflection," in *Frank Gehry, Architect*, ed. Ragheb, 12.

19. Ragheb, "Sites of Passage," 341. Rosalind Krauss (quoted, ibid., 346) has spoken of modern art's prevailing tendency toward the "fetishization of sight."

20. Muschamp, "The Miracle in Bilbao," 59.

21. Michael Sorkin, "Frozen Light," in *Gehry Talks: Architecture + Process*, ed. Mildred Friedman (New York: Universe Publishing, 2002), 47.

22. Jan Greenberg and Sandra Jordan, *Frank O. Gehry: Outside In* (New York: Dorling Kindersley, 2000), 9–10.

23. Sorkin, "Frozen Light," 42.

24. William J. Mitchell, "Roll Over Euclid: How Frank Gehry Designs and Builds," in *Frank Gehry, Architect*, ed. Ragheb, 354.

25. Friedman, *Gehry Talks*, 17.

26. It's instructive to read Mitchell's analysis of the tremendous difficulties posed for draftsmen, engineers, and construction contractors alike by Utzon's design. See Mitchell, "Roll Over Euclid," 357–58.

27. Mitchell, "Roll Over Euclid," 359. As Gehry himself has remarked: "Many artists over time have thought about movement, talked about flow. The only thing that holds back or restricts shape is technology and money . . . In our culture technology has evolved so that it's cheaper to build a rectangular building. But if you can figure out a way to make technology work for you, you can explore curved shapes and make them possible at competitive costs." Quoted in Greenberg and Jordan, *Frank O. Gehry*, 35.

28. Comparisons are sometimes made to Gaudí's Church of the *Sagrada Familia* in Barcelona, Utzon's Sydney Opera House, and Frank Lloyd Wright's Guggenheim Museum in New York, but none of these buildings comes even close to the level of structural complexity achieved by Gehry.

29. Greenberg and Jordan, *Frank O. Gehry*, 44.

30. Sorkin, "Frozen Light," 47–48.

31. Ragheb, "Sites of Passage," 343.

32. Space limitations prevent analysis here of more than a handful of Gehry's finished projects. See *Frank O. Gehry: The Complete Works*, eds. Francesco Dal Co and Kurt W. Forster (New York: The Monacelli Press, 1998).

33. See Greg Critser, *Fat Land: How Americans Became the Fattest People in the World* (Boston: Houghton Mifflin, 2003), 20ff.

34. On behavioral economics, see Daniel Kahneman and Amos Tversky, *Choices, Values, and Frames* (Cambridge, UK: Cambridge University Press, 2000); and Richard H. Thaler, *The Winner's Curse: Paradoxes and Anomalies of Economic Life* (New York: The Free Press, 1992). Kahneman received the 2002 Nobel Prize for Economics for his groundbreaking work with Tversky in challenging the rationalist basis of choice presented in classical economic theory. What Kahneman, Tversky, Thaler, and other so-called behavioral economic theorists show is that individual choices and preferences are constructed in context, typically as a result of "framing" effects.

35. See Critser, *Fat Land*, 20ff. As Critser makes clear later (53ff.), by midcentury, there had been some loosening of the prohibition against gluttony, particularly among more fundamentalist branches of Christianity. But evidently the biblical injunction remained strong enough to restrain people from being seen buying two servings in public.

36. See W. K. C. Guthrie, *A History of Greek Philosophy* (Cambridge, UK: Cambridge University Press, 1962), vol. I, 293–295.

37. See George Johnson, "Here They Are, Science's 10 Most Beautiful Experiments," *New York Times* (Science section), September 24, 2002.

Chapter 9

1. Steve Kemper, *Code Name Ginger: The Story Behind Segway and Dean Kamen's Quest to Invent a New World* (Boston: Harvard Business School Press, 2003).

2. On the subsequent influence of this commercial, see Nat Ives, "Poverty, Chastity, Marketability: Advertisers Turn Monks into Pitchmen," *New York Times*, August 25, 2003.

3. "Hang on Lads, I've Got an Idea," *The Economist*, December 31, 1999. Interestingly, unbeknownst to Bacon, all *three*, including printing, were Chinese inventions.

4. Jared Diamond, "Invention Is the Mother of Necessity," *New York Times Magazine*, April 18, 1999.

5. See John Man, *Gutenberg: How One Man Remade the World with Words* (New York: Wiley, 2002), 5ff. I have relied on Man's excellent, highly readable account—currently the only full-length biography of

Gutenberg in English—for many of the historical details concerning the invention of printing, and have also been stimulated by his ideas. Man's book explicitly sets out to answer the questions posed here.

6. Diamond, "Invention of Necessity," 18. Diamond's remark is made in relation to Gutenberg himself, but in the context of the article clearly applies to the whole history of printing.

7. John Chadwick, *Linear B and Related Scripts* (London: British Museum Press, 1987), 57.

8. The secret of papermaking spread to Japan and Korea via Buddhist monks, and thence to the world of Islam via Chinese prisoners captured in Samarkand. It was probably brought to Europe at the beginning of the fourteenth century by returning Crusaders who had learned the art as prisoners in Arabian paper mills. See Theodore Lustig, "Gutenberg: First Modern Inkmaker?" *Graphic Arts Monthly* 74, no. 2 (February 2002). The first paper mill opened in Germany in 1390, in Nuremberg, less than 200 kilometers from Mainz. See Blaise Agüera y Arcas and Adrienne Fairhall, "Archeology of Type," *Nature*, June 28, 2001, 997. By the time Gutenberg had started developing his press, there were already six paper mills operating in Germany.

9. Man, *Gutenberg*, 105.

10. See Diamond, "Invention," and "Hang on Lads, I've Got an Idea." A precise description of Pi Sheng's technology and its subsequent improvement is given in Man, *Gutenberg*, 105–106.

11. Man, *Gutenberg*, 8, 50.

12. On the development of a suitable ink for printing, see Lustig, "Gutenberg," and "The World of the Renaissance Print Shop," by Merry Wiesner-Hanks, in "The Infancy of Printing: Incunabula at the Golda Meir Library," University of Wisconsin–Milwaukee, 1996, http://www.uwm.edu/Dept/Library/special/exhibits/incunab.

13. See Wiesner-Hanks, "The World of the Renaissance Print Shop."

14. Man, *Gutenberg*, 48. In 1419 King Sigismund gave Mainz the right to mint a new set of imperial coins (p. 40), giving rise to a consequent demand for new punches.

15. See Man (ibid., 45ff., and chapter 5, "The Secret Revealed") for a clear description of the process and its relation to typecasting. Recently, the claim that Gutenberg used this method has been challenged. Using computer-enhanced image analysis, Paul Needham and Blaise Agüera y Arcas found minute variations in different occurrences of the same letter, suggesting Gutenberg may not have mass-produced his type using the same matrix, but instead used sand molds, an older technology. It's hard to see how Gutenberg could possibly have made the forty-two-line Bible using such a cumbersome technology; scholarly opinion currently appears to be waiting for further evidence to resolve the matter. See Dinitia Smith, "Has History Been Too Generous to Gutenberg?" *New York Times*, January 27, 2001; and Arcas and Fairhall, "Archeology of Type."

16. I'm paraphrasing Man, *Gutenberg*, 132, here.

17. Figures throughout this section are drawn from Man, *Gutenberg*, chapter 7, "The Bible."

18. Paul Needham, "The Invention," *Calliope*, February 2003.

19. Man, *Gutenberg*, includes Hoffmann's estimate as an appendix.

20. Efforts at secrecy continued, however. When Anton Koberger set out to print the *Nuremberg Chronicle*, a highly popular work purporting to be a world history, he locked his workers in their workshop for fear of plagiarism. The book was produced in a pirated version anyway, soon after publication. *Plus ça change . . .*

21. On the issue of timing in general, see Anthony J. Mayo and Nitin Nohria, *In Their Time: The Greatest Business Leaders of the Twentieth Century* (Boston: Harvard Business School Press, 2005).

22. Man, *Gutenberg*, 2.

23. Albert-László Barabási, *Linked: The New Science of Networks* (Cambridge, MA: Perseus, 2002), 35–37.

24. Paul Needham, "The Invention."

25. This same matrix of ideas is also more or less present in German, including the language Gutenberg himself spoke. I'm grateful to Roger Bevan for verifying this for me.

26. One might reasonably object that most of these arguments don't apply to Pi Sheng, the original inventor of movable type. However, Chinese characters are not cursive, and so stand on their own more easily than alphabetic writing. Admittedly, the calligrapher's craft demanded creating each sign as a unique, though recognizable, aesthetic object. But the relatively crude craft of woodcut printing must already have significantly reduced this aesthetic dimension, leading inevitably to a certain amount of standardization.

27. John Seely Brown and Paul Duguid, *The Social Life of Information* (Boston: Harvard Business School Press, 2000).

Chapter 10

1. G. H. Hardy, *A Mathematician's Apology* (Cambridge: Cambridge University Press, 1967), 89.

2. John Walker, *Joseph Mallord William Turner* (New York: Abrams, 1976), 68.

3. Sam Smiles, *J. M. W. Turner* (Princeton, NJ: Princeton University Press, 2000), 51.

4. Walker, *Turner*, 55.

5. Ibid. The frequent accusations of madness, as one commentator drily notes, "may well have struck a nerve with an artist whose mother had been committed to Bedlam" (Smiles, *J. M. W. Turner*, 52). James Hamilton, in his recent biography *Turner* (New York: Random House, 2003, 285), notes of the late 1820s that "claims that Turner is mad now become an accepted part of society lore."

6. Kenneth Clark, *The Romantic Rebellion: Romantic Versus Classic Art* (New York: Harper & Row, 1973), 223. Without always being in agreement, I have drawn mainly on Clark's interpretation of Turner in this and subsequent works cited, as well as on Walker's, for the conventional judgment of his art.

7. Walker, *Turner*, 116. Eastlake judged the paintings to be "unfinished." On the extent to which this was so, see note 8.

8. Kenneth Clark, *Civilization: A Personal View* (New York: Harper & Row, 1969), 284–288, emphasis added. The French critic Edmond de Goncourt remarked on one of Turner's late paintings, *A Landscape with a River and a Bay in the Distance* (1835–1840), "It makes you despise the originality of Monet and the innovators of his kind" (Walker, *Turner*, 124). Walker (116), echoing Clark, remarks regarding Turner's so-called unfinished paintings: "Nothing like [these] pictures . . . would be painted for over a hundred years."

9. Ibid.

10. Standard art histories typically vary as to when they date the origins of modern art. Cézanne is often mentioned, although some go back as far as Manet. With the possible exception of Lawrence Gowing and Monroe Wheeler (see note 49), most historians would reject any claim on Turner's behalf. I believe, however, that the recent revelations about Turner's integration of current scientific discoveries into his art in James Hamilton's *Turner and the Scientists* (London: Tate Gallery Publishing, 1998) cast Turner's achievements in an entirely new light.

11. See, for example, Kenneth Clark, *Landscape into Art*, new edition (New York: Harper & Row, 1976), 231: "[Art] may always be given a new direction by individual genius: but beyond this point art will reflect the fundamental assumptions, the unconscious philosophy of the time."

12. Hamilton, *Turner and the Scientists*, 9. As Smiles (*J. M. W. Turner*, 75) notes, "More perhaps than any nineteenth-century artist, [Turner's] work bears full and comprehensive witness to its own cultural situation, to a world changing from one social, political and technological understanding to another."

13. Walker, *Turner*, 72.

14. Ibid., 74.

15. Ibid., 59.

16. Clark, *The Romantic Rebellion*, 223.

17. Smiles (*J. M. W. Turner*, 73ff.), for example, discusses Turner's habit of completing his paintings at the Royal Academy on so-called Varnishing Days as though it were a typically Romantic manifestation of the artist's egotism in displaying his creativity. Walker (*Turner*, 59) claims that "of the basic principle of Impressionism, the truth to the optical effect, there is scarcely a trace. For Turner was a poetic, rather than a scientific, painter."

18. Lawrence Gowing, *Turner: Imagination and Reality* (New York: Museum of Modern Art, 1966), 27. I have found Gowing's interpretation of Turner to be the one closest to my own, and have benefited from his many astute insights about Turner's modernity.

19. See Hamilton, *Turner and the Scientists*, 1998. I have drawn heavily on Hamilton's groundbreaking account of Turner's enthusiastic involvement, hitherto largely ignored, with industrialization, technology, and science. I should add that my own interpretation of this involvement probably goes well beyond anything Hamilton would probably feel comfortable in attributing to Turner.

20. Hamilton, *Turner and the Scientists*, 76.

21. Contemporary critical opinion was as usual harsh: Clark (*The Romantic Rebellion*, 272) reports that it was part of a series of pictures of the same period generally referred to as "Mr. Turner's little jokes." One critic judged it "a snow storm of most unintelligible character—Neither by land or water was such a scene ever witnessed." (See Frederick Brill, *Frederick Brill on Turner's* Peace—Burial at Sea [London: Cassell, 1969], 25.)

22. Hamilton, *Turner*, 355.

23. Smiles, *J. M. W. Turner*, 74.

24. Hamilton (*Turner and the Scientists*, 84ff.) recounts in detail Turner's enthusiasm for a variety of inventions that made seafaring safer, including distress flares developed by Capt. George Manby. I am following his interpretation of the picture here.

25. Hamilton, *Turner*, 355.

26. Hamilton, *Turner and the Scientists*, 128.

27. Ibid.

28. Hamilton (*Turner*, 355), doubts for that and other reasons that the story is literally true, but grants the metaphoric association with Ulysses. If Turner in fact made the story up, it merely adds force to the apparent symbolic significance he attached to the painting.

29. Ibid.

30. See Walker, *Turner*, 88. Walker notes: "These cones of light and shade appear from this time on in Turner's works, and in scale and grandeur are without precedent in art."

31. Ibid., 112.

32. Gowing, *Turner*, 13.

33. As Turner's sketchbooks reveal, he often deepened his knowledge of reality through repeated observations that he recorded in a form that begins to resemble a scientist's lab notebook. In one sketchbook, Turner includes no less than sixty-five different views of the moment-by-moment changes in color and light in the same patch of sky, recorded over a period of three days. See Hamilton, *Turner and the Scientists*, 64.

34. Gowing, *Turner*, 13.

35. Hamilton, *Turner and the Scientists*, 17. See also, regarding the infinite, the following passage from Somerville's *Mechanism of the Heavens* (a copy of which Turner owned), in which the author "conjures up imagery that would have been deeply impressive to an inquiring mind like Turner's: 'The heavens afford the most sublime subject of study which can be derived from science: the magnitude and splendour of the objects, the inconceivable rapidity with which they move, and the enormous distances between them, impress the mind with some notion of the energy that maintains them in their motions with a durability to which we can see no limits'" (Hamilton, *Turner and the Scientists*, 69).

36. Clark, *Civilization*, 284.

37. Clark, *The Romantic Rebellion*, 245. See also 223: "Turner's [post-Venice] pictures depend for their effect entirely on light and colour and have no identifiable subject—nothing to distract us from the pure sensation. They are modern painting." This is a distinctly quirky view of modern art, to say the least, starting with the omission of Picasso's low-keyed palette and preference for line over color.

38. Clark, *The Romantic Rebellion*, 245.

39. Ibid., 263.

40. Clark, *Landscape into Art*, 189.

41. Gowing, *Turner*, 21.

42. See Gowing, *Turner*, 27: "Many of his pictures after 1840 are . . . balanced on an incandescent central axis . . . It was in fact a bold defiance of convention. The essence of the picturesque was asymmetry . . . The cone of sunlight in [pictures of this period] was designed to give radiance its natural symmetry. There is a Platonic geometry in it, which Turner no doubt recognized."

43. For details, see Brill, *Francis Brill*, 19.

44. See Gowing, *Turner*, 16. Farrington, a contemporary of Turner's, described his early watercolor technique as follows: "Turner has no settled process but drives the colours about till he has expressed the idea in his mind."

45. Turner's habit of completing most of the detailed work on his paintings at the Royal Academy on Varnishing Days (he often submitted little more than a barely colored background) is further support for this interpretation, as opposed to the Romantic egotist version preferred by many critics. Turner was simply demonstrating that, as in science, what is universal and lasting in art resides in the *process* of emergence, not in the subject itself.

46. Turner told Mary Lloyd, a close friend, "People talk a lot about *sunsets*, but when you are all fast asleep, I am watching the effects of *sunrise* far more beautiful; and then you can see the *light* does not fail." Hamilton, *Turner*, 272, emphasis in the original.

47. See Turner's reference to Akenside's remark about "matter's mouldering structures," quoted in Gowing, *Turner*, 27.

48. Even today, the spiritual dimension of abstract art is all too rarely recognized. See Maurice Tuchman et al., *The Spiritual in Art: Abstract Painting 1890–1985* (New York: Abbeyville Press, 1986), published in association with a landmark exhibition at the Los Angeles County Museum of Art. See especially essays

by Tuchman, Judi Freeman, and Linda Dalrymple Henderson for discussion of the spiritual dimension in painters like Barnett Newman, Mark Rothko, and Jackson Pollock, among others.

49. Another important connection with twentieth-century art was Turner's view of paint itself as a focal point of attention. As Gowing (*Turner*, 10) notes: "It was not only a conventional code of figuration that was breaking down under Turner's relentless pressure. The whole condition of painting was in question. It had been founded on an axiom derived from classical sources, the axiom, as Fuseli put it, 'that the less the traces appear of the means by which a work has been produced, the more it resembles the operations of nature.' The traces of Turner's means were unconcealed . . . Painting was now required to resemble itself before anything else; the operations portrayed were first and foremost the painter's." In regard to Turner's proto-abstract painting, Monroe Wheeler, introducing an exhibition of Turner's paintings at MOMA, noted (Gowing, *Turner*, 5) that MOMA from time to time includes "exceptional productions of other periods of art history in which the modern spirit happened to be foreshadowed or by which modern artists have been influenced. We have no precedent for a one-man show of an artist who died more than a century ago . . . [Turner] found himself revolutionizing his art, eliminating from it linear draughtsmanship and classical composition . . . Transcending the concepts of romantic art, he reached out into the borderland between representation and the abstract . . . Presumably none of the present-day abstract painters whose principal means of expression is light and colour had Turner and his life-work in mind; but looking back upon their revolution, more than a hundred years later than his, we see a kinship." Gowing goes on to laud Turner's anticipation of abstract painting.

50. Quoted in "Andy Grove: 'We Can't Even Glimpse the Potential,'" *BusinessWeek*, August 25, 2003.

51. Quoted in Denise Caruso, "Technology Has Made Some People Money, but Is That All There Is?" *New York Times*, March 27, 2000.

52. When it first appeared, Kevin Kelly's *New Rules for the New Economy: 10 Radical Strategies for a Connected World* (New York: Viking Penguin, 1998; references are to the 1999 Penguin paperback version) was greeted with hyperbolic praise: "Mr. Kelly's elegant description of the new economy may one day rank it alongside *The Organization Man* as the book that defined an economic era," spouted the normally sober *Wall Street Journal* (as quoted on the book jacket). George Gilder was even more effusive: "The canon law of the new economy. Kevin Kelly has defined and decreed the rules for success . . . in this handbook for happening entrepreneurs." Wow!

53. It is extremely hard to do justice to Kelly's full case, which is both intricate and lengthy, in such a summary. For the sake of clarity and brevity I have sometimes expressed his arguments slightly differently from the way he does, although I trust without seriously distorting his intent. For example, Kelly doesn't speak precisely of the new economy resulting from the convergence of three subeconomies—the digital, the network, and the demassified—even though this is surely what he is arguing.

54. Kelly, *New Rules*, 10. This idea owes much, as Kelly freely acknowledges, to George Gilder.

55. Ibid., 5, emphasis in the original.

56. Ibid., emphasis in the original.

57. See Jeff Madrick, "Wal-Mart may be the new model of productivity, but it isn't always wowing workers," *New York Times*, September 2, 2004.

58. Kelly, *New Rules*, 73, 75.

59. Ibid., 75.

60. Ibid., 9, and 65.

61. "Everyday [sic] we see evidence of biological growth in technological systems. This is one of the marks of the network economy: that biology has taken root in technology. And this is one of the reasons why networks change everything." Kelly, *New Rules*, 32.

62. "Until very recently economics has gravitated to an understanding that settled on an equilibrium, primarily because anything more complex was impossible to calculate." Ibid., 115.

63. Ibid., 94, and chapter 7.

64. Ibid., 96.

65. Ibid., 119.

Chapter 11

1. Quoted in Larissa MacFarquhar, "The Gilder Effect," *The New Yorker*, May 29, 2000.

2. The aim of this type of research includes building robots that can be sent into extreme environments ranging from hostage situations to collapsed buildings destroyed in terrorist attacks, thereby avoiding jeopardizing emergency personnel. See the interview with Professor Full in the *New York Times*,

April 4, 2002. See also Clark, *Being There*, 12ff., 31ff., on the work of Rodney Brooks at MIT's Mobile Robot Laboratory.

3. Ibid., 180.

4. T. S. Eliot, *The Sacred Wood* (London: Methuen, 1920); the quotations are from the introduction and the essays "Tradition and the Individual Talent" and "The Possibility of a Poetic Drama."

5. See AnnaLee Saxenian, *Regional Advantage: Culture and Competition in Silicon Valley and Route 128* (Cambridge, MA: Harvard University Press, 1994).

6. See Kevin Kelly, *New Rules for the New Economy: 10 Radical Strategies for a Connected World* (New York: Penguin, 1999), chapters 2, 5, and 7.

7. Kelly (*New Rules*, chapter 2) has his own version of this law, "the law of increasing returns," although he is wrong in claiming that Bob Metcalfe was the first to notice this mathematical tendency of networks to explode in value (Cantor long preceded him). Elsewhere, Kelly advances the interesting idea that networks obey what Stephen Jay Gould calls "the Great Asymmetry," that is, the tendency of evolution to create more than it destroys in ecological webs (see chapter 10). Whether such an asymmetry holds in cultural and economic webs is not entirely clear, but certainly a question deserving of further investigation.

8. Notice that a hotspot doesn't have to be *hot* in the sense of being trendy or popular, but rather in the sense of being highly fit. Tim Berners-Lee used an extremely obscure branch of mathematics to make the radical breakthrough involved in creating the World Wide Web. It just happened to be conceptually highly relevant to solving the problem at hand.

9. "When We Were Worms," *New Scientist*, October 18, 1997.

10. The idea that nature proceeds not smoothly but by creative leaps was originally put forward by Stephen Jay Gould and Richard Lewontin in their well-known theory of *punctuated equilibrium*.

11. See Alex Kucynski, "Menopause Forever," *New York Times*, June 23, 2002.

12. See Louis Menand, "Profiles: The Reluctant Memorialist," *The New Yorker*, July 8, 2002. I have based the details of this account on Menand.

13. See Howard Gardner, "Too Many Choices?" review of *Kingdom of Children: Culture and Controversy in the Homeschooling Movement*, by Mitchell L. Stevens, *New York Review of Books*, April 11, 2002.

14. His two most popular books, *How Children Fail* (1964) and *How Children Learn* (1967), both still in print, have together sold over 1.5 million copies and been translated into fourteen languages. For a succinct introduction to his life and ideas, see Patrick Farenga, "John Holt and the Origins of Contemporary Homeschooling," *Paths of Learning* 1, no. 1 (Spring 1999): 34–37.

15. The process whereby basic assumptions in a domain change, persistent problems can be restated more insightfully, and new solutions evolved when placed in the dynamic context of a new field of ideas is often referred to by creativity researchers as *reframing*, a concept that has roots in gestalt psychology. See Robert J. Sternberg, ed., *Handbook of Creativity* (Cambridge, UK: Cambridge University Press, 1999), and especially David Perkins, *Archimedes' Bathtub: The Art and Logic of Breakthrough Thinking* (New York: Norton, 2000), 132ff. See also Charles Spinosa, Fernando Flores, and Hubert L. Dreyfus, *Disclosing New Worlds: Entrepreneurship, Democratic Action, and the Cultivation of Solidarity* (Cambridge, MA: MIT Press, 1997), especially sections dealing with what they call "cross-appropriation," and "reconfiguration."

16. See James Tobin, "To Fly!" *Smithsonian*, April 2003, 50–62.

Chapter 12

1. Calvin Tompkins, "Everything in Sight. Robert Rauschenberg's New Life," *The New Yorker*, May 23, 2005, 68–77.

2. Larry Bossidy and Ram Charan, *Confronting Reality: Doing What Matters to Get Things Right* (New York: Crown, 2004), 171.

3. See, for example, Eric Bonabeau, "Don't Trust Your Gut," *Harvard Business Review*, May 2003, 116–123.

4. See Colin McGinn, *Mindsight: Image, Dream, Meaning* (Cambridge, MA: Harvard University Press, 2004).

5. Ibid., 5.

6. See especially ibid., chapter 10.

7. Bossidy and Charan, *Confronting Reality*, 9.

8. Ibid., 53.

9. See, for example, ibid., 78, 179, and 218; the authors approvingly cite Intel CEO Andy Grove's book *Only the Paranoid Survive* as advocating the right attitude to the current hypercompetitive business environment.

10. Ibid., 192.

11. Gary Hamel and C. K. Prahalad, *Competing for the Future* (Boston: Harvard Business School Press, 1994); see also Gary Hamel, *Leading the Revolution* (Boston: Harvard Business School Press, 2000).

12. Hamel, *Leading the Revolution*, 120.

13. Bossidy and Charan, *Confronting Reality*, 192, 223.

14. See, in addition to Bossidy and Charan, *Confronting Reality*, Jeffrey Pfeffer and Robert Sutton, *Hard Facts, Dangerous Half-Truths, and Total Nonsense: Profiting from Evidence-Based Management* (Boston: Harvard Business School Press, 2006).

15. Hamel, *Leading the Revolution*, 120. I am quoting Hamel at some length because no one has been a more prescient champion of the value of imagination in business.

16. See Tim Berners-Lee (with Mark Fischetti), *Weaving the Web: The Original Design and Ultimate Destiny of the World Wide Web by Its Inventor* (New York: HarperSanFrancisco, 1999).

17. See Randy Kennedy, "With Irreverence and an iPod, Recreating the Museum Tour," *New York Times*, May 28, 2005.

18. See "The Lowdown on Podcasting," *BusinessWeek* online, May 24, 2005, http://www.businessweek.com/technology/content/may2005/tc20050524_9688_tc_211, and David Kiley, "Mad Ave.'s Rush to Podcasts," *BusinessWeek* online, May 25, 2005, http://www.businessweek.com/technology/content/may2005/tc20050525_8984_tc_211.

19. On Gilbert's Web site, see Kennedy, "With Irreverence and an iPod."

20. See "Podcasting Explosion," *BusinessWeek* online, www.businessweek.com/technology/tech_stats/podcast050523.htm.

21. See Philip B. Evans and Thomas S. Wurster, "Strategy and the New Economics of Information," *Harvard Business Review*, September–October 1997.

22. See Philip J. Kaplan, *F'd Companies: Spectacular Dot.com Flameouts* (New York: Simon and Schuster, 2002), 16–17.

23. The original Atkins diet had been regarded as too far out in left field to be a serious threat, but the revised version could be more easily assimilated into the mainstream nutrition discourse.

24. Gary Taubes, "What If It's All Been a Big Fat Lie?" *New York Times*, July 7, 2002.

25. For discussion of Sony's strategy, see Nicholas G. Carr, "Top-Down Disruption," *Strategy and Business*, Summer 2005.

26. Bossidy and Charan, *Confronting Reality*, 23ff.

27. See Clive Thompson, "The BitTorrent Effect," *Wired*, January 2005. For details of the company, see www.bittorrent.com.

BIBLIOGRAPHY

Agüera y Arcas, Blaise, and Adrienne Fairhall. "Archeology of Type." *Nature*, June 28, 2001, 997.

Anderson, Walter Truett. *Reality Isn't What It Used to Be: Theatrical Politics, Ready-to-Wear Religion, Global Myths, Primitive Chic, and Other Wonders of the Postmodern World*. San Francisco: Harper & Row, 1990; paperback, Cambridge, MA: MIT Press, 1995.

Barabási, Albert-László. *Linked: The New Science of Networks*. Cambridge, MA: Perseus, 2002.

Berners-Lee, Tim, with Mark Fischetti. *Weaving the Web: The Original Design and Ultimate Destiny of the World Wide Web by Its Inventor*. New York: HarperSanFrancisco, 1999.

Bernstein, Peter L. *Against the Gods: The Remarkable Story of Risk*. New York: Wiley, 1996.

Blau, Eve, and Nancy J. Troy, eds. *Architecture and Cubism*. Princeton, NJ: Princeton University Press, 1997.

Bonabeau, Eric. "Don't Trust Your Gut." *Harvard Business Review*, May 2003, 116–123.

Bossidy, Larry, and Ram Charan. *Confronting Reality: Doing What Matters to Get Things Right*. New York: Crown, 2004.

Bowers, K. S., et al. "Intuition in the Context of Discovery." In *Cognitive Psychology* 22 (1990): 72–110.

Brill, Frederick. *Frederick Brill on Turner's Peace—Burial at Sea*. London: Cassell, 1969.

Briscoe, Bob, Andrew Odlyzko, and Benjamin Tilly. "Metcalfe's Law Is Wrong." *IEEE Spectrum Online*, July 2006, http://www.spectrum.ieee.org/jul06/4109.

Brockman, John, ed. *The Greatest Inventions of the Past 2,000 Years*. New York: Simon and Schuster, 2000.

Brown, John Seely, and Paul Duguid. *The Social Life of Information*. Boston: Harvard Business School Press, 2000.

Buchanan, Mark. *Nexus: Small Worlds and the Groundbreaking Science of Networks*. New York: Norton, 2002.

Carr, Nicholas G. "Top-Down Disruption." *Strategy and Business*, Summer 2005.

Chadwick, John. *Linear B and Related Scripts*. London: British Museum Press, 1987.

Chomsky, Noam. *Cartesian Linguistics: A Chapter in the History of Rationalist Thought*. New York: Harper & Row, 1966.

Christensen, Clayton M. *The Innovator's Dilemma: When New Technologies Cause Great Firms to Fail*. Boston: Harvard Business School Press, 1997.

Christensen, Clayton M., and Michael E. Raynor. *The Innovator's Solution: Creating and Sustaining Successful Growth*. Boston: Harvard Business School Press, 2003.

Clark, Andy. *Being There: Putting Brain, Body, and World Together Again*. Cambridge, MA: MIT Press, 1997.

———. "Magic Words: How Language Augments Human Computation." In *Language and Thought: Interdisciplinary Themes*, edited by Peter Carruthers and Jill Boucher, 162–183. Cambridge, UK: Cambridge University Press, 1998.

———. "Minds, Brains and Tools." In *Philosophy of Mental Representation*, edited by Hugh Clapin. Oxford, UK: Clarendon Press, 2002, 66–90.

———. *Natural-Born Cyborgs: Minds, Technologies, and the Future of Human Intelligence*. New York: Oxford University Press, 2003.

———. "Reasons, Robots and the Extended Mind (Rationality for the New Millenium)." *Mind and Language* 16, no. 2 (2001): 121–145.

Clark, Kenneth. *Civilization: A Personal View*. New York: Harper & Row, 1969.

———. *Landscape into Art*, new edition. New York: Harper & Row, 1976.

———. *The Romantic Rebellion: Romantic Versus Classic Art*. New York: Harper & Row, 1973.

Crick, Francis. *What Mad Pursuit: A Personal View of Scientific Discovery*. New York: Basic Books, 1988.

Critser, Greg. *Fat Land: How Americans Became the Fattest People in the World*. Boston: Houghton Mifflin, 2003.

Dal Co, Francesco, and Kurt W. Forster, eds. *Frank O. Gehry: The Complete Works*. New York: The Monacelli Press, 1998.

Dennett, Daniel. *Kinds of Minds*. New York: Basic Books, 1996.

Diamond, Jared. "Invention of Necessity." *New York Times Magazine*, April 18, 1999.

Downes, Larry, and Chunka Mui. *Unleashing the Killer App: Digital Strategies for Market Dominance*. Boston: Harvard Business School Press, 1998.

Engell, James. *The Creative Imagination: Enlightenment to Romanticism*. Cambridge, MA: Harvard University Press, 1981.

Evans, Harold. *They Made America: From the Steam Engine to the Search Engine: Two Centuries of Innovators*. New York: Little, Brown, 2004.

Evans, Philip B., and Thomas S. Wurster. "Strategy and the New Economics of Information." *Harvard Business Review*, September–October 1997.

Farenga, Patrick. "John Holt and the Origins of Contemporary Homeschooling." *Paths of Learning* 1, no. 1 (spring 1999): 34–37.

Fauconnier, Gilles, and Mark Turner. *The Way We Think: Conceptual Blending and the Mind's Hidden Complexities*. New York: Basic Books, 2002.

Florida, Richard. *The Rise of the Creative Class: And How It's Transforming Work, Leisure, Community and Everyday Life*. New York: Basic Books, 2002.

Frampton, Kenneth. *Modern Architecture: A Critical History*. 3rd ed. London: Thames and Hudson, 1985.

Frank, Robert H. "Economic Scene: If Firmly Believed, the Theory That Self-interest Is the Sole Motivator Appears to Be Self-fulfilling." *New York Times*, February 17, 2005.

Freiberger, Paul, and Michael Swaine. *Fire in the Valley: The Making of the Personal Computer*. 2nd ed. New York: McGraw Hill, 2000.

Friedman, Mildred, ed. *Gehry Talks: Architecture + Process*. New York: Universe, 2002.

Gardner, Howard. "Too Many Choices?" Review of *Kingdom of Children: Culture and Controversy in the Homeschooling Movement*, by Mitchell L. Stevens. *New York Review of Books*, April 11, 2002.

Geertz, Clifford. "Culture War." *New York Review of Books*, November 30, 1995.

———. "The Legacy of Thomas Kuhn: The Right Text at the Right Time." Chapter VII in Clifford Geertz, *Available Light: Anthropological Reflections on Philosophical Topics*. Princeton, NJ: Princeton University Press, 2001.

Gentner, Dedre, Keith J. Holyoak, and Boicho N. Kokinov, eds. *The Analogical Mind: Perspectives from Cognitive Science*. Cambridge, MA: MIT Press, 2001.

"George Gilder's Telecosm: Metcalfe's Law and Legacy." *Forbes ASAP*, September 13, 1993.

"Get Creative: How to Build Innovative Companies." *BusinessWeek*, August 8, 2005.

Gladwell, Malcolm. *Blink: The Power of Thinking Without Thinking*. New York: Little, Brown, 2005.

———. *The Tipping Point: How Little Things Can Make a Big Difference*. New York: Little Brown, 2000.

Gleick, James. *Chaos: Making a New Science*. New York: Viking, 1987.

———. *Isaac Newton*. New York: Pantheon, 2003.

Gould, Stephen Jay. "Humbled by the Genome's Mysteries." *New York Times*, February 19, 2001.

Gowing, Lawrence. *Turner: Imagination and Reality*. New York: Museum of Modern Art, 1966.

Granovetter, Mark. "The Strength of Weak Ties." *American Journal of Sociology* 78, no. 6 (1973): 1360–1380.

Graves, Robert. *The Greek Myths*, 2 vols. London: Penguin, 1960.

Green, Hardy. Review of *The Last Lone Inventor: A Tale of Genius, Deceit, and the Birth of Television*, by Evan I. Schwarz. *BusinessWeek*, June 30, 2003, 20.

Greenberg, Jan, and Sandra Jordan. *Frank O. Gehry: Outside In*. New York: Dorling Kindersley, 2000.

Guthrie, W. K. C. *A History of Greek Philosophy*, vol. I. Cambridge, UK: Cambridge University Press, 1962.

Hacking, Ian. "The End of Captain Cook." Chapter 8 in Ian Hacking, *The Social Construction of What?* Cambridge, MA: Harvard University Press, 1999.

Hamel, Gary. *Leading the Revolution*. Boston: Harvard Business School Press, 2000.

———, and C. K. Prahalad. *Competing for the Future*. Boston: Harvard Business School Press, 1994.

Hamilton, James. *Turner*. New York: Random House, 2003.

———. *Turner and the Scientists*. London: Tate Gallery Publishing, 1998.

Handler, Ruth, with Jacqueline Shannon. *Dream Doll: The Ruth Handler Story*. Stamford, CT: Longmeadow Press, 1994.

Hayashi, Alden M. "When to Trust Your Gut." *Harvard Business Review*, February 2001, 59–65.

Hippel, Eric von. *Democratizing Innovation*. Cambridge, MA: MIT Press, 2005.

Holt, Jim. "To Infinity and Beyond." *The New Yorker*, November 3, 2003, 85–87.

Holt, John. *Teach Your Own*. New York: Delacourt, 1981.

Holyoak, Keith, and Paul Thagard. *Mental Leaps: Analogy in Creative Thought*. Cambridge, MA: MIT Press, 1995.

Howe, Michael. *Genius Explained*. Cambridge, UK: Cambridge University Press, 1999.

Ives, Nat. "Poverty, Chastity, Marketability: Advertisers Turn Monks into Pitchmen." *New York Times*, August 25, 2003.

Jencks, Charles A. *The Language of Post-Modern Architecture*. 6th ed. New York: Rizzoli, 1984.

John, David. "History of Western Architecture: 20th-Century Architecture: The Modern Movement." *Encyclopedia Britannica Online*. http://www.search.eb.com/eb/article?eu=119576.

Johnson, George. "From Here to Infinity: Obsessing with the Magic of Primes." *New York Times*, September 3, 2002.

———. "Here They Are, Science's 10 Most Beautiful Experiments." *New York Times*, Science section, September 24, 2002.

Johnson, Steven. *Emergence: The Connected Lives of Ants, Brains, Cities, and Software*. New York: Scribner, 2001.

Judson, Horace Freeland. "Annals of Science: DNA I-III." *The New Yorker*, November 25–December 11, 1978.

———. *The Eighth Day of Creation: Makers of the Revolution in Biology*. New York: Simon and Schuster, 1979.

Kahneman, Daniel, and Amos Tversky. *Choices, Values, and Frames*. Cambridge, UK: Cambridge University Press, 2000.

Kahnweiler, Daniel-Henry, et al. *Picasso in Retrospect*. New York: Praeger, 1973.

Kandel, Eric R. *In Search of Memory: The Emergence of a New Science of Mind*. New York: Norton, 2006.

Kandybin, Alexander, and Martin Kihn. "Raising Your Return on Innovation Investment." http://www.strategy-business.com.

Kaplan, Philip J. *F'd Companies: Spectacular Dot.com Flameouts*. New York: Simon and Schuster, 2002.

Kauffman, Stuart. *At Home in the Universe: The Search for Laws of Self-Organization and Complexity*. New York: Oxford University Press, 1995.

———. *Investigations*. New York: Oxford University Press, 2000.

Kelly, Kevin. *New Rules for the New Economy: 10 Radical Strategies for a Connected World*. New York: Viking Penguin, 1998.

———. "The Economics of Ideas." *Wired*, June 1996.

Kemper, Steve. *Code Name Ginger: The Story Behind Segway and Dean Kamen's Quest to Invent a New World*. Boston: Harvard Business School Press, 2003.

Kennedy, Randy. "With Irreverence and an iPod, Recreating the Museum Tour." *New York Times*, May 28, 2005.

Kim, W. Chan, and Renée Mauborgne. "Creating New Market Space." *Harvard Business Review*, January–February 1999.

Kivy, Peter. *The Possessor and the Possessed: Handel, Mozart, Beethoven, and the Idea of Musical Genius*. New Haven, CT: Yale University Press, 2001.

Kucynski, Alex. "Menopause Forever." *New York Times*, June 23, 2002.

Kuhn, Thomas S. *The Structure of Scientific Revolutions*. 2nd ed. Chicago: University of Chicago Press, 1970.

Lakoff, George, and Mark Johnson. *Metaphors We Live By*. Chicago: University of Chicago Press, 1980; afterword, 2003.

Lakoff, George, and Mark Johnson. *Philosophy in the Flesh: The Embodied Mind and Its Challenge to Western Thought*. New York: Basic Books, 1999.

Lax, Eric. *The Mold in Dr. Florey's Coat: The Story of the Penicillin Miracle*. New York: Henry Holt, 2004.

Lee, Rupert. *The Eureka! Moment: 100 Key Scientific Discoveries of the 20th Century*. New York: Routledge, 2002.

Lewis, Peter H. "State of the Art; Napster Rocks the Web." *New York Times*, June 29, 2000.

Linzmayer, Owen W. *Apple Confidential: The Real Story of Apple Computer, Inc*. San Francisco: No Starch Press, 1999.

Lord, M. G. *Forever Barbie: The Unauthorized Biography of a Real Doll*. New York: Morrow, 1994.

Lustig, Theodore. "Gutenberg: First Modern Inkmaker?" *Graphic Arts Monthly* 74, no. 2 (2002).

Maddox, Brenda. *Rosalind Franklin: The Dark Lady of DNA*. New York: HarperCollins, 2002.

Madrick, Jeff. "Wal-Mart May Be the New Model of Productivity, but It Isn't Always Wowing Workers." *New York Times*, September 2, 2004.

Man, John. *Gutenberg: How One Man Remade the World with Words*. New York: Wiley, 2002.

Mann, Charles C. "The Heavenly Jukebox." *The Atlantic*, September 2000.

Markoff, John. *What the Dormouse Said: How the 60s Counterculture Shaped the Personal Computer*. New York: Viking, 2005.

Mascetti, Manuela Dunn. *Aphrodite—Goddess of Love, Goddess of Wisdom*. San Francisco: Chronicle Books, 1996.

Mayo, Anthony J., and Nitin Nohria. *In Their Time: The Greatest Business Leaders of the Twentieth Century*. Boston: Harvard Business School Press, 2005.

McDonough, Yona Zeldis, ed. *The Barbie Chronicles: A Living Doll Turns Forty*. New York: Simon and Schuster/Touchstone, 1999.

McGinn, Colin. *Mindsight: Image, Dream, Meaning*. Cambridge, MA: Harvard University Press, 2004.

Menand, Louis. "Profiles: The Reluctant Memorialist," *The New Yorker*, July 8, 2002.

Miller, Arthur I. *Einstein, Picasso: Space, Time, and the Beauty That Causes Havoc*. New York: Basic Books, 2001.

———. *Insights of Genius: Imagery and Creativity in Science and Art*. Cambridge, MA: MIT Press, 2000.

Mokyr, Joel. *The Lever of Riches: Technological Creativity and Economic Progress*. New York: Oxford University Press, 1990.

Moore, A. W. "How to Catch a Tortoise." *London Review of Books*, December 18, 2003, 27–28.

Morford, Mark P. O., and Robert J. Lenardon. *Classical Mythology*. 2nd ed. New York: Longman, 1977.

Murray, E. L. *Imaginative Thinking and Human Existence*. Pittsburgh, PA: Duquesne University Press, 1986.

Muschamp, Herbert. "The Miracle in Bilbao." *New York Times Magazine*, September 7, 1997.

Needham, Paul. "The Invention." *Calliope*, February 2003.

Nichols, Peter. *Evolution's Captain: The Story of the Kidnapping That Led to Charles Darwin's Voyage Aboard the "Beagle."* New York: HarperCollins, 2003.

Nickles, Thomas, ed. *Thomas Kuhn*. Cambridge, UK: Cambridge University Press, 2002.

"Now You See It, Now You Don't." In "A Survey of Information Technology," *The Economist*, October 30, 2004, 7–8.

Obeyesekere, Ganath. *The Apotheosis of Captain Cook: European Mythmaking in the Pacific*. Princeton, NJ: Princeton University Press, 1992.

Olby, Robert. *The Path to the Double Helix*. New York: Doubleday, 1974.

Ortony, A. *Metaphor and Thought*. 2nd ed. Cambridge, UK: Cambridge University Press, 1993.

Perkins, David. *Archimedes' Bathtub: The Art and Logic of Breakthrough Thinking*. New York: Norton, 2000.

Pfeffer, Jeffrey, and Robert Sutton. *Hard Facts, Dangerous Half-Truths, and Total Nonsense: Profiting from Evidence-Based Management*. Boston: Harvard Business School Press, 2006.

Picasso, Pablo. "Discovery of African Art: 1906-1907." In *Primitivism and Twentieth-Century Art: A Documentary History*, edited by Jack Flam with Miriam Deutch, 32–33. Berkeley, CA: University of California Press, 2003.

Pinker, Steven. *How the Mind Works*. New York: Norton, 1997.

Popper, Karl R. "Back to the Presocratics." Chapter 5 in Karl R. Popper, *Conjectures and Refutations: The Growth of Scientific Knowledge*. New York: Basic Books, 1962.

Price, A. Grenfell, ed. *The Explorations of Captain James Cook in the Pacific, as Told by Selections of His Own Journals, 1768-1779*. New York: Dover, 1971.

Ragheb, J. Fiona, ed. *Frank Gehry, Architect*. New York: Guggenheim Museum Publications, 2001.

Read, Herbert. *A Concise History of Modern Painting*. London: Thames and Hudson, 1959.

Richardson, John. *A Life of Picasso: Volume I, 1881–1906*. New York: Random House, 1991.

———. *A Life of Picasso, Volume II: 1907–1917*. New York: Random House, 1996.

Richerson, Peter J., and Robert Boyd. *Not by Genes Alone: How Culture Transformed Human Evolution*. Chicago: University of Chicago Press, 2005.

Romer, Paul. "Economic Growth." In *The Fortune Encyclopedia of Economics*, edited by David R. Henderson. New York: Warner Books, 1993.

———. "Increasing Returns and New Development in the Theory of Growth." In *Equilibrium Theory and Applications: Proceedings of the 6th International Symposium in Economic Theory and Econometrics*, edited by William Barnett et al. Cambridge, U.K.: Cambridge University Press, 1991.

Rorty, Richard. "Thomas Kuhn, Rocks, and the Laws of Physics." In Richard Rorty, *Philosophy and Social Hope*. New York: Penguin, 1999.

Rosenblum, Robert. "Picasso and the Typography of Cubism." In *Picasso in Retrospect*, by Daniel-Henry Kahnweiler et al., New York: Praeger, 1973.

Sahlins, Marshall. *How "Natives" Think, About Captain Cook, For Example*. Chicago: University of Chicago Press, 1995.

———. *Islands of History*. Chicago: University of Chicago Press, 1985.

Saxenian, AnnaLee. *Regional Advantage: Culture and Competition in Silicon Valley and Route 128*. Cambridge, MA: Harvard University Press, 1994.

Schrage, Michael. *Serious Play: How the World's Best Companies Simulate to Innovate*. Boston: Harvard Business School Press, 1999.

Schwartz, John. "New Economy: How Reality Fits with Fantasy in Cyberspace." *New York Times*, December 11, 2000.

Smiles, Sam. *J.M.W. Turner*. Princeton, NJ: Princeton University Press, 2000.

Smith, Dinitia. "Has History Been Too Generous to Gutenberg?" *New York Times*, January 27, 2001.

Smith, Douglas K., and Robert C. Alexander. *Fumbling the Future: How Xerox Invented, Then Ignored, the First Personal Computer*. New York: Morrow, 1988.

Smith, Patricia R. *Modern Collector's Dolls*. 7th series. Paducah, KY: Collector Books, 1995.

Sorkin, Michael. "Frozen Light." In *Gehry Talks: Architecture + Process*, edited by Mildred Friedman. New York: Universe Publishing, 2002.

Spinosa, Charles, Fernando Flores, and Hubert L. Dreyfus. *Disclosing New Worlds: Entrepreneurship, Democratic Action, and the Cultivation of Solidarity*. Cambridge, MA: MIT Press, 1997.

Sternberg, Robert J. *Handbook of Creativity*. Cambridge, UK: Cambridge University Press, 1999.

———, and Janet E. Davidson, eds. *The Nature of Insight*. Cambridge, MA: MIT Press, 1995.

Strogatz, Steven. *Sync: The Emerging Science of Spontaneous Order*. New York: Hyperion, 2003.

Taubes, Gary. "What If It's All Been a Big Fat Lie?" *New York Times*, July 7, 2002.

Thaler, Richard H. *The Winner's Curse: Paradoxes and Anomalies of Economic Life*. New York: Free Press, 1992.

Thompson, Clive. "The BitTorrent Effect." *Wired*, January 2005.

Tobin, James. "To Fly!" *Smithsonian*, April 2003, 50–62.

Tompkins, Calvin. "Everything in Sight. Robert Rauschenberg's New Life." *The New Yorker*, May 23, 2005, 68–77.

Tuchman, Maurice et al. *The Spiritual in Art: Abstract Painting 1890–1985*. New York: Abbeyville Press, 1986.

Walker, John. *Joseph Mallord William Turner*. New York: Abrams, 1976.

Watson, James D. *DNA: The Secret of Life*. New York: Knopf, 2003.

———. *The Double Helix: A Personal Account of the Discovery of the Structure of DNA*. New York: Atheneum Press, 1968.

———, and F. H. C. Crick. "Molecular Structure of Nucleic Acids: A Structure for Deoxyribose Nucleic Acid." *Nature* 171 (April 25, 1953): 737–738.

Watts, Duncan J. *Six Degrees: The Science of the Connected Age*. New York: Norton, 2003.

Westenhouser, Kitturah B. *The Story of Barbie*. Paducah, KY: Collector Books, 1994.

"Western Painting: Cubism and Its Consequences." *Encyclopedia Britannica Online*, February 4, 2004. http://www.search.eb.com/eb/article?eu=115377.

"When We Were Worms." *New Scientist*, October 18, 1997.

Wiesner-Hanks, Merry. "The World of the Renaissance Print Shop." In "The Infancy of Printing: Incunabula at the Golda Meir Library." University of Wisconsin–Milwaukee, 1996. http://www.uwm.edu/Dept/Library/special/exhibits/incunab.

Winograd, Terry, and Fernando Flores. *Understanding Computers and Cognition: A New Foundation for Design*. Reading, MA: Addison Wesley, 1987.

Wolf, Gary. *Wired—A Romance*. New York: Random House, 2003.

Womack, James P., and Daniel T. Jones. *Lean Thinking: Banish Waste and Create Wealth in Your Corporation*. New York: Simon and Schuster, 1996.

Wood, Gaby. "Dream Doll." *New Statesman*, April 1, 2002.

Wysocki, Bernard Jr. "For Economist Paul Romer, Prosperity Depends on Ideas." *The Wall Street Journal*, January 21, 1997.

Young, Jeffrey S. *Steve Jobs: The Journey Is the Reward*. Glenview, IL: Scott, Foresman, 1988.

INDEX

relying on external help for, 10–12
self-organizing emergent systems and, 21–22
Crick, Francis, 27. *See also* DNA structure discovery
cubism
    absence in architecture, 163
    as an example of coevolutionary change, 134
    impact on the art world, 131
    influence on Gehry, 171, 174, 176, 177
    law of spontaneous generation and, 133–134
    reframing of art due to, 19, 133
    techniques used by Picasso, 131–132
    triggering of exponential growth, 134–135

Darwinian networks, 97–100, 104, 106–110
Delbrück, Max, 38, 47
Demoiselles d'Avignon, Les (Picasso), 8–9, 131, 133, 149
Dennett, Daniel, 12
Desmond, Paul, 5
Diamond, Jared, 183, 184
Dichter, Ernest, 146
discontinuity, 19–22, 61, 184
DNA structure discovery
    Chargaff's experiment-based idea-space, 39–40
    Chargaff's ratios, 31–32, 36, 42, 43
    complexity of the problem, 29–30
    Crick and Watson's backgrounds, 27–28
    Crick's theory-based idea-space, 45–46
    cross-disciplinary nature of idea-spaces involved, 30
    discovery of the DNA structure, 37–38
    dynamics of reason and imagination, 50–52
    evolution of the idea of a genetic code, 47–49
    Franklin's experiment-based idea-space, 40–41
    individuals failure to see beyond their own idea-space, 32–37, 41–43, 45, 46
    interplay of Crick's insights, 48–49
    interplay of spaces of ideas, 46–47, 49–50
    Pauling's theory-based idea-space, 44–45
    relevant history of genetic research, 30–31
    Watson's experiment-based idea-space, 41–43

Doerr, L. John, 78
Dompier, Steve, 76, 92, 94–95
Donohoe, Jerry, 38
Downes, Larry, 20–21
Duguid, Paul, 64, 84, 206, 230

Einstein, Albert, 17, 68, 130, 134, 136, 170
Eliot, T. S., 237–239
embedded idea-spaces. *See* idea-spaces
embedded intelligence. *See also* intelligence
    communities of practice and, 84
    creative leaps and, 4–5, 67, 141, 245
    cultural/social forms of, 12, 54, 55
    extended mind and, 17
    genius and, 12–13, 16–17, 67
    idea-spaces and, 2
    imagination interfacing with, 6, 73, 114, 261
    integration of, 149, 226
    law of the fit get fitter, 166
    law of hotspots, 168, 225
    law of minimal effort, 237
    leadership's need to scan for, map, 252, 260
    lens of, 61
    paradigms as forms of, 64
    space to think with created by, 55
    technological artifacts/systems and, 12
    transfer between idea-spaces, 4–5, 67, 108, 136, 158, 225, 245
    weak ties, 108, 136, 225, 245
emergence
    of creative breakthroughs, 81, 135, 238
    of higher-level pattern, 111–112, 116, 119
    of idea-space/hub, 23, 166
    law of hotspots and, 166, 238
    law of small-world networks and, 205
    law of spontaneous generation, 119–121
    laws of fitness and, 100, 124
    order for free/spontaneous order, 127–130
    paradox of, 112–114
    tipping points, 112–114
Encarta, 24
Encyclopedia Britannica, 24, 253–254
Engelbart, Douglas, 77
Eratosthenes, 180–181
Esposito, Joseph, 253

ABOUT THE AUTHOR

Richard Ogle is a veteran educator and business consultant. He has a PhD in linguistics from UCLA, and has taught at the University of Essex (UK); the University of California, Davis; and in the Evening MBA Program of the School of Economics and Business Administration at St. Mary's College, California. His consulting clients include Simon and Schuster, The Discovery Channel, The Electric Power Research Institute, Pfizer, Wells Fargo Nikko, The Axelrod Group, and Kaiser Permanente.

His current research and consulting activities focus on breakthrough creativity in entrepreneurial business organizations. He can be contacted through his Web site, richardogle.com.

Born and raised in England, he came to the United States in 1968. He currently lives with his wife, Laura Bonazzoli, and daughter, Elizabeth, in Camden, Maine.